The Popular Theatre Movement in Russia, 1862–1919

The Popular Theatre Movement in Russia, 1862–1919

Gary Thurston

NORTHWESTERN UNIVERSITY PRESS / EVANSTON, ILLINOIS

Northwestern University Press
www.nupress.northwestern.edu

Printed in the United States of America

ISBN 978-0-8101-3484-3

The Library of Congress has cataloged the original, hardcover edition as follows:

Thurston, Gary.
The popular theatre movement in Russia, 1862–1919 / Gary Thurston.
p. cm. — (Studies in Russian literature and theory)
Includes bibliographical references and index.
ISBN 0-8101-1550-6 (cloth)
1. Theater—Russia—History—19th century. 2. Theater—Russia—History—20th century. 3. Theater and society—Russia—History—19th century. 4. Theater and society—Russia—History—20th century. 5. Popular culture—Russia—History—19th century. 6. Popular culture—Russia—History—20th century. I. Title. II. Series.
PN2723.T5 1998
792'.0947'09034—dc21

98-24479
CIP

In Loving Memory: O.W. & J.L.C.T.

Очень бы и очень хорошо было, если б кто из наших изыскателей занялся новыми и более тщательными, чем доселе, исследованиями о народном театре, который есть, существует и даже, может быть, не совсем ничтожный.
—Достоевский

It would be very, very good if one of our researchers undertook a new and more thorough investigation than has yet been done of popular theatre, which exists, is functioning, and is perhaps not completely without value.
—Dostoevsky

Широко распространенное суждение опекунов народного театра:

«Народ хочет сказки, а не быта.»

П.П. Гайдебуров:

«Чего хочет народ, знает только народ—да и завтра он может захотет лучшего, большего и, во всяком случае, иного, чем он хочет сегодня.»

In response to those who insisted that popular audiences wanted only amusing entertainment and not reality in the theatre, P. P. Gaideburov replied: "Whatever the people want, only they know—and tomorrow they may want something better, bigger, and, in any case, different from what they want today."

Contents

Acknowledgments

For the undimmed first pleasure of afternoon rehearsals and exciting evenings in the theatre, I have my high school drama coach to thank. Carol Houghton Hollingsworth combined high energy, an infallible instinct for quality in dramatic texts with community appeal, and rare dedication to her charges and their personal development. Interestingly, her ancestors at Hoghton Tower employed, then protected William Shakespeare in a connection that is just now understood sufficiently to clarify aspects of his originality that have puzzled scholars for nearly four hundred years.

At Grinnell College I left off playing to explore the dazzling possibilities of historical explanation. Sam Baron encouraged me to believe that I could make a living while studying European history, and commended Russian history as a specialization. He also revealed a brilliant teaching method that challenges me still.

Two of my teachers at Columbia, mentors, respectively, in Russian history and Russian literature, have been nobly generous with their time and attention. Marc Raeff and Robert Maguire, successively holders of the Bakhmetieff Chair of Russian Studies (created after I had left New York), have been available at the shortest notice to discuss any quandaries or snags. The latter has shown me many kindnesses, including providing material from his personal library for use in the present study. Marc Raeff, a European-American who embodies the attributes of courtesy, civility, and civilization, is an inspiration. I am particularly grateful for his persistent encouragement to write my own book rather than fill in a square in the grid of Slavic studies.

Elsewhere I have thanked Eugen Weber for the very stimulating National Endowment for the Humanities summer seminar he gave at UCLA just after publishing *Peasants into Frenchmen.* I should add here that, among other things, he put me on to Continental historians it would have taken me years to find on my own.

The International Research and Exchanges Board afforded me ten months in the Soviet Union, without which any proper appreciation of popular theatre's significance in Russian history would have been impossible. The University of Rhode Island Council for Research enabled me to return to Moscow when the political climate changed, and Nikolai Ivanov graciously assisted me in gaining access to archival materials I had not been able to see under IREX auspices. The Harvard Ukrainian Research Institute and Russian Research Center gave me affiliation for a sabbatical year, maximum Widener Library privileges, and the opportunity to try out my ideas on critical audiences. The University of Illinois Slavic Lab twice provided accommodation while I availed myself of their library's superb reference facilities and extensive collection. The University of Chicago Library let me roam in the papers of Samuel Harper. (I have to credit the Department of Special Collections for permission to quote from them.)

Joel Cohen, as chair of my department, vigorously endorsed my work on popular theatre and enlisted his dean's material support. Joan Neuberger took time to discuss Habermas with me. Friends who have read various versions of the manuscript—Sam Baron, Patricia Herlihy, Denise Youngblood, Marilyn Malina, and Marc Raeff—all called attention to problems and shortcomings, yet have sustained me with their warm encouragement. None bears responsibility for how everything was finally resolved.

G.J.T.
Wakefield, Rhode Island
January 1998

Introduction

EUROPEAN POPULAR THEATRE

It was in the eighteenth century that Europe harnessed literary theatre to the project of Enlightenment. Literary theatre denoted performances of fixed, written texts by known authors. Such texts had first appeared in classical Greece, and the Greek tragedies and comedies were thought to constitute part of an irreplaceable European inheritance. There was folk theatre as well, with looser performances, following something closer to scenarios than authored texts, and adjusting readily to the moods and responses of particular audiences. Europeans fancied that Greek drama bespoke a civic unity that had been lost sometime in the past. The scientific revolution and rationalism in the seventeenth century, above all, had left Europeans living in "two different worlds of the mind."[1] It was hoped that a reconstituted theatre would (1) restore unity to the public and (2) correct social "problems"—like drunkenness—related to urbanization and population growth. Folk theatre had no role to play, given its not infrequently antagonistic relationship to high culture and the progress of manners.[2] But literary theatre, revitalized and regulated, could generate texts defining a nation's genius.

The argument of this book is that the popular theatre phenomenon in Europe united aesthetic achievement and aspiration to community in an endeavor of lasting significance. The Russian manifestation is, of course, my main concern here. But Russian popular theatre must be understood from the outset as part of a process encompassing distinct (and predictable) phases, a process played out—with variations—in several European countries. Therefore I lay the groundwork by considering the process as experienced outside Russia. Next I offer a brief description of popular theatre's progress in Russia with consideration of a theory that helps explain the rising and falling fortunes of theatre for enlightenment. I close with a consideration of theatre's essential function from its inception.

In France, central and northern Europe, England, and Russia advocates emerged for popular theatre and organizers appeared to bring theatre to those not served by commercial or state-supported enterprises. The French experience and discussion is of particular interest because it served as a reference point for other Europeans who would subsequently take up the cause.

The Enlightenment debate on theatre's educational potential can perhaps be traced to Voltaire, who settled in Calvinist Geneva in 1754 and began to give amateur theatricals at home. He invited local young people, whose theatrical exposure had been limited to street fairs, the only form of the medium to survive in the Protestant city.[3] D'Alembert, in his entry on Geneva in volume 7 of the *Encyclopédie,* argued for the right of theatre to exist (under careful regulation and censorship). Rousseau, in his *Letter to d'Alembert on Theatre* (1785) insisted that the theatre could arouse passions that cause viewers to forget virtue, but was powerless to improve manners and morals: "The empire of opinion . . . does not depend on theatre at all, for, rather than giving the law to the public, the theatre receives the law from it."[4] The theatre of the Greeks, Rousseau conceded, had inspired sentiments of honor and glory in the breasts of the people. Their plays were "a constant source of instruction." But contemporary theatres functioned differently, having been built for "personal aggrandizement," and presenting modern plays full of "nastiness."

Diderot, in his *Deuxième entretien sur le Fils naturel,* echoed this theme of the vast difference between the theatres of antiquity and the contemporary stage. But he considered that a modern drama depicting middle-class people in domestic situations with authentic feeling could, by developing sentiments of tenderness and compassion *(sensibilité),* prove far more useful to viewers than the remote issues and grand passions of classical tragedy.[5] His disciple, the critic Louis-Sébastien Mercier, in his *Du théâtre: ou nouvel essai sur l'art dramatique* (1773) and *Nouvel examen de la Tragédy française* (1778) called for plays that would mold the manners and morals of citizens. Deploring the cultural separation of the people from the elite, Mercier demanded a people's theatre that would "illuminate and arm the people with reason."[6]

Republicans in the French Revolution took up Mercier's ideas of theatre as a school for the people. Legislation in 1791 abolished corporate monopolies of the Comédie-Française, Opéra, and Comédie-Italienne, authorized new theatres to open without established sponsors, and made actors citizens. It envisioned theatres that would be sources of moral edification as much as the school and the church.[7] Because the state had strictly regulated the establishment of theatres since 1402, this new freedom represented a great novelty. As many as thirty-five theatres opened by late 1791, and by the end of 1792 more than two hundred had sprung up.[8] With the sudden increase in audience numbers in the 1790s, the theatre became for the first time what might be regarded as a mass medium.[9] In March 1794 the Committee of

Public Safety acted on recommendations to create a national theatre that would render men more virtuous and enlightened. Yet somehow the new theatres failed to live up to the revolutionaries' expectations. Robespierre saw betrayal by playwrights. Others lamented a dilution in quality of productions as the quantity had increased so rapidly. The raising of a revolutionary citizen army of course distracted attention from educational endeavors. The conquests of the Revolution—the rights to establish a theatre and to adopt any repertory—were finally lost. Censorship returned, and by the time of the Consulate repertories of the approved theatres were being reviewed by authorities weekly.

Napoleon restored state regulation of theatre in 1807, much to the relief of entrepreneurs struggling in an overcrowded market. In fact the market for theatre exploded in nineteenth-century France: the transportation revolution vastly increased any theatre's potential audience within Paris and attracted regular spectators from the provinces. Indeed, the theatre of the era has been characterized as an *industry* that efficiently matched resources to demand. New construction techniques altered the class balance of audiences, with iron framing making it possible to put nearly a third of the viewers in cheap amphitheatre seats.[10] As urban laborers became more numerous they found more affordable theatre seats available. In 1864 Napoleon III did away with the licensing system and again freed commercial theatres to multiply and compete with the subsidized state theatres. The supply of plays expanded, with as many as thirty-two thousand being written in the nineteenth century. And audience deportment changed in the last third of the century. Even as the theatre audience quadrupled, the rowdy behavior of the gaslit theatres—marked by whistling and stamping—gave way to passive, "civil" reception of the fare, however insignificant it might be. The decorum (or indifference) of the auditorium may have been a factor in working-class audiences' desertion of the theatre by 1910.[11]

After the Paris Commune of 1871, Jules Bonassiès published *Le Théâtre et le peuple* (Paris, 1872), in which he defined the people as all of society and argued for theatre as a mechanism of reconciliation. He envisioned expanded state support to assure excellence of production and fund a system of decentralized theatres *(théâtres populaires)* in outlying districts, hosting municipally subsidized troupes. In the realm of practice rather than theory, a much more influential development for popular theatre came from André Antoine, a clerk in a Paris gas company. In this case dramatic texts provided the stimulus, and a loophole in the censorship law created the opportunity. Private amateur performances went unregulated, and Antoine hit on the fruitful idea of financing a company of amateur players from contributions by "honorary members, theatre lovers" and giving open performances of new, usually naturalistic, works, to which the leading critics of the day were invited. He scored a major triumph in February 1888 with the first production in France of Tolstoy's *Power of Darkness*, given first as a private, then a public performance for paying viewers. After introducing French audiences to Ibsen's *Wild Duck* and *Ghosts* and Strindberg's *Miss Julie*, and touring abroad, Antoine directed a commercial theatre (renamed Théâtre Antoine), then in 1906 assumed directorship of the Odéon, "which he succeeded at last in transforming into a truly popular theatre."[12]

The central figure in the French popular theatre movement that began in the 1890s was Romain Rolland, who published critical comment on all the various projects and chronicled the movement in *Le Théâtre du peuple*, a book that attempted to "renew the tradition interrupted by the Revolution."[13] Rolland credited the historian Jules Michelet with bringing the ideals of eighteenth-century figures and the Revolution down to contemporaries. He quoted the appeal "to find your souls again in the people's theatre" from Michelet's 1847–48 lecture course: "Give [the people] the supreme teaching which constituted the education of the glorious city-states of antiquity: a theatre that was truly of the people. . . . The theatre is the most potent agent in education and goes far to establish closer relations between man and man. . . . Before I die I wish to see a spirit of national fraternity in the theatre."[14] For his part, Rolland believed that "the people's manner of perceiving is entirely different from that of the elite." He had a definite idea of the working man's mentality: "[His] mind normally rests while his body labors. . . . The people are more foolish than malicious—and malicious on account of their foolishness." He counted on theatre to bring order to confused minds: "It should cast some light into the terrible brain of man, which is full of sinkholes, shadows and monsters" (113–16).

Rolland dated the beginning of the new people's theatre movement from a rural celebration in 1892 commemorating the centennial of the revolutionary Republic. Maurice Pottécher had translated Molière's *Le Médecin malgré lui* into the Haute-Moselle dialect and produced it in the Vosges town of Bussang. When townspeople of all classes responded enthusiastically, he opened a people's theatre there in 1895 with a play of his own composition on the perils of drink.[15] A popular theatre opened in Poitiers in 1897; peasant actors performed at Ploujean, Brittany, in 1898; and similar theatres functioned in Grenoble, Orange, Nîmes, and Béziers. Pottecher also wrote on national (as opposed to regional) popular theatre, arguing for mixed audiences where the elite could help correct the taste of the crowd.[16]

French theatres specifically for working-class audiences at times set out to facilitate access to the classics, augmenting dramatic fragments with anything at all that might stimulate the audiences' sense of their own identity. At the end of the 1890s Adrien Bernheim, inspector general in the Ministry of Education, formed the Oeuvres de trente ans du Théâtre to introduce the laboring classes to the national classics, using professional actors performing in whatever facilities were available in worker districts. Louis Lumet's Théâtre

Civique presented a program on the theme of justice at the height of the Dreyfus affair.[17] The *Revue d'art dramatique* in 1899 offered a prize for the best proposal for a working-class theatre. In 1903 a Théâtre Populaire devoted to workers opened in the Belleville suburb of Paris. It offered plays by Rostand, Ibsen, and Hauptmann, and its director was committed to Rolland's goal of stimulating "spiritual energy" while providing enlightenment and relaxation. All these enterprises folded by 1905. An essay by J.-R. Bloch in 1910 entitled "Le Théâtre du peuple: Critique d'une utopie" explained that industrial workers could not be interested in theatre because no plays were being written by or for them.[18]

Thus on the eve of the First World War, France's renewed interest in theatre for the people had given way to disappointment. The 1890s enthusiasm for popular theatre differed somewhat from the Enlightenment enthusiasm: the first was concerned with mass attainment of national identity; the latter, with rationality and civility. In this era also the role and status of the dramatic text became the subject of intense debate. Some activists maintained faith in the power of national classics to edify and unify, while others insisted that theatre required fresh works to stimulate reflection on contemporary political and economic issues. In a diverse society the uniform achievement of *sensibilité* no longer seemed supremely desirable; nonetheless, theatre still appeared capable—if only suitable texts were forthcoming—of stimulating civic vitality.

In the German-speaking parts of central Europe, folk theatre still flourished in the eighteenth century. Saxon Professor J. C. Gottsched proposed, in his *Critical Art of Poetry* (1730), that the courtly virtues of propriety and regularity be brought to bear on a medium characterized by crudity and improvisation.[19] Gottsched recommended the classical French court drama of Racine as a model. But in the 1750s he lost a polemical battle with Lessing, who wrote successful domestic tragedies along the lines of Diderot's. From 1775 Goethe wrote for and participated actively in the ducal court theatre at Weimar. He came to see that published dramatic texts focused the attention of widely scattered German-speaking intellectuals on important philosophical and social issues. Around 1782 he began to dictate *Wilhelm Meister's Theatrical Mission,* the story of a young man of the middle class who throws himself into theatrical life and travels with a touring company. In book 6 of the novel, completed in 1785 (the year of Rousseau's letter to D'Alembert), Goethe came to a new understanding of the connection between artist and audience. "According to this new view, the audience is to be addressed for the sake of the loved one hidden within it; though it is a 'mass' . . . it is affected by art not collectively, but individual by individual."[20] By the late nineteenth century the Germans had an important body of dramatic texts, spanning Lessing, Schiller (who embraced the notions of Mercier), Goethe, Kleist, Grillparzer, Büchner, Hebbel, Nestroy, and Hauptmann.

Urbanization and industrialization by the end of the century were producing new audiences and a market for new dramatic forms. Middle-class patronage developed in Munich in the 1880s and 1890s, for example, for skits and one-act plays, performed first on small stages in beer halls extolling the joys of rural life and community.[21] Industrialists found theatre useful as an entertainment for workers in large-scale facilities, as exemplified in the Franz Joseph Theatre Arthur Krupp built at Berndorf near Vienna in 1899. Still, as in France in the 1890s, a body of challenging dramatic texts representing a national literary achievement, augmented by accessible naturalist dramas that addressed contemporary issues, encouraged the belief that theatre could inspire and uplift working-class audiences.

New theatres of high quality opened in Berlin in the late 1870s and 1880s, but ticket prices remained beyond the reach of the working classes. Moreover, a political censorship that banned plays dealing with poverty and social problems stood in the way of an issues-oriented theatre. The naturalistic plays of Ibsen, however, were widely read and the social problems they raised were debated in working-class discussion circles.[22] (Literary circles were legal at a time when Social Democratic political associations were not.) In 1890 theatre critic Otto Brahm unveiled a scheme not unlike Antoine's to establish a subscription society to circumvent the censorship and provide private performances of naturalist works. The professional classes rallied to this "Free Theatre's" subscriber ranks. Within months Bruno Wille was addressing an inaugural meeting of the "Free *People's* Theatre" subscription. He said that "Art for the People" had been the motto of the best minds of ancient Greece and that now working people needed access not only to the new drama that addressed social issues but to the plays of Goethe and Schiller.[23] Late in 1892 the Free People's Theatre split over whether its mission should be the education of individual viewers or class consciousness and preparation for revolution. When Max Reinhardt took over theatrical management of the New People's Free Theatre in the 1905–6 season, production standards rose and membership leapt from six thousand to ten thousand. By 1912 the organization was distributing half a million tickets a year. After facing increasing pressure from the state censorship, it merged with the surviving People's Free Theatre, and they constructed a building seating nearly two thousand. Funds for the structure, which boasted advanced stage machinery and lighting, had come from thousands of small contributors. It opened in December 1914, the motto "Art to the People" incised across its facade.

The popular theatre movement had less impact in England than in either France or Germany. Provincial theatres did well in the late eighteenth and early nineteenth century but experienced the same sharp decline in theatregoing as did London from the 1840s to the early 1870s. The working classes cheerfully populated pit and gallery in commercial theatres, but from the

1860s resorted to music halls. Birmingham's first theatre dated from the 1740s, but by 1774 leading citizens of what was by then England's third-largest provincial town built "a much grander theatre, one more commensurate with the growing economic and social importance of the town, and one which would 'tend to improve the morals, the manners or taste of the people.'"[24] Douglas Reid, looking into the behavioral differences between working and the middle and upper classes attending the Theatre Royal in New Street notes that "in the eighteenth century (indeed into the nineteenth) theatre boxes were often quite as noisy as the galleries, but the reformation of manners which worked through all sections of society in these years led to a new sensitivity about . . . manners, particularly in the popular sections of the theatre."[25] He also finds that performances of Shakespeare nearly filled pit and gallery, while leaving the boxes and stalls sparsely populated. At one time the Birmingham pit had known their Shakespeare "so well that they could prompt any actor who went astray" (83).

The music halls, which could be operated by limited liability companies after 1862, flourished by offering varied entertainment to the working-class public. Tableaux figured in their stock-in-trade, and they installed stages, then prosceniums and fixed seating in rows. Yet their campaigns to be allowed to play legitimate drama came to naught.[26] In the 1880s they began to phase out the sale of strong drink, while raising admission prices. By the 1890s middle-class families began to patronize them, now that respectability had become their rule and business had tamed the sociability of expanding leisure time while making it pay.

The early, rowdy music halls challenged reformers to contrive an alternative with the entertainment centered on drama.[27] The Old Vic, in the Waterloo Road, had offered "bloodbath melodrama" to the working classes of Lambeth and Southwark in the decades of theatrical contraction. When a significant new competitor, the Elephant and Castle Theatre, opened in 1872, the Victoria reinvented itself as "the people's theatre."[28] Emma Cons reopened the establishment as the Royal Victoria Coffee Music Hall in 1880.[29] Cons came to the district in connection with a program that built housing for the poor and rented flats at modest rates to approved tenants. She took on the Victoria as a temperance project. Several temperance music halls in the north of England had already proved successful. And by 1880 there existed fifty-six companies like the Coffee Tavern Company, offering competition to public houses and pubs. George Rowell, who consulted the archives of Royal Victoria Hall, admits, "What was actually presented on the stage of the Old Vic during the first 25 years of Emma Cons' regime is often difficult and sometimes impossible to establish."[30] The manager she hired to run the music hall in 1881, William Poel, had played Hamlet and was "dedicated to 'purified' drama and to the theatre as a means of instruction and improvement, rather than mere diversion." He is known to have specialized in spectacles and tableaux vivants. Later the Hall found a large audience for heavily abridged operas.

In her 1902 annual trustees report Cons observed, "The workers at this hall have been labouring for 23 years to provide . . . a 'people's palace'—one that should furnish only innocent amusement, and educate its visitors to take their pleasures apart from drinking and betting."[31] For the author(s) of one account of her management, "Their inspirations were religious rather than aesthetic. . . . [Cons' niece, Lilian Bayliss] persuaded actors, managers, directors, dancers, singers and choreographers to forego West End salaries to take part in what was a labor of Christian love."[32] The importance of the theatre may hinge on its function as a burgeoning community center. Bayliss said that the Old Vic was built by battered wives who knew they could come there and find refuge and decent manners. One model for Cons was perhaps the People's Palace in the Mile End Road, built with a bequest from a local resident. The Palace favored entertainment such as amateur concerts, choirs, and competitive shows; it evolved into Queen Mary College. Cons too raised money to establish a "College for Working Men and Women." The 1891 Order in Council that set down the regulations for Morley College spelled out the responsibilities of the theatre under the new trust: "The theatre shall be for the holding there of public lectures and musical and other entertainments and exhibitions suitable for the recreation and instruction of the poorer classes."[33] Cons and her philanthropist friends secured for the Victoria Coffee Music Hall a grateful, loyal local audience. But what earned the institution a place in theatre history was the Shakespearean productions initiated in October 1914.[34]

Proposals to create a subsidized national theatre as a Shakespeare memorial gave proponents occasion to praise the high standards of the subsidized French theatres. Lady Julia Pollock wrote in 1871 that government assistance was needed to save British drama, and a decade later Matthew Arnold joined in the call for a subsidized national theatre presenting Shakespeare and modern British drama—arguing that the national character could only suffer from the performances that currently passed for drama on the English stage.[35] In 1900 Poel petitioned the London County Council for a site on which to build a replica of an Elizabethan theatre. In April 1913 a Private Member's Bill to establish a national theatre subsidized by the state failed to pass in Parliament by four votes.[36]

This brief survey of European popular theatre suggests some common tendencies. While early proponents saw popular theatre as a way to address the rift between the cultivated and uncultivated, later activists hoped it could somehow address specific social antagonisms. In fact, motives of presenters ranged from sharing pure aesthetic pleasure, to philanthropy and uplift, to propagation of a particular political outlook. A central concern from the beginning was the state's proper role. Should it merely regulate? Should it censor plays to protect audiences? Should it subsidize, guarantee high standards, establish a national theatre for the benefit of all the people? Debate raged over repertory as well. Should popular theatre limit itself to acknowledged classics that could affect and to some extent improve audiences in predictable ways—for instance, providing a perspective on the passions that might facilitate self-mastery, or present heroism or honor, or even civic virtue in the best light? Or should it be conceived as a laboratory for the creation and testing of plays addressing contemporary problems? Should popular theatre attempt to manipulate audiences to improve them, as some temperance advocates insisted? A classic repertory with its emphasis on self-mastery might prove more effective in achieving the desired result. Should popular theatre engender class consciousness? Or should it stimulate individual self-consciousness, or national consciousness? Over time several European nations accumulated a body of dramatic texts in the national language that revealed the identity if not the genius of the national character. What use could be made of them? The passage of time also brought an increase of wealth that made possible new methods of financing and supporting popular theatres. New institutional forms appeared, such as the community centers that combined popular theatre with formal instruction for those formerly lacking access to more than elementary education. Each of these issues and developments would figure in the Russian popular theatre movement.

RUSSIAN POPULAR THEATRE

Russia's first popular theatre went up on Red Square in Moscow in 1701. Peter the Great desired that it educate common people in the capital by showing them through drama how other Europeans lived and comported themselves. This, Europe's first theatre for popular enlightenment, soon failed, proving incapable either of educating or amusing. Its viewers could not make sense of what they saw nor find any benefit in attending. The tsar would shortly move the capital to the north and ultimately achieve success in transforming his subjects' manners and mores by focusing his Westernization efforts on a small, privileged segment of the population.

By the last third of the eighteenth century some Russian noble families acquired such a strong partiality to European amusements that they set up their own private theatres with serf actors and production assistants.[37] Although the last of the serf theatres were liquidated in the 1840s, Dostoevsky could observe in the early 1860s that they had laid the foundations for "a national dramatic art."[38] From the old serf theatres he traced a succession of dramatic traditions handed down from generation to generation, with attendance by soldiers, factory workers, people in small towns, and servants from noble houses.[39]

Almost as if to confirm Dostoevsky's impression of a "national dramatic art," a landowner living 150 miles north of Moscow built in 1862, the summer after the year of serf emancipation, a wooden theatre for the local peasants. He invited them to a production by members of his family of a play written eight years earlier in Moscow depicting the manners and ways of unwesternized Russians. The landowner wanted to share the pleasure of amateur performance with the former serfs of the neighborhood but also sought to satisfy his curiosity about peasants' ability to follow and enjoy an enactment of a dramatic text. He found his guests' enthusiastic response gratifying and followed up with a few more productions, but his experiment contributed little to Russia's popular theatre movement, remaining unpublished for a quarter of a century.

Russia's imperial theatres enjoyed state subsidies, just as the select French theatres did. But by the 1860s the imperial theatres could not accommodate even all the merchants who would like to have attended. In 1872 a metropolitan authority resorted to theatre to amuse and improve the common folk. The governor-general of Moscow, considering "healthy entertainments" conducive to improved order in the city, made a building site available to a civic commission concerned with the welfare of workers. The City Council supported the project and erected a 2,000-seat theatre as part of its contribution to the celebration marking the two hundredth anniversary of the birth of Peter the Great. The theatre was intended for all classes. But the director who took charge of it set out to appeal to audiences that lacked any theatregoing experience. A. F. Fedotov assembled excellent actors, emphasized ensemble playing, and maintained production standards higher than those prevailing at the imperial theatres. He scheduled challenging plays that encouraged viewers to think critically. After Tsar Alexander II attended a performance of Gogol's famous satire on bureaucratic administration, *The Inspector General,* the Theatre of the 1872 Polytechnic Exposition lost official support. When the exposition ended, the building was sold cheaply to private entrepreneurs.

After Alexander II died in 1881, A. N. Ostrovsky, the original and prolific Russian playwright, petitioned his son for authorization to establish a Russian national theatre. Alexander III was known to be an enthusiastic proponent of all kinds of art produced by ethnic Russians. Ostrovsky argued in his appeal that Russia, which had achieved a characteristic school of painting and a recognizable style in orchestral music, had the resources to achieve a unique dramatic tradition as well; a national theatre would signify her achievement of cultural maturity among the peoples of Europe. Moreover, Ostrovsky reasoned that the peasants who in the nineteenth century became middling traders, rich merchants, artisans, and factory workers could profit from the "civilizing influence" of theatre as they worked on eliminating coarseness from their behavior. Though nothing came of his proposal for a national theatre, within a generation Russian theatre would achieve a distinct national style that would command attention and respect abroad.

Professional actors began taking plays to the countryside in the summer. Amateur dramatic circles appeared in a few communities that reached beyond the ranks of the educated and drew common folk into productions. Scattered landowners continued to build theatres for local popular audiences. And school theatre appeared. In 1888 the central government acknowledged this rising tide by creating a special Popular Theatre Censorship for theatres serving uneducated audiences. Its aim was to protect simple people from observing immorality and violence on the stage, to avoid politicization and class antagonism.

Meanwhile, the older folk theatre was expanding and adapting. In Russian the same phrase, *narodnyi teatr,* is used to designate both literary theatre performed to educate the public and folk theatre, with its performances directly adapted to the mood and ongoing responses of the audience. Folk theatre, which had been a staple in booths *(balagany)* at fairs, became a fixture of permanent garden theatres in cities by the 1880s.[40] Entrepreneurs at these garden theatres began to incorporate into their fare short authored texts or single scenes from plays that were standard in the repertoires of the edifying popular theatres. In the 1890s the government-sponsored temperance theatres hired these entrepreneurs to bring their flair for the spectacular to the new improving theatres. Thus by the turn of the century the lines between these two very different kinds of Russian popular theatre began to blur.[41]

The devastating famine of 1891 made educated Russians regard with new urgency the cultural gulf separating them from the masses. But if the enlighteners of the 1860s had assumed that their culture of science and abstract values contained everything the uneducated needed, intelligentsia activists now sought to learn from theatrical presentations how their less fortunate brethren reasoned in their own terms. Now the proponents of popular theatre began to organize. Journal articles described various experiments in rural theatres for the people and attempts to interpret audience responses. In 1895 the All-Russian Agricultural Exposition in Moscow featured an exhibit on popular theatre. Shortly thereafter a thick compendium of articles and essays appeared, *Popular Theatre: A Collection,* which sold out immediately. In 1896 the Congress on Technical and Professional Education considered a proposal to follow the example of Paris and establish a series of small theatres in working-class districts of Moscow. In 1897 the Moscow Art Theatre was founded, with one of its main objectives the delivery of quality theatre to workers and villagers. Before the government forced it to stop offering blocks of seats to workers at reduced prices, it called itself The Moscow Artistic General Access Theatre and The Moscow People's Theatre.

Yet if the government feared theatre that might encourage critical thinking, it nevertheless did much in the 1890s to encourage popular theatre that entertained and distracted in rapidly growing cities. As part of its industrialization program it dedicated certain tax revenues for the provision of "rational entertainments" that would compete with taverns and created a Trusteeship for Popular Temperance in 1894. This board granted subsidies to temperance societies across the empire desiring to establish tea rooms (often with stages) and popular theatres. By 1900 Temperance trustees had helped construct public facilities (People's Houses) with theatres in Kiev and Cheliabinsk. Their showcase Nicholas II House of the People, opened in Saint Petersburg in that year, contained a theatre seating fifteen hundred.

Government-promoted rapid industrialization caused many large-scale factories and plants to be built, with the result that Russia had the highest proportion of enterprises employing more than five hundred workers in all of Europe. Owners of these new factories often found it useful to construct theatres on their premises. A factory theatre near Iaroslavl, for example, seated one thousand. In Petersburg industrialists helped organize the Nevsky Society, which established a park for workers with summer theatre, winter theatre, and children's theatre; eventually it constructed a 2,000-seat stone theatre.

At the very time Emma Cons ran London's Old Vic as a "People's Palace," philanthropist Countess S. V. Panina constructed a far more palatial public facility in the Petersburg Obvodnyi Canal working-class district that likewise combined theatre and formal instruction for adults and young people. To operate her 500-seat theatre (opened in 1903), Panina hired an energetic young married couple steeped in the naturalist and symbolist drama of the 1890s. P. P. Gaideburov and N. F. Skarskaia patiently worked to develop their mixed audience and challenge it with the latest Russian and foreign plays. They also formed a touring company that took productions to the four corners of the empire during the summer months. Panina's community center became a clearing house for requests for information on establishing People's Houses. A survey it conducted in 1914–15 found that theatrical performances were given regularly in sixty-one out of ninety People's Houses across Russia.

An important factor in the proliferation of People's Houses was the new interest taken in them after the turn of the century by the *zemstvos,* the indirectly elected district and provincial agencies of self-government. Zemstvo tax revenues could now be tapped by public-spirited Russians interested in constructing community centers. Many of the new People's Houses coordinated activities in association with the Free University movement to offer lectures and courses of instruction.

By 1905 Russia already had at least 361 popular theatres. But the most influential development in the Russian popular theatre movement would come out of the revolution of that year. A 1906 law that went some distance toward establishing freedom of assembly permitted amateur circles to form and present plays simply by informing local authorities of their intention to do so. By 1908 rural circles began to proliferate. Worker drama circles became more numerous after the legal workday was cut to 9–10 hours in 1913. In Moscow a private organization of theatre lovers dedicated itself to supporting these groups by lending scripts, sets, props, and wigs. The Section to Promote Village, Factory, and School Theatre also offered instruction in play selection, scenic design, and theatre business management. In 1915 it completed a substantial headquarters building near the Zoological Garden with a 250-seat theatre where volunteers experimented with new methods to simplify production and reach new audiences.

Professionals who made a living in theatre also took an interest in popular theatre through their associations, such as the Russian Theatrical Society. Thus the All-Russian Congress of Theatre Personnel scheduled reports on popular theatre over the years. In 1915 the First All-Russian Congress on Popular Theatre convened in Moscow with the blessing of the Ministry of the Interior. With the introduction of national prohibition at the beginning of the war in 1914 the central government saw a need for the provision of entertainments to replace the distractions of drink. As grain exports stopped and government purchasing raised rural incomes, new resources went into the construction of People's Houses with theatres. The war also stimulated the cooperative movement, which invested in cultural development programs and used theatrical presentations to explain cooperation and recruit new members.

Theatre mania was rampant in the army as well, where soldiers often organized amateur productions in their spare time. After Panina's People's House became a military hospital, her displaced theatre company arranged to tour for the soldiers at the Northeastern Front. Their meticulously recorded data on soldier responses to their presentations describe the moods at the front in the weeks before the October revolution.[42]

The Bolsheviks expanded theatrical activity after folding it into the work of their "Commissariat of Enlightenment." In 1919 the commissar of theatre nationalized the Section to Promote Village, Factory, and School Theatre. The authorities took command of all decisions concerning selection of plays for presentation and thereby ended the autonomy of grassroots theatres that had emerged after 1906.[43]

In sum, popular theatre in Russia resembled popular theatre in the rest of Europe but was much more important in the larger cultural development of the nation. After emancipation, members of educated society regarded it as a vehicle of acculturation. The state intervened to regulate any theatre for the masses that had higher ambitions than amusing them or making them more orderly. In the 1890s naturalist works with grim depictions of social conflict provided a fresh impetus to take theatre to the burgeoning working classes. But subscription schemes of the sort that put theatregoing within reach of working-class audiences in Paris and Berlin did not develop in Russia. Nor did Russian workers become disillusioned with theatre before the war, as they had in France. If fewer first-rank playwrights wrote in Russian than in German, by 1914 the Russians still had a substantial corpus of major plays to be proud of, thanks to Gogol, Ostrovsky, Tolstoy, Chekhov, and Gorky. With the Bolshevik centralization and state funding of theatre it could be argued that Russians achieved their national theatre well before England. But nagging questions remain concerning the fulfillment of drama's enlightenment promise: its efficacy in altering mentalities. No history of Russian popular theatre can be written without a context for evaluating the achievements of its protagonists and their lofty dreams of reconciling individualism and social harmony.

THE THEORY OF A "PUBLIC SPHERE"

Popular theatre in Russia involved the state, educated society, and a new kind of sociability that developed around the writing, viewing, and criticism of plays (which in turn represented a critique and exploration of current states of affairs.) The rapid growth of this new sociability (that is, the way it was taken up by the common folk who readily found uses for it) is a puzzling phenomenon that demands some explanation. The search for an explanation leads directly to the fascinating subject of mentalities: the content of the plays most often selected, and the recorded reactions of viewers who attended them, open a window into the self-, social, and political consciousness of several consecutive generations of Russians. A theory worked out by Jürgen Habermas in the early 1960s to describe the emergence of public opinion in western Europe and the subsequent expansion, decomposition, and collapse of the "public sphere" offers a perspective from which to approach Russia's popular theatre movement.

Habermas's *Strukturwandel der Öffentlichkeit* (Darmstadt and Neuwied, 1962) appeared in English translation in 1991.[44] Until recently, American historians of Russia have paid little attention to the theory of structural transformation—perhaps because a book dealing with "bourgeois" attitudes would seem to have little relevance for a country whose middle class was notoriously slow to develop. But recent books on late nineteenth- and early twentieth-century Russia have begun to correct this oversight.[45] Among veteran Russian specialists, Daniel Brower has made the fullest use to date of Habermas's theory of the public sphere in his interpretation of the origins and development of municipal affairs.[46] Habermas's theory happens to be extremely useful for explaining both the spectacular trajectory of Russia's popular theatre movement and its essential connection to such matters as legal consciousness and personal autonomy.

The argument of *The Structural Transformation* may be summarized fairly briefly. When European society was ordered according to estates, performance arts like theatre and music usually served to grace special occasions. The court and the church patronized these arts, which had an "aura of extraordinariness" and aimed to impress the public by *representing* qualities such as majesty, excellence, highness, dignity, honor, and fame. In the baroque festival, dance and theatre "retreated from the public places into the enclosures of the park, from the streets into the rooms of the palace."[47] These representative occasions found a new form in Florence (then Paris and London) as the humanistically cultivated courtier supplanted the knightly courtier. Then representation ceased, as a "public sphere" appeared. Driving this change was the development of the modern tax-supported state, with its bureaucracy, standing army, and regular communication. New people linked to the modern state first constituted the public sphere. Under mercantilism the state encouraged private initiative through regulation. Merchants, bankers, entrepreneurs, and manufacturers gathered in novel associations, such as salons, coffeehouses, literary societies, and Masonic lodges, where they freely discussed a wide range of issues. As state authority became depersonalized, civil society came into existence. Subjects began to see civil society as properly theirs, not the authorities'.

Not the least of the charms of Habermas's theory is the centrality it accords to literary activity in the flowering of the public sphere. He argues that the novel was born to facilitate exploration of the "private sphere" that mirrored and made possible the public sphere. With the fading of court society and "representation," and the rise of regularly circulating commodities, money, and information, artworks began to become common, and so lost their exceptional aura. Theatrical and musical works came to be presented for their own sake and were widely discussed by the educated. Tension between the administering state and the administered public stimulated the use of reason among the latter. When theatre, for example, became publicly accessible as a commodity, it sparked psychological interests and critical discussion (29). The "public sphere" is simply Habermas's name for the thinking, discussing part of society that took literature, theatre, music, and museums seriously.

Once theatre and music, freed from the court, produced their own public, "taste . . . became manifest in the assessments of lay people" (40).

> But since the true judgment was supposed to be discovered only through discussion, truth appeared as a process, a process of enlightenment. Some sectors of the public might be more advanced in this process than others. Hence, if the public acknowledged no one as privileged, it did recognize experts. They were permitted and supposed to educate the public, but only inasmuch as they convinced through arguments and could not themselves be corrected by better arguments. (259 n. 32)

This reasoning, discriminating public gave rise to "public opinion." Habermas finds Rousseau to have been the first to use the term, but credits Louis-Sébastien Mercier with having been the first to think through its implications; it was Mercier who remarked (1797): "the good books are dependent on the enlightened people in all classes of the nation . . . they enlighten the government about its duties" (93, 95, 269 n. 23). It would not be long before public opinion legitimated itself as the "rationality that strove to discover what was at once just and right" (51–52).

Here it becomes necessary to consider Habermas's explanation of the role of the "private sphere." From the foregoing it should be clear that reasoning in the public sphere gave rise to assurance in matters of moral judgment and not just syllogistic logic. Habermas finds Europeans' discovery of humanity to have constituted the core of enlightenment.[48] The Greek city-states had employed critical reason in the law courts and in discussion, he notes, but they could go only so far. "The conduct of the [Greek] citizen was agonistic merely in the sportive competition with each other that was a mock war against the external enemy and not in dispute with his own government" (52). In Habermas's view, it was in the bourgeois family that Europeans discovered autonomy, freedom, and "interiorized human closeness." This family (unlike the family in the classical Greek model) came into existence through free choice of individuals, maintained a loving atmosphere, and encouraged the disinterested development of all the faculties of its members. And the modern European was instructed through literature in the family life that opened awareness to the humanity inherent in all mankind. "The relations between author, work and public . . . became intimate mutual relationships between privatized individuals who were psychologically interested in what was 'human,' in self-knowledge, and in empathy" (50).

Habermas traces the path by which public opinion discovered itself while reasoning about sovereignty and the state. Locke and Hobbes distinguished between power exercised arbitrarily and the executive power that merely implements the abstract, permanent norms of justice. Habermas thinks that the criteria of generality and abstractness characterizing legal norms had a resonance for privatized individuals who in their communication confirmed each other's subjectivity and shared the equality of cultivated persons. Kant, of course, represented the high point of optimism about the general development of talents and refinement of taste and the enlightened public's ultimate ability to guarantee the rule of law. Kant's definition of property is of particular interest to us, because it is broad enough to show that educated nineteenth-century Russians who were not merchants or landowners could readily join the Public Sphere: a citizen must have some property to support himself "which can include any skill, trade, fine art or science."[49] It was precisely here that Hegel discovered a fatal flaw in the concept of a steadily expanding public of independent critical minds. He showed how civil society rewarded superior skill and resources, with the result that those so established set the terms of employment for the rest in ways that limited access to self-improvement. Habermas describes the theories of Mill and Tocqueville, conceived as civil society appeared to be losing its coherence, as an attempt to rescue the expanding public sphere from itself by substituting compromise for consensus.

Habermas's description of the expansion, decomposition, and collapse of the public sphere is dramatic indeed. He finds the very character of sociability changed as the societies and associations died out and clubs went into eclipse. In the twentieth century it came to be marked by "abstinence from literary and political debate" (163). Individuals focused their energies on occupation, leisure, and consumption, and changed their attitude toward the state. Private interests took control of legislation, so that the laws no longer could be vindicated as regards their elements of truth. The taxing state survived by becoming the welfare state. The notion of the public good was lost as people looked to the state to advance their particular interests. And literature and art ceased to be vehicles of communication for the educated public, as individuals became consumers of entertainments and passive receivers of messages. "The sounding board of an educated stratum tutored in the public use of reason has been shattered; the public is split apart into minorities of specialists who put their reason to use nonpublicly and the great mass of consumers whose receptiveness is uncritical" (175).

Habermas's American publisher brought out a volume of papers discussed at a conference to reconsider *The Structural Transformation* on the occasion of its appearance in English nearly thirty years after it was first written.[50] Contributors pointed to matters the author would have to address if he were rewriting the book today. Concerns were expressed about the work's "gender blindness." The author was faulted as well for his failure to credit the rise of scientific method for providing a model of "disinterested" discourse. Specific suggestions from two contributors significantly enhance the usefulness of Habermas's theory for our analysis of the Russian popular theatre movement. Craig Calhoun recommends two changes in Habermas's presentation of the undermining of the public sphere. First, he notes that while its standards of debate were still high the public sphere itself took up the question of *social* justice: "the inequalities always present in civil society ceased to be 'bracketed' and became instead the basis of discussion and action" (21). Second, he faults Habermas for including Mill and Tocqueville in his discussion of Hobbes, Kant, Hegel, and Marx on the public sphere. He considers that they belong at the end of the book because they represent the basic theory of the *post*-transformation sphere. "Mill and Tocqueville accepted an individualism without a notion of the whole. . . . They worried about the possibility of protecting free critical thought from public opinion itself. Here we see an initial theoretical response to the structural transformation of the public sphere" (20). Geoff Ely finds that the value of Habermas's perspective has been "fundamentally borne out by recent social history in a variety of fields" but considers that his book could nevertheless be improved by incorporating Gramsci's concept of "hegemony."[51] Ely also believes that Habermas overstated contention with the state as the defining factor for the public sphere: "The emergence of a bourgeois public was never defined solely by the struggle against absolutism and traditional authority. Also it necessarily addressed the problem of popular containment as well" (52). These suggestions point to the enhancement of a theory already well suited to interpret a large body of empirical evidence.

THE ORIGINS OF EUROPEAN THEATRE

One last preliminary remains. Because our subject is the impact of theatre in Russia it seems appropriate to ask whether something intrinsic to the art itself might have made some audience members change the way they looked at themselves. Might it have motivated not insignificant numbers to want to become participants in its perpetuation? Europeans who wrote about theatre's potential in the eighteenth and nineteenth centuries could rarely do so without referring to its meaning for classical antiquity. In inventing theatre the Greeks had constructed a mechanism that seemed to extract higher truths from tangled and conflicted human interaction. And modern Europeans continued to accord high prestige to such an invention.

Greek theatre evolved out of the rituals of various agricultural festivals, including those honoring Dionysus. Procession probably provided its starting point; other elements from ancient festivals included "dances, scenes between characters separated out from the chorus . . . *agon,* death and lamentation . . . the wedding."[52] A critical turning point came with the fusion of elementary units into sequences, then the genres of tragedy, comedy, and satyric drama, and the professionalization of the performers. As cities became established in Greece the performers found that the rite that had spoken to a rural audience could no longer command sufficient compensation to sustain them. Redefining themselves as actors, they severed their ties with ritual. "We know," wrote Bruno Snell, "that this step met some resistance, on the grounds that tragedy 'no longer seemed to have any business with Dionysus.'"[53] Froma Zeitlin explains the proverb "nothing to do with Dionysus" as a comic quip against the growing complexity of comedy, tragedy, and lyric performed at the Athenian Festivals of Dionysus.[54]

Tragedy and comedy crystallized at a time when what G. E. R. Lloyd calls "the new rigorous thinking" was changing the lives of citizens in Greek city-states.[55] Many Greeks gained extensive experience in the evaluation of evidence and in applying the notions of justification and accountability in the law courts. Lloyd calls attention to the combative atmosphere that developed as various claimants asserted the superiority of their particular branches of knowledge. Paul Veyne also addresses the turmoil that ensued when literate Greeks began to discriminate between different kinds of speech and adopted a nuanced attitude toward levels of meaning. But he concerns himself mainly with those left behind: those "who are docile when faced with another's word, because they are possessed of a virtuous and respectful mentality."[56] The end result of this combat over employment of the new modes of thinking was incredulity arising among the people in what he terms "an upsurge of intractability in response to the word of the other."[57]

The ultimate source of the "new rigorous thinking" was of course written language. Debate continues to rage over the implications of literacy. Eric Havelock propounded the view in numerous books and articles that its impact was revolutionary, direct, and relatively quick. He probably overstated the speed and directness of its impact. But his bold description of a "before" and an "after" underscores the intellectual turmoil of the age in which theatre was born. Greek civilization before alphabetic writing, he asserts, depended on an "oral storage mechanism," which combined exhortation, admonition, proverb, fable, and ritual celebration to transmit accumulated wisdom. In this way, authority was embodied in a voice that repeats and repeats, that captivates by incorporating rhythms, cadences, gestures, and turns of phrase. "You do what you are told to do . . . by a voice which is collective, a voice of the community."[58] A special, privileged kind of speech was employed to preserve the community's codes on diet, hygiene, marriage, and morals. This speech was shaped by a need to facilitate memorization. The voice always preferred a connected story, usually narrating action. A dynamic syntax elaborated "goings-on." The voice ranged freely in a timeless present, with chronology either blurred or irrelevant.

According to Havelock, "Pure, mature phonetic writing" shattered this traditional oral culture and threw society into disarray. It converted the Greek spoken tongue into an artifact, "*thereby separating it from the speaker* and making it into a 'language,'" that is, an object available for inspection, reflection, and analysis.[59] With a symbolic storage device it became possible to scrutinize and reorganize the transmitted codes, to compare and reconcile different accounts. Chronology could be established and cross-checked; it became possible to write in a historical rather than a timeless present. The character of language itself began to change. Syntax adapted to state propositions rather than describe events. Narration of "goings-on" made way for presentation of static facts. Vocabulary expanded to include a number of abstract terms that made possible such disciplines as history and law. Instead of embracing "the right thing to do," an individual with access to the new storage mechanism could develop an autonomous value system.

Without addressing Havelock's work, Francisco Adrados emphasizes the central role of the word as theatre developed out of rite: "The process by which an entire ritual is made anthropomorphic and mimetic, the process which leads to theatre, implies that words acquire greater and greater importance."[60] Words not only become more prominent; they gradually shift away from the collective. If the chorus represented the wisdom of the community through continual repetition, its decline in relation to dialogue may reflect rising social conflict. Oddone Longo believes this to be the case.

> The reduction of the choral element in favor of the actors' debates might be seen as the product of the progressive integration of the drama into the more pluralistic system of the *polis*, where division of labor, social stratification, and class struggle reduce precisely the area of unanimity in the community. As a result dialectical distinction increases, and along with it the opposition of roles and parts.[61]

Longo in fact concludes that the theatre born in Athens developed a fine balance between the spectator's identification as an individual person who assumes the contradictions of the tragic character and the audience's consciousness of its social integration and the claims of the group.

While arguing against a sharp distinction between orality and literacy, Rosalind Thomas notes a shift from the private symposium as a locus for oral performance "and the transmission of memory of the past to the public sphere (agora or public festival)."[62] She also takes pains to show that literacy did not suddenly engender a new legal consciousness. Writing began to be used publicly in the city-states in the mid-sixth century. Thomas contends that at first written laws merely attempted to supplement the revered oral customary law. Even though the Athenians established a central archive in the last decade of the fifth century, "the 'rule of law' remained heavily dependent on individual memory and commitment" (96). Only in the second half of the fourth century did written documents come to be considered adequate proof by themselves, and this was a "result of the ever-present distrust in an increasingly complex society" (3, 149).

A parallel timetable for the theatre would note that plays only began to be reperformed—that is, to become plays—in the fifth century.[63] The oldest Greek tragedy known to us by title and author dates from 493. Authoritative texts of the great fifth-century tragedies were only fixed in the second half of the fourth century.[64] But theatre reflected or perhaps somewhat anticipated Athenians' acceptance of written law. Little more than a decade before Athens established its central archive, Euripides argued for the first time (in *The Suppliants* [c. 420] 433) that written laws could serve as a protection against injustice. Euripides is also generally credited with shifting the focus of drama from large political matters to the private sphere. His *Cyclops*, the only surviving satyr play, shows the difference between proper and deviant manners, between what is human and what is gross and monstrous. Alfred Burns, who believes Euripides' fragmentary *Palamedes* testifies to fairly widespread literacy in Athenian life, stresses the intellectual implications of framing written laws:

> The formulation of written law raises concerns from the specific to the general. The writer must anticipate and categorize future cases. The lawgiver must define a class of events (A) and prescribe action (B) which will invariably follow any event which falls into class (A). This is a decided advance towards more abstract thought.[65]

As the written language generated more and more abstract concepts, "value words" like justice, honor, and goodness, truth suddenly came to be seen as complex. The central characters in their drama are ambiguous figures, somehow distanced from reality by the need to fathom the depths of truth's newly discovered complexity.[66]

THE PLAN OF THIS BOOK

The history of popular theatre in Russia hardly lends itself to straightforward narrative. The institutional developments are easy enough to describe, but form only part of the story. The impact of popular theatre on mentalities is extremely interesting, but the evidence is intermittent and often inconclusive. Work on Athenian theatre helps to illuminate Russian reactions to playgoing: to know that theatre gave audiences a sense of an underlying truth behind the interplay of human affairs, and the impression that what is right and just is clear to anyone who cares to look closely. And, the European experience of popular theatre alerts us to the crucial role of manners. Not only did plays explore the relationship between manners and personal distinction, but audience behavior in theatres—first that of the upper and middle classes and then of the others—in time became decorous and reserved. From start to finish, the propagation of "good" manners motivated presenters of popular theatre.

The literary dynamic is engrossing—what Paul Fussell calls "the simultaneous and reciprocal process by which life feeds materials to literature while literature returns the favor by conferring forms on life."[67] An account can be given of how specific Russian plays were constructed to comment on contemporary issues and customs and were viewed from a different angle when seen after circumstances had changed. The literary aspect is somewhat complicated by the shifting objectives subsumed under sentimentalism, romanticism, realism, naturalism, and symbolism.

It is intriguing to watch humanity emerge in the theatre for inspection, discussion, and speculation. The preconceptions of any narrator of the story of a nation's popular theatre will determine whether that humanity is presented as useful and self-enhancing for individual spectators or a distracting illusion.[68] In fact Russian popular theatre flourished because humanity in the theatre seemed conducive to the development of individualism. The authorities liked the prospect of enhanced self-control that went with individualism, while intelligentsia types liked the idea of an expanded public sphere, where individuals could reason together about laws, public policies, and social arrangements. There is evidence to suggest that spectators were pleased to think of themselves as part of an evolving humanity increasingly characterized by dignity and mutual respect.

Perhaps because of the confrontational structure of its dialogue, theatre fostered the development in some of its viewers of the practice of anticipating how those of different backgrounds will interpret and respond to one's actions. Educated Russians thought this particularly desirable for peasants who appeared to them to be little more than an extension of the landscape in their traditional communities. Anthropologist Daniel Lerner supplies a vocabulary to explain why the empathic skill carried little value in such communities. "There people are taught to handle the ego with minimum awareness of alternatives to current practices—in the technical sense, compulsively."[69]

This skill is related to what Francis Fergusson termed "histrionic sensibility," the mimetic perception of action.[70] For people accustomed to doing as their parents had done, literary theatre revealed a vastly greater range of occupation and behavior. The Moscow Art Theatre, an important part of the popular theatre movement—which grew directly out of the impulse to civilize the folk—intrigued Fergusson because it trained actors to free their minds from the clichés of their own times and the specific limitations of their own personalities. It challenged its audiences to transcend the mores of their times and practice a certain kind of concentration that makes it possible to respond fully and freely to any given situation. The result of this kind of spiritual exercise (Fergusson compares the Art Theatre's methods to the training given by Ignatius Loyola) is the flexibility to lift one's self in its full integrity out of the contingent, to size up any situation critically, and respond to it with intelligence and emotion. Eugen Weber emphasizes in his discussion of what he calls "cultural mimicry" in provincial France how the mimetic skill could be manipulated to make people fit in. "This *mimétisme* . . . could also be used to didactic ends—not only to spread the use of French, but to spread the mentality approved by official culture: to moralize, to civilize, to soothe the savage breast."[71] This "mimicry" is directly related to the "respectability" that overtook English music halls, and the *"kul'turnost'"* that so obsessed Russian enlighteners.[72] It demonstrates yet again the importance of the commentator's vantage point—from within or without—on the enterprise.

In any case, the matter of intellectual skills that pave the way for a new kind of social interaction brings us back to the development of a public sphere in Russia. Geoff Ely denies that such a thing existed:

> Nineteenth century Russia provides an excellent counter-example for the growth of the public sphere. It displayed the absence of all those processes—particularly the emancipatory impulse of free associational initiative, which under Tsarism was precluded by a combination of social backwardness and repressive state authority—that Habermas's concept of *Öffentlichkeit* presupposed.[73]

But Ely lets the tsarist attempt to repeal public opinion and shore up the estates [*soslovie*] system—a forty-year campaign that retreated from a program of public education in the countryside and harassed outspoken members of educated society—obscure the vitality of those forces that finally erupted in the 1905 revolution and secured legal protection for qualified freedom of association and freedom of speech.

The division of this book into two parts reflects two distinct phases of the public sphere in Russia. In the first era of public opinion, from 1856 to 1863, the core plays of the popular theatre repertory were completed and the very first step was taken to present literary theatre to common people in the countryside. Educated society, encouraged to take private initiative by the state, undertook to make itself the agency of Enlightenment. The prospect of free and open public discussion seemed to eliminate the last obstacle to "the rationality that strove to discover what was at once just and right." The reunification of society, the elimination of "two worlds of the mind" through universalization of the rigorous thinking of scientific rationality, the propagation of good manners, morals, and legal consciousness among the common folk, seemed achievable at last. But the result of heightened tensions between the educated public and the state in this case resulted in the state's severely restricting open public discussion for two generations.

At the turn of the century the state could restrain the tide no longer. The transformation of the public sphere began in Russia. As literary theatre (and other forms of art) became a ubiquitous commodity entertainment for the folk, several things happened. Massive resistance arose to the enlightenment project from below, manifested in bitter rejection of "good" manners and taste. Resentment of the educated and their attainments found its voice, along with an upsurge in "intractability to the word of the other." The educated themselves began to doubt that society could be reunified or that civil society could produce consensus. And yet, even as society began to resolve itself into specialists and consumers, theatre in Russia remained an arena for the presentation and criticism of ideas about personality, justice, and relations between individuals. Some peasants and workers took up the presentation of plays themselves as a means of investigating the possibilities inherent in all mankind. In this second era of public opinion in Russia popular theaters began to form the nuclei of community centers, even as the coherence of the larger society fragmented.

Part One

Chapter One

The Birth of Russian Popular Theatre

TWO RUSSIAN NOBLEMEN on diplomatic missions to Italian city-states in the seventeenth century recorded impressions that register the progress in the West from baroque festival sociability to a "public sphere." Tsar Alexis sent one Likachev on a mission to Florence in 1659 as part of his campaign to establish relations for the first time between Russia and the less important European states. A spectacle presented in honor of the special occasion of his visit clearly delighted the ambassador. But his report revealed that he lacked the intellectual framework to make much sense of its representation of majesty, highness, and fame.

> The Prince ordered the play to begin. A palace appeared and then sank out of view. There were six changes of scene in all. . . . A sea appeared, with waves breaking, and in it fish with people riding on them. Above . . . , the sky, with people seated on the clouds. And the people on the clouds began to descend. Picking up the people on the ground, they again ascended and disappeared. Those who had been sitting on the fish also ascended. Then there descended from the sky a cloud with a man in a carriage, and opposite him another carriage containing a beautiful maiden. The horses pulling the carriages were lifelike, their legs moving to simulate running. The prince said that one was the sun, the other the moon. And many marvelous youths and maidens in gold came from behind the curtain and danced.[1]

Likachev's ingenuous account bespeaks an inability to interpret, discuss, or criticize the play he had seen.

Nearly forty years later, early in Peter I's reign, Peter Tolstoy went to Venice as part of a mission to study shipbuilding and other military and civil engineering techniques. He mastered map reading, and learned Italian and the abstruse terminology of seamanship. In his diary he commented on the self-control of Venetians, the absence of public drunkenness, and the civil society his hosts had achieved. "[A]lways cheerful, never blackguarding each other, and with nothing to fear from each other; each one does as he likes according to his wishes. There has always been this freedom in Venice, and Venetians always live without fear."[2] He generalized beyond his evidence, but he situated what he saw in a context. His identification of a society of individuals suggests a critical, comparative bent.

In the 171 years between the theatre Peter I ordered to be built on Red Square and the temporary government-authorized Moscow theatre constructed in connection with Peter's bicentenary the Russian state promoted literary theatre as a civilizing institution. This eighteenth-century regulating state promoted new forms of association for its subjects, and members of the service nobility embraced theatre as a pastime—some devoting enormous resources to the erection of serf theatres in the decades after state service became optional. The passion for theatre among nobles may have been related to its usefulness in addressing the cultural responsibilities the state set them. Plays facilitated consideration of abstract concepts, levels of language, manners, and they stimulated reflection on role-playing among the estate obliged to set an example. The serf theatres would finally disappear, but only after creating a demand for exacting standards in acting and production and for native dramatic texts.

When the state encouraged public opinion in order to debate the renovation of existing institutions, Russian authors of books exploring freedom in the nurturing family took the opportunity to address the public on the need for national cultural reunification. Habermas has been faulted for overemphasizing the centrality of the struggle against absolutism and traditional authority in the emergence of the Public Sphere. But the Russian case bears out Habermas's emphasis. In 1863 Alexander II sharply curtailed public discussion of political reform. But if the autocracy effectively stalled public opinion, it could not halt the private application of reason to the problem of creating a just society. If anything, it deflected such reasoning into belles lettres, where the issues were worked out ingeniously in the context of the private sphere. Theatre profited from this deflection of energy in the form of challenging new plays. Theatre in Russia also advanced as associations the state had earlier encouraged its Westernizing subjects to join pressed its civilizing claims. The state could not approve the critical independence literary theatre promoted; neither, however, could it resist theatre's potential to propagate respectful openness to new worlds of experience.

STATE AND THEATRE IN THE EIGHTEENTH CENTURY

Peter the Great ordered a public theatre constructed in the capital in 1701. His father, Alexei Mikhailovich, established a court theatre in 1672. Here the "most quiet" tsar had taken pleasure from plays written in German until his death in 1676. But a quarter-century later Peter wanted something different, a public theatre "with willing viewers . . . [and] the majority of the audience drawn from the ranks of all the people." He ordered a "temple of comedy" constructed on Red Square inside the Moscow Kremlin near the

Foreign Affairs Department, equipped with stage machinery and sets and seating 450 on benches.[3] A provincial German company was engaged to perform every Monday and Wednesday, and eventually Russian language performances alternated with German. The plays' subjects came from French, Italian, and German plays, popular legend, and events out of contemporary history. The free-admission theatre (to anyone properly dressed) attracted a motley audience of men from the commercial districts, resident foreigners, and clerks from the Foreign Affairs Department (whose education Peter intended it to further).

The tsar had attended a comedy with his retinue the day after he arrived in Amsterdam in 1697, and he frequented the theatre in London in 1698.[4] During his months in the West he had inspected innumerable institutions. He returned home determined to impart to his countrymen something of the vitality he found in Western societies. The location he chose is suggestive. Peter is known to have admired the civility of common people he encountered in the West, and a public theatre in the Kremlin may have seemed to him a way to send a shaft of light into the heart of medieval Muscovite barbarism.

If so, the Holstein ambassador's description of his theatre's ambience should be read with caution.

> In Moscow there is a theatre, but barbaric: only dark people visit it. . . . From time to time arguments flare up. In one corner someone loudly complains that his pockets have been picked, in another corner a Swedish servant, not noticing the stern warning not to smoke in the "temple of comedy," lights his pipe and dumps his ashes on the floor carelessly. His neighbor tries to stop him but he declares that nobody forbids him to smoke.[5]

The diplomat deplored the uncouth audience and seemed to regret the absence of polite society. But if Peter's aim was to educate public taste these were the viewers the "temple" had to attract.

The theatre languished. Peter disbanded the company and closed the building in 1706, after chronic poor attendance made it clear that no public was developing for such a diversion. The acting had proved unsatisfactory. Performers declaimed, and either bored viewers with pathetic monologues or regaled them with buffoonery in slapstick farces. Simon Karlinsky succinctly summarizes the more fundamental reasons for its ineffectiveness: "there were no Russian plays, no suitable literary language into which foreign plays could be translated, and hence no interested audience."[6] He explains that all translated plays were rendered into chancery language (itself a hybrid of archaic biblical style and legalese), and illustrates by noting the impossibility of translating a Molière comedy into Russian at the time: "Not only were there no ways of conveying the notions of pretensions, affectation, flirting, or *préciosité* in Russian, but the concepts themselves had no counterparts in anyone's experience."

The linguistic impediment is crucial. If Renaissance theatre had galvanized spectators by offering an image of ego projecting itself into a variety of experiences involving specialized technical vocabularies, then the audience had to grasp as well at least something of the abstract terminologies and required terms referring to the self's putting on and taking off masks, slipping into and out of roles.[7] During Peter's reign the Russian language added vocabulary at a staggering rate through the incorporation of foreign terms, perhaps doubling its endowment. It incorporated almost two thousand new legal terms alone.[8]

Peter could not wait for the general public to expand its vocabulary sufficiently to appreciate translated European plays. He instead focused on changing the customs, norms, and behavior of the nobility. Besides requiring the nobility to serve the state, he gave them the added responsibility of mastering proper deportment, as defined by western European society. In this he relied on association with foreigners to help his nobles develop the requisite skills. His manifesto of 16 April 1702 inviting foreign specialists to Russia specified as one objective, "to institute changes for the greater training of the people, so that our subjects may be conveniently made into trained people in manners the longer and more thoroughly they are exposed to every kind of society and intercourse with all other Christians."[9] By 1718 Peter was ready to force his modernizing subjects to come together for polite conversation in a form of association modeled on the French *assemblée.* His decree explained:

> Assemblies is a French word which cannot be expressed in Russian by one word, but to speak in detail: a free assembly or gathering in a house not only for amusement, but also for business, for one may see each other there and talk over every need, and also hear what is going on somewhere else, and at the same time amuse oneself. And in what manner these assemblies are to be arranged, this is defined below this point until it will become a custom.[10]

After giving the sets, costumes, and scripts from his Kremlin theatre to his sister Natalia, who established a private theatre at Preobrazhensk, Peter took up school drama. Feofan Prokopovich, whom he brought from Kiev to administer the Russian Church, used plays to explain and propagandize for the reforms. Drama figured as a teaching device in new clerical schools sponsored by the Church and was encouraged as well in the exclusive Infantry Corps for Nobles—where it apparently stimulated the fancy of A. P. Sumarokov, the first Russian dramatist. At the Slavic-Greek-Latin Academy in Moscow it became a tool for explaining misunderstood state policies (like Peter's wars) and even his personal life (his marriage to Catherine I).[11]

Palace grooms and stable boys gave performances from around 1710, according to Jakob von Stählin, the first chronicler of eighteenth-century Russian theatre, but they apparently did less to spread an interest in theatre than did the schools.[12] F. G. Volkov, organizer of what became Russia's first professional acting company, for example, received his early schooling at the Slavic-Greek-Latin Academy. The amateur troupe he assembled also reached out to popular audiences. His father, a Kostroma merchant, died when he was young, and his mother married a Iaroslavl merchant and factory owner. With his four brothers, beginning when he was around twenty, Volkov became involved in the management of the factory and supervision of its workers. There is evidence that they gave plays in the factory in 1750–51.[13] The business itself failed.

As it happened, the state rescued Volkov—thanks to a sovereign's whim—and turned his hand to public theatre at the center. Peter's daughter, Empress Elizabeth, a lover of all forms of theatre, opera, and pageant, learned that Volkov's company was drawing large and enthusiastic crowds in Iaroslavl and invited him to Saint Petersburg to perform. After putting him and his leading players through the Infantry Corps of Nobles (Shliakhetnyi korpus) to complete their education, Elizabeth commanded him in 1756 to organize a public theatre in the capital for performances of secular plays in Russian. By this time the literary language had developed sufficiently, along with the numbers of those who functioned in it, that a market appeared capable of supporting several theatre companies and stimulating in turn the writing of new plays.

Elizabeth's successor, Catherine II, further patronized theatre and playwriting and even wrote plays in Russian herself. Although fond of referring to theatre as "the School of the People," in this as in most of her reforming activity she concentrated her constructive efforts mainly on advancing the sophistication and discernment of the Westernized elite.[14] Russia now had its own theatre, but the common folk knew it not—except, of course, for those serfs removed from agriculture by their masters, employed in domestic service, and specifically trained as actors to provide entertainment in manor house theatres.

Magnates with vast resources began to establish their own private theatres in the first decade of Catherine II's reign. In doing so they consciously or unconsciously emulated their sovereign. The empress augmented the Italian opera first established by Anne in 1732 and made it one of the leading lyric theatres in Europe. And in her passionate devotion to theatre, she did not overlook its value for socialization. In the 1760s all ranks of the nobility (both sexes) were admitted free of charge to the court theatre and opera. In the decade following, the best seats were distributed according to rank, but people without rank were admitted to the upper gallery.[15] The Palladian Theatre she would eventually build for her Hermitage at the Winter Palace and her Chinese Theatre at Tsarskoe Selo remained entrancing foci for court life. In the provinces theatre became the state's preferred instrument for socializing and enlightening the local nobility. According to Priscilla Roosevelt,

"Catherine's desire to enlighten the Russian provinces hinged on her 'children' the nobility, whose own cultural education she had overseen, acting as culture-bearers in the provinces. There, they were to take on the role of tutor, to bring new ideas and manners . . . , precisely through theatre and spectacle."[16] She cites orders in 1776 to the new vice-regent of Kaluga province to build a theatre that would "bring people together, for the spread of social life and politesse" and notes the construction of similar theatres by imperial order in Tula, Kharkov, and Penza. Poet and administrator Gavrila Derzhavin recalled that when he served as governor of Tambov province he found that only a few of the gentry—those who lived much of the time in Saint Petersburg or Moscow—knew how to "dress, move and comport themselves as a well-born person should." He therefore arranged for young volunteers of both sexes from the nobility to give theatrical presentations in his residence on holidays and festive occasions in order to disseminate the requisite skills.[17]

Nobles in the capitals had long since turned their attention to the minute details of self-discipline. Manuals defining correct behavior, similar to one that had enriched book publishers in the West since the sixteenth century, sold well for decades. Between 1717 and 1767 the famous etiquette manual, *Honorable Mirror for Youth (Iunosti chestnoe zertsalo)*, went through many editions.[18] In fact, the authority accorded texts like etiquette manuals and aesthetic works because of the Petrine reforms effectively turned the lives of many nobles inside out by charging formerly mundane matters like dress and hairstyle with significance.[19] When Iuri Lotman investigated the changing self-image of the Westernized as revealed in the memoirs and correspondence of the period, he found that late in the eighteenth century some individuals broke with the generally accepted norms and styles of behavior and began to indulge themselves in playing roles, like "eccentric," "Jester," "ramrod," and "sharp-tongued prankster."[20] The role of *bogatyr*, for example, signified superiority in eating, drinking, lovemaking, physical strength, luxury—a squandering of human potential. Others indulged their taste for the dramatic by organizing serf theatres on their estates.

SERF THEATRE AND SHCHEPKIN

The first, and the grandest, of the serf theatres grew out of amateur theatricals given in the 1760s at the Saint Petersburg home of Count Peter Borisovich Sheremetev, the son of one of Peter the Great's famous generals.[21] Married to the daughter of Elizabeth's chancellor, A. M. Cherkassky, he was counted among the wealthiest landowners of the time. Over the years Catherine paid four visits to the serf theatre he created at Kuskovo, near Moscow, where he gave free open-air performances in his park that attracted upward of thirty thousand visitors—enough to engage all the conveyances in Moscow. By the 1770s Kuskovo was considered the equal of the court theatre in the capital. At Peter's death his son Nikolai became the greatest landowner in Russia and built a theatre at his Ostankino estate near Moscow only slightly smaller than the contemporary Dresden Opera House.[22] Famous in the 1790s for the two serf architects who designed its great stage, its serf actresses named after precious stones, and its serf technicians, the Ostankino theatre had a Paris agent to keep its owner abreast of the latest developments of the French stage. At Ostankino the operatic side of the repertory predominated over the dramatic. Guiseppi Sarti, one of several gifted Italian composers working in Russia under Catherine, trained Sheremetev's serf composer.

It is impossible to estimate how many serf theatres existed from Catherine's reign to the middle of the nineteenth century. Tat'iana Dynnik documented 173: forty-five for the eighteenth century, twenty-six for the turn of the century, sixty-nine for the nineteenth century, and thirty that could not be dated.[23] The theatre of Count Sergei Mikhailovich Kamenskii, "His Highness the Petty Tyrant," survived in Orel province until the middle of the nineteenth century. A continuous line of serf theatres can be traced in Nizhni Novgorod province down to the 1840s; but the famous fair that attracted merchants from all over Russia lured the company of a Prince Shakhovskoi and converted it during the fair's season into a lucrative commercial proposition. Plays with house serf actors began in Kursk province in the 1760s and continued into the 1840s. Yet serf theatres evidently came to an end in Penza province in the 1830s. In Vladimir province they existed only from the 1780s to the turn of the century. "The 1840s," Dynnik concluded, "must be considered the last, already inglorious days of the *pomeshchik* [landlord] stage" (47).

At Catherine's death in 1796 all the serf theatres closed for ten months' mourning. When they reopened, the empress's son and successor, Paul, issued a rescript prohibiting them from performing any plays that had not been approved by the drama censor and played in a public theatre.[24] This significant restriction does not seem to have stifled the private theatres, for theatre mania swept a new generation at the turn of the century. At the beginning of the nineteenth century, Lotman found, the theatre "invaded life—actively restructuring people's everyday behavior."[25] The generation that sensed, thanks to the Napoleonic Wars, that it participated actively in the historical process began to view life itself as a spectacle, shaped by a plot. The enthusiasm for serf theatres declined steadily from about 1825.

The enormous gentry expenditures on serf theatres require some explanation because they seem to fly in the face of economic rationality. The costs of maintaining the Ostankino enterprise to the highest international standards bankrupted the Sheremetev estate by 1810. Catherine Wilmot described the theatrical offering that followed a dinner given at an estate near

Moscow by a man who had been ennobled after his father had made a fortune in Siberia:

> In the interval of Play & Farce they danced a Ballet, nevertheless [the host] made the humblest apologies about the miseries of everything we witness'd "because all his people were engaged at the Harvest & it was impossible to him to assemble any except the few we saw!"[26]

Presumably this landlord's agricultural serfs had no training in acting and could not have contributed to the entertainment except as extras. But his remark indicates at least a dim awareness of the connection between his theatre and his estate's agriculture, and the incident underlines the point that the apparently free labor extracted from serf orchestras and valets entailed real opportunity costs. Lesser gentry with relatively few serfs never lost sight of the fact. For the richest landlords the labor factor would have been virtually free only if the population of agricultural serfs had become so dense that underemployment existed in farming. This can hardly have been the case in the eighteenth century. Laurence Senelick offers a theory that speaks indirectly to the economic question. Gentry theatre buffs trained serf actresses and had them perform for their neighbors. "By means of this exhibitionism, the owner raised their value."[27] This may in fact represent a persuasive motivation for serf owners in the hinterland who took up the pastime after the grandees. But for the court society that aimed to present theatre of the highest quality, the best motive was surely to capture the empress's attention. As long as she had rich steppe lands acquired during the Turkish wars in her gift to disburse to favorites, mastery of her majesty's favorite entertainment may have guaranteed access to her very valuable attention. Once Catherine was gone and financial pressures more realistically perceived by her grandsons curtailed the grants, the theatre as an economic gamble no longer made any sense whatever.

Yet more was at stake than economics. Serf theatre evoked real gentry enthusiasm. The delightfully nutty whim of Count Skavronskii, who indulged his taste for Italian opera by making his servants address him in recitative, offers a good example.[28] Theatre may have been widely adopted because it lent itself to an established pattern of traditional behavior, like open-handed hospitality. It may have represented a tonic against boredom in the remotest countryside. It may have offered scope for organizing, which became a habit for nobles in state service. In fact, it was not at all unusual for serf theatres to overlap significantly with one or another of three institutions prominent in eighteenth-century noble life: the *assemblée*, the barracks—with its regimented efficiency—and the serf harem. Richard Wortman stresses the way in which power permeated the pastime. "The theater was a sign of the power of those who occupied lofty positions in the social hierarchy and high positions in the Table of Ranks. By participating in the magical transformations on the stage, they imitated and assimilated an attribute of absolute power."[29] All of these motives are evident in Count Kamenskii's serf theatre.

I. S. Zhirkevich, an officer transferred to a company in Orel in 1816, left an account of the Kamenskii theatre.[30] He met the count soon after arriving in the city. The count took a liking to the young man and sent complimentary tickets to all his productions during the three years he was stationed there. The Kamenskiis were a military family. Sergei Mikhailovich, an infantry general and decorated war hero, had inherited seven thousand souls on the death of his father, the field marshal. He dressed his two choirs in military garb. The actors and dancers lived under something like a military regime. The former he required to have their lines word-perfect and to work without a prompter. During performances he wrote notes on their errors and omissions.

> On the wall behind him [in his loge] hung several whips, and after every act he went backstage and settled up with the guilty, whose cries were sometimes audible to the audience. . . . And woe to anyone who stumbled or hesitated. As for the acting itself, he seldom complained. (568)

The female house serfs in training to become actresses had to attend every performance. The following day the count required each of them to recite some monologue from the work they had seen. Kamenskii kept four hundred domestic servants, including his actors. He exercised minute control over their work, but the result was a mindless and ultimately unproductive discipline.

> A whole cavalry of lacky trash was installed in the entrance hall—seventeen lackies who were obliged . . . to bring the count his pipe, his glass of water, his shawl, to inform him of the arrival of a guest or of the director. Not one of them could fill any other's assignment, and in their spare time sitting in the antechamber they made nets and knitted stockings. (570)

Despite the size of the staff, rooms went uncleaned, broken windows remained unrepaired. Nonetheless, the count entertained lavishly. Formerly he had lived "like a grandee of old," setting a table for sixty on Sundays and welcoming anyone at all who came properly dressed. It still pleased him to have uninvited guests for dinner. They dined well on excellent food and wine. "After dinner he liked best to talk about his theatre and the talent of his artists" (570). He personally dispatched free tickets to those in the vicinity who enjoyed his favor. When it came to the stage, a need for self-assertion seemed to count for more than any desire to render dramatic texts faithfully. His *Caliph of Bagdad* consumed thirty thousand rubles with its lavish costumes, sets, and decorations. Yet for one who saw it, it was "a crazy entertainment and not real theatre" (565). The productions pleased most of those who attended, but the "highest circle" in the district came only to laugh at

Kamenskii's actors and the impresario himself. On one occasion he took note of their gibes, ordered all the lamps extinguished but one—which resulted in the whole room becoming enveloped in oil smoke—and stopped the presentation. Indeed, it can be argued that precisely now, when serf theatre fell into decay and disrepute, it was because the theatre had produced its own discerning public, skilled in critical discussion.

To Russians of refined tastes, such an approach to dramatic art as Kamenskii's could not produce satisfying productions. After A. S. Griboedov pilloried what might be called "power theatre" in his magnificent play, *Woe from Wit,* serf theatres quickly began to become unfashionable. Kamenskii continued his, buying serf actors from other nobles who were liquidating theirs. In *Woe from Wit* (1824) Griboedov's hero Chatsky, returning to Moscow after travel in the West, finds the ways of the city hopelessly quaint. Ticking off some local characters that signify the city's provinciality, he asks about a nobleman with a private theatre:

> And what of our illuminator, our paragon?
> The one with Theatre and Masquerade written on his forehead?[31]

Griboedov's play steps back to take a disdainful look at the ethics of a court society. It assesses the psychic price to be paid for currying favor, seeking and giving patronage. It sounds a retreat from frivolous socializing, heralds the rise of respect for the rights of the individual personality, and laughs the notion of caste off the stage. As gentry taste matured, all but the most expensive serf theatres ran the risk of looking ridiculous. Most noble impresarios who could not do full justice to the theatre arts found themselves hoist on their own petard. Chatsky discredited not theatre itself, but the misguided attempts of base spirits to exploit it. Absolute aesthetic integrity had nothing to fear from his strictures; it was the very ground of his being. Real nobles could continue to devote themselves to theatre as long as they met it on its own terms rather than attempting to use it to advance other interests.

When the idea that art alone could ennoble any theatrical enterprise gained currency, a door opened for serf actors to engage in their craft on an equal footing with their masters. Almost no direct evidence has come down from serf actors before this opening to reveal how they felt about their employment. Liubov Pavlovna Nikulina-Kositskaia, an actress who started in a commercial theatre in Nizhni Novgorod some years after her father had bought the family out of serfdom, ended her professional career in Moscow. In her memoirs she described an encounter with a serf actress she met when traveling in a remote area. The *pomeshchik* who extended hospitality to her party kept ten maidens whom he had taken from their parents, taught them to read and write so that, as one of them explained to her, they "could play various jests in the *kiatr.*" The girls were known as the master's "concubines." When he had finished with one he married her off "to some disgusting peasant." The distraught source of this information confided that "the peasants and the domestics are all worn out and have to play in the *kiatr* on demand."[32] Nikulina-Kositskaia stumbled on this establishment in the early 1840s, decade of the *pomeshchik* theatres' end-game. But as described to her, it appears to have been more harem than theatre.

The age when masters claimed exclusive right to determine the artistic truth of theatrical productions passed quickly enough. Two well-known literary works have contributed to the illusion that we understand how serf actors felt about practicing their art in bondage. Nikolai Leskov published his "The Make-up Artist" in 1883. This abolitionist tale opened with the image of "the dark and somber ruin" of the structure that had housed Count Kamenskii's theatre, "an enormous gray wooden building with false windows painted in lampblack and ochre."[33] Based on local legend he heard in his youth, Leskov's story hinges on the theatre-obsessed landlord's shocking disregard for his serf performers' interests and personalities. Its epigraph reads "In memory of that blessed day, 19 February 1861" and announces the work's intention as a celebration of the passing of serfdom and routine exercise of arbitrary personal power by one estate over another. Leskov's tale did not, unfortunately, offer any fresh insights into the effects of literary texts on shaping the mentality of serf actresses.

One other literary work responsible for the impression that serf actors' mentalities are well understood is Alexander Herzen's "The Thieving Magpie" ("Soroka-vorovka") published in 1848. His tale describes the life of Kuz'mina, a serf actress assiduously educated in French, German, and English by her affectionate owner, P. V. Esipov, whose serf theatre in Kazan inclined to the brothel type. When Esipov died suddenly, his heirs sold the whole troupe to Count Kamenskii for three hundred thousand rubles. Kuz'mina found herself in precisely the same position vis-à-vis her new owner as Constanze to Pasha Selim in Mozart's *Abduction from the Seraglio.* Kamenskii, somewhat less patient than the Pasha, if just as importunate, distributed her starring roles to others and sharply curtailed her freedom of movement. Herzen based his work on a polished narration frequently given by the famous serf actor Mikhail Semenovich Shchepkin, who had seen Kuz'mina play in the melodrama *The Thieving Magpie.* In fact, Shchepkin's oral version of her plight was well known in literary circles and arguably superior to Herzen's, as can be seen from A. N. Pleshcheev's account in an 1849 letter to Dostoevsky: "I can assure you, Herzen's story does not produce even half the effect of Shchepkin's oral narrative, because there is more sincerity in his . . . the tears glistened in his eyes when he talked of meeting the actress."[34] In this case the declamation, its author, and what he made of serf theatre are far more important than Herzen's outraged account of legally sanctioned villany.

Shchepkin's own writings are an essential source on serf theatre. He compiled a memoir, at Pushkin's urging, and in his later years he corresponded with actors and exchanged information that marks an important step in the evolution of Russian theatre. Strictly speaking, he was a serf whose acting talent secured him his freedom. This would seem to make him the ideal reporter on serf theatre. But he was a most atypical serf. Learning his craft among enlightened nobles who were theatre amateurs, he enhanced his stature by identifying with an art claiming a central place in high culture. His study of that art led him to form a view of human character formation and of Russian society in all its complexity.

Born in 1788, he played his first role—in a Sumarokov play—at the age of eight.[35] He was cast as the only serf in a company of gentry children because he happened to be doing well at school. When they repeated the play for a nobleman celebrating his daughter's wedding, Shchepkin was kept from returning home for a school holiday as planned. He recalled in his memoirs that after the performance the governor of the town kissed each of the other actors and said "Good." To Shchepkin he presented his hand to be kissed and said, "Good lad! You will make a fine servant for your master." From his earliest experience, Shchepkin identified theatre with important social occasions. In 1802 he was sent to the provincial school in Kursk, where he quickly went to the head of his class. The governor noticed him and admired his talent. From 1808 to 1816 he acted regularly with a company in Kursk.[36] He met the Barsov brothers, serf actors, the elder of whom had already bought his freedom. He observed that they were both treated respectfully by noblemen and townspeople—not like serfs. And from this time on he determined to become a professional actor. In 1818 the theatre-going public in Kursk raised 5500 rubles to buy Shchepkin's freedom, and in 1821 he accumulated the last remaining 2500 rubles of the price set by his owners. Having left his master's service, he put himself in the service of the theatre.

The Shchepkin family's enrollment in the serf estate represented a kind of historical anomaly. Documents dating from the mid-seventeenth century show that they were then registered in the clerical estate. Peter the Great and his daughter Elizabeth legislated to require subjects attached to the clerical estate but not actually serving the church to be subscribed to *pomeshchiki.* The Shchepkins became enserfed in 1748 when Count Vol'kenshtein, commander of the Izmailovsk regiment, subscribed Shchepkin's grandfather because he liked his voice. Shchepkin's father became the manager of the Vol'kenshtein estate, overseeing twelve thousand working peasant males. His background explains why young Mikhail would have been sent to school at all. In the course of his tuition the boy felt keenly the disability his status conferred. He was not permitted, for example, to study French. On the other hand, he was permitted to get instruction in drawing, another subject normally unavailable to peasants, specifically because he could put it to use in his master's service.

The theater Count Vol'kenshtein established in his home demonstrated that all serf theatres need not function as harems nor be organized in quasi-military fashion. His had moral and educational objectives and appears to have been motivated by ideas popularized in his day by Nikolai Novikov on the upbringing of children, which called for molding character while protecting from idleness and vicious influences.[37] As Shchepkin recalled in his memoirs, the count was also extending his solicitude to another suggestible, undeveloped creature: the house serf.

> [The count] had an excellent orchestra and a good choir, so he decided to set up a small domestic theatre for the amusement of his children, who were ten and twelve years old: also for the entertainment of the household serfs. . . . His idea was to provide simple amusement for the children, practice for the musicians, and, for the numerous serfs who swarmed all over the house, an opportunity to spend their time more profitably than in gambling or drinking. And I must confess . . . I never met domestics less spoilt and uncouth."[38]

Shchepkin's larger vision of theatre seems related to Vol'kenshtein's serf theatre. There the usual luxury and glitter of household theatre were replaced by the uncompromising demands of an aesthetic. Military regimen gave way to the internal dynamic of an entertainment that stimulates a sense of individual responsibility. In making theatre his calling, Shchepkin assigned it an edifying mission for society as a whole.

Shchepkin traveled widely during the reign of Alexander I while performing. Commercial audiences were so sparse that a company had either to offer fresh plays quickly or move on. In the course of his career Shchepkin appeared in more than six hundred plays, most of them only once or twice.[39] Performing in this way quickly made him aware of the paucity of strong Russian plays. When he eventually found himself working in metropolitan theatre he undertook to coax new scripts from Russian writers.

At the Maly (Small) Theatre in Moscow Shchepkin found a more sophisticated audience, but one still very much in a state of becoming. At the peak of his career, in the 1830s and 1840s, the foundations of Russian literature were being laid in the capitals. First came an awareness of a potential readership for gifted writers who would dedicate themselves to defining and explaining what made Russia and Russians unique. What could be made of theatre audiences and readers of imaginative literature? They could of course be entertained and exploited. But they could also be enlightened, uplifted, educated—formed into a conscious moral entity. Donald Fanger emphasizes Nikolai Gogol's own program in discussing his famous essay on the theatre:

> Comedy, defined as "a true copy of society," mirrors the audience at the same time that it makes of them in their shared reaction a newly authenticated entity, a society in microcosm. Recognizing themselves in what is exposed on stage, moreover, the spectators . . . emerge emotionally and morally elevated.

> This is plainly . . . anachronistic, harkening back . . . to . . . Aristophanic "Old Comedy." Gogol's own *Inspector General,* as Vyacheslav Ivanov has shown, conforms to the model not only in its social emphases but in its designs on the audience. . . . If Gogol's comedy aspired to be Aristophanic, however, his audience was hardly Athenian.[40]

Yet Gogol's choice of an Athenian analogy in attempting to grasp the potential of a Russian audience is astute nevertheless. The Athenians may have identified with a land as small and sunny as Russia was vast and forbidding. They may have had a state as unlike Russia's bureaucratically administered autocracy as possible. But they had been the first people to embark on the path to general literacy, and they had been remembered down the ages for their self-consciousness. Shchepkin and Gogol grasped that advancing literacy and developing audiences presented them the opportunity to become founders.

In fact, the new literature offered far more of the middle-class roles that Shchepkin's friend, the critic Vissarion Belinsky, thought he excelled at than did the existing neoclassic drama.[41] Belinsky defended the "types" approach to characterization by calling attention to the primitive condition of the Russians who formed the subject of the new national art. "The concept of personality among us," he wrote in 1847, "is only just taking shape, and therefore the Gogolian types *for the time being* are the most authentic Russian types."[42] In his acting Shchepkin drew on the people he had observed in his travels. He attempted to project the basic dignity in whichever person he played and to elicit the audience's sympathy for it. He worked out every detail of his characters in advance, giving each its own distinctive voice, manner of speaking, and body language.[43] Whether his goal was to define psychological types, as D. S. Mirsky thought, or social types, he paid close attention to social distinctions and their influence—as can be seen from advice he gave Aleksandra Schubert in 1848.

> Try to mix in society as much as time permits, study man *en masse,* attend to every anecdote that comes your way and always try to understand why something worked out as it did and not in some other fashion: you can substitute this living book for theories, which, regrettably, do not exist in our art as yet. That is why you should observe all ranks of society, without prejudice to any one of them, . . . and this will enable you in your acting to give each social stratum its due.[44]

The relatively new experience of traveling across Russia in the service of theatre enabled Shchepkin to see the country and its society whole; "I know Russian life from the court to the lackeys," he boasted.[45]

The idea that dignity for all was advancing, along with general respect for the rights of others, formed the basis of Shchepkin's sense of historical dynamic. He identified a powerful civilizing force in drama. A. N. Afanas'ev, the collector of folk tales, attested that the actor liked nothing better than to hold forth concerning Russia's forward momentum, which he illustrated by comparing contemporary morals to those of bygone days (as in his account of Kuz'mina).[46] He saw theatre as a medium of communication in the service of progress. General Bariatinskii learned something of these beliefs when Shchepkin replied to his inquiry about constructing a theatre in Tiflis:

> I hope that your excellency's concern on account of the theatre *is not only for its entertainment value* . . . but would also develop an art which is so beneficial for the people. In every century art has always been ahead of the masses, but in the process of contemplating it actively, the masses advance imperceptibly.[47]

A contemporary observed the lengths to which Shchepkin carried his exaltation of theatre: "There was something almost sacred and religious about Shchepkin's love of art; to persecute dramatic art would have been like persecuting Christianity in days of old, and he would be its first martyr."[48]

As a serf, Shchepkin gained access to an art that served the nobility as a means of educating itself. Given Russia's rigid social structure, he could never become a member of "the quality" himself. But he could make a profession of his craft. He had much to transmit in the way of knowledge and technique—not least his legendary understated style of acting, which contributed significantly to reception of literary drama in Russia.[49] His own theatrical discipline adumbrated a professional ethos. In thirty years he was never late for a rehearsal, and he almost never spoke to other actors offstage during a performance, lest he break his concentration.[50] In his teaching, rehearsals were sacred. His objective was not of course to train specialists in re-creating particular kinds of roles, but to nurture creators discerning in their own right, sensitive and faithful to particular texts, playwrights, and conventions of dramatic genres. Late in life he brought into his home and adopted a fifteen-year-old actress, Glikeriia Pozdniakova, who in turn had an influence on the founders of the Moscow Art Theatre.[51] In this way many of his concerns were transmitted to the makers of Russia's theatrical revolution at the end of the century. Through the tradition of professional training he established, the notion was reinforced generation after generation that theatrical literature is somehow a very special, privileged discourse. Shchepkin lived to see the emancipation of the serfs. His remarkable career represented a quite unexpected outcome from serf theatre; a triumph of the values of dignity and self-respect rooted somehow in the literary texts and the practice of their presentation to audiences.

THEATRE POLICY IN THE ERA OF THE GREAT REFORMS

The state's increasing reliance on bureaucracy during the reign of Nicholas I (1825–55) is well known. Less well known is the way in which "enlightened bureaucrats," applying the methods of German administrative science, had begun to collect and organize masses of concrete information about conditions in the empire in the 1840s.[52] Germans had in fact pioneered the systematic collection of "remarkable facts about the state" *(Statistik)*, and German professors had lectured on the comparative economic conditions of European nations.[53] This branch of knowledge that appeared late in the eighteenth century is not unrelated to the circulation of news and goods discussed by Habermas. The Russian ministries under Nicholas began to publish their own journals, in which some of the data they collected were printed and thus became available to the critics and reviewers of the "thick" literary journals that began to appear in the 1830s.

After the Crimean War demonstrated Russia's economic inferiority vis-à-vis France and England, Nicholas's successor, Alexander II, set about to revamp Russian institutions. He determined that reforms should be made based on detailed information, and to facilitate the gathering and review of the information he instituted a policy of "publicity" or "openness" for the first time in Russian history. *Glasnost'* entailed publicizing deliberations of the bureaucratic agencies, co-opting certain members of the nobility and intelligentsia into committees charged with producing reform legislation, and soliciting proposals and memoranda from the general public.[54] Alexander threw open the press. Where it had been nearly impossible to secure a license to start a new publication in the years before his father's death, 150 new newspapers and journals were chartered from 1856 to 1860. Censorship remained, but the administration relied far more than before on responsible behavior from publishers.

For Habermas, "Civil society came into existence as the corollary of a depersonalized state authority."[55] No one claims that *glasnost'* at the beginning of the Great Reforms ushered in a full-grown civil society, but public discussion did soon take up the recent work of Tocqueville and his writing on the decline of estate consciousness at the end of the Old Regime in France.[56] In a book he published in 1862 Prince P. V. Dolgorukov warned that the "despotism of the provincial governors" represented a threat to building a new society from the bottom up. For Dolgorukov the only sure guarantor of grassroots development was legal consciousness, or legality, facilitated by *glasnost'*: "with a free press with the existence of publicity and public opinion giving a stabilizing force, decentralization will be immensely healthy for Russia."[57] He asserted that dismemberment was a real possibility for the Russian Empire unless local initiative could be coaxed into existence.

Thanks to *glasnost'*, the ideas of publicist N. G. Chernyshevsky would become influential among educated Russians who identified with the Enlightenment project for the transformation of society. A seminarian from Saratov, Chernyshevsky had written a graduate thesis at Saint Petersburg University on the power of art to communicate through images. By 1856 he had assumed some editorial responsibilities at the venerable journal *The*

Contemporary (Sovremennik). He quickly exploited *glasnost*'s eased censorship restrictions and announced that in 1858 the publication would become primarily a "social-political" journal.[58] Targeting a new, younger audience that included many students and junior officials, he expanded *The Contemporary*'s paid circulation from 3000 in 1856 to slightly more than 6500 in 1860. In 1858 he also became editor of the government's new military journal *Military Compendium (Voennii sbornik).* The fact that Alexander approved a substantial subsidy for this latter publication suggests the tsar agreed with those who considered that a periodical could help overcome intellectual deficiencies in the officer corps.[59] By the time Chernyshevsky was dismissed as editor at the end of 1858, *Military Compendium*'s circulation had raced ahead of *The Contemporary*'s (with most of the individual subscriptions taken by officers). Chernyshevsky's journalism presumed to interpret the latest developments in science.[60] This was just one of its claims to authority, but helps explain why it was read and studied so carefully by so many.[61] By late 1861 an internal government report excoriated his relentless criticism of the existing social order in *The Contemporary:* "in regard to society [his articles] show contempt for the higher social classes, a peculiar idealization of woman, and an extreme devotion to the lower class of people."[62] Chernyshevsky urged his readers to take education to the people and endorsed the new secular Sunday schools, where university students and army officers volunteered to teach reading and writing in classrooms the government put at their disposal.[63]

Glasnost' ended because a public whose ideas on politics and society had not been permitted to circulate freely in print before 1857 became intoxicated with the prospect of radical reform.[64] At a "literary musical evening" on 2 March 1862, organized to mark the thousandth anniversary of the founding of the Russian state, "advanced progressives" active in publishing staged a kind of antigovernment demonstration. Pandemonium broke out as Professor Pavel Pavlov, one of the founders of the Sunday school movement, began to speak. One observer noted:

> it always seemed to me afterwards that this evening marked the . . . culmination of our dream revolution. . . . The government, consistently wanting to preserve a liberal form of activity, was put in a very difficult situation. It seemed that every liberal measure excited in society a movement which used this measure for its own ends, which were not liberal but completely radical.[65]

In May 1862, after a student strike closed Saint Petersburg University and a fire of mysterious origin destroyed an area three miles in circumference in the capital, the Council of Ministers closed the Sunday schools and issued a stringent new law on private presses.

The 1863 January Revolution in Poland marks the apogee of Russian public opinion's initial launch. Alexander determined to proceed with institutional reform, but exclude the public and leave the design to bureaucrats. The tsar clamped down on the circulation of critical ideas in part by offering educated Russians productive employment within the system. Bruce Lincoln emphasizes the role of hiring policies in changing the minds of many young critical thinkers.[66] Reforms of 1864 creating a zemstvo empowered to levy taxes to provide myriad local services and a renovated court system with adversary proceedings and lawyers also offered significant new opportunities for constructive employment for the educated.

Official consideration of a proposal to open metropolitan theatre production to private entrepreneurs coincided precisely with the first *glasnost'* era. The tsar's secret decision to reject the recommendations of his investigating committee paralleled his decision on the Great Reforms—to proceed under the imperial bureaucracy, eliminating public opinion. As with the Great Reforms generally, financial issues loomed large in the decision to review the status and management of the imperial theatres. A committee appointed in 1856 to consider measures to end the substantial deficits at the heavily subsidized theatres, which enjoyed a monopoly in Moscow and Saint Petersburg, dispatched a representative to study the administration of the principal French and German theatres. This comparative approach to institutional review would continue to figure until the reforms were completed. Although the potential audience for theatre had expanded steadily as the Westernized element in society became more numerous, high ticket prices kept the entertainment beyond the means of many who would have liked to attend. The appointees proposed decentralization, a solution favored by framers of other reforms. The theatre committee's report, submitted to Alexander in 1858, ascribed the deficits "to the fact that the exclusive direction of all the theatres in the capitals is in the hands of the government" and proposed a radical reform of the nation's theatrical life.[67] It recommended theatre in other European countries as a model and suggested permitting private theatres to open.

Count V. F. Adlerberg, minister of the court, whose father had been a trusted adviser to Nicholas, transmitted the report to the tsar. But in a secret memorandum outlining his own views, he argued that because Russian literature had become so political and was so inimical to the present order, it would be dangerous to permit "completely free theatres for all classes in the capitals." Private theatres would immediately become platforms for antigovernment political propaganda and would provide convenient access to the simple folk *(prostoi narod)* for those desiring revolution. Alexander evidently concurred, for he jotted on the memo his decision that private theatres would not be allowed in the capitals. Significantly, no announcement was made of his rejection of this recommendation from his committee's report. But Adlerberg informed the director of the theatres on 2 April 1862 that for the time being public presentation of theatrical works would remain the monopoly of the imperial theatres, with exceptions made only for groups like merchants circles and the German Club.

Vasilii Sleptsov, a man of the theatre, reflected perceptively on the removal of public opinion from the reforming process. A talented mime and monologist who went on to participate in club theatricals in the 1870s and seriously contemplated assembling a model company for popular theatre, he wrote a piece called "About the Theatre" in 1864 in which he tried to explain the abruptness with which this powerful force had vanished. "Public opinion," he said, "suddenly found itself in the same situation as mustard passed around after supper: nobody had a use for it any longer."[68] He alluded to an 1855 play by Alexander Ostrovsky, *A Profitable Post (Dokhodnoe mesto),* to make the point that when the government authorized public opinion it had been responding to a sense that the educated public was rapidly growing in maturity. A character in the play related the creation of public opinion (even before Alexander actually permitted new journals to be founded) to "a sense of justice . . . beginning to be felt by the young, a feeling of responsibility." In Sleptsov's opinion, Ostrovsky had identified a real and striking advance in the educated public's perception of official corruption. But before the educated could become accustomed to regarding their collective insight as a legitimate force in the nation's politics, the central government had raised its ethical standards for officials and quietly punished the worst offenders. Nevertheless, receiving better government appeared to Sleptsov a poor bargain for sacrificing participation in the process of shaping change.

In another essay seized by the Third Section at the time of his arrest in 1866, Sleptsov recalled how the very texture of urban life had changed. "Our life suddenly broke in the middle and fell into two pieces: work and idleness, weekdays and holidays. . . . And now it is another year and where are we? Public lectures have been replaced by public balls, Sunday schools by card playing" (71:361–63). As he saw it, corruption at the center had been succeeded by cynical manipulation that blunted the development of public spiritedness.

> The most important [new] form [was] the dance evening, which continues the whole winter and provides a way to spend the evening in dancing and conversation with girls, who for the great convenience of the public are admitted free. Moreover, at designated public dance halls they had buffets where one could get every kind of appetizer and vodka of the best quality, to say nothing of the fact that at almost every public house it was possible to have private rooms for relaxation and intimate conversation. . . . For the working classes the price of liquor was cut substantially and the number of public houses greatly expanded. (71:366–67).

Sleptsov looked to the theatre to regain in the future something of what had been lost in the public-opinion debacle. In an unpublished essay he wrote for *Fatherland Notes (Otechestvennie zapiski),* he insisted that for the theatre to flourish it needed moral and financial independence, and he referred to theatre's potential as a school of morals and "the great influence it can exercise on the masses" (71:149).

While Sleptsov worked off his anger by writing unprintable articles, less reflective souls pressed for permission to create new theatres. Because Alexander's policy of prohibiting private theatres remained secret, proposals to charter them were received, then rejected. V. F. Mordvinov submitted a project to create one in 1862. A proposal was filed to establish a permanent popular theatre in Kronstadt in 1865.[69]

But it became increasingly difficult to ignore requests to expand the available supply of theatrical entertainment. For one thing, the methods described by Sleptsov that had been employed in Saint Petersburg to ensure the docility of workers carried a price. Encouragement of alcohol consumption could hardly enhance long-term social stability. No less an authority on public order than Saint Petersburg Police Chief F. F. Trepov proposed construction of a public theatre as an alternative that might distract peasants from drunkenness and function as a safety valve for letting off steam that might otherwise go into "social disorders."[70] Adlerberg, now head of the imperial theatres, condemned the recommendation. Censorship could not make plays safe, he insisted, because a phrase or even an image might ignite the dark peasants: "Theatres, like Sunday schools, would only be powerful and true weapons for revolutionary propaganda."

By 1870 one of Russia's most venerable independent organizations, the Free Economic Society, took up the idea of popular theatre and did much to make it more acceptable. Chartered in 1762 by Catherine the Great to encourage nobles to interest themselves in the economics of estate management, the Society focused in its early publications on the peasant as agricultural laborer. By the 1860s it manifested its curiosity about peasant culture by sponsoring a folk song collection. Now its Committee on Literacy, in compiling a list of more than 124 plays, demonstrated interest in a pastime that could benefit peasants. It noted that many works of literary theatre had appeared recently that were valuable and accessible.[71] Besides listing works by fifty Russian dramatists, the committee's report explained that the appearance of Ostrovsky—fourteen of whose plays it included—constituted nothing less than a turning point in the Russian drama. He had brought the merchantry, which, "[consists], in the majority of cases, of simple folk who have grown rich," flocking to the theatre in droves. The potential of popular theatre "to distract the people from crude and immoral pastimes and give them no less entertaining but wiser amusements" was plain to see. The report spoke of popular theatre's "right to exist," and justified it with reference to taking the customers away from the taverns. Such theatre could also "heighten the patriotic feeling of the people."

Addressing concerns about the theatre's incendiary potential, the committee proposed the creation of a special censorship, such as that already existing for the imperial theatres, to make necessary cuts in plays presented to popular audiences. The Free Economic Society had been created to permit the nobility to pursue its interests as an estate. It is noteworthy that the censorship proposed by the committee could function as a mechanism to screen out texts that might incite class conflict. In a review of the report entitled "Nashi Manilovy" (after Gogol's landowner in *Dead Souls* who dreamed of peasant women on his estate dressed in beautiful sarifans, situated in a transformed landscape, selling delicious cakes) social reformer M. O. Shchepkin faulted the committee for omitting the works of authors whose plays portrayed landowners in an unfavorable light.[72] Although criticized for overcautiousness in its selection of plays, the committee endorsed the medium, and this endorsement undoubtedly contributed to the impression that popular theatre might have much to offer and represented no real danger to the social order.

Despite the 1858 committee recommendation that the Imperial Government terminate its monopoly over theatre productions and allow private entrepreneurs to produce plays, as in the West, the monopoly survived. The upheavals of 1862 apparently strengthened Alexander's determination not to open this potential forum of communication as he had opened the periodical press. But if the government demonstrated that it could complete the reshaping of national institutions without guidance from public opinion, it could not in the end resist claims made for theatre by serious persons who spoke for its capacity to uplift while entertaining.

DOSTOEVSKY AND TOLSTOY WEIGH THE TWO CULTURES

Even before Russia's first era of public opinion began, Dostoevsky and Tolstoy had put into circulation books that stimulated reflection on family as the nexus for personal development, the private sphere that Habermas found so important in defining a Public Sphere. Dostoevsky's *Poor Folk* appeared in 1846. Tolstoy brought out *Childhood* in 1852 and *Boyhood* in 1853.

In 1858 Feodor Mikhailovich Dostoevsky and his brother Mikhail applied for and received permission to publish a "political and literary" weekly. Their *Time (Vremia)* printed fiction, intellectual news, and comment. From his editorial platform Dostoevsky in 1861 defined "the major problem of our time" as the dissemination of enlightenment from the upper class to the masses.[73] Yet he cautioned those who advocated simply taking knowledge to the people, "we do not know how to go to the people. . . . Either we exhibit a coarseness beyond all belief, or the pitiful, sugar-sweet manner of Manilov. . . . [The people] will not tolerate . . . a politeness *à la française* which they take as an insult."[74] Besides addressing the issues of the day as a journalist,

Dostoevsky contributed a major fictionalized work on his experiences as a political prisoner in Siberia, which was published in installments from September 1861 through 1862. *Notes from the House of the Dead (Zapiski iz mertvogo doma)* was written as a comment on the sociocultural situation of the early 1860s.

While incarcerated in Omsk from 1850 to 1854, Dostoevsky had experienced a range of behavior generally unknown to Russian writers or readers of the cultured classes. He presented *House of the Dead* as fragments of a manuscript left by a recently deceased landowner who had spent ten years in penal servitude in Siberia. The chapters, written in the first person, purport to be selections from a larger text made by an editor who introduced the work. The memoir rests squarely on the premise that the Westernized classes have no idea how abysmal their ignorance of the peasant is.

> [The gentry] are divided from the peasants by the deepest abyss, and this is *fully* evident only when *a member of the privileged class* suddenly finds himself, due to the action of powerful external circumstances, completely deprived of his former rights, and turns to the common people. It does not matter if you have dealt with peasants all your life, if you have associated with them every day for forty years in a businesslike way, for instance in regularly prescribed administrative transactions, or even simply in a friendly way, as a benefactor, or, in a certain sense, a father—you will never really know them.[75]

The narrator repeatedly emphasizes that it took imprisonment at close quarters with peasant convicts to make him see how much he took accustomed social roles and privileges for granted. He experienced the greatest difficulty in being treated by the peasants as a person. "The hatred which I as a member of the gentry, continually experienced from the convicts during my first few years became intolerable, poisoning my whole life" (176).

He found his value system to be almost completely alien to that of the peasant prisoners. As he observed them closely he discovered that they were intemperate, blasphemous, and irreverent. Not only were they unrepentant of the crimes that had put them in prison: they seemed immoral beings at heart! To be sure, he found some appealing characteristics, like their shrewdness at sizing people up, and their essential personal dignity. But there was no possibility of abandoning enough of his own cultural sensibilities to merge into the peasant community that welcomed and integrated each new peasant within hours of arrival.

The narrator found association with peasants in the prison so loathsome and debilitating that he regularly retreated into the neutral space of the prison hospital.

> During those first few years, I often used to go into the hospital, though not unwell, simply to avoid being in prison, simply to escape from this relentless, unflagging, universal hatred. . . . It was oppressive [in the prison itself], harder

> than here [in the hospital], morally more oppressive. The malice, enmity, back-biting, envy, the ceaseless attacks on us, the gentry, the spiteful, menacing faces! Here . . . all were more on an equal footing and lived in a more friendly way. (176, 164–65)

Were hospital conditions the only ones that permitted members of the two groups to meet in an atmosphere of mutual acceptance? Dostoevsky glimpsed one possible basis for cultural reunion.

Smack in the middle of *House of the Dead* stands an account of a Christmas theatrical given by some of the convicts. The chapter, entitled "The Theatrical Production" *(Predstavlenie)*, concludes part 1 of the book. In an introductory statement he points to "unmistakable signs of a national dramatic art," and a succession of dramatic traditions handed down from generation to generation, attended by soldiers, factory workers, poor people in small towns, and servants of the wealthier gentry in the country and in provincial cities—all traceable to the old serf theatres, and well worth studying.

> In our remote towns and provinces there are actually . . . plays which nobody seems to know anything about, which may never have been published, but appeared from somewhere and are the necessary appurtenance of our popular theatre in . . . Russia. Yes, I said "popular theatre." It would be very, very good if one of our researchers undertook a new and more thorough investigation than has yet been done of popular theatre, which exists, is functioning, and is perhaps not completely without value.[76]

The prison theatricals function momentarily as a bridge between the peasant actors and the narrator, who has seen professionals perform one of the plays on the bill, *Filatka and Miroshka,* in Moscow and Saint Petersburg. Because of their innate sense of quality and the narrator's expertise, for once the peasant convicts seek his approval.

> They recognized that in this [theatregoing] I was better able to judge than they, that I had seen and knew more than they. Even those who were least well disposed toward me were (I know for a fact) anxious now for my approval of their theatre, and without the least sacrifice of dignity they put me in the best place. I see that now, recalling my impressions at the time. It seemed to me at the time—I remember—that in their correct estimate of themselves there was no deprecation whatever, but a feeling of their own worth. The highest and most salient characteristic feature of our people is their sense of justice and their thirst for it. (121)

His judgment on the peasant who played Filatka ("magnificent . . . a born actor with great talent") contains a criticism of the professional actors he had seen in the part: "By comparison with him they were too much *paysans,* and not real Russian peasants. They were too anxious to impersonate the Russian peasant" (124). Even more than the acting, he was interested in the reactions of the audience, who were transported and in complete rapture over one of their own dressing up and playing a gentleman. As he watched the spectacle he could not help pondering how much power and talent in Russia were sometimes wasted in servitude and poverty. He saved his most optimistic conclusion for his summing up of the theatrical: "These poor people were only rarely permitted to live on their own, to enjoy themselves in a human fashion, to live for an hour without care—yet the person was morally changed, if only for a few minutes."[77]

Dostoevsky's text, constructed around a binary opposition between the native culture of the oppressed masses and the alien culture of the Westernized masters, was designed to challenge his readers' historical, cultural, and psychological assumptions. While *House of the Dead* offered no prescription for closing the culture gap, one reading of the Christmas theatricals chapter offers some hope. Could the two sides not meet halfway? The Westernized would have to surrender their privileged status and approach their peasant brethren in a spirit of true equality. The peasants would have to build on their conception of personal dignity and learn some manners (internalize mechanisms of self-restraint and self-control, abandon violence). Given their freedom, they would have to build on their innate sense of justice and develop morality. They would have to build on their respect for quality (as demonstrated in their competitive but objective attitude toward acting) and move toward a Westernized value system where individual achievement counts for so much. Dostoevsky did not assert that the cultural chasm could be bridged; he merely posited peasant qualities that could serve as the basis for development in the direction of civilization. He did not present a program, but rather held out a possibility.

Here was the germ of Dostoevsky's conception of a common culture. The gentry, abandoning their claims to status and social superiority could profit from adopting the peasant culture's premise of the essential natural equality of every person. They in turn could teach the peasants the advantages of self-control and self-possession, could reveal a plane of action where responsibility and freedom went hand in hand. The peasantry could build upon their respect for quality and perhaps eventually overcome their bitterness over centuries of oppression. The two cultures could merge on the basis of exploring a common humanity, and the theatre seemed—to Dostoevsky, at least—the most obvious place for the process to begin.

Lev Nikolaevich Tolstoy established his first peasant school two years after coming into the Iasnaia Poliana estate in 1847. He took no part in its instruction, nor did he ever refer to it in his published writings. During the Crimean War he sought and was refused government license to publish a military journal. To his editor he wrote: "A good half of the reading public consists of military men, *yet we have no military literature,* except the official military literature, which for some reason has not earned the trust of the public and which therefore cannot give nor reflect the direction of our military society."[78]

By the summer of 1858 Tolstoy had adopted the dress and gestures of local peasants. He also read the recently published correspondence of Nikolai Stankevich, and conceived a great admiration for this humanitarian who rejected role-playing of any kind and cultivated simplicity and authenticity. Among other things, Stankevich's example inspired Tolstoy to struggle to break his habit of resorting to physical violence in dealing with peasants. Tolstoy opened his second Iasnaia Poliana school in the autumn of 1859, but interrupted his teaching to accompany his ailing brother to western Europe, where he traveled from May 1860 to March 1861. While abroad he investigated the latest pedagogical theories, inspecting schools and interviewing educators in England, France, Belgium, Switzerland, and several Italian and German states. In London in the spring of 1861 he secured a letter of introduction to Matthew Arnold, then a senior official in the Department of Education, which concluded, "Count . . . Tolstoi is particularly anxious to make himself acquainted with the mode of teaching Natural Science, in those schools where it is taught.[79] When he met social theorist P.-J. Proudhon in 1860 he informed him that Russian society had come to see that without popular eduation no state structure could be secure. Upon his return he hurried to Saint Petersburg, applied for and received permission to publish an educational journal. In 1862 he brought out *Iasnaia Poliana,* an account of his pedagogical activity, which he would discontinue after twelve issues.

The reasoning behind Tolstoy's decision to drop everything and run a school for peasant children was simple. Rapid strides in science and technology at midcentury were widening the gap between the native and Westernized cultures in Russia. In a letter to E. P. Kovalevskii concerning popular education Tolstoy said the signs of progress in Russia, like telegraphs and academies of art, were premature and misleading, when only one percent of her seventy million people could read. "Marfutka and Taraska," he opined, "must learn at least a little bit of what we know."[80] Bridging this gap was vital to the national interest. Educated society did not understand the mentality of the people, and existing educational theories that called for molding the child provoked great resistance from peasants and made real learning impossible. Nobody knew how to teach the people. He could perform a brilliant feat by discovering the way.

Tolstoy conceived his school as a laboratory, for he regarded pedagogy as an *experimental* science (he had earlier spoken of his estate as a laboratory for the study of management).[81] He found works on chemistry, biology, zoology, and geology to be superior to those in all other disciplines in the West.[82] In his diary he expressed his powerful faith in science to achieve his great goal of cultural unification: "We know nothing. The only hope for knowing is for all to know together—to merge all classes in the knowledge of science."[83] One reason for emphasizing its experimental character was to distinguish his scientific faith from that of Chernyshevsky, who understood science to be a collection of discovered truths that could be applied to revolutionize human life and relations through rationalization and simplification of all institutions. To bait Chernyshevsky, Tolstoy flatly insisted that university students could not make good teachers of peasants.[84]

To establish an environment conducive to learning, the Iasnaia Poliana school functioned without corporal punishment. Visitors were astonished at how much learning could be accomplished without beatings. Realizing that peasants had their own body language and gestures, Tolstoy adjusted to his young charges: "Everybody who knows anything about peasant children has noticed that they are not accustomed to any kind of caresses—tender words, kisses, being touched with a hand, and so forth—and that they cannot bear these caresses."[85] Understanding that they had their own time sense, he refused to structure the school day in fixed periods demarcated by the ringing of a bell. The class would study a given subject only as long as its interest remained high. When attention flagged they would move on to another. Even the length of the class day should remain flexible. If the pupils became restless and nothing was being accomplished, they were cheerfully dismissed.

Yet despite his solicitude for their learning environment, he found to his dismay that his pupils could assimilate almost no science! Tolstoy concluded that it would take them a long time to outgrow the conceptions of the physical world they had learned at home and adopt a scientific worldview. They could absorb no geography at all. Abstractions of all kinds gave them difficulty. Three weeks after Tolstoy worked with them for hours explaining the concept of law not one of them could tell him what law was. They had no historical interest whatever. Lacking autonomy, they had no reason to situate themselves in historical time or any larger world. He made excuses, relating their deficiencies with regard to geography and history to their never having traveled beyond the village that was their universe and to lacking any sense of participation in politics without newspapers or opinions. And he redoubled his efforts to coax his pupils to leap the chasm to his cultural heritage.

One of Tolstoy's most instructive misadventures involved his choice of an English literary classic for reading to his charges. As a reflective European he found it perfectly natural to turn to a literary work to sharpen thinking on how one faces the world.[86] But they found the adventures of *Robinson Crusoe* virtually incomprehensible. He dragged them through the work by paraphrasing, but it took a month, and they left it in disgust. Some of the boys wept because they could not understand and retell the story in their own words. On the face of it, the choice of this particular novel seems innocent enough. After all, Tolstoy had achieved a free and easy rapport with his class, and an action-filled adventure story would have seemed just the sort of entertainment they could share. Moreover, the book enjoyed continued high reputation among the literate of the lower orders in England, where it remained one of the two or three books most likely to be read by people who read only a very few in the course of a lifetime. Yet one can only wonder whether Tolstoy was fully cognizant of why he selected Daniel Defoe's first novel for this experiment.[87] It seems an unlikely choice for people who could not fathom geography because they had never gone anywhere. *Robinson Crusoe,* firmly rooted in seventeenth-century English empiricist epistemology, and incorporating formal techniques developed in the genre of autobiographical memoir, represented a landmark in the representation of individualism. Could anything have been more puzzling to lads from extended families in communes in the precapitalist Russian countryside? Surely Tolstoy expected his peasant pupils to go far more than halfway in meeting Western culture if they were to comprehend the outlook that informed this book. Ian Watt observes that *Robinson Crusoe* offers, "for the first time in the history of fiction . . . a hero whose day-by-day mental and moral life is fully shared by the reader."[88] Did a desire to stimulate self-scrutiny, with its implications for self-control, perhaps motivate Tolstoy to choose a completely inappropriate book—or did the writer's fascination with craft and technique cloud his judgment?

Remarkably, Tolstoy's failure to teach *Robinson Crusoe* led in an indirect way to his one major breakthrough in the school. In requiring the children to retell the story in their own words he concluded that it was the literary language of the (translated) original that impeded comprehension.[89] To demonstrate his hypothesis that the peasants were as adroit, creative, and original in their own colloquial Russian as the educated were in literary Russian, he found it useful to shift the focus of teaching back to the content of peasant culture. It occurred to him that folk proverbs expressed the tensions felt by peasants in everyday life, and he decided to choose one at random from his copy of Snegirev's collection and ask his class to "compose a little drama on it."[90] The results astounded him. When it came to making a narrative faithful to the details of peasant life, each of the students concocted a story superior to the one he himself produced on the theme. Two of the boys stayed late and together with Tolstoy they crafted a story he considered to have real artistic merit, by virtue of its simplicity, its action, and its trueness-to-life.[91] He declared victory, publicized the talent and ability of the best pupils—and closed the school.

Having determined that peasant scholars could accomplish most if they worked from what they knew and concentrated on developing their self-expression, Tolstoy returned to literature and began writing *War and Peace.* It has been said that "everything [he] learned of and from the peasants up to the closing of his school, found a place in his literary works."[92] He may have revealed his disappointment at the peasant children's inability to leap across the culture gap from the warm and responsive environment he had created for them, when he remarked in 1863, "I can feel sorry for [the peasants], but it is hard for me to understand how I could love them so strongly."[93] In the magnificent failure that was his school Tolstoy had stumbled on his pupils' dramatizing impulse. He would go on working to build a common Russian culture and would one day write for the popular theatre, long after rejecting science as the central component of the world view of the educated.

POPULAR THEATRE AT THE 1872 POLYTECHNIC EXPOSITION

Tension between the state and educated society persisted after *glasnost'* ended in 1863. But some officials considered that literary theatre could usefully be made available to popular urban audiences. By the beginning of the 1870s authorities allowed themselves to be persuaded to permit a public theatre to open on a trial basis. For one thing, significant new ground continued to be broken in Russian theatrical literature (as in Russian literature generally), and it seemed mean-spirited to keep works by highly talented authors from a wider native audience. This literature seemed to embody desirable progressive values that promised to contribute to the moral development of those who consumed it. But if the Popular Theatre of the 1872 Polytechnic Exposition affirmed for many the vitality of performance art in Russia, it also increased the awareness of some high in government—a government only slowly becoming depersonalized—of theatre's potential as a provocative and dangerous social instrument.

Civic-minded Moscow philanthropists formed an association to establish a theatre that would serve the urban lower classes (townspeople, in the estates system of classification). Municipal government, reorganized and strengthened as part of the Great Reforms, supplied material support. Management drew on the highest professional wisdom of the Shchepkin tradition to present productions of exemplary quality. The participants in the venture regarded its audience impact with the utmost curiosity and optimism.

The central government authorized an all-class theatre to be created during the Polytechnic Exposition of the summer of 1872 as part of the festivities commemorating the two hundredth anniversary of the birth of Peter the Great. In the background of this ambitious public theatre stood a (rejected) proposal for a people's theatre submitted to Alexander by Saint Petersburg's chief of police, F. F. Trepov, in 1868. Anthony Swift has assessed the project shrewdly:

> Since June 1866, when the tsar had ordered the police to curb the growing "debauchery, depravity, and especially drunkenness" of the city's lower classes, the police had been attempting to restrict public drinking. . . . Now that the problem . . . was under control . . . it was time to take more positive measures to raise "the moral level of the common folk." Having limited the opportunities of the "uneducated milieu" to indulge in "crude pleasures," the police had the obligation to provide them with "the opportunity for a different, more sub-

> lime means of satisfying their need for amusement." In Trepov's mind, drunkenness and immorality were cultural rather than social problems.[94]

Several of Trepov's assumptions found official support, and a People's Theatre was finally authorized for a celebration "meant to be . . . a demonstration of the country's modernity."[95]

A commission appointed from members of an unchartered group to discuss construction of a popular theatre in Moscow, The Society on Behalf of Workers (Obshchestvo popecheniia o rabochikh) first met in January 1871. Prince V. A. Dolgorukov, governor-general of Moscow and former head of the Third Section (1856–66), put a site at its disposal. The commission, headed by M. Ia. Kittary, served under a committee appointed to plan the Polytechnic Exposition. Its members included theatre director A. F. Fedotov and Prince V. A. Cherkasskii (then mayor of Moscow). Kittary persuaded Peter Shuvalov, Dolgorukov's successor as director of the Third Section, and Interior Minister A. E. Timashev that such a theatre would not threaten domestic tranquillity. Alexander II gave his permission on condition that Timashev approve the plays to be performed. N. M. Shchepkin, son of the late actor, wrote a long article defending the idea of popular theatre.

In the course of ten public meetings held in the library of Moscow University, the commission reviewed the Society's original project. It called for a reading room, school, tea room and lunchroom for the people in addition to a theatre. Though the commission started with only 400 rubles, it secured an interest-free loan of 10,000 rubles from the Moscow City Duma and proceeded to commission architect and painter V. A. Hartman (whose work would be immortalized by Mussorgsky's *Pictures at an Exhibition*) to design a fully equipped theatre seating two thousand.[96] The theatre of the Polytechnic Exposition opened its doors on 4 June and closed on 1 October.

By several measures, it triumphed. One critic wrote that the actors gathered by director Fedotov enabled him to "introduce a new element into our national culture."[97] Nearly everyone who attended the Polytechnic Exposition took in a theatre performance as well. With ticket prices ranging from five kopeks to one ruble fifty, it was technically a "general access" *(obshchedostupnyi)* rather than exclusively popular theatre. A full house brought in 860 rubles—enough to hire good actors. Fedotov assembled a troupe of forty-five, which included many well-known performers from the provinces. He introduced important innovations that gave this short-lived institution a lasting place in Russian theatre history.

Aleksandr Filippovich Fedotov had joined the company of the Maly Theatre in 1862, after being expelled from Saint Petersburg University for participating in a student demonstration. The following year he married Glikeriia Pozdniakova, Shchepkin's adopted daughter. (He too instructed Stanislavsky, who said in his autobiography that acquaintance and rehearsals with Fedotov were his best school.)[98] At the Maly, Fedotov absorbed Shchepkin's natural, undeclamatory style of playing, and he made his Polytechnic company in 1872 work in that tradition. He considered that this naturalness and the respect with which the company treated the audience created a bond after the first few performances. Challenging plays were of the utmost importance in reinforcing this bond. He insisted that the simple folk could perfectly well understand Gogol, Pisemsky, and Ostrovsky. Vaudeville, he predicted, would bore them; and when the audiences proved him correct, he virtually eliminated it from the repertory. Like Shchepkin, he insisted on fidelity to the author's text. At a time when the Maly still relied on all-purpose sets, Fedotov's Polytechnic Theatre had sets especially designed for each play. He also gave unusual attention to costumes and makeup. The seeds of what came to be known as ensemble playing can be discerned in his direction.[99] The production values were noted by literally all the writers who reviewed the work of the Polytechnic Theatre.[100]

Did audiences respond well to the challenges of serious Russian theatre? The evidence was inconclusive. On the one hand, audience taste as reflected in ticket sales left something to be desired. A grandiloquent melodrama by S. A. Gedeonov, *Liapunov's Death (Smert' Liapunova),* which played twenty-two times altogether, loomed as the Polytechnic Theatre's most demanded offering. Nevertheless, Fedotov declared the experiment a success. "The *simple* Russian viewer, after the popular theatre had been in existence a short time, succeeded in showing the people studying him that he was far from being as simple as the gentlemen philanthropists thought who up to that time had insisted that Shrovetide *balagany* and other such fare were sufficient to amuse the folk." He explained the mixed results with reference to his mixed audience, which included the educated—"for whom theatre is only an illustration of life, a fresh combination of occurrences long familiar"—and the uneducated, "the petty trader, the member of an *artel* [communal association of laborers], the foreman or factory worker" who needed to know "how to think, to feel, to suffer and to enjoy, how to live in the light."[101]

The tsar formed his own impression of this theatre for the people at the end of its first week. He arrived in the middle of the second act, accompanied by Interior Minister Timashev, for the special performance he had requested of *The Inspector General (Revizor).* They left in the middle of the third act. As soon as Timashev returned to Saint Petersburg, he telegraphed Dolgorukov in Moscow proposing that the Gogol play be withdrawn from the stage of the Polytechnic Theatre, inasmuch as "the impressions produced in the production of this play by the stage atmosphere are not in complete accord with the positive goals for which the popular theatre was established—that is, raising and improving the morals of the people."[102] The fact that Alexander chose to be present for this play in particular suggests that he questioned whether allowing uplifting entertainment for the masses might be detrimental to the state's authority.

Gogol's "Old Comedy" approach to his audience in this play, seeking to form it into a microcosm of society so that it could in turn judge a society, was not at all what the authorities wanted; they reasoned that sober and reflective models of behavior on stage would stimulate imitation of that behavior by simple folk. In the end they reached a compromise on *The Inspector General.* Rather than risk offense by forbidding it altogether, the officials curtailed the number of performances. At the end of the season decisive steps were taken to liquidate the institution. The theatre was turned over to commercial promoters who stripped away all the professional features from the Shchepkin legacy. The Ministry of the Court secretly gave permission to two businessmen, F. M. Urusov (who had been a member of the commission) and S. V. Taneev, to open a private general-access theatre in Moscow.[103] The Duma sold them the building at a knockdown price. Urusov and Taneev raised ticket prices, thus excluding from the audience the simple folk for whom it had originally been intended.

The prehistory of Russia's popular theatre movement can be seen to have begun with Peter the Great. His Red Square Theatre of 1701 was just one of the tsar's innumerable projects. He was in fact a quintessential "projector," as defined in Daniel Defoe's *An Essay upon Projects.* Defoe allowed that only about the year 1680 had the real "art and mystery of projecting" begun to creep into the world.[104] Projectors were those who, urged by some pressing necessity, turned their thoughts to "honest invention, founded on the platform of ingenuity and integrity"; the fundamental objective of a project consisted of "public good and private advantage."[105] Peter's attempt demonstrated that the modern state could not command a public for literary theatre. But the private advantages enjoyed by the "new men" connected to the modern mercantilist state included new forms of association, and literary theatre quickly commended itself to their attention.

By the late eighteenth century the Russian nobility showed a marked affinity for literary theatre. They had also incorporated literature into their lives as regular consumers of printed texts. Gary Marker found that a surge in book sales during the later 1780s confirmed an expansion of literacy among segments of society beyond gentry and educated priests. The literature that appears to have sold uniformly well at the time was moral fables and stories.

> Readers had extensive practical concerns about the laws but quite limited interest in the principles or philosophy of law. They were more likely to be drawn to literature or general interest non-fiction that presented easy and concrete examples or guides to personal behavior and fulfillment than they were either to abstract considerations of ontology and epistemology or to discussions of . . . general social issues. They were eager to read descriptions of other times and other places, whether real or imaginary, but complex analyses of other

societies, cultures or politics left them cold. All this points to a reading public with an overriding concern for . . . how they themselves should behave."[106]

The same dynamic seems to have operated in the serf theatres, where the performers themselves became absorbed by the challenges to prevailing norms presented in the dramatic texts. This accords with the emphasis Habermas gives to the influence of the circulation of literary texts. Dramatic texts emerged, like Griboedov's, which called attention to the very processes that were leading individuals who had been connected to the state to adopt independent objective value systems and a critical attitude toward privilege.

It was a peculiarity of Russia's estate system that deflected an unusual serf like Shchepkin—from a literate, even bookish, family—to professionalize theatre practice early on. Had Shchepkin been born a noble he might happily have devoted himself to a serf theatre of his own as he perfected his taste. As it was, the more reactionary elements of Moscow society "saw something subversive in [his] progress to full acceptance as a citizen."[107] This scion of educated clerics raised theatre itself to a kind of religious status and assigned it a mission to define Russia's state of grace and national progress.

When the state finally sanctioned public opinion in Russia, the educated predictably began to enlighten the government about its duties. But within the ranks of the educated, differences appeared concerning the course of popular enlightenment. Dostoevsky and Tolstoy rejected Chernyshevsky's faith in the mechanical transmission of abstract reason to the ignorant. While agreeing on the vital importance of cultural unification, they urged an empirical approach to determine what the simple folk might *select* for assimilation.

For the government's part, even after the autocrat terminated the general-access theatre of the Polytechnic Exposition (which embodied the professional standards established by Shchepkin), it could not leave theatre alone. Just four years later a provincial governor-general raised funds to construct a theatre and concert hall in Viatka. In a letter to a prospective donor appealing to local civic and individual pride, he explained that theatrical productions could have value in raising public consciousness and morals.

> Everyone knows that in theatrical performances society sees, as in a mirror, the good and evil sides of life. . . . No moral book, no moralistic lecture can have the kind of powerful corrective influence on a person as [can] a play in which all the ugly and beautiful actions of the human soul are shown . . . by means of living examples.[108]

Theatre had by now attained a prestige that simply begged to be exploited.

Before leaving the period of first *glasnost'* we must verify that it produced a drama capable of speaking immediately and directly to the common folk. The evidence confirms that by the time serfdom ended, Russian plays existed that could galvanize peasants in the countryside and elicit their comment and reflection.

Chapter Two

Essential Ostrovsky

THE CAREER OF Alexander Nikolaevich Ostrovsky spanned three very different epochs in Russian history, and each left its mark on his work. In the 1840s Nicholas I perfected the regulating state Peter I had imagined. But his regimentation, bureaucratization, and supervision stimulated intellectuals to see civil society as *their* business.[1] After the Crimean War, under Alexander II, came the appearance of a public sphere, which entailed freedom to circulate observations and comments on the recent Nikolaevan order in literary texts. After Alexander II's assassination his son Alexander III vacated some of the Tsar Liberator's commitments to public education and limited public participation in national politics; nonetheless, he patronized Russian artists and indulged in what could legitimately be called Great Russian cultural chauvinism.

Boris Pasternak said in his autobiographical meditation on creativity that every work of art is the story of its own creation.[2] This was never truer than in the case of Ostrovsky. Like Dostoevsky and Tolstoy, he saw in the rapidly changing marketplace of Russian literature the opportunity to establish himself as a founder. To his generation, literature beckoned as a branch of philosophy whose potential audience included most of Russia's educated public and whose potential rewards evoked the strikes of the California gold fields.

Ostrovsky's work, considered as a whole, conforms to an overall design. Iuri Lotman described the development that had created the intellectual climate in which the playwright labored: "The psychology of ambition underwent substantial alterations around the end of the eighteenth century. Side by side with the ideal of self-assertion, of changing one's own status in an unchanging world . . . arose the ideal of activity in the name of changing the world."[3] Ostrovsky's program can only be identified with modernism. For convenience, a list of characteristics drawn from a discussion of Habermas's defense of modernism (against postmodernist criticism) will indicate its main features.[4] Modernity is denoted by a consciousness of novelty, accelerated technological advance, subjective freedom, democratic self-determination.

Habermas, following Walter Benjamin, insists that the modern age rooted its legitimacy ultimately in the past.

> The modern age does not rigidly imitate the past . . . nor does it appropriate the past with a view to solving the problems of the present. Rather, the past is creatively invoked to counteract "homogenous and empty time," the evanescence of the everyday, the oppressive continuity and normalcy of the routine, in a revolutionary correspondence with the unredeemed hopes of former generations.[5]

Besides the temporal, the spatial aspects of modernity intrigued Ostrovsky—like the disappearance of gendered space. As Henning Beck puts it, "the modern world is not partitioned off in two spheres with but tangential points of contact, as is still the rule in some Arabic countries, where 'public life,' from pavement cafés to government agencies, is a male enterprise."[6] Ostrovsky's modernist preoccupations will become clearer with reference to specific plays and his proposals for a national theatre.

His plays succeeded in the marketplace because they seemed to offer sensible guidance for dealing with the changing "feel" of time and space. Other themes proved attractive. The tension between the claims of authority and the community as against the claims of the autonomous self to personal fulfillment in the family loomed large in his work. So did the need to belong, to associate with a community beyond the family. The costs of dependency—weighed against the costs of increasing self-control—and the question of rights and the ideals of justice and dignity returned again and again. An examination of his methods, his particular sort of realism, and its precise situation within the procession of literary "isms," reveals how he lowered barriers to identification for popular audiences.[7] Responses to his work are particularly well documented.

INVENTING THE POPULAR THEATRE

Ostrovsky (1823–86) would leave a legacy that included forty-seven original plays, five written in collaboration with others, several translations of foreign classics, and seven historical plays written in verse. Before he had finished, he touched on all walks of life through the seven hundred characters he created. Although the corpus he left retained the power to grip popular audiences long after his death, the very first plays he wrote held the strongest attraction for the *narod.*

Clerical respect for learning and service to the regulating state intermingled in the playwright's background. Ostrovsky's father came from a well-educated priestly family and was graduated from the Moscow Theological Academy but chose to enter the civil service. He practiced law in one of the city's poorer sections. When his first wife died, he married a baroness of

Swedish extraction who taught young Alexander music (which he read easily) and, with the help of tutors, languages. The youthful language studies may have heightened his sensitivity to language itself. Alexander told the playwright A. F. Pisemsky, "In our family we studied languages with unexampled diligence. Especially French. Ancient ones too—Greek, for instance, and Latin—oh, how we did grind at them."[8]

After two years in the Law Faculty at Moscow University, where his studies took a back seat to frequent attendance at the Imperial Maly Theatre, Alexander failed his exams. This did not keep him from entering the civil service, and he soon found employment in the Moscow Commercial Court, where he became intrigued by the language and customs of "Over-the-River," Moscow's merchant quarter south of the Kremlin. The law attracted his attention to the merchantry because of their peculiar attitude toward it, which bespoke an astonishing lack of any underlying sense of justice to undergird the rights enforceable by the court.

In 1847, as a government fearful of revolutions tightened its regulation of intellectuals and artists, he published *Scenes from Life Over-the-River (Stseny iz zamoskvorechskoi zhizni)*. One of those scenes, "The Bankrupt" ("Nesostoiatel'nyi dolzhnik" [Bankrut]), was judged by the authorities to present a distasteful picture of unredeemed viciousness in Russian society and brought Ostrovsky a stern lecture prepared by an Extraordinary State Commission—and termination of his government employment. Although an investigation revealed nothing to suggest subversive or malign intent on his part, he was nevertheless put under surveillance. Undeterred, he expanded the scene into *It's a Family Affair—We'll Settle It Ourselves (Svoi liudi, sochtemsia)* in 1849. Though it was highly unlikely he could obtain permission for production, he was of course free to read from it in private homes.

Retirement from the bureaucracy freed all his energies for the theatre, and the government made no effort to interfere actively with his talent. *Don't Get into Somebody Else's Sleigh* was his first play to secure performance. The Maly mounted it in 1853 as a benefit for Nikulina-Kositskaia, who possessed a remarkably rich voice and a superb reputation for expressive singing. Nicholas I attended its second performance and left the theatre enchanted. He remarked, "There are few plays that have given me as much pleasure as this one. This is not a play, it is a lesson."[9] Nonetheless, he took no action to cancel the surveillance on the dramatist.

The literary salon proved important for Ostrovsky's advancement. Evenings in private homes provided an outlet for his dramatic composition, brought him into contact with new people, and gratified his taste for Russian songs. Restraint characterized his vocal performance. When he read, he changed his voice hardly at all for the various characters, bringing them to life by altering his intonation instead. On one occasion he read "The Bankrupt" at the home of publisher Mikhail Pogodin in the presence of Gogol and M. S. Shchepkin. Partly on the strength of his reading, Pogodin appointed Ostrovsky editor of his Slavophile journal *The Muscovite (Moskvitianin)* in 1850. Ostrovsky shared the Slavophiles' interest in traditional Russian culture, and his early plays are often referred to as belonging to his "Slavophile period."

He socialized with several friends who came to be known as the "young editors" *(molodaia redaksiia)* of *Moskvitianin,* men like him who were ten to fifteen years younger than the Slavophiles and Westernizers. In 1847 he met Tertiev Filippov, a protégé of Pogodin, in a student tavern. Filippov taught Russian literature and Church Slavonic at the First Moscow Gymnasium. He invited a colleague, Apollon Grigoriev, to a party at Ostrovsky's. Grigoriev begged to join the circle and was accepted.[10] In 1851 Pogodin turned over the belles lettres and literary criticism sections of *The Muscovite* to the young editors.

The folk song was one of the interests the editors shared. Under the aegis of Romanticism the Russian folk song had followed the art song into the literary salon in the 1840s. Slavophile Peter Kireevsky published a collection of Russian folk songs in 1848. From 1846 Ostrovsky had trained himself in the art of singing. Grigoriev, an accomplished guitarist with an inadequate voice, specialized in gypsy songs. Filippov possessed the most extensive repertory of songs and perhaps sang them with greatest accomplishment.

Singing formed part of the appeal of the taverns for the young editors. Gypsies who performed there were also noted exponents of the Russian folk song. Carousing was a related attraction. Several of the editors, Grigoriev and Ostrovsky among them, had reputations as heavy drinkers. Wayne Dowler, Grigoriev's most recent biographer, tells of how Grigoriev prowled the taverns and back streets of Moscow in search of talented folk performers and coerced embarrassed friends into going to listen to them.[11] He quotes from a letter written by Grigoriev from Florence at carnival time in 1858 that reveals something of the magnetism the tavern exerted on the circle:

> Our [Shrovetide] sketched itself before my eyes, our good, intelligent and capacious people with their sprees, hard drinking and colossal dissoluteness. . . . A winter snowstorm came to life in my memory, the Novinskoe, the wit of the conversation of the factory workers with the clowns, the *samokaty,* the songs of my fatherland, the cellars in which I . . . spent the night. (106)

In the same letter he mentioned hearing a rumor that the drunkenness and debauchery of Ostrovsky and Pisemskii had in recent times reached Herculean proportions.

The theatre represented another common interest of the editors. Several actors figured as members. And two important playwrights stood at the circle's fringe. A. A. Potekhin and A. F. Pisemskii, who had served together in the Kostroma provincial administration, were both close to Grigoriev and

Ostrovsky. Members of the circle who wrote also had the habit of appropriating Russian proverbs to title their works.[12]

Ostrovsky's early plays pursued Russian singularity through avenues of particular interest to the young editors. Folk songs and proverbs belonged to the merchant lifestyle, because the merchant class had until that time largely avoided the Western influences that had affected noble and clerical estates.[13] Ostrovsky had started with the merchants because he wrote what he knew. Their culture still appeared exotic from the standpoint of readers of Russian literature.[14] Grigoriev had grown up in the Over-the-River district, and so had a basis for judging how well Ostrovsky had captured the texture of merchant life there. The future jurist A. F. Koni tutored in the district while preparing for a legal career; he observed that the merchants in Ostrovsky's play generally taken to be caricatures were in fact true-to-life.[15] Ostrovsky frequently gave readings to groups composed exclusively of Moscow merchants, where he received expressions of gratitude for the precision with which he presented their class, including the revelation of their vices.[16]

The young editors also sought to establish a new relationship to the Russian past. Muscovite culture was to a certain extent preserved among the merchantry and the *narod.* Outstanding personal achievement never became an ideal in old Russian culture, nor did a code of pure, disinterested behavior develop for the conduct of business in old Russian civilization.[17] Ostrovsky set no store by triumphs of acquisition and possession—another attitude typical of old Russian culture.

The young editors believed the merchant class had used the Russian language to the full extent of its richness.[18] Ostrovsky captured much of that linguistic originality in his early plays, but continued this line of search for a usable past in historical dramas. Liberal historian A. A. Kizevetter would testify on behalf of his skill:

> Whoever has an acquaintance from the documents with the speech of our sixteenth- and seventeenth-century ancestors will find in Ostrovsky's historical dramas an incomparable artistic delight, for there one sees how much Ostrovsky is at home among the treasures of authentic old Russian speech that he is able effortlessly and with perfect ease to intertwine the rough diamonds of this speech into his poetic language in such a way that the antique expressions neither mottle nor burden the literary language of the poet.[19]

Another connection with the Muscovite past which Ostrovsky exploited was the surviving rituals of everyday life. *Byt* lent itself beautifully to dramatic depiction.

> *Byt,* that little chest of treasure accumulated by the people, preserves everything rooted in a given environment and established customs—methods for relating to surroundings, things and persons, methods of relating to the self, the upbringing of the family . . . ordinary modes of thinking and feeling. All this creates its own kind of ritual, the everyday practice of our life.[20]

The ritualization of everyday life harkened back to sixteenth-century Orthodoxy. Ostrovsky depicted sympathetically the behavior patterns that had stood the test of time. If he worked whole verses of folk songs into his 1850s plays, it could easily be justified by the centrality song still retained in the life of the folk.

The tension in his plays often came from ancient customs colliding with the modern claims of the individual personality. Over and over Ostrovsky counterpoised the charm of tradition, which offers everyone a comfortable place in harmony with his surroundings, and the claims of the autonomous individual possessed of rights (whose power he had witnessed firsthand during his service in the commercial court). Despite its charm, tradition stifled individual choice. The patriarchal autocrat of the family—Ostrovsky christened him *samodur*—could claim the justification of tradition when he kept his wife in seclusion, arbitrarily arranged the marital or educational futures of his children against their wishes, or brutally enforced his will on any matter. Women as well could abuse the power they enjoyed by virtue of their position in the hierarchical family structure, and poisonous relationships frequently developed between mothers-in-law and daughters-in-law. In Ostrovsky's estimation, individualism and the traditional culture were not inimical. He suggested that the traditional ways, whose essential goodness he never doubted, could somehow be restored to their original glory by respecting the claims of the individual personality. Both the perpetrators and victims of *samodurstvo* could affirm their dignity and correct themselves if they could be made to see more clearly into themselves.[21] A course of guilt is not prescribed for the errant, for in a way they are victims of tradition and therefore deserving of pity. The goal is a restoration of harmony with the group, consonant with individual rights and dignity.

What started with an inquiry into merchant life naturally extended itself to the life of the peasantry. Indeed, Ostrovsky is said to have advised A. A. Potekhin to write his first play, *Man's Judgment Is Not God's Judgment (Sud ludksoi—ne bozhii),* which appeared in *The Muscovite* in December 1854.[22] It utilized folklore and was the longest dramatic work dealing with the portrayal of the peasantry to date.

An unsympathetic critic writing after the turn of the century called Ostrovsky's plays "as authentically Russian as a tavern with foul-mouthed drunken talk and songs in the background."[23] His censure misses the point entirely. Authenticity, racy repartee, music, and the conviviality of the tavern had the utmost value for the young editors. And if Ostrovsky could fix all this in texts that invited review and correction of the surviving traditional folkways, he deserved to be celebrated.

The playwright's dramatic strategy underwent a decisive change after the success of *Sleigh* in 1853. He perceived that he could employ photographic realism to capture the attention of an un-Westernized Russian audience and hold up the surviving folkways for critical examination, should those living in the traditional culture care to correct their management of everyday life. Thus his plays could accomplish for the *narod* what his readings had achieved for Moscow merchants. As he wrote to Pogodin:

> I don't want to do anything for *It's a Family Affair* (1) because I don't want to make enemies, (2) because my ideas have begun to change, (3) because my vision of life in my first comedy seems callow and too cruel, (4) better the Russian get pleasure from seeing himself on stage than to be depressed by it. Reformers will come forward without us. In order to have the right to correct the *narod*, without offending, it is necessary to show that you know what is better for them. That is just what I am working on now, in uniting the elevated and the comic.[24]

This new approach, conceiving the play as a social instrument linked to compelling depiction of the homely genius of Russian life led to a burst of activity that produced some of his most beloved plays. In 1854 he created *Poverty Is No Vice (Bednost' ne porok)* and *You Can't Live Just As You Please (Ne tak zhivi, kak khochetsia)* both rich in musical interpolation and notable for some of the most picturesque, idiomatic language he ever wrote for the theatre. The latter bore a defect in the form of the unconvincing ending wherein the pealing of the church bells brought the enraged central character to his senses before he could kill his wife. This escape hatch may have represented an unconscious response, in the twilight of the Nikolaevan era, to the stiff reprimand he had received for leaving vice unpunished in *Family Affair.* In any case, he never again furnished a psychologically false resolution to give a play a happy ending by rehabilitating a sinner.

Apollon Grigoriev was the first critic to grasp the importance of Ostrovsky's dramatic texts. He wrote that with Liubim Tortsov, the drunken but honest hero of *Poverty Is No Vice,* Ostrovsky had "spoken a new word."[25] Then in March 1855 he explained the national significance of his friend's achievement in *The Muscovite.* With *Poverty, You Can't Live, Family Affair,* and *The Poor Bride (Bednaia nevesta)* (published in *The Muscovite* in 1852 and first performed in 1853—presumably antedating Ostrovsky's change of strategy and perhaps more cruel and depressing than the two beginning with *Sleigh*), Ostrovsky had "created the popular theatre."

> [These plays and the advance in acting that they engendered] awakened the sympathy of *all* classes of society; they altered the way many looked at Russian everyday life, they acquainted us with types whose existence we did not suspect . . . , with the most novel and dramatic relationships, with the most complex aspects of the Russian soul—its deep, touching, tender and wild sides, which no one had concerned himself with before.[26]

He went on to explain what he meant by popular:

> Strictly speaking, literature is popular when it either (1) adapts itself to the views, conceptions and tastes of the undeveloped masses, for their instruction, or (2) studies this mass as *terra incognita,* its morals and ideas as something strange, becoming familiar with their development. . . . In either case, such a literature is premised on the historical fact that the *narod* are out of synchronization [with the rest of society following its transition from the old Russian language to European-Russian in the time of Peter the Great]. (57)

Challenged by *Fatherland Notes* to define *narodnost'* more precisely, he said that the concept would have to be worked out gradually.[27] But he did explain that "the 'word' of the young editors was respect for tradition and for everything achieved by Russians."[28]

Not all of the theatre public or theatre establishment approved of Ostrovsky's program or his plays. Europeanized viewers often found his depictions of Russian ways simply grotesque. Ostrovsky's realism was too stark to be appealing to some who were interested in the advancement of the civilizing process. Shchepkin was still at the Maly when his new and original style of drama began to triumph in that company's productions. As a Westernizer, he found Ostrovsky's Slavophile associations distasteful. The plays' directness and coarseness repelled him and violated the sense of dignity with which his image of Russia was suffused. His method of acting in fact better suited the earlier plays by native authors that depicted personality in a fundamentally different way. Neoclassic drama reduced it to a few basic humors; while sentimentalist drama exalted a sensitive self that could be cultivated—the human organism finely attuned to emotion, experiencing and empathizing with the greatest intensity. Shchepkin selected from his gallery of types to find the character closest to what he thought the author intended. He found Ostrovsky's new photographic style, with its insistence on precise reproduction of manners and dialect, uncongenial.[29] It remained to be seen what peasants would make of Ostrovsky's delineation.

By the time Nicholas I's successor had laid the new foundations for his administration, Ostrovsky had established himself as an important Russian artist.[30] When Alexander II's brother, Grand Duke Konstantin Nikolaevich, now head of the naval ministry, decided to employ gifted Russian writers to study and prepare reports on Russian river towns and local boating skills, A. A. Potekhin received a commission to study the Oka from Saratov to its mouth. He recommended Ostrovsky to the ministry, which assigned the playwright a stretch of the Volga.[31] The ministry's expenditure would be more than justified by the impact of just one play that grew out of his travel. His tour afforded Ostrovsky the opportunity to research the pure, indigenous customs of Russians living along the Volga and probably inspired his determination to picture in a series of plays the total national community, showing its diversity of customs across regions and across the whole social spectrum.

A PLAY FOR THE REFORM ERA

But before undertaking his literary ethnographic expedition, he wrote a biting, topical play that marked the dawn of the Great Reform epoch. It appeared in *Russian Colloquy (Russkaia Beseda)*, a recently founded Slavophile journal, in January 1857. V. Sleptsov appreciated the work's importance; its appearance marked the beginning of Ostrovsky's difficulties with the drama censorship that precisely coincided with the *glasnost'* era.

A Profitable Post (Dokhodnoe mesto) describes a rising tide of personal consumption ("luxury") among civil servants and of education among the young. This education imparts a faith in progress and a desire to succeed on the basis of honest hard work, and of legality in the regulation of civil administration. Three corrupt officials who have grown wealthy through defalcation understand that the younger generation, with their idealism and their belief in the possibility of succeeding "by the book," will swamp them. "Such times are coming it will be impossible to live," says bureaucrat Iusov.[32] Indeed, in the last act an investigation uncovers the wrongdoing of the old timers and topples their empire. The ringleader is obliged to make restitution to the full extent of his personal wealth. Iusov cannot regard their fall as the inexorable working of justice, for he sees life as "nothing but a wheel of fortune" (110). The promising young man who embraces progress in this play, Zhadov, happens to be the nephew of one of the malfeasants. A somewhat priggish character, he amuses the clerks with his high principles and insists on succeeding on his own merit, without any favors from his uncle. He marries for love, believing that he can educate his young bride and provide the necessities for her in a state service career through earned promotions.

The play comes alive when he finds he cannot communicate his ideals to his wife, whose upbringing has predisposed her to admire only leisure, wealth, status, and fashion, and who envies her sister living in luxury thanks to a bribe-taking husband. Zhadov finally breaks, worn down by work and poverty, despairing when his wife threatens to leave him. They go together to his uncle to beg him for a lucrative position, only to find that the powerful official has just been indicted. Zhadov answers Iusov's taunts by saying that he never believed one generation to be more honest than another, only that some people in each generation are honest and that

> society is little by little throwing off its indifference to crime, heeding the energetic cries protesting social evil . . . that gradually a consciousness of shortcomings is arising, and in that consciousness is hope for a better future . . . that a feeling of justice has been inculcated in young people that is growing and bearing fruit. . . . Don't rejoice in my weakness. I am no hero. I am an ordinary, weak man. (116)

Tolstoy grasped the importance of the play's message, its comment on bureaucratic reform and the idealistic efforts of the young generation of civil servants at self-improvement. Shortly after its publication he wrote Ostrovsky congratulating him: "This is an enormous thing in its depth, comment on prevailing reality, and in the superbly realized character of Iusov."[33] Later the same year he praised the play to V. P. Botkin for its powerful protest against contemporary mores and pointed to the parallel of its central situation in Griboedov's *Woe from Wit* (*Gore ot uma* [1824]), where a young civil servant learns how the system really operates by observing his superiors.[34] *A Profitable Post*'s thematic similarity to Griboedov's masterpiece—arguably the greatest of all Russian plays—would not have gone unnoticed by most cultivated Russians. In the earlier play an idealistic young man applies critical reason to the world of power and discovers that flattery and deceit advance careers, while qualities of virtue are despised and crushed. Surely Ostrovsky counted on the *differences* in his version to serve as a comment on the real possibilities for change in Russia now, as opposed to the 1820s when *Woe from Wit* circulated in manuscript. He pointed to two promising new factors that might prove decisive: the post–Crimean War spirit of reformism at the center (coupled with a new faith in the possibility of regulating and rationalizing administration), and a more sophisticated understanding of social processes and social forces. Griboedov's hero, Chatsky, saw through sham and hypocrisy with the greatest clarity. But his commitment to uncompromising honesty and integrity doomed him to Romantic isolation. Finding the woman he thought he loved to lack his penetration and discernment, finding everyone in the ruling elite critically incapacitated by complicity with the reigning ways, he fled in the end. Ostrovsky's Zhadov, despite his failure and shame, offers more promise at the close of his much grittier odyssey. He was willing to work within the system, confident that in time his ideals would enable him and those of like mind in his generation to transform that system. Instead of walking away because a perfect love with a critical, committed intellectual equal failed to present itself, he married on the hunch that he could transmit his values and convert his mate. The disgrace of Ostrovsky's central character somehow appears less threatening than the system's complete failure to comprehend Chatsky's moral critique, but the implication remains that the new people, committed to work and struggle, can triumph if they preserve their integrity in the quotidian battle to teach and inspire.

What could simple folk make of a groundbreaking play like this who knew nothing of its dialogue with *Woe from Wit?* Because a gifted intelligentsia enlightener, Khrista D. Alchevskaia, published the reactions of villagers to whom she read it in 1887, it is possible to make an informed inference. Despite their inability to understand much of it, the dominant theme of personal virtue and right conduct in *A Profitable Post* sustained the Alekseev villagers' interest. They processed much of the play's content in a way that would be expected of a community with an oral culture, laying blame and extracting proverbial wisdom. But the issue of personal development clearly captured their imagination. At a fairly basic level, the auditors were perplexed as to what a university-educated official might be. One explained to his puzzled neighbor, "The university is to civilians what the model regiment is to soldiers."[35] The term "student" actually functioned as a curse in their region. (Alchevskaia recalled that a local university student home for the holidays heard the term inserted in a string of profanity; he introduced himself to the speaker, and was told, "Don't joke about being a student!") Alchevskaia's listeners, vaguely troubled by the notion of university, evidently failed to connect it to students. They responded to Zhadov's line, "I won't give up a millionth part of those convictions which I am obliged to hold by virtue of my education," with expressions of incomprehension. They also failed to comprehend the cynical, tipsy lawyer who tells Zhadov soon after meeting him that he makes his living by writing petitions for tearful merchants, secretly mocking and laughing at them while they cry and sob. The listeners sided with the weeping merchants.

The peasants understood the play's theme, the evils of bribe-taking. A few auditors thought Zhadov's fellow officials right to call him a half-wit for not taking bribes. But Demian defended him, "he's not like the people talking about him." Grandpa Brusko picked up on one of Zhadov's fiery speeches, adding, "It used to be that when you told a lie everybody avoided you. . . . Now it's not that way." Another added, "He investigates everything and gets to the bottom of everything. Lying makes him indignant." Alchevskaia believed that if this public had had a knowledge of applause they surely would have drowned out the reading of Zhadov's speech in praise of the power of honest work.

The scene in which Zhadov's future mother-in-law instructs her daughters on how to snare husbands produced the following interchange: "Such instructions!" remarked one, "Such a mother to teach well! If only she can sell them off her hands. No, it's not like that with us; with us a mother doesn't come out with such edification." Another objected, "Well, it happens among us the same way. People are instructed that a [potential] husband be given consideration, and who can know what is said behind closed doors?" As the drama unfolded, the auditors generally blamed the mother for her daughter's ultimatum to Zhadov either to set her up in luxury or live apart from her.

Alchevskaia observed that the women in her audience reacted differently to Zhadov's dilemma than the men. When he tells his wife that in every generation there have been people who reject outmoded customs, because they subscribe to more honorable principles than the prevailing ones and that the welfare of posterity depends upon them, that without them lying and wickedness will grow until they block out the sun, one woman leaned over to her neighbor and said, "I didn't get that." Her neighbor explained, "In the world things don't happen the way you learn in books." The men were more deeply affected by Zhadov's decision to abandon his honor in order to keep his wife. Demian and Grigorii cried, and the blacksmith Kiril, who was known to work exceptionally long hours to keep his wife among the best-dressed, covered his face with his hands.

The listeners displayed great impatience early in the last act to learn whether Zhadov would go through with his decision to solicit his uncle for a position. Just about half of them appeared to understand a subplot involving a society intrigue. Demian was the first to figure out that the uncle's malfeasance has been uncovered by the authorities and that he is ruined: "The money they squandered on drink ran out like sap—that's what." The auditors fully expected Zhadov to return to the path of virtue and speculated on whether his wife would remain with him. But if the conclusion startled them they nevertheless found a certain fitness in the uncle's death offstage. When it is announced that he has suffered a stroke, one of the peasants rose slightly from his bench, crossed himself, and said loudly and clearly, "Glory to Thee, our Lord. Truth has triumphed." The others all involuntarily crossed themselves.

With *A Profitable Post,* Ostrovsky appeared to abandon the Slavophile camp. He now published mainly in left-leaning journals and only occasionally in more moderate publications like the *Library for Reading* and the Dostoevskys' *Time.* Chernyshevsky's *The Contemporary* announced in its first number of 1857 that it would henceforth dedicate its issues to four first-class writers: D. V. Grigorevich, Tolstoy, I. S. Turgenev, and Ostrovsky. In October, Apollon Grigoriev wrote Pogodin that *The Contemporary* was upset that Ostrovsky, Tolstoy, and Turgenev "may be ours" and added that he hoped that Ostrovsky's connection with the "reds" would not continue long.[36] But Ostrovsky did part company from those of his generation pressing to extract the greatest gains from the climate of openness that developed in the late 1850s.

Apparently at least some in government feared the effect that performance of his plays might have on the public. While the drama censor, on 19 September 1857, passed *A Profitable Post* for production with only the most minor cuts, that approval was suddenly withdrawn on the eve of its premiere at the Aleksandrinsky Theatre in Saint Petersburg on 16 December, and an order went out to the only provincial theatre playing it—in Kazan—to terminate performances forthwith.[37] Ostrovsky was furious at this crude arbitrariness and his friends agreed, but advised him not to make an issue of it under the present circumstances. His 1859 play *A Ward of the Mistress (Vospitannitsa),* a study of the corrosive influence upon character of unrestricted power over others—be they serfs or gentry—failed to secure the censor's production approval in October. Even his patriotic play, *K. Z. Minin, the One-Armed,* published in *The Contemporary* in 1862, was denied permission to be performed. The representation of clergy and its "ultrademocratic tendencies" counted against it. Ostrovsky applied much energy and resourcefulness to get these decisions reversed, petitioning authorities, mobilizing friends, and enjoining actors seeking benefit performances. When permission finally came in 1863 to perform *A Profitable Post* drama censor I. A. Nordstrem asserted that it was not entirely clear why the original authorization had been withdrawn. Part of the reason was objection to conversations about bribe-taking in the play.[38]

DEBUT IN THE COUNTRYSIDE

When emancipation drastically changed the relationship between peasants and landlords it was an Ostrovsky play mounted as a local entertainment that formed the first known Russian effort to present contemporary literary theatre to a peasant audience. The 1861 legislation's most important short-term result was to remove agricultural peasants from the jurisdiction and oversight of gentry landowners. With nobles unable any longer to stand in loco parentis, they had to find new ways to relate to the rural masses. It could be left to essayists and writers of fiction to redefine the peasant, but some landowners liked to look for themselves.

In 1862 S. A. Iur'ev decided to offer Ostrovsky as a kind of test to the villagers of Voskresensk, some 150 miles north of Moscow.[39] Because *You Can't Live Just As You Please* featured situations, mores, and language accessible to peasants, it simply begged to be acted before the people. Although it had enjoyed only moderate success when it premiered seven or eight years earlier in Moscow and Saint Petersburg, some of its admirers believed it had yet to find its proper audience.

Iur'ev, an ardent and knowledgable devotee of Moscow theatrical life, had two sons. He engaged as their tutor a student of the Medical Faculty of Moscow University who was also a passionate thespian. Enthusiasm for drama engulfed the household, and they decided to present a play as a family affair, with the tutor acting the lead and preparing the production. Iur'ev experienced nothing but positive cooperative support from Voskresensk peasants when he made known his intention to put on a public show. They regarded his proposal as a grand gesture of seigneurial hospitality. The group of carpenters employed on the estate charged him the lowest possible price for constructing a wooden theatre, a structure with prompter's box and footlights designed to accommodate two hundred in raked seating.[40] They also volunteered to police the crowd that came to see the play. Iur'ev's household servants joined family members in filling some of the roles. The female servants were literate, but his coachman, who was not, had to get his part by repetition. Not only did the local priest not interdict the presentation, one of his relatives took part.

As the theatre and the production approached completion, the determined host distributed free tickets to local peasants along with invitations specifying that no drink would be allowed on the premises. On the appointed July Sunday he became alarmed when the yard filled by noon with peasants in holiday dress, drinking, singing, and playing games. They proved an amiable and orderly throng, but by the 5:00 P.M. curtain time some five hundred had arrived to crowd into the theatre—far more than had received tickets. His fears of an obstreperous or disorderly audience subsided quickly. Especially moving moments in the play caused some peasants to start laughing, but they responded to the carpenters' requests to quiet down so that the show could continue. After the performance Iur'ev received no end of thanks from the peasants for the handsome way they had been treated as his guests. Some remarked that nothing could be better than this, neither beer nor wine. (He later learned that his spectacle had ruined the local tavern's trade that day.)

Few old men appeared for this first performance, some staying away fearing it might be sinful to attend. But one who did come touched Iur'ev when he approached him afterward for two tickets to the next performance. He explained that his son, who would soon be back from the mowing, "had started drinking crazily, got mixed up with some slut in Moscow, grown tired of his wife and ruined his home," just like the central character in Ostrovsky's play (49). The father wanted his son to see the play and recognize his guilt.

In *You Can't Live Just As You Please,* Peter has eloped with a girl whose parents run an inn and set up housekeeping in Moscow. But he has begun to drink heavily, ignore business, and absent himself for long periods. He speaks abusively to his visiting father, who complains of the lad's loose conduct and inattentiveness to his wife, and the old man departs in anger. It turns out that Peter is spending his time in another part of the city pretending to be single and courting another woman. His wife wants to return to her parents on account of her husband's coldness, but her father refuses to take her back, saying it is a woman's duty to stick with her husband no matter what. When the woman Peter courts learns that he is married, she orders him out. He consults a sorcerer on how to get rid of his wife ("She's my wife, she's my slave!"), then in a drunken rage sets out with a knife on the frozen Moscow river to kill her. The ringing of the church bells brings him back to his senses in a surprise ending, and he begs everyone's forgiveness and promises to turn over a new leaf.

The Voskresensk peasants regarded the play as a real happening, and it became the subject of conversations and deliberations from every angle. Yet some thought the play insufficiently realistic in certain respects and lingered after the performance to complain to Iur'ev. One woman objected that had she been Peter's girlfriend when she learned he already had a wife, "She would have torn at him and not let him get away alive." But the main objections concerned the play's ending and reflected difficulty with melodramatic convention. A middle-aged peasant said:

> In this play Peter drank away his whole life, sold his soul to the devil . . . and then, because of the ringing of a bell, he, though totally devoted to his belly, began to whine. You don't break this devil with the pealing of a bell; you don't cut somebody down with a bell. It doesn't work that way. (49)

A woman offered an alternative ending, which those who stayed to talk agreed was "more like things really are":

> He is on thin ice. He begins to move slowly, so as not to fall through a hole in the ice, but without feeling any regret. And he thrusts his knife into her. She begins to bleed from the heart. Either he comes to his senses from this, or perhaps people run him down and bring him to his senses. Here the beast in him is vanquished, because an innocent Christian soul was squandered; his faithful wife, such a dove, was murdered. Inside he changes completely and sees God. And afterward it gives him comfort that his wife's faithfulness, even unto death, saves him from hell with her heart's blood. (49)

At the second performance, which attracted six hundred viewers—some from as far as ten miles away—Iur'ev actually substituted this ending for Ostrovsky's. Though not very artistic, he said it proved quite moving.

The following summer, 1863, A. F. Pisemsky's *A Bitter Fate (Gor'kaia sudbina)* was presented. Many peasants had begged to be given parts, and because of the difficulty of teaching lines to illiterates, Iur'ev also introduced improvisations in the manner of commedia dell'arte on a scenario of his own based on the folk saying "Thank God, the peasant weaves bast sandals." They threw themselves into their parts, transferred all their likes and dislikes to the stage, and played to the point of self-oblivion.

Iur'ev's experiment revealed things about the peasant that would have surprised many educated contemporaries. Besides the fact that such a large spontaneous gathering demonstrated they could behave in an orderly fashion, there was their obvious ability to follow the play and the wit and curiosity to discuss and criticize it. In one respect the recorded reactions bear out the common preconception that peasants were accustomed to violence and took it for granted, and that they tended to act impulsively. And the Voskresensk peasants failed to appreciate some of the nuances of Ostrovsky's text—for example, whether Peter's wife's smothering attention played any part in souring their relationship. They saw only a black-and-white case of someone falling under the influence of irrational forces and causing suffering to another who is perfectly pure and innocent.

What became of Iur'ev's theatre is unknown. He probably tired of the enterprise and abandoned it.[41] What is most striking about this first presentation of literary theatre to Russian peasants is the speed with which its sponsor deconstructed it. Russian historian V. O. Kliuchevsky claimed that emancipation ended the alienation responsible for the falsity of relations between peasants and nobles that prevailed from the eighteenth century.[42] No alienation whatever is evident in Iur'ev's account of his theatre for peasants. This was emphatically not "power theatre," and there was nothing luxurious about it. Iur'ev observed the peasants' customs and reactions with interest. He seemed genuinely impressed by their sensitivity to the ethical issues raised by Ostrovsky's play. The telling thing is that in his zeal to accommodate the peasants' conception of reality, and their limitations, he immediately retreated from literary theatre for the people to improvisation. Did his concessions bespeak the insecurity of landowners generally following emancipation? He met the Voskresensk villagers more than halfway. The peasants' reworking of the denouement of *You Can't Live . . .* represented a predictable result of the collision of a literate and an oral culture. When the popular theatre movement eventually got under way, it was with the expectation that the oral culture would finally expire in extended confrontation with the literate.

This premier event in the history of Russian popular theatre demonstrates the allure of mimetic performance, the attraction of a text that depicted characters familiar by virtue of their speech and manners and the choices they confronted in their personal lives. Ostrovsky's text immediately stimulated community discussion. If the community in this case had little say in the policies by which it was governed, its members had some control over their own behavior. It seems significant that the Voskresensk community responded to the play not by acting to change the circumstances that constrained them but by "correcting" the aesthetic object so that it more accurately mirrored the constraints under which they operated.

OBJECTIVITY AND INSTRUCTION

Ostrovsky himself was enough a man of his time to believe in science and objective truth. He constructed his dramas so that the ideals were clear and the audience should have no doubt where its sympathies belonged, considering that an accurate picture of a social or moral milieu had the power to convey its own truth *(istina)*. A Soviet scholar noted that he believed that life, and therefore a play, should arouse the same impression in different people.[43] This attitude made his plays popular with audiences who sought guidance from the artist and problems that admitted of correct interpretations.

Considering the didactic (but emphatically not preachy) dimension of Ostrovsky's enterprise, it is hardly surprising that he would turn his attention to the creation of a Russian national theatre. The case he made is important because his assumptions about acculturation, the civilizing process, and essential capacity of drama were shared by enlighteners who went on to lead the popular theatre movement in Russia.

The opportunity to prepare such a sweeping proposal came with the forced retirement of top bureaucrats in the wake of Alexander II's assassination. In August 1881 Adlerberg was replaced as minister of the court by I. I. Vorontsov-Dashkov, who brought in his own man as director of the imperial theatres. The two quickly formed a commission to draw up new rules for the imperial theatres (which enjoyed a monopoly in Moscow) and consider the legal status of private theatres elsewhere.[44] Ostrovsky and A. A. Potekhin were among the appointed members, and Ostrovsky "worked night and day" to prepare the memorandum he submitted to the body in September 1881. His "Note on the Situation of Dramatic Art in Russia at the Present Time" excoriated Adlerberg's policy of promoting translated French melodrama and operetta at the imperial theatres, without naming him.[45]

Ostrovsky pitched his proposal to Alexander III's well-known cultural chauvinism. "There is a Russian school of painting, there is Russian music. We may be permitted to hope for a Russian school of dramatic art as well. . . . A national theatre is a sign of a nation's maturity, like an academy, universities and museums" (183). To create a sense of urgency, he argued that an alien force might still block the emerging non-Westernized Russian audience from educating itself on the one "true, eternal [dramatic] art." An "advanced, but anti-artistic nation," France, had provided Russia with a counterfeit dramatic art:

> melodrama, with its impossible events and inhuman passions . . . operetta, where pagan gods and priests, kings and ministers, armies and nations dance the can-can . . . fairy play, where the decorations change twenty-four times, and in the course of an evening the spectator manages to visit every corner of the earth and the moon besides, and where in all twenty-four scenes there are the same naked women. (154)

The inescapable imperative: establish a national theatre in Moscow serving all classes of society. Ostrovsky submitted an abridged version of his proposal to Alexander III—who notoriously did not read lengthy documents—in October 1881. The tsar noted in the margin, "It would be very desirable to realize this idea, which I share entirely."[46] Yet before the committee could complete its work, the government ended the monopoly of the imperial theatres in Moscow. Anna Brenko opened the first private theatre in Russia for the general public.[47] Others, like Korsh and Lentovskii, quickly followed. No national theatre was forthcoming. But the terms of Ostrovsky's argument for a national theatre came to be widely accepted.

The "Note" assumes "the civilizing" (literally, "humanizing") influence of theatre, and posits a need for its services by a significant portion of Moscow's inhabitants and by the visitors from other cities now arriving daily in droves. Ostrovsky offers a demographic analysis of the city's growth since the 1820s, when peasants built textile factories around Moscow and became wealthy (townsmen). The gentry had dominated the city until the 1840s and 1850s. The manufacturers and their people kept to themselves, rarely went out, seldom even socialized with relatives. But their sons and grandsons began to break out of this stifling patriarchal culture. "Office assistants who hadn't dared to go to public places lest they be seen by the master, now instituted their club. Some went to taverns."[48] The Imperial Maly now served the rich Moscow merchants.[49] Ostrovsky, who had traveled widely in western Europe describes them as "much less developed" than their European counterpart. Their family fortunes had been laid down by men who "considered freedom from science and learning to be a privilege of their estate" (177). They were "unable to understand abstractions quickly," were morally and intellectually sluggish. Fortunately, however, many "continued to be Russian," concerned "more about intellectual education than about imitating Europe."

This brought Ostrovsky to his third assumption. Moscow had grown, incorporating a substantial laboring element; now the middle and lower middle classes were developing intellectually. "They were all peasants not long ago and are now a public for Moscow theatres." The working man "wants to forget boring reality, wants to see another life, another environment, another form of society." Dramatic spectacles can counteract "excessive sensuality in the spirit of an undeveloped person," provide "spiritual occupations to make him *forget time and place*" (172, 174; emphasis added). A particular body of plays—what he called the "repertoire of everyday life," demonstrated the ability to show the "powerful but coarse peasant multitude . . . that there is good in the Russian person, that one must look after and nurture it in oneself and that wildness and coarseness exist within oneself which must be fought."[50]

Ostrovsky's "Note on the Present State of Dramatic Art" represents an extension of the concerns in his plays. He sees thought and action as taking place in a universe of social and economic givens that are solid and hard but not perdurable, because subject to historical change. And he anticipates tremendous advantage for the nation from drama's capacity to stimulate independent judgment, to appeal to conscience. The objectivity of his created world served consumers of his drama by confirming their assessment of how things work now. What he showed was clear and recognizable; but to arrive at the truth behind it required the viewer to master abstractions, touchstones essential to achieving stable self-identity and maintaining self-respect in a challengingly complex and changing world. His art is radically democratic, and he essays to overturn barriers keeping it from the largest possible public. He seeks nothing less than social recognition for the *narod*'s right to learn, know and question—an endorsement without which they cannot emerge from the uncertainty and doubt being aroused in them.

THE TRUE AND ETERNAL DRAMATIC ART

"Inside he changes completely and sees God." The Voskresensk peasant woman proposing an alternative ending to *You Can't Live Just As You Please* after seeing landowner Iur'ev's production in 1862 imagines what would be required to bring Peter "to his senses" in the world as she understands it. She is perfectly familiar with the interior life, but in her view the spirit, the conscience, operates under religious governance. Far from conceiving an ego that navigates by making endless real-time calculations of personal advantage, she understands the individual as either in or out of compliance with Christian ethical commandments. To her, Peter's conquering "the beast in him" would demand that he actually carry out the contemplated murder of his wife and squander "an innocent Christian soul." Nor does she approach the question of personality from the standpoint of rights—least of all a civil right like that of Peter's wife to life. In her thinking the wife's faithfulness to her husband redeems his lapse and saves his soul from hell. A religious outlook informed the judgment of village people, and they naturally criticized the motivation and plotting of *You Can't Live Just As You Please* from that standpoint. Ostrovsky wrote his plays for a national community acquiring fresh critical skills.

Ostrovsky noted in his 1881 memorandum that there were among the undeveloped folk some with serious thoughts and potential and that they deserved to partake of the true and eternal dramatic art. When he used the word *eternal* as a qualifier it seems safe to assume that he had in mind nothing more ancient than Athenian drama at its pinnacle in the fifth century B.C. Certainly classical Greek drama had anchored western European thinking about social regeneration since before the French Revolution. Urbanization figured in his analysis, and he must have known that the birth of theatre in the Greek city-states had something to do with accelerating urbanization. Postemancipation Moscow also had advancing literacy in common with Pericles' Athens. Ostrovsky's vision of a theatre to educate and develop members of the audiences possessed of good instincts and a desire to change bespoke drama demanding and exalted in the manner of Aeschylus, Sophocles, and Euripides. His memorandum indicates a grasp of the singular nature of the performed text's capacity to elicit speculation and contemplation of life's problematic complexity.

Pythagoras attributed superiority to people who approach life as though it were a spectacle. Identifying himself as "a philosopher," he explained that life is like the Great Games, where some go to compete for the prize and others go with wares to sell, "but the best as spectators [*theatai*]; similarly, in life some grow up with servile natures, greedy for fame and gain, but the philosopher seeks for truth."[51] Out of roots denoting speculation and contemplation of performed texts grew the term *theory*.[52] Theatre always invited a contemplation not just of the surface action, but of the complex text invisible to the characters but visible to some members of the audience.[53] And Ostrovsky insisted that common folk with good aesthetic instincts were as likely as nobles to contemplate the spectacle with penetration.

Ostrovsky's memorandum staked bold claims for the capacity of demanding dramatic texts to produce effects on spectators unachievable through any other art. It is not his business to explain just how this is achieved, but recent classical scholarship does offer a persuasive hypothesis. The language of such texts, argues Charles Segal, is dense and complex.[54] He cites, for example, a brief passage from *Oedipus Tyrannus* that mixes the specialized vocabularies of hunting, scientific investigation, sophistic rationalism, and the courts. It is this language operating at the frontier, probing the depths, employing irony, abrupt reversals and novel dialogic structure that enables tragedy to represent "two or more levels of significance simultaneously," "a double perspective," "a division between a surface world of illusion and a truth which lies beneath . . . rest[ing] in part upon the presence of two sign systems in its background, a verbal and a visual, a hidden text of written signs and a public, open performance."[55] Like Ostrovsky, J.-P. Vernant stresses the dramatic author's unparalleled ability to communicate with the spectator through the text.

> It is only for the spectator that the language of the text may be transparent at all its levels, in its polyvalence and its ambiguities. From the author to the spectator, the language recovers this full function of communication which it has lost on the stage between the characters in the drama. . . . At the very moment when he sees the protagonists adhere exclusively to one sense, and in consequence be blinded, disoriented, or lost, the spectator must understand that in reality there are two or more possible meanings. The language becomes transparent to him, the tragic message communicable only as he makes the discovery of the ambiguity of words, of values, of man, where he recognizes the universe as conflicted, and where, abandoning old certainties, he opens to a problematic vision of the world.[56]

Ostrovsky as playwright deployed language to confront spectators with the ambiguities facing individuals choosing for themselves. He was impatient or intolerant enough to disdain theatrical texts with other objectives.

Ostrovsky said in his theatre proposal that Russia's awakening middle and lower classes saw their identities as constituted by their histories and communities and therefore would happily go to the theatre to learn the history of the nation. But in most of his own dramas he pictured unheroic people establishing their individuality by exercising rights, demanding justice and behaving as though an objective truth exists that can be arrived at by reflection. Whether individualism is an illusion, the self-creating, choosing person a mirage, is not at issue here. The integral, self-controlled personality is real in one branch of literary theatre. Ostrovsky gave the audiences of his plays much to ponder about personal identity and the interior life, and this democratic tendency connects him to the great dramatists of classical antiquity.

Yet Ostrovsky's plays are wines that do not travel. Only a very few have been translated from Russian into other languages. Because they are so concerned with social distinctions and the cultural differences (or "manners") of the various social groups at a particular historical moment, they are easily misapprehended without some considerable knowledge of Russia's estates and their phylogeny. Western Europeans who knew how their social classes thought and related to each other could cast about in vain for familiar hooks on which to hang Ostrovsky's merchants, for instance. In *Even the Wise Can Err* Ostrovsky frolics with the often-noted Russian obsession for rank and position within a pecking order. Ten of the sixteen characters have noble status but hold a different rank *(chin)* in the Table of Ranks. Each attempts either to ingratiate himself with or displace the character at the next higher rank. To complete the circle, the highest-ranked noble pursues the (peasant) fortune-teller![57] Can this sort of joke not fail to be lost in translation? In the same play Glumov's diary presents a problem that only a knowledge of the play's larger intellectual context can solve. To a viewer possessing a general knowledge of European civil service at the higher levels in mid-nineteenth-century Europe, Glumov would seem no more than an oily fop who stupidly (and unconvincingly) keeps a written account of the genuine opinions he so sedulously conceals in his dealings with the people around him. Without some knowledge of the context, of the belief that words on paper can capture an objective truth that is elusive at best and impossible to achieve in oral discourse, a basic tension in the play's dynamic is missing. (In an English adaptation by Rodney Ackland, the document displaces the wise man and the unwariness in the title: *The Diary of a Scoundrel* [1948].) Without the topical context that so interested Ostrovsky, his plays too easily appear inept.[58]

What makes his plays difficult for foreign playgoers makes them fascinating for the historian. Social and historical processes captivated Ostrovsky. He identified the ones he considered influential and estimated their potential. Occasionally he admitted to miscalculating the speed with which they gathered force. Zhadov's assertions about the influence of the people in Chernyshevsky's generation who think for themselves and reject outmoded customs required reconsideration at the end of the Reform era, for instance. The personal tragedy of Katerina in *The Storm* is set in an elaborate review of the new things and ideas that promised to change Russian life after the Crimean War. The railroad has begun to shrink the country. Electricity is beginning to be understood. A woman who has traveled widely on pilgrimage calls attention to the fact that life in the cities is astonishingly speeded-up. In Moscow people rush to and fro, and the noise in the streets is deafening. The seasons used to drag by but now time flies. She calls it "the end of the world." The merchant family Katerina Kabanova has married into is ruled by a matriarch who grinds her obedient son down "like rust on iron" and insists on observance of the old customs. Another merchant, rude and abusive, terrorizes his family and clerks. By "greasing the wheels" of town government he is able to avoid paying all he promises to the hundreds of peasants he employs. The clerks engaged by merchants write denunciations, which give rise to lawsuits that keep the courts and lawyers busy. The image of the impending storm serves as a comment on the advance of science, self-control and manners, civic-mindedness, and personal rights that must sweep away the dominance of the moneyed authoritarians.

Ostrovsky was right to emphasize the transforming power of urbanization. Although Russia's urban dwellers numbered a scant ten million in 1880, that number would triple by 1914. Daniel Brower insists that already by the 1890s the process of urbanization had become irreversible.[59] One concomitant was agricultural peasants' discovery, or rediscovery, of the value of education for the rural population.[60] As migrant laborers found more and more urban employment, what they reported when they returned represented a major determinant in changing prevailing attitudes and assumptions. Tolstoy had in 1874 bemoaned the disappearance of the village "literacy schools" that had sprung up like mushrooms, often on peasant initiative, after emancipation. He had later thrown himself into publishing massive editions of cheap reading material to facilitate the advancement of literacy among the folk. He told Alchevskaia that when he read her book, published in 1881, on reading Ostrovsky to the people, he felt moved to resume his acquaintance with the playwright, which had lapsed in the mid-1850s. "He suddenly appeared before me again in his full stature, and I became so excited that I made up my mind to get dressed and go to him to share my impressions."[61] Moreover, he interested Ostrovsky in the *Posrednik* (Intermediary) venture, which subsequently printed large editions of his plays.[62] The novelist also reread Ostrovsky's works in order to study the craft of play construction, and he wrote his first play for the popular theatre *The Power of Darkness (Vlast' t'my)* in 1886, the year of Ostrovsky's death.

Besides his writing and his labors on behalf of a national theatre, Ostrovsky devoted himself to the training of actors starting out or already established in the provinces. From 1865 to 1883 he served as president of the Artistic Circle. At the Maly he taught actors to build up their characters from the rhythm of the language they were given to speak. A. N. Pleshcheev recalled, "In the Maly Theatre they did not act, they performed a rite. It was not a production but a concert." These multifaceted activities in the service of Russian theatre came at a price. Ostrovsky worked himself to the point of exhaustion and died of heart failure before he could see popular theatre develop as a movement.

Ostrovsky's plays written in the 1850s and 1860s were found by educated Russians to appeal strongly to Russians with no prior experience of literary texts. Their popularity must have had something to do with the familiar material they incorporated. At midcentury Ostrovsky had determined that theatre should give pleasure by showing Russians to Russians. But by the end of the century, when about twenty of his plays had emerged as the backbone of the popular theatre repertory, his work began to fall out of favor with the intelligentsia. One writer remarked that his plays had become dated in forty years and that people could no longer relate to those "old merchants."[63] Another complained that he gave actors of the new psychological type nothing to do.[64] A third found him "external," "elementary," "deeply uncultivated," and incapable of depicting true dynamics.[65] Successful creators of literary theatre found new points of departure. What had been invented in the 1850s could of course no longer satisfy highbrow curiosity about the people. Realism had been superseded, and literary evolution had rendered his plays obsolete for the cultural elite.

At the apogee of Russia's first *glasnost'* Ostrovsky wrote a play that addressed the cultural gulf that so exercised Dostoevsky and Tolstoy. *The Storm* resonates with social processes that attended the birth of Greek drama and with certain ramifications of the scientific rationality that had given rise to the "two worlds of the mind" in western Europe in the seventeenth century.

In nominating *The Storm* (1859) for the Uvarov Prize, I. A. Goncharov remarked on its "lofty classical beauty."[66] He probably had in mind its structural elegance, its temporal unity, its neatly symmetrical arrangement of spaces and oppositions. But *The Storm* also shared some thematic concerns with the earliest Greek tragedies. Richard Seaford has argued that tragedy appeared in the wake of a money economy supplanting self-sufficient household management and regular judicial procedure that offered an escape from vendetta and blood feud.[67] "Tragedy," he explains, "a product of the polis at a later stage of its development, takes the royal individuals of myth, calls them *tyrannoi* and concentrates on stories in which their unlimited desire gives rise not just to reciprocal violence but also to killing of kin, attacks on religion, perversion of ritual, and the delusion that results in action being reversed into the opposite of its intention" (233). Ostrovsky's two Volga merchant families in *The Storm* adhere to the old ways. They are manifestly tyrannical. Dikoi, given to insulting, abusive speech in all his dealings, takes out on his family the frustrations he experiences in his public affairs. At one point he avoids going home because of the fighting he knows he will encounter there. Old Kobanova, a matriarchal tyrant, arguably presides over a perversion of ritual *(byt).* She takes in female pilgrims and feeds them well but "swallows up" her own family through domination and compulsion; her daughter-in-law, Katerina, came from a home where such women joined with the female household members in sewing, narrating the lives of the saints, and singing spiritual verse. Old Kobanova's refusal to allow Katerina any autonomy or personal freedom ultimately drives the girl to suicide.

In Seaford's view the god of the polis reverses excessive female adherence to the household by imposing a frenzy that destroys the household (259). An aspect of his theory is the notion that tragedy's invention coincided with the emergence of a civic cult that brought together as a community people unrelated by blood, urged the practice of self-restraint, and counseled the superiority of a happy daily life over attaining mastery over enemies (402–3). *The Storm* juxtaposes the tyrannical family destroyed by frenzy against orderly, polite, prosperous, civic life.

Given *The Storm*'s composition in the midst of first *glasnost'* it should come as no surprise that the rise of civic life and a public sphere figure explicitly in the text. This subject is treated spatially, with great theatrical panache. The private space in the play is the Kobanovs' house, the street in front of it, and the garden and ravine below (acts 2 and 3). The public space is "a public garden high on the banks of the Volga" (acts 1 and 5) and an ancient arcade next to a relatively new broad street or promenade *(bul'var)* (act 4). Kuligin, a self-taught watchmaker of the lowest estate of townsmen *(meshchanin)*, speaks for civic improvement, science, and community life in the open.

> Here it is, sir, our hole of a town. They built a promenade, but nobody goes for walks on it. It's only used on holidays, and then with a single view in mind: to be seen by the other strollers. . . . Poor people never go there, sir, because they are working day and night. . . . And the rich? You would think they'd want to relax in the fresh air, but that isn't the case. Long before dusk they've locked their gates and unleashed their dogs—not for fear of thieves, but because they don't want people to see how they browbeat their servants and how they tyrannize [*tyraniat*] over their families. Everything is behind closed doors. Nobody sees or knows anything. Only God sees! When the rich man is in the street he says "Look at me as much as you like, but my family is none of your business. . . ." "The family," he says, "is a private matter, secret! . . ." The only people who use the promenade are young couples who steal an hour to go strolling.[68]

It seems apposite that Kuligin, the first character to speak in act 1, should mention the English early on, for it was England, of all European countries, that had first established public walks and gardens in most of its towns.

Peter Borsay finds that London pioneered the trend between 1605 and 1616, with Oxford and Cambridge the first provincial towns to take up the fashion.[69] By the mid-eighteenth century, when the proportion of the population living in communities with more than five thousand people had grown to 20 percent, "there were probably few country towns, regional centers or resorts that were unable to boast at least one set of public walks or gardens."[70] He concludes that because many of these promenades were located along rivers or at the edge of towns, at the borderline between urban and rural worlds, their rise was linked to the upsurge of interest in the natural world that Keith Thomas investigated in early modern England.[71] Borsay relates the promenades to the institutions described by Habermas as giving rise to the Public Sphere in modern Europe: "Promenades were the outdoor arenas to parallel the interior ones provided by the burgeoning theatres, assembly rooms, coffee-houses, and luxury shops."[72] Without mentioning the work of Habermas or Eugen Weber, he summarizes the social significance of the new public spaces thus:

> The élite, and those who aspired to join them, were increasingly withdrawing from their participation in traditional culture, which all society had to some degree shared, and were turning to the exclusive but expanding world of fashionable urban leisure. The former, deprived of its prestigious support became essentially popular in character, while the latter emerged as the foundation of a new polite culture. Formal walks . . . helped forge among the promenaders those cultural bonds of refined behavior that welded together élite society, and separated them from the perceived barbarism of plebeian life. (131)

This background helps clarify Ostrovsky's intentions in the spatial organization of *The Storm*.

As the play begins Kuligin (the name suggests a clearing free from forests) claims that he has gazed at the Volga every day for fifty years and still can't get enough of it; he chides his companion for failing to appreciate the joys of nature. Later in act 1 he says he'll catch it for his idle talk: "I can't help it, I love to converse with everyone." The patriarchal merchant, Dikoi, cannot speak to anyone without being rude and insulting. Still, Kuligin approaches him in act 4 to "do something for the town." If Dikoi will provide the materials, Kuligin will build a sundial to beautify the promenade. The many travelers who came to the town would add the ornamental sundial to their list of beautiful sights. Dikoi replies that Kuligin is a "bandit" and a "worm."[73]

At the end of act 4 Katerina appears on the promenade. There she meets Boris, the educated lover she has taken while her merchant husband has been away drinking. She asks Boris to take her with him to Siberia; he declines, remarking furtively "I hope nobody finds us here." Katerina, who has earlier informed her mother-in-law "Whether there are people around or not, I am always the same. I don't show off," now leaves to throw herself into the Volga. When her husband learns she has been seen on the promenade he says to his mother, "Who would have thought that she would come here, a place with so many people? Who would think of concealing oneself here?" Kobanova replies, "Consider what she is doing! What a venomous person she is! She persists in hanging on to the kind of character she has!" (280, 232, 282). An extensive literature exists from the second half of the twentieth century on the projection of individual personality into public spaces, but it is significant that Ostrovsky made this a central axis of his greatest play in 1859.[74] It is also significant that the investigation of family life as the nurturing ground for the individual free personality (which Habermas believes the novel was invented to explore) was in Russia being carried forward in plays.

Having established the richness and the topicality of Ostrovsky's dramas that formed the core of the popular theatre repertoire in Russia, we are now prepared to examine two enlighteners' discoveries about the people as they employed native plays in their educational work.

Chapter Three

Plays for Schooling: Resistance and Response

PLAYS DEPICTING the manners and fortunes of recognizable commonplace Russians became available in the 1850s; by the 1870s they had begun to take on a life of their own. Even before the acting profession and commercial entrepreneurs brought them to rural Russia, Westernized intellectuals committed to the Enlightenment project and motivated by a desire to go "to the people" incorporated them into their teaching. The most famous of these educators left accounts of such plays' impact on village culture that throw light on peasant thinking and adaptive capacity in the 1880s and 1890s.

N. F. Bunakov (1837–1904) and Khrista D. Alchevskaia (1841–1920) organized inventive rural schools that received national attention. Young adults in the first *glasnost'* era, they lauded the general thrust of the Great Reforms.[1] Russia's expanding market economy furnished the means to pursue their enlightening activities. They dedicated themselves to imparting the culture of science and reason. Rooted squarely in realism, they practiced an empirical approach that started with the world as it was.[2] But they studied the peasants they tried to serve primarily so that they could disseminate concepts and skills with maximum effectiveness. Their carefully documented trial-and-error experiments in teaching contributed significantly to the educated public's image of peasant mentality and potential for learning.

Both Bunakov and Alchevskaia considered changing peasants' orientation to language critical to Russia's future. They believed that they could play a historical role by modernizing peasant outlooks. This they sought to do by propagating literacy and implementing a sense of individualism. In their long, arduous search for effective methods they tried and discarded various approaches to breach the defenses of a self-sufficient traditional culture with its own logic and reward structure.

Government policies impeded and exasperated both enlighteners, but in an unexpected way reinforced the consciousness each had of representing an exalted mission. The work of Bunakov and his companion L. I. Mikhailova and of Alchevskaia reveals the steadily changing climate of peasant resistance to the learning of Europeanized Russians. They found increasing receptivity to their educational projects by the 1880s, as villagers communicated more with the outside world and began to adapt their internal relations to conform to the local judicial institutions established after emancipation. Their discoveries about drama's appeal to the people set in motion the last preparations for a popular theatre movement.

Recent American scholarship on postemancipation development of peasant village justice has exposed enlighteners as mere cultural imperialists. Evidence suggesting rapid peasant adjustment to an individual-rights approach, at the expense of patriarchal family authority or village security determinations, has been underestimated. But were Russian peasants in fact indifferent then to improvising community-focused practices according respect for diverse individual interests? They have been reproved for wasting energy on working out local standards for local circumstances when they could simply fall in line behind the national legal norms framed by the bureaucracy and legal professionals. Or, they have been presented as victims of cultural colonizers imposing alien notions of time, work, sanitation—"progress." The evidence of the Bunakovs and Alchevskaia deserves to be reviewed because it suggests the intellectual or mental stimulus exerted by a certain kind of linguistically complex but accessible text. New thinking about individualism in traditional communities—and not just in cities—had immense political implications. Even if these enlighteners occasionally deceived themselves, and even though they underrated regional differences, their findings suggest that dramatic representations of modern life and choices exerted a civilizing influence quite apart from the authority of the agents who delivered them.

THE BUNAKOVS' ENLIGHTENMENT

One of four sons of a minor official, N. F. Bunakov lacked the means to attend a university. But on the strength of his gymnasium course he secured the promise of a teaching position at Petrozavodsk and moved to Saint Petersburg in 1864. When the job failed to materialize, he attempted to support himself there through writing.[3] He met K. D. Ushinskii, a Russian educator who had just returned from Switzerland, and F. F. Rezener, who had just opened an experimental, tuition-free school on Vasilev Island. Their conversations aroused Bunakov's interest in the science of teaching, and he learned German so that he could acquaint himself with the latest pedagogical theory. The Vasilev Island school particularly intrigued him, because it functioned without any coercion whatever and imposed no discipline from above.[4] While lecturing there at Rezener's invitation, he found that he could not hold the students' attention; they wandered to the windows after half an hour. Abashed, but challenged, he would eventually contrive ingenious ways to motivate children whose parents could not afford school fees. It was Rezener who arranged for Bunakov to tutor N. G. Chernyshevsky's son Alexander in the Russian language the summer before the boy entered a gymnasium.[5]

Bunakov shared with other men of the sixties the conviction that the critically thinking individual, through work, could exert a powerful influence for social betterment. Like others of his generation, he held that personal sincerity and commitment always took precedence over established niceties and formalities. He hated hereditary rank. The Russian gentry, he firmly believed, had oppressed the peasantry for years and bore responsibility for their present sorry condition. While asserting his superiority to the titled elite by championing humane values, he remained impatient, cantankerous, and contemptuous of everything he considered impeded the good.

The institutional restructuring of the Great Reforms gave Bunakov his first important teaching position, in the Voronezh Military Preparatory Gymnasium. Progressives around Dmitri Miliutin in the War Ministry created a new system of military gymnasia for cadet corps, which emphasized general education. This reform overturned the Nikolaevan practice of training officers in obedience rather than thinking for themselves. By special examination Bunakov won an appointment in 1866 to teach Russian language and literature in the Voronezh Gymnasium, where he remained for five years.[6] Bunakov recalled that when he began there, he found a pedagogy in transition: from "the stick to teaching under principles valuing personality, freedom, humanism" (Z 71). Even before Bunakov arrived, programs in the Russian language and in mathematics became the basis for all other studies in the gymnasium. Though unable in his Voronezh years to start a school for peasants, Bunakov did indirectly advance the cause of acculturation by impressing upon his gymnasium pupils that they all had a duty to the Russian people.[7] He did not consider the Russian peasantry intellectually inferior to the Westernized elite: men of the folk—Nikon, Pososhkov, Lomonosov, Shchepkin, Nikitenko, Kramskoi, and Shevchenko—had been moved by science, culture, literature, and enlightenment. Rather, he saw the peasanty as exploited.[8]

Soon after his arrival in Voronezh he founded a private primary school based on these new principles; he directed the school for fourteen years.[9] He dreamed of starting a village school, but would have had to find a financial backer. Or he could have gone to work for the Ministry of Education as a school inspector. But he supposed the officials there considered him insufficiently trustworthy for such service. To be sure, he had little sympathy for the way it was run.

In the 1870s Bunakov suffered a series of personal misfortunes. His marriage frayed as he revised his textbooks and lavished time on his Voronezh school. In 1876–77 the leadership of the gymnasium changed, and his employment there ceased. The Education Ministry banned his teacher-training courses. His health broke down, and he found himself completely paralyzed on the left side. He was seriously ill in 1879. He and his wife separated. Urban life became increasingly distasteful to him. Nevertheless, his enthusiasm for the cause of popular education burned bright as ever. He finally determined to realize his dream of establishing his own village school where he could test his teaching methods on peasant children. Sales of his textbooks gave him the means to buy a small estate near a village just a few miles from Voronezh in 1884.[10]

Its relative backwardness made Petino, on the high bank of the Don in the southernmost of the central black earth provinces, attractive to someone bent on testing theories of acculturation. The village had a repartitional commune and adhered to the three-field system.[11] Only two or three of the thousand villagers could read and write. Petino had no prereform school tradition to distort contemporary teaching results, no lingering memories of "Books of Hours and boxed ears." Moreover, Bunakov relished the challenge of teaching in a milieu where no inclination toward literacy existed. He hired an architect and erected a building that combined a two room school with adjoining lending library, a surgery with a small pharmacy, and a dwelling for himself and L. I. Mikhailova. As it went up, the peasants thought the structure must be an inn. The zemstvo board joined him as trustee in the school. In its first decade he spent 12,000 rubles equipping and maintaining the school, compared to 3,000 from the zemstvo—which paid the salaries of one teacher and the religion instructor. A priest from Vladimir was the first to hold the latter office, and he warned Bunakov that the Petino peasants were "heathenish and accursed"; scoundrels, thieves, and drunkards; as bad as the Vladimir peasants.

Bunakov hoped to convert the village to literacy by winning the hearts and minds of the younger generation in his school. But he understood the need to involve their parents in the process as well. This he sought to do by arranging "evenings" on the school premises. He showed lantern slides, gave readings from Russian literature, directed choral singing, and lectured on Russian writers. At first chaos reigned. Visitors broke glasses and banisters. He hired guards to keep order. The lack of elementary civility shocked him, and one of the first lessons he undertook to impart was that "one does not force one's way into another's house, and that good deportment is as necessary in school as in church." He concluded that the Petino peasants "were not of high moral development." Nor, he found, did they much care to take up books and learning, which they considered to be the business of the landowner class. The adult generation more often than not regarded schooling as useless, boasting that they themselves were illiterate, like their ancestors, and "none the worse for it."

He instituted the school confident that he and Mikhailova could gain acceptance among the peasants because they came as philanthropists, wanting nothing for themselves but proffering something of inestimable value.

But could it be valuable if peasants had no use for it? Tolstoy had proved that acculturation could not proceed unless peasants wanted to learn what the would-be teachers offered. Bunakov acknowledged the point, to the extent of mouthing the platitude that the rural school must teach only what would be useful to the peasants in life. Yet he persisted in believing that his mission was to lead peasants to "a higher level of being" the advantages of which they could not appreciate in their "degraded" condition. He would begin with components of their own culture and demonstrate the superiority of these same elements as configured in the high culture, where they were treated with seriousness or even reverence. His program for singing offers a good example:

> I am convinced that singing is necessary in the public school as the most accessible and most easily understood of all the arts, as an excellent method not only for possible and necessary aesthetic development but also for the intellectual discipline of the students. . . . The Russian people sing at work, in church, on a spree. Of course this singing is rather wild. In school it must be improved, ennobled.[12]

He approached the Russian language in the same way. If peasants could be made to respect it from their earliest years, they could be transformed. Language had always stood at the center of his teaching.[13] He supposed that social factors accounted for the decline of vernacular Russian. During centuries of oppression, he hypothesized, "swearing became the peasants' all-purpose conversational speech" (Z 157).

Bunakov took pride in the fact that his pupils, beginning their letters in October, were reading by December. Despising the officially endorsed dictation method to teach and test writing, he devised an alternative to stimulate creativity rather than overwhelm with formal conventions. To arouse in his pupils an individualized awareness as quickly as possible he had them compose letters addressed to him. He corrected their mistakes and wrote each pupil a reply. Thus they immediately found their sense of themselves as part of a collective challenged in his school. The ongoing exchange of letters focused the learners' attention on the thinking and organizing process, and orthographic accuracy fell into place relatively painlessly.

His goal was nothing less than to evoke fluent and structured statements of his scholars' knowledge, feelings, and desires. Recalling his first graduating class in 1886 (two boys and three girls) in his memoirs, he underlined the superiority of their language instruction by virtue of its employment as a vehicle for the exploration of experience:

> Among us it seems that no one wants the people to have useful knowledge, far less to have their own thoughts, feelings, and desires. Expressions that are foisted upon one are not necessary in the free and independent use of language. Overeducated phrases of the senseless literary kind, the sort with which the Russian army smothers its recruits, I can proudly say that my Petino students [did not have]. (Z 177)

In the late eighties he believed that peasant parents were coming to value literacy more highly. He insisted in an article he published in 1889 that parents now expected their children to come out of a three-year school with the ability to write intelligently and clearly, and he quoted from a study of peasant attitudes toward school and learning in Orlovsk province to make his point.[14] "The literate person is accepted everywhere—among merchants, in shops, in taverns; they make money quickly. . . . [The literate person is] friendly and wise, he is able to go farther than an illiterate and commands a higher price." He cited another step forward in the erosion of peasant insularity in an 1890 article. Villagers, he wrote, were coming to respect peasants who had returned from military service as "mental persons because they had attained some external polish and learning."[15]

But the famine of 1891 altered Bunakov's image of the local peasants, and he substantially revised his optimistic assessment of their progress on the path of enlightenment. No rain fell on Petino's fields in the summer of 1891, and the crops failed. When rain finally came after the fall planting the peasants had nothing to eat until the spring harvest.[16] Bunakov and Mikhailova served on a local committee to distribute food. By December the committee was feeding the school children, and a dining facility had been organized in their kitchen to feed the youngest children in the village. Bunakov praised the governor and his wife and the district zemstvo for their relief efforts. Villagers were given employment on modest public works projects. The educator stressed that this lifted peasant morale, and even marked the beginning of a consciousness of the connection between sanitation and health in Petino. But the experience seems to have caused him to reassess the difficulty of redeeming the peasantry through education.

In lectures he gave in Voronezh and Riazan in 1892 Bunakov called attention to the peasant's "ox-like" lack of discrimination when it came to work, which he equated to "a lack of desire to construct a life that is human for oneself" (Z 202–3). He found the peasant's "Christian" feelings like love for members of the family circle and goodwill toward neighbors to be weakly developed. "On the contrary, feelings like envy, petty self-love, joy in the misfortune of others, almost a hatred of mankind, are quickly aroused in him." By 1893 his inability to persuade a neighboring village with the means to do so to build a school led him to conclude that in the years since emancipation the local peasants had not come to see any need for literacy. "We are living well enough," someone always insisted when the commune met to consider construction. Bunakov devised a historical analysis of the impasse. Peter the Great had forced the gentry to acculturate, but that class was now in decline and could offer no leadership. The bureaucracy remained incompetent, for the most part. Centuries of serfdom had killed the peasant spirit, and the peasant generally lacked faith in any intelligentsia initiative. Although Bunakov did not speak explicitly of a civil society, he lauded the "consensus" that had made emancipation possible in 1861. And he lamented the peasant's lack of a consciousness of individual rights.

> The peasant does not know what he can do and what he cannot, in which circumstances and in what measure his personality and property are guaranteed, where and in what cases he may apply for explanations, for security, for protection, for medical attention. He does not have any clear and distinct conception of [the competence of authorities like] the zemstvo board, land captain, head of the county constabulary, head of the district police, village constable, marshal, governor, etc.

He decried their credulity.

> There is nothing easier than to deceive, to harm, to rob, to ruin a peasant. He does not know whom to believe and whom to avoid. Often he does not believe the people who truly wish him well, curses them and orders them to get out, but believes the kulak userer who entices him into debt and poverty. Or someone who is passing through with a story of seizing landowners' and merchants' land and dividing it among the peasants. Or about a secret visit to the village by the tsar or heir apparent to check on how the lords are feeding peasants who suffer from famine and crop failure.

It is revealing that this condition he deplored was typical for an oral culture, with its innate respect for the word of the other. He also regretted their apparent inability to come to grips with facts, without stopping to consider how the fluxion of an oral culture is inimical to fact. Bunakov continued to see an introduction to individualism as the peasant's best hope and continued to regard written self-expression as central to such an education. As it became clear that peasants were choosing this course for their children too slowly, Bunakov considered compulsory schooling to be the solution for Russia. Peter the Great had coerced the privileged to learn, and to Bunakov a similar measure now seemed required for the common folk.

Bunakov's own test results, when he brought back the first decade's graduates from his school to check their retention, should have made him question the wisdom of putting mastery of the written word at the center of his program to entice peasants to individualism. Of 101 alumni, 46 returned to Petino for a reunion and examination. They wrote an essay, solved arithmetic problems, read from the Gospel, answered questions about Russia and Russian history, and recited poetry that they had memorized as students. Their writing had slipped badly. Nor did they remember much of the religious instruction they had received. But they did well in arithmetic, recalling poetry, and especially reading. Bunakov's sober assessment of the school's progress blamed the inertia of the village rather than his teaching methods for the modest gains. "The work of the school can and must continue with its former energy, even though the adult population is little changed for the better, even though the exaggerated expectations with which I embarked on this work ten years ago are hardly vindicated."[17] He continued to hope that the change of a single generation would usher in for the village "a different life, different ideas, and morals." His faith may have been sustained by educated society's newfound consensus in the 1890s that universal literacy represented the key to national salvation.[18]

RUSSIA'S FIRST SCHOOL THEATRE

Another reason for optimism was the appearance of an attractive entertainment as an adjunct to primary education: school theatre was recognized for its great potential to arouse peasant curiosity about the larger world beyond the village. The idea for importing theatre into the school came from a pupil in 1887 who asked, "What if we put on this Koz'ma Zakhar'evich?"[19] He was referring to the play by Alexander Ostrovsky the class had just read from a Ministry of Education anthology, *Kozma Zakhar'evich Minin, Sukhoruk* (K. Z. Minin, the one-armed). Thus it was the text of a historical drama, an account of national renewal set in the Time of Troubles, that itself suggested a reenactment of the spectacle. The class divided the parts and learned the lines, but did not present this work. They did, nonetheless, dramatize a fable by Krylov at their Christmas party. This first Petino presentation freely incorporated peasant customs and manners, and was discussed in the village for a long time.

It was L. I. Mikhailova who first suggested casting pupils and former pupils in plays for presentation to peasant audiences (Z 183). They chose a children's play the following year, P. Vasil'ev's *Sirotka* (The little orphan girl). The parts were copied out and assigned, and ten rehearsals held. The villagers liked the production so much that a second performance had to be scheduled. The classroom, which could accommodate only sixty, served as auditorium until 1892.

Sirotka would have been broadly accessible to villagers who knew little of the outside world. The cast consists mainly of children—eleven with speaking roles—and two adults. The play includes several songs. Indeed, the choral music may have made the script especially appealing for a first production in the Petino school, given the trouble that Bunakov had gone to to engage instructors experienced in teaching singing. The setting, at the edge of a forest near the Volga, would have been familiar to the Petino villagers. So would the dialogue, which is peppered with sayings like, "When you live as an orphan, tears come down in torrents," "Misfortunes don't last a century," and "God reaches into his own pocket for an orphan." Bunakov considered that it "captured rather accurately, without falsification or exaggeration, and without a crudely stenographic character," the tone of popular speech.[20] The power of the peasant commune is manifest in the predicament of the central character, an orphan whom it has assigned to the miller as a servant in return for payment of her parents' arrears. And there is superstition in the form of talk among the boys about "diabolical force." Because of the critical role played by this particular text in establishing an important new institution, *Sirotka* merits close examination.[21]

The action takes place on a summer holiday. The plot hinges on the orphan's estrangement from the other village girls. She avoids them because she is ashamed of her poverty and shabby dress. They think her "stuck up" because she happens to be literate. The second act opens deep in the forest at night. Village boys are seated around a campfire in a clearing. Their horses are asleep. (The obvious reference to Turgenev's *Bezhin Meadow* is reinforced by another to *Kasian from the Beautiful Lands* in the boys' talk about a local man who knows all the birds in the forest and can capture nightingales at will.) First they speak of the moon and its mysterious power. One lad explains that there is nothing mysterious about it, that its apparent facial features are mountains and craters, that it is a "planet" like the earth, but without water. He knows all this because the teacher told him.

STEPA: "Well, and how did the teacher himself come to know this?"

IASHA: "You numskulls—through his head, his head! You see, he's a mental person. And it's well known that a mental person has to know everything. And he has books in which everything is written. In school he showed a picture of the moon and everything on it."

The boys' discussion of natural phenomena drifts to wolves, birds, and the forest itself. Senia tells of a village girl hunting mushrooms who lost her way in the depths of the forest. Wandering for hours, she kept coming back to a beautiful grassy clearing covered with pale blue and yellow flowers. She finally gave in, went out to pick the flowers, and has never been heard from since. Some of the boys are certain it was the work of the Devil, but Iasha explains that it was no such thing. The grassy clearing was simply turf over a bog, and she fell in. "There were no unclean forces here at all." And in answer to Senia's challenge, Iasha replies, "Me? I'm not afraid of sinister forces, that's for sure: because there's nothing to that."

The boys dash for their horses when an offstage voice calls to them that the miller's girl has disappeared, probably a victim of wolves. Then the old forester wanders in, wondering how the boys could have left their campfire burning and lamenting that he is alone in the world, without wife or children. The orphan girl, who has lost her way looking for the heifer, stumbles into the clearing. Telling the forester of her misery, the orphan learns that he has found the heifer and put it with the other cattle. In the fourth act everyone is reconciled. The girls apologize, and the orphan happily agrees to let the forester adopt her.

In his account of the choice and production of *The Little Orphan Girl* Bunakov said nothing of the challenges the play presented to traditional peasant culture. Yet the seemingly innocuous drama can clearly be seen to function as a Trojan horse. Jeffrey Brooks's study of the popular Russian prose preferred by the newly literate in the second half of the nineteenth century demonstrates that those who learned to read re-imagined themselves and redrew the boundaries demarcating self from the world.[22] Two of the chief themes Brooks identifies in the burgeoning popular literature figure prominently in Vasil'ev's play: freedom and rebellion. These themes, which constitute the most important motif in this material, juxtapose the interests of the individual and the collective. To mute the conflict, Russian writers often resorted to the device of casting their central figures as orphans:

> Many of the heroes and heroines . . . were orphans. Their lack of ties to family and community allowed them to succeed without violating obligations to parents left behind in the village. Orphans were peripheral members of the community and hence did not have to share their good fortune with the collective. (286)

Vasil'ev's orphan feels herself unwanted and out of place in the village, and at the beginning of the play considers leaving to go to cook and clean for the Volga boatmen. The village, in the person of an older woman who warns the orphan off by counselling her about the roughness and even depravity of these laborers she has romanticized in her imagination, mediates some of the dangerous tendencies of individualism. And in the end it is luck rather than individual action that secures this particular orphan a happier place in the village society than the commune arranged for her. But the village here is seen responding to individual feelings and interests in an uncharacteristically attentive way.

Brooks finds a clear difference between the treatment of science and superstition in the Russian popular literature of the period and the contemporary European and American popular reading. Because superstition figured only incidentally, if at all, in French and English popular literature of the period, he says, the unmasking of devils and sorcerers could have no place there (265). But with science and superstition functioning together so routinely as a binary opposition in the Russian works, the kind of debunking seen in the campfire scene is relatively common. "In the Russian stories," he explains, "all characters except the hero generally assume supernatural explanations and then are convinced otherwise as the story unfolds" (267). Vasil'ev's orphan girl successfully asserts her claim to some kind of emotional satisfaction, and literacy is vindicated over the gibes of the village youth (a male—the males—leading the way) in this simple play, although the changes cost the village none of its allure as the personal tensions are resolved within the collective.

The Petino production of *Sirotka* had its flaws. For one thing, the girl who played Dunia frequently broke character and laughed. Bunakov found it difficult to tell how the village public understood the presentation, how much they liked it, and what precisely they liked about it. Because tickets were free, it was unclear from demand whether the villagers set much value on the entertainment. Henceforth they would charge admission of between one and twenty kopeks per seat, the take of five or six rubles being divided among the participants according to the size of the role they played. Players could earn as much as nine rubles per season. Some regarded the work as a commercial proposition, but others seemed to Bunakov to take it more seriously and threw themselves into their playing. The cheapest seats proved the most popular, and those who sat in them the most interesting, he noted.[23]

L. I. Mikhailova followed up this beginning by inviting an intelligentsia amateur company to perform Ostrovsky's *You Can't Live Just As You Please* for the school at Christmas. Bunakov considered this the ideal play for peasant audiences, and over the life of the Petino theatre it remained the second most popular drama they performed. The intelligentsia production stimulated discussion locally of the desirability of involving peasants in literary theatre. His neighbors voiced uncertainty as to whether local audiences could understand the best Russian literary drama, whether tolerable performances could be secured, or even whether any locals would care to attend. Some thought peasant participation could be helpful, because neither the amateur nor the professional theatres in the area had enough participants. Others feared breaking down the cultural barriers that kept villagers apart. Bunakov paraphrased their objections.

> And why should we introduce this foreign diversion to people living in the Russian countryside? Already the Russian countryside was noticeably contaminated by unhealthy urban tastes and preferences: little by little dress was losing its native character, popular Russian songs were dying out, and the patriarchal purity of village manners and morals was disappearing. The public house or inn, freakish city fashions, the cigarette, cheap manufactured concertinas and songs, the willfulness and dissoluteness of young people—all this boldly invaded Russian village life, which not long ago was still so pure, simple, filled with poetry, naivete and patriarchal simplicity.[24]

To these local opponents Bunakov riposted that Russian peasants had long ago demonstrated an affinity for theatre, that it was a healthy recreation, and that they needed something from which they could derive satisfaction. To his readers he remarked that the people who were most vocal in their opposition to public schools, popular reading, and popular theatre were those with a vested interest in keeping the peasantry poor, ignorant, and lacking in self-control.

With the initiation of regular Sunday theatre performances during the school year, the Petino company encountered resistance from a different quarter. The students performed *A Life for the Tsar* (in four acts and six tableaux) from a version based on Glinka's libretto that had just appeared in a reader for public schools. The audience was particularly impressed by the death of Ivan Susanin, the tableau showing a Kremlin interior, and the last choral number, complete with bells.

The student acting improved markedly. One of the youths insisted that they perform Fonvizin's *The Minor,* which found warm reception in 1891 and provoked laughter. Bunakov thought they did a good job with N. A. Polushin's *Omut* (The whirlpool), which contrasted city and village life, but it did not appeal to the audience. They scored another major success, on the order of *You Can't Live . . .* , with A. A. Potekhin's *Chuzhoe dobro v prek ne idet* (You cannot profit from someone else's property) (1855).[25] Potekhin's third play, a drama of Russian peasant life, raised issues that remained significant: the limits of patriarchal authority, the desirability of dividing extended households (with nuclear families setting up on their own), and the appropriateness of gentlefolks' manners for peasant emulation. The play is worth a brief look because it is representative of works enjoyed by rural audiences but lacking any particular literary distinction.[26] It resolves its issues in a thoroughly conservative fashion, with virtue restored and temptations to change rejected. Threatened by the blandishments of the Great World, its peasant family wobbles, then recovers and rejoices that it can supply everything necessary for the good life. Bunakov presumably chose the play because he wanted something villagers could identify with, enjoy, and discuss among themselves.

The peasant family in *You Cannot Profit . . .* is not engaged in agriculture. The father has two sons who transport passengers to a nearby town in a troika—a good business, especially during the long fair season. He has put his hopes in his firstborn, who is thirty; the younger son is a bit slow. But Mikhail has a weakness for expending his tips at the puppet booths, drinking vodka, and buying gingerbread and nuts for the girls who sing at the fair (and "honor[ing] them by kissing them"), even though he has a wife and two young sons at home.

Bunakov may also have found *You Cannot Profit . . .* appealing because of its sharp delineation of the mores of three distinct social groups. Most members of the family recall classic peasant stereotypes. The daughter-in-law grumbles that she wears herself out around the house every day. Her husband, Mikhail, refuses to confide in her, considering her "lower" than himself. She takes orders from a mother-in-law who is pleased that they live well and speaks often of God's will. The father insists that his word is law in the family and tells Mikhail that he lived with his old man until he was thirty and had no will of his own. "I am great in the home, I am head of the household. . . . As long as I live, everything is in my hands."[27] The younger son gladly gives his tips to his father: "[A]ll is from father . . . his money."

Two merchants appear briefly in the first act. The liveryman and his wife receive them ceremoniously. She regards their visit as a great honor.

They are invited to take tea. One of them asks for beer instead, which has to be sent for. On no account can they be accused of aping the manners of polite society. One inquires why the younger son is not married, and rejecting the explanation of shyness, he theorizes that the lad's reason may be weak. They want to know the going price for oats, and upon getting a quotation, volunteer that it is most reasonable. One asks about the cost of the malt that went into the beer. After they depart, the mother remarks on the quality of their guests. The merchants' visit furnishes the incident that drives the play's action. After they leave, Mikhail finds a purse containing fifty thousand rubles in banknotes. The father seizes the trove, announces his intention to keep the money, and warns that they must not spend excessively, lest they arouse suspicion in a community where the scale of everyone's income is known to all.

The manners of the educated play a pivotal role in this Potekhin play, even though none of the characters is educated. At the fair Mikhail meets Leonid, who has served as a butler for the local landowner. With money in his pocket and a thirst for the good things of life, Mikhail begs to be accepted as a friend by the cigarette-smoking young man in a cutaway. "But you are a simple peasant lout," he is told. "You've never been anywhere, never seen anything beyond your village." Still, the dogged Mikhail wants to treat him to a drink. Leonid takes only sherry and madeira, libations unknown to Mikhail. When Leonid sees some of the merchants' cash, he proposes that he and Mikhail play cards. Mikhail does not know how. In the course of the next three months the two run through five hundred rubles and the proceeds from the sale of one of the troika horses. They visit the city.

When they return, Mikhail tells his furious wife that his new friend has found him "such amiable women! *Madamy*, as they are called." Having met the rest of the family, Leonid pronounces his verdict: "It is clear, brother, that you are a peasant and all your female relatives are peasants, fools."[28] He requests a corkscrew to open their last bottle of vodka. "What the hell is a corkscrew?" wonders Mikhail, as he smashes the neck of the bottle against the table. They plot to take the remaining money from Mikhail's father while he is asleep that night and split it. Leonid conjures up a shimmering vision of the pleasures money can buy in a city. There is theatre. In the capital it attracts ten thousand spectators, and its lamps burn five times brighter than the sun. (Mikhail calls it *kiatr* and knows it has something to do with comedy.) There is ballet. One can be admitted anywhere if one is properly dressed. Mikhail confides that he used to think the best thing in life was to build one's own home, raise one's children, order the wife around, and eat sweet things. But having seen something of the outside world, he knows that it is better than his wife. Leonid confirms that he "shouldn't have to live with that trash." He assures Mikhail that children remain with the father, though he wonders how he can think of children if he is "receiving the great satisfaction of making a person out of" himself.

You Cannot Profit . . . ends happily, if not convincingly. The plotters break in on the sleeping father carrying an axe. But they are surprised and disarmed by the younger son before any violence can occur. He tells his father of observing Mikhail's unwillingness to strike him and persuades the old man to return the money to the understanding merchant. His mother, who earlier recalled the saying that "treasure comes from the devil," exults and agrees to forgive her daughter-in-law for insubordination. Mikhail promises henceforth to obey his father in all things, if only he will purge his heart of all ill will toward him. They agree not to divide the household, and Mikhail calls his brother the wisest of them all.

Thus Potekhin's play exalts precisely the "patriarchal simplicity" that seemed to be disappearing from the countryside in the 1890s. The challenge of urban ways and egoism, a fit subject for a play written on the eve of the *glasnost'* era, had by now penetrated to deepest Voronezh province. Its theme that money and dress make it possible to go anywhere contrasted nicely to the rising realization noted by Bunakov that it is literacy that makes it possible to go anywhere. *You Cannot Profit* . . . stimulated so many conversations and so much interest in the theatre at Petino that older villagers overcame their prejudice and began to attend.

Bunakov read a paper on their theatre in December 1891 to the Saint Petersburg Committee on Literacy. It renewed interest in popular theatre as an instrument of education and sparked the formation of a commission charged with exploring entertainments that could be useful to the people in their leisure time.[29] The paper quickly appeared in the *Russian Primary School Teacher,* which reprinted it for sale as a brochure.

In 1895 Bunakov and Mikhailova decided to have a fifty-seat theatre constructed as an addition to their school and domicile. They also organized an independent company of young peasant adults from the actors they had trained in their school theatre. When the Moscow Literacy Committee organized a popular theatre exhibit at the Fourth All-Russian Agricultural Exposition in December, it distributed copies of Bunakov's brochure and picture postcards of the just-completed Petino theatre. The exhibit displayed a simple stage that could be built cheaply anywhere, along with playbills, costumes, decorations, props, and materials on popular theatres in Petersburg. It greatly helped to publicize the idea of popular theatre in Russia, as did *Narodnyi teatr,* a volume initiated by its two directors, P. Tinkovskii and N. A. Popov, to which Bunakov also contributed.[30] When the rather expensive book appeared and sold out almost immediately, Bunakov noted in his diary that "it meets a real need in Russian life" (Z 248).

Clerical opposition plagued the Petino theatre. As it happened, a high ecclesiastical official summered in Petino. In church he warned the peasants that it would be a great sin if they attended a comedy. Then when he opened a parish school in a neighboring village he said, "Beware, lest ye be present at that comedy given at Petino." Bunakov thought the priest made little impression on the peasants, who scarcely understood what he was talking about (Z 218). But it did stick in the head of the Petino sexton, a poorly educated seminarist who came out against the theatre when the company prepared a production of Tolstoy's comic sketch *Pervyi vinokur* (The first distiller). The play, based on the story "The Imp and the Crust," concerns the misfortunes of a Devil's agent ordered to tempt an honest peasant and secure a bargain for his soul. Lavish staging in the new theatre revealed the Prince of Darkness dressed all in black, seated on a throne surrounded by golden fire. Though he and his various agents figured prominently in their superstitions, Russian peasants were unaccustomed to real-life realizations of the Devil. The sexton threatened the grandmothers and children that the theatre and the school and the whole village were going to fall into damnation because of this endeavor. The production had to be withdrawn when the parents refused to allow their children to participate.

Nevertheless, this incident represented only a single setback, and Bunakov believed they were making substantial progress against religious obscurantism. Over time the villagers came to question and reject the authority of local figures who opposed the theatre. One of the theatre's persistent difficulties had been finding women to act. At first the village elder had forbidden women to have anything to do with it, but he withdrew his order in the face of strong public support for the enterprise. There remained, however, a taboo on married women acting. Bunakov related it to the prohibition on married women singing in the church choir, and noted that Petino peasants had no prejudice against actors or acting in general.[31] As the fame of the Petino theatre spread and Bunakov received invitations to visit popular theatres in other regions, he noted that female acting was generally superior elsewhere. A breakthrough of sorts came in Petino in 1897 when for the first time a young woman in the company decided to continue to act after marrying. Her husband and his relatives supported her decision. To Bunakov it represented an important step in challenging local customs and changing behavior patterns.

The effects of acting and reading plays were astonishing. After her husband's death, L. I. Mikhailova confessed, "We were soon convinced that the theatre offers much more for the development of the people than our wretched school, where . . . children forgot their letters after a year."[32] For one thing, plays stimulated students to read. First-time actors were motivated by a desire to learn their parts quickly. Seasoned actors ransacked the library for the very best plays and recommended their discoveries to their friends. Soon they had become too sophisticated to be satisfied with childish plays and entreated the Bunakovs to let them perform Ostrovsky and Gogol. Moreover, the school's method for preparing plays promoted examination of alien ways of living, and thereby disclosed an image of personality defined by autonomy and choice. In the mornings the teachers worked with each student individually to clarify the spirit and moral qualities of his role; evenings were for general rehearsals. In their assumed roles the students could live, if only briefly, alternative lives; and this experience altered their conception of themselves.

> After each play they felt a powerful urge to escape from the beastliness of their lives and remain in the clothes of the intelligentsia and live a human life. The peasant actors attempted to transfer these preferences of cultured persons into their personal and family lives. They had handkerchiefs and kept their own homes and clothes cleaner. Convinced from the plays how easy it is to have the external appearance of a *barin,* they could not help feeling at the same time that the externals count for little, and that without the development and education of a *barin* one could not be a *barin* and one's life would not change. This consciousness in them could never die. It explains why the peasant actors read much more and strove much harder for education and clung so fearfully to us. They could not help feeling that the theatre made them developed and intelligent people; the theatre opens to them a way to the stage of human form.[33]

The actors altered their habits of dress. The young men began to wear jackets and the women blouses and skirts. Mikhailova observed a "softening of manners" of the whole peasant population in the village, and noted that even the grandmothers began to curse less. "Becoming dissatisfied with their situation, [the peasants developed] a critical relation to their surroundings—this great engine of all progress. . . . Of course they were no longer passively complacent as formerly."[34] As Bunakov saw it, theatre paralleled the work of the church and affected participants accordingly. Far from corrupting young people's morals, it developed their critical ability to distinguish between good and evil, to evaluate people, to go into a strange situation.[35]

With the new hall, a broader repertory, and improved acting the Petino audience expanded. Intelligentsia types and popular theatre activists came from some distance to observe the phenomenon. Village teachers, scribes, *fel'dshers* (surgeon's assistants), their wives and families came to escape from the deadly monotony of village life. Clerks and others employed in Voronezh drove out, bringing their wives and children for the entertainment. Peasants from surrounding villages came, often on foot. Petino ticket buyers became more discriminating, demanding seats for their favorite plays. The audience also became more demonstrative and began to show its approval with applause.

In 1898 Bunakov considered that his actors were ready to benefit from exposure to professional performers and took his troupe of thirty to see Ostrovsky performed at a commercial theatre in Voronezh. The director took them backstage, described theatrical life, and even treated them to refreshments specially laid out in the foyer. "They began to understand," Bunakov surmised, "that the work and calling of the actor and actress are honorable and deserve respect and manifestly increase their human worth" (Z 278). It seemed to Mikhailova that this visit stimulated their actors' striving for self-education through reading. She also thought their acting improved to the point where they played better than any amateur group, indeed, as well as professionals. As the audiences swelled, the Bunakovs found themselves turning away peasants who had come from as far as ten miles away. After the Petino season ended, the company tried performing in the neighboring village of Devitsa, where a large new school had just been built. But when they arrived, the teacher became frightened of offending the local clergy and turned them away.

The Bunakovs decided on a step almost as bold as their original move to Petino. They determined to build, on a plot of their own in the village, a People's House with a theatre seating five hundred. The structure, decorated by a student of the painter Ilia Repin, would be completed in the autumn of 1902.

KH. D. ALCHEVSKAIA AND THE PROPAGATION OF LITERACY

The labors and discoveries of Kh. D. Alchevskaia parallel those of Bunakov in suggestive ways. Like Bunakov, Alchevskaia began from the assumption that pedagogical work could raise the masses and usher them into the ranks of the enlightened. She too felt privileged to have acquired certain intellectual and rhetorical skills associated with general education and saw a challenging calling in transmitting them. And she too felt confident of her ability to find and develop untried methods of teaching. Over the years a thousand women would teach in her Kharkov Private Women's Sunday School. Like Bunakov, she displayed an early personal interest in theatre, then incorporated it into her teaching. After running a clandestine Sunday school in her home for some years and achieving success teaching urban women there, she attempted a rural school for peasants. Like Bunakov, she modified techniques that worked in an urban setting for the countryside.

And like Bunakov, Alchevskaia published. Her remarkable volumes *What to Read to the People?* (1884, 1889, 1906), a compilation of reactions by pupils drawn from the common folk to literary and scientific material read to them, attracted widespread attention from educated Russians who were curious about the thinking processes and potential of the folk. If Bunakov gained professional recognition from his textbooks, seminars, Petino school, and finally candid political speech, Alchevskaia too became a public figure. The Sunday school she established in Kharkov ignited a revival of the Sunday school movement and would operate for decades, eventually providing instruction for fifteen thousand pupils. She would travel to the Chicago World's Fair of 1897 and the Brussels Exposition of 1900 to proselytize on behalf of mass literacy and would remain in the public eye right up until World War I.

Born in Ukraine in a remote town a hundred miles northeast of Kiev, Alchevskaia was the daughter of a district school teacher.[36] Her maternal grandfather had been a general and a hero of 1812. Her mother came from a gentry family in Moldavia and had completed the course of instruction provided at the Smolny Institute in Saint Petersburg founded by Catherine the Great. Her father quickly ran through his wife's fortune. He beat her serfs cruelly, and his children often interceded to stop him. He hired a seminary student to tutor his two sons but considered a daughter unworthy of education. Khrista learned to read and write by eavesdropping on her brothers' lessons through a door. When her father was transferred to Kursk province and her brothers entered a gymnasium, she studied with them and even wrote their compositions for them.

Before she was seven she was reading to the family servants in the kitchen for their amusement. At the age of twelve she began, with her mother's help, to declaim heroic roles at home for invited guests. Among her appreciative audience was one Krinitsyn, a neighboring landowner who loved the theatre and had trained a local girl who became a celebrated actress. He proposed to do the same for Alchevskaia, but her father forbade her to act professionally. He did, however, permit her to take part in amateur theatricals given in Kursk for charity. She garnered rave reviews in the local papers, and her appearance in a play always guaranteed a good box office. The amateur dramatic circle specialized in French melodramas, which failed to challenge her; but they opened local gentry society to her. She became acquainted with a landowner who had studied the condition of the peasants and was concerned about their needs and desperate poverty. It was at this time, when she was sixteen, that she first began to teach reading and writing to country children.[37]

Two years later, in 1859, she wrote a revealing letter about her experiences to Alexander Herzen's crusading reformist paper published in London. In her letter to *The Bell,* signed simply "Ukrainka," she addressed two subjects. She begged the famous expatriate to publicize the condition of women in her area, who, she said, were treated little better than cattle and deserved to be raised to the status of persons. She also described her teaching of peasants, pointing out that her school differed sharply from the usual gentry schools for peasants in its informality and relaxed discipline:

> This is how I conceived the possibility of developing our peasants: at first I started with children, every day their numbers grew, then adults began to come. Within a week or two the majority of the people were coming to me each day at dusk and listening to me greedily. I undoubtedly owed my success to the fact that I did not constrain them, did not give them lessons and tried with all my ability to get them to discuss [*rassuzhdat'*].[38]

Though written at the height of press freedom under Alexander II, Alchevskaia's message concerning women in Ukraine could only be addressed to European—not Russian—public opinion.[39] Her letter never appeared in *The Bell.*

In 1862 Alchevskaia married and moved to Kharkov, where she immediately began to feel the currents eddying from the capital at this crucial juncture in the Great Reform era. In May she joined the Kharkov Women's Sunday School as an unpaid volunteer. The school was free, accepted illiterates and those receiving primary instruction, and besides the three R's, taught geography, history, jurisprudence, natural history, agriculture, and hygiene from its opening in 1860. But the Ministry of Education ordered that all but basic literacy and numeracy and moral principles be dropped from the curriculum, lest the Sunday school encroach on gymnasia subject matter. Then three Kharkov instructors were arrested for subversive teaching, and in June the government closed all existing Sunday schools, pending new legislation on their competence. At considerable personal risk, Alchevskaia organized an underground Sunday school in her home with some fifty pupils. When the new legislation issued in 1864 required that all Sunday school teachers have a degree with specialization in teaching she determined to continue the school illegally while seeking a special dispensation. She approached the Kharkov Society for Literacy, but they could not adopt her without a diploma. Finally she arranged to take a special examination and received official certification to teach in 1870.

The cultural gap dividing the *narod* and educated in Russia prompted her mission. In her memoirs she spoke of "the impenetrable, lying ignorance that separates us, the literate, from the illiterate."[40] When she described her background in a letter to the populist writer on the peasantry, Gleb Uspenskii, after he praised the first volume of *What to Read to the People?* she explained that as a young woman she had asked herself what she could do in life and answered: "I must drag insofar as possible many people to the point of intellectual and moral existence where I find myself."[41]

That the radicalism of the early 1860s left a lasting impression on her can be seen from Alchevskaia's attempt in the following decade to organize a sewing workshop for young women reduced to prostitution and begging. In this venture she imitated utopian socialist fiction, taking as her model Vera Pavlovna's cooperative of seamstresses in Chernyshevsky's novel *What Is to Be Done?*[42] After arranging a subscription and gathering funds, she rented lodgings—furnishing them with items from her own apartment—and recruited her girls in the poorest neighborhoods and dens of iniquity. Though it started harmoniously enough, the experiment in socialism failed when a woman expert in cutting material and "more developed" than the others gained control and turned the workshop into a fashion salon, introduced wage differentials, and began to exploit the labor of the others.

The project highlights her idealism and her concern for the condition of women in Russia. It may have had an eventual educational objective as well, for Chernyshevsky's seamstresses devoted part of their earnings to tuition. She had settled upon a women's school and chosen to concentrate on literacy for women, she later told Uspenskii, because they had more influence in the home and therefore on the younger generation than men.

Ironically, her husband was a businessman whose personal fortune flourished in the economic expansion of the period. When they moved to Kharkov their only income came from a tea room. But her husband went into banking and bought land. (He would overextend himself and commit suicide after going bankrupt in the crash of 1900.) Bunakov, who met Alchevskaia at the 1872 Polytechnic Exposition, would remember her as "a rich woman" with an original way about her (Z 99). New money enabled her to indulge her passion for social reform.

Another of her passions was for Ukrainian culture. She said that she must have imbibed her love for her native Ukraine and for the Ukrainian people in the milk of her wet nurse. Upon coming to Kharkov she quickly mastered Ukrainian, her goal being to teach the Ukrainian people in their own language. In 1862 she joined the Kharkov branch of the "Hromada" circle, which her husband headed.[43] An organization of liberal landowners and intelligentsia, which existed in Kiev, Chernigov, and other Ukrainian cities from the 1860s to the 1890s, it published legal and illegal literature in Ukrainian and gathered material on folklore and ethnography. The Imperial Government first outlawed school instruction in Ukrainian and the publication of anything but belles lettres in the language, then declared "Hromada" separatist and made it illegal in 1876. Alchevskaia continued to try to put Ukrainian literature into the hands of her pupils, but she found certain Russian literature more useful than Ukrainian in her acculturation mission. She said that her charges understood and enjoyed plays in Ukrainian, but that these did not make such a deep impression as Ostrovsky's.[44] Some Ukrainian nationalists reproved her for letting her educational activities submerge her interest in their cause.

In her Kharkov Sunday school Alchevskaia perfected a haphazard and time-consuming but often effective method of instruction. The format enabled her to disregard the convention of the graded class. In essence, her technique encouraged illiterates to apply their intellects immediately to the intricacies of written records. She started from the premise that the pupils had to be kept interested above all. Instead of drilling pupils on the mechanics of language, she and her staff read to them, encouraged discussion, and asked them individually to retell and interpret what they had heard. They could expand the listeners' intellectual horizons by explaining what was puzzling as they went along. Alchevskaia believed the culture of the literate to be so obviously fascinating and superior that if its richness were simply revealed to the uncultivated, those who could would master the mechanics for themselves in order to establish a personal acquaintance with books. The object was to get students to go to the school library—which Alchevskaia referred to as "our pride and joy"—and choose what they wanted to read at home.[45]

In one sense the method seems absurd. How could it hope to achieve literacy if it did not train people to master the process of reading? Yet it embodied a brilliant insight. She took the culture of the book and presented it orally for the delectation of those firmly rooted in an oral culture. She harbored no illusions that all who encountered the literate culture would want or be able to function in it, but she made it available for the minority that would make the leap and embrace it.

The technique proved itself in the 1860s and 1870s in an urban setting. The Kharkov Private Women's Sunday School, visited and studied by educators intent on setting up similar institutions, attained national eminence. Nor was there any dearth of pupils. Whether because of the intrinsic value of even this cursory introduction to the outlook of the Westernized stratum, or because of the commonly held belief in Kharkov that women who had studied there got better husbands than those who had not, is unclear. Having established the workability of the technique, she reverted to her early interest in teaching peasant villagers and attempted to try it on a small scale.

OSTROVSKY IN ALCHEVSKAIA'S TEACHING

After many years of successful teaching in an urban setting, Alchevskaia established a rural school.[46] She discovered widespread parental recognition of the value of literacy and quickly overcame her initial doubts about the teachability of village children. In the school she organized with zemstvo help she turned the connection between drama and literacy to good account. She experimented with reading plays by Ostrovsky, and a few by other authors to serve as a control. Her accounts of pupils' reactions and discussions, published beginning in 1881, helped build support among the educated in Russia for teaching peasants. They make possible some inferences by way of what has come to be called textual pragmatics, the study of the actual reception of information coded in literary texts. Alchevskaia's records disclose village auditors engaged in a process of translation of the dramatic material into a more familiar framework, often through the use of nature metaphors. The discussants reveal willy-nilly their attitudes toward personality. While they find individualism appealing, their preference is for autonomy and rights without egoism. They identify personal goodness with sacrifice for the group. What they cannot comprehend in the plays is as revealing of their mental state as what moves them. They have difficulty, of course, sorting out incidents from issues, because they lack the systematizing skill that comes from literacy and mastery of a range of abstract concepts.

The idea of village instruction presented itself when Alchevskaia summered in the countryside in 1878 on property owned by her husband in Alekseev ("Istoriia" 217). Located between Kharkov and Voronezh, the settlement seemed remote at twenty miles from the nearest railway station. When she learned that the district had not a single school, she inquired of a neighbor on the zemstvo board about the feasibility of building one. In September the zemstvo offered a subsidy of 400 rubles to any society or person who would pledge 200 rubles toward construction of a school and commit to working on behalf of its interests. Alchevskaia filed a request with the district school inspector, but then had second thoughts. Her neighbors told her there would be no pupils, because the local folk were not disposed to send their children to school. She decided to test the waters by offering instruction in her home, as authorized under the 1864 statute regulating public primary schools. As she recalled her motive later, she wanted to show that a person from the gentry was ready to help peasants, even though she doubted whether peasant children were educable. She remained fascinated by Russia's seemingly absolute cultural dichotomy: "We, with our bookish sympathies, seem foolish to them, and they, being practical, take joy from their fundamental skepticism" ("Istoriia" 202).

In May 1879, a local tailor complained to her that he had a son who desperately wanted to learn to read but that there were absolutely no schools. She invited the boy to come to her for instruction. Her steward, yardman, gardener, and coachman all sent their children, and peasant neighbors sent theirs as well. Within three days she had thirty pupils. The oldest were two boys twelve and thirteen, whose parents removed them from employment herding cattle and working in a mine in order to take advantage of the opportunity. She started by passing out combs and explaining the importance of cleanliness, went on to explain the Lord's Prayer and moved to the alphabet. Within a month she knew that a school could succeed here ("Istoriia" 201).

The local police inspector, however, intervened to halt her teaching, asserting that she operated an unlicensed school. He also ordered her to stop tending the sick, on the grounds that that too was forbidden by law. One mother of a sick child reacted bitterly to his interference: "Sure, they don't forbid the damned yids to open taverns and rob the people, but when a kind person turns up, they raise hell. What of it that we're cattle, to be wasted like illiterate dogs, to rot without relief from our sores?!" ("Istoriia" 206). Word of official interference in her benevolent activities spread quickly. She received requests from Saint Petersburg periodicals to tell her story. A prominent attorney offered to argue her case gratis if it came to trial. She did have to appear in the *volost'* court, but after her pupils were interrogated about what she taught them, the case against her was dropped. Vindicated, she returned to the zemstvo school project. Her contribution of five hundred rubles helped complete the building's construction. From its opening in 1881 she applied her method of reading and questioning there. She included peasant responses collected there in *What to Read to the People?* and in a special volume she published on the impact of Ostrovsky's plays in 1881.[47]

Alchevskaia's experiment in the Alekseev school represented a departure from her Kharkov teaching in several respects. The class, which stabilized at around thirty-five pupils, was mixed in sex, age, and social standing. Ostrovsky's early plays were chosen, she explained, because they presented a picture of reality perfectly familiar to every illiterate hearer (*Ccn?* 1:314). The characters were simple Russian people, the kind one meets everywhere. She was also attracted by the way his plays stimulated thinking about the claims of family and the rights of the individual. "Being startled by the injustice, arbitrariness, and harm brought by the family despots to those who depend upon them," she advised, "the readers . . . value more highly the good, wise, honorable people, better esteem and love justice and legality and thus get . . . an understanding to transfer to their own families."

The peasant reactions she published reveal that the insularity of Alekseev village had already begun to break down. The residents came to her readings possessing considerable knowledge of the outside world. Institutions new since emancipation, like the peasant *volost'* courts and an army that filled its ranks through conscription after 1874, plainly touched them. Economic expansion was creating jobs in nonagricultural pursuits like mining, which drew able-bodied village males to foreign parts from time to time. Villagers in this region had a potentially wide range of vision. Being bilingual in Ukrainian and Russian gave them entrée into two distinct cultures. Their knowledge of Russian society remained fragmentary: while they were acquainted with Russian merchants and could identify with them, they apparently were unfamiliar with the world of officialdom. They knew colloquial Russian but had trouble following the Russian of the bureaucracy. Obliged to teach in Russian, Alchevskaia was pleased that they knew enough to follow as well as they did. They knew enough to be curious. But she was keenly aware of their limited knowledge, and as she bumped up against the limits of their comprehension, she tended simply to omit the plays that gave the most difficulty.

At an initial reading, Alchevskaia explained what plays were and why people valued them so highly. Then she described acting, which the auditors could comprehend because they knew a local coachman who possessed unusual abilities as a mimic and amused people with scenes of his own invention, in which he imitated everyone from lord to laborer. After the reading of their first Ostrovsky play, *A Ward of the Mistress*, two new auditors appeared, one the brother of a charter member and the other the bailiff's wife, who came in holiday dress. The original group continued to feel at home and treated the newcomers with friendly condescension, even though they were of higher rank. Though the dialogue form proved somewhat difficult to follow at first, the play proved a powerful attraction.

Emboldened by this success, Alchevskaia decided to read *The Storm* next. After a description in the play of the merchant's unethical conduct and complete lack of civic feeling, one auditor remarked, "The merchants are the same [here]—all the usages and customs are [the same]." "But," objected the listener Grigorii, "merchants are not everywhere as they are here." Auditor Ivan Pozniakov said, "all the same, they are polished people, while we are tearing ourselves apart." All the listeners disapproved of Boris's romantic involvement with the young Katerina, whose authoritarian mother-in-law rules the family as a matriarch and completely dominates her spineless, hard-drinking son. Grigorii compared Katerina, who has come from a happy upbringing into this joyless and oppressive household, to a caged bird that talks to and amuses itself. When Katerina's husband leaves on business, she is persuaded by her girlfriend to meet Boris, with whom she has fallen desperately in love, by the river late one night. This compromising situation the listeners treated as a harmless prank. When Katerina, guilt-ridden over her relationship with Boris, feeling nothing for her pathetic husband, and unable to endure her mother-in-law's insults, finally cast herself into the Volga, one hearer burst out, "Oh, my God, save her!" Another listener, who had lost a daughter of her own, sobbed, "But what about your mother, whose daughter has drowned!" At the end, Alchevskaia reports,

> The majority of hearers, men and women, sobbed quietly. No one stirred from his place until someone clapped and said, "Enough sadness!" Then they all started talking at once, nervously and louder than usual, telling each other their views of the play and trying to prove the rightness of their interpretation. We had never seen anything like it in our classroom. (*Dp* 11)

The hearers' discussion focused on who was to blame. Was the mother-in-law guilty, or the children because they did not love her? One blamed Katerina's husband for not taking her along on his business trip, knowing what his mother was like. (Rather unrealistically, for it would apparently have run counter to custom.) Another indicted the friend who arranged the assignation. Another called the mother-in-law "a real Baba Iaga," identifying her with the witch from Russian folklore. Still another chided his fellow listeners for talking so loudly, "like real drunkards." Demian, still with tears in his eyes, replied, "we may be like drunkards, but we still have good hearts." An old man drew an abstract moral from the play, saying, "It seems to me that one can get along without love in order to avoid burning." An old woman shot back, "You've survived with it; it's a fine thing for you to talk."

You Can't Live Just As You Please especially intrigued the Alekseev audience. Although it is set in a city and its characters are merchants, they recognized the types and had strong opinions on the issues raised. Alchevskaia's auditors sympathized more and more with the suffering young wife, Dasha, as it became clear that she has done nothing to merit her husband's neglect. An aunt lives with them, and when she chides Peter the auditors advise her to keep quiet, both because she is a guest in the household and because her remarks cannot bring Peter to reform himself. At the point where Dasha flees to her parents, the auditors interrupted the reading to argue over whether her father or her mother would suffer more upon learning of their daughter's fate: "A father is never as wounded by a child's fate as a mother is, and that's true the world over." "You always put yourself higher." "A mother simply dies for her child." "But the father feeds it." (Alchevskaia notes that they often argued heatedly and passionately over the rights, obligations, and relations between men and women and with their children.) When Dasha's father tells her that he will send her back to her husband, the listeners generally agreed that she belongs with her spouse even if he treats her coldly. One remarked, "She could at least take from home the property listed in [her parents'] commune. All the same, on the run she'll be subject to summons at every step."

In the play the woman Peter courts discovers that he is married and angrily rebuffs him. A blacksmith who witnesses the scene offers to put Peter in touch with a sorcerer who can cast a spell on her that will cause her to submit. Alchevskaia observes that although her pupils greeted this proposal derisively, "deep in their hearts they believed in the existence of a world of dark forces" (*Dp* 24). She explains that they were completely unsympathetic to Peter. One voiced their common sentiment, saying, "He is a willful man! He grumbles and gets drunk in order to acquire wisdom. Just look at what a wise man he is! There is more wisdom in him than the whole village." (Interestingly, the play has nothing to suggest that Peter is part of a commune—the hearer is imagining the independent merchant in a village context.) They anticipated a catastrophe, and when Ostrovsky has Peter repent at the last moment they still do not like him, believing his repentance unmotivated by love or genuine renunciation; they expected him to pay with his life for tearing up others'. They had empathized with Katerina in *The Storm* and hoped to the very end that she would be saved—even though she had gone farther with her lover than Peter had with his—because she had not a trace of egoism in her heart.

Their reaction to one Ostrovsky play, *The Poor Bride,* included responses so different from what the author must have intended that the reading called into question the basic assumptions of the enterprise. Alchevskaia omitted the work from a list of plays recommended for performance in popular theatres or for reading to semiliterate simple folk, contending that too many of the characters were not understood. Reactions to this play add significantly to our picture of Alchevskaia's audience (*Dp* 19–22).

In *The Poor Bride* a widow who had lived well with her bureaucrat husband now finds herself facing poverty and nags her daughter to marry someone of means. The suitors who are relatively near in age to the girl all prove unsatisfactory. Two have no money, and the one the daughter falls in love with turns out to be an adventurer. Dobrotvorskii, an old lawyer friend of the family, assists the mother in her defense against a lawsuit. When the court rules against them, she redoubles her efforts to persuade her daughter to marry someone useful.

First, the auditors agreed with the mother that it was a misfortune to have a daughter of marriageable age still unwed. They accepted completely her arguments on behalf of marriage to an older man of means. One of the hearers speculated approvingly that such a marriage could provide the mother a home as well. They credited her relentless protestations that she is "a weak woman," and agreed with her that a household without a man—with only an old woman to run it—is undesirable. The unctuous Dobrotvorskii is taken by the auditors at face value; one of them proclaimed, "Here is a good man." This family friend's solution is to introduce Benevolenskii, a prosperous, clever official who will both fix the lawsuit on appeal and marry the daughter. Far from pitying the daughter when she learns that the young man she loves has no intention of marrying her, the listeners considered her fortunate to have Benevolenskii in reserve.

Benevolenskii's proposal, written in stilted chancery style, was received by the listeners as intelligent and businesslike. "Now he's obviously an educated man," one said. They liked Dobrotvorskii's stupid witticisms, laughing, for example, when he tells that his sister-in-law had six fingers on her right hand but still found a good husband. They expressed a positive feeling toward Benevolenskii as a serious person and man of affairs. When he excused himself for missing the only play he ever tried to attend because he sat drinking in a tavern with friends, they responded indulgently: "He forgot himself over a little vodka. Well, that's nothing." And they accept as perfectly legitimate his explanation to the daughter that he has a tender heart and is quite capable of love, but is at present indisposed, by reason of business. "Will he have time to think about it?" one asked gravely. They missed the mood of frustration Ostrovsky establishes when the daughter realizes her love was not reciprocated, agreeing that she should quickly accept Benevolenskii: "She should make up her mind at once and shoulder her fate." When she does just that they express surprise that the mood of the wedding should be so sad. "Look—it's time for enjoyment, but she is crying." Never mind that the text makes it clear that the groom has accumulated his wealth by taking bribes and that his mistress of five years' standing shows up to make a scene.

Responses to Gogol's *Getting Married* (*Zhenitba* [1833]) also reveal misunderstanding. The reading started well. The listeners laughed until they cried at the conversation between Podkolesin, the bachelor who has decided he should get married, and his servant. His soliloquy about his future children also amused them greatly. One remarked, "He's discussing them and they don't even exist yet" (*Ccn?* 2:493). They did not, however, find anything comical in the competition, of two matchmakers specializing in women of different classes, for his commission; nor did they think it odd for him to arrive at the home of one prospect to find himself among a crowd of other suitors. When Podkolesin, attempting to converse, comes out with some nonsense about the weather, one listener thought he was making an intelligent comment on the crop prospects. They wish him well but see in him merely a strange person rather than someone facing up to a cosmic dilemma. When he finds himself alone with the would-be bride and can't think of anything to say, one old woman explained, laughing, "He doesn't know how to catch hold." The listeners sense impending disaster when Podkolesin, alone, begins to reflect on whether or not he should go through with it. "If only he didn't think it over," someone said. Not everyone understood why he jumps out of the window at the end. And one was satisfied with the matchmaker's explanation, that he backed out because of his friend's meddling.

When Alchevskaia read Ibsen's *A Doll's House,* the audience drank in every detail at first but soon became bored and finally found the play completely incomprehensible (*Ccn?* 3:219-21). One old woman suspected Nora of maintaining a liaison with Dr. Rank in another house. The others found her guilty of lies, hypocrisy, and unfaithfulness. The women responded unsympathetically when she decides to leave her family and undertake self-education: "She's come unstrung! She even repudiated her own children!" Grandma Parashka said impudently, "If I were her husband, I would kill her."

They exercised remarkably effective self-censorship in excluding works whose assumptions they were not prepared to share. Alchevskaia prepared to follow *A Doll's House* with a reading of Ibsen's *An Enemy of the People,* cutting the text heavily so that it might be understood. But before she could begin, "a rumor reached me that [the auditors] were dissatisfied with my reading. . . . The idea that I was driving my rural listeners away . . . frightened me into deciding to stop this undertaking, despite the fact that I had spent much time on it and had so sincerely dreamed what effect these works would have on the heart of the reader from the *narod.*"

In reviewing Alchevskaia's published presentation of her play reading to Alekseev villagers a sort of program begins to emerge. She emphasized the peasants' sensitivity, their warm feelings, the keenness and range of their emotional response to literary drama. She went to some lengths to suggest that they were alive to discrepancies in moral, social, and family life underlined by dramatists and hinted that they were ready and willing to "work on" their own personalities in a mature and reflective way. She emphasized their concern with individual rights and suggested that they were moving quickly toward a sense of personal autonomy, legal consciousness, and respect for the rights of others. She insisted that they had a modern conception of time and a notion that customs and mores are constantly changing.

Alchevskaia emphasized discussion in her teaching method, implying that talking and reasoning about problematical arrangements could lead to considered action—as opposed to compulsive behavior—on the part of her auditor discussants. Did contemporary educated Russians who had personal experience of Russian peasant villagers confirm Alchevskaia's finding that peasants confronting discrepancies between their needs and their aspirations had the capacity to adjust their own behavior? Two influential writers in fact found sharp regional differences among Russian peasants and conceded that the auditors in the particular area Alchevskaia chose for her village school could likely have been more attentive to dramatic representations of the problematics of power relations within the family than peasants elsewhere. Aleksandra Efimenko, an ethnographer who lived for many years in Archangel province and conducted research on the commune and peasant family, moved to Ukraine in 1874. She found that because the communal family had broken up much earlier in Ukraine than in Great Russia, a division of labor and conception of obligations and rights had appeared significantly earlier there.[48] She reasoned that economic opportunities and work alternatives swamped "the patriarchal, clan principle" that had held the individual personalities of family members in thrall.[49] In Little Russia she was impressed by the emotional richness of peasant life: "The tender and refined feelings with which [Ukrainian] popular poetry sparkles are completely alien both to the morals and poetry of the northern peasantry."[50] S. A. An-skii (Rapaport), a populist writer who traveled among and read to miners and peasant laborers, also subscribed to the notion of regional differences among Russian peasants. Although he had not tried reading literary drama, he warned that Alchevskaia's findings should be used cautiously because her village was not in the central provinces.[51] He quoted enlighteners who read to the people in Moscow province and asserted that "dramatic works are read nowhere [here] and are not understood."

Alchevskaia's lively interest in peasant conceptions of justice happened to coincide with Efimenko's. The ethnographer recommended perusal of decisions of *volost'* courts, created in 1861 in connection with peasant emancipation, to get a sense of the peasant understanding of what is just.

> The decisions of the *volost'* courts . . . in . . . Archangel province . . . throw light on the role of women. . . . The *volost'* courts almost never refuse to take up cases dealing with property or personal disputes between spouses, though, strictly speaking, they have no jurisdiction in them. No other Russian court besides the *volost'* can do anything for a woman. The *volost'* court often reaches verdicts completely at odds with the spirit and letter of the law, and it must be said that many of these verdicts are in favor of the woman, in defense of her rights and personality.[52]

Alchevskaia's record of her auditors' reactions to plays likewise gives the impression of a developing sense of justice and its identification with individual rights enforceable by courts. The Alekseev peasants did not laugh at a passage in *The Storm*, meant to be funny, about the courts being unjust (*Dp* 9). And during *Poverty Is No Vice* someone remarked that younger brothers stay poor all their days, suggesting perhaps that they were routinely cheated out of their inheritances (*Dp* 37). Yet the listeners know Dasha's property rights in *You Can't Live Just As You Please* better than she does. And in the course of *The Poor Bride* they shouted out advice on how to manage the lawsuit (*Dp* 21). During a reading of A. F. Pisemskii's *A Bitter Fate* (*Gor'kaia sudbina* [1860]) one speculated that it might be possible for the peasant to take the landlord to court for impregnating his wife! (*Ccn?* 2:529).

The statements of Alchevskaia's auditors concerning women's rights appear deeply equivocal. Although the Alekseev peasants believe the widow's daughter in *The Poor Bride* should make a loveless marriage to guarantee her mother's security, they oppose Liubim Tortsov's marrying his daughter to a much older man in *Poverty Is No Vice.* Someone piped up, "Don't marry her to the old man. It's a sin," and found assent (*Dp* 39). An older female pupil retelling *A Poor Bride* felt the daughter was being sold and recalled a similar experience in her own life (*Ccn?* 1:320). The claims of the individual are recognized, but may be superseded by the interests of the family.

As they struggle to weigh individual rights against family and community interests, Alchevskaia's listeners appear to be developing a sense of historical time. They possess a keen awareness of how times can change in such a way as to require a basic reassessment of assumptions and expectations. For them the emancipation formed the great divide between the old days and the new, an event that marked a sharp change in customs and manners. At a reading of *A Ward of the Mistress,* when the heroine is deceived, one of the girls remarked, "All *barins'* sons were like that then" (*Dp* 4). At a reading of *A Bitter Fate* when they learned that the peasant's wife had given birth to the landlord's child, someone remarked that it must have taken place under serfdom.[53] In reference to Peter's disregard for any authority outside himself in *You Can't Live Just As You Please,* someone observed, "It used to be different, but now everything happens in the open."

Alchevskaia became known among the cultivated, educated classes for her conviction that the uncultivated could be moved by plays. She well understood that many better-off Russians doubted that the lower orders could even comprehend drama, and she used that condescension to challenge a group of her Kharkov Sunday school pupils in 1898 after they had been taken to see a professional production of Ostrovsky's *Jesters* (*Shutniki* [1864]): "You know that some people doubt whether someone who cannot read and has never been to the theatre can understand a play and recount what happened in it; we teachers think otherwise and take every opportunity to prove to them that they are wrong."[54] Their answers to her questions satisfied her that they had "understood it down to the last detail." One older pupil told her something that confirmed her observations about Ostrovsky's special power. A year earlier the pupil had seen a play by someone else. When she retold it at home, nobody said a word. But when she retold *Jesters*, everybody cried over the fate of the father and the daughter. Another of the Sunday school teachers took a group to see *The Forest*. They had so many questions about the first act that the intermission was not long enough to answer them.

> We talked about the characters, their relationships, about what the author wanted to express, about the influence of environment, about the *difference between the characters*, about education, about social outlooks and ideals, about the place of artists in society. . . . For the most part, the ideas expressed were fine and true. They understood the more complicated spiritual developments, and if one or another expressed a not completely accurate view, the rest immediately corrected them, *pointing out the inconsistency of their judgments*.[55]

Clearly, the method employed by her teachers in Kharkov consciously exploited the aspect of playgoing that raises the viewer's consciousness of his individuality for the purpose of educating children. She could feel vindicated in her insistence on the progress of acculturation from the rapid development of Kharkov itself and its amenities.[56] The city happened to possess what has been called one of the three best theatrical enterprises in all the provinces, a place where actors enjoyed the best possible working conditions.[57] Its owners, the Diukov family, regularly distributed free tickets to schoolchildren for Sunday matinees. And Kharkov seemed to have a special affinity for Ostrovsky. In 1876 some eighty-one Russian provincial cities enjoyed performances of at least one Ostrovsky play; Kharkov topped the list with no fewer than twenty-three performances of Ostrovsky works.[58] Ten years later, 203 provincial cities performed Ostrovsky, and Kharkov still led with 31 performances (Kazan had 23, Kiev, 19).[59] By 1899 Kharkov had a Society for Establishing Popular Theatres.[60] Moreover, whole layers of Russian society had transformed their folkways by the end of the century. By now some of the social realities depicted by the native dramatist whose plays had attracted simple Russians to theatre had become outdated. Alchevskaia needed to explain that the merchantry had changed since Ostrovsky's time and now boasted some shining personalities who built hospitals and aided famine relief.[61]

Alchevskaia left the image of *peasant* acculturation through theatre a bit fuzzy. After all, she had not taken Alekseev peasants to see plays. But by insisting that peasants still captives of the village could follow plays, she had performed a signal service for the movement. Surely it followed from her experiences that great feats could be accomplished with peasants who migrated to cities where they could directly experience cultural institutions like

People's Houses with their public reading rooms, the free universities and other formal educational institutions, and popular theatres.[62]

American scholars over the last decade have debated the meaning of Russian enlighteners' ministrations to peasants.[63] A close look at recent disagreement over peasant conceptions of justice may serve to clarify current thinking on the "humanizing" project. In a 1987 article Cathy Frierson discussed the peasants' "schizophrenic" attitude toward law and order. Their legal consciousness took a traditional form when applied to the maintenance and prosperity of the village community and a modern form with respect to "recognition of law as a system of norms to be applied across the empire."[64] Peasants continued to practice *samosud,* or summary justice to maintain order in their village settings. But she found the formal, individual rights–based notion of law to be gaining on family- and commune-oriented *samosud* as the century ended. "By 1903," she noted, "many local observers reported that the civil code had become so much the authority for the *volost'* court that the latter had virtually ceased to represent local customary law" (57).

Frierson had described the *volost'* courts in a 1986 article focusing on attitudes of educated Russians toward peasant customary law.[65] She explained, but could not support, Efimenko's position that peasant legal consciousness as manifested in *volost'* court decisions had genuine cultural value and encompassed a respect for community that could profitably inform the national statutory law (532–35). Frierson concluded instead that the survival of these courts designed to accommodate subjective, personal justice, represented something of an anachronism by 1912: "one can only wonder at the insistence on retaining a court of customary law for a rural population that was experiencing economic, social, and thus cultural transformation. The migration of labor between city and countryside, the rise of a money economy, the break-up of the extended patriarchal household—all of these trends operated against the rule of custom and tradition" (544).

Stephen Frank soon identified Frierson's perspective as one "unfortunately" continuing "to figure uncritically in studies of the Russian peasantry."[66] For him, *samosud* represented not "'lawless violence,' as outsiders claimed," but creative action designed to restore peaceful relations between villagers. Customary peasant justice, he proposed, should be regarded as "a language poorly understood by representatives of the dominant culture."[67] In a 1992 paper Frank insisted that study of the "oral culture [which] served as the primary medium through which villagers expressed their world and organized their lives . . . demonstrates that Russian peasants were conscious participants in the making of their society, not just 'upholding tradition.'"[68] Christine Worobec found "patriarchal ordering" and "oppressive power relations" endemic in the village, but discerned a logic of survival operative there that explained the persistence of customary law in the face of the rise of money economy and individual choice that so impressed Frierson.

> The family, with its productive, reproductive, and cultural functions, and the community, embracing all families in a network of economic and social relations, were at the root of peasant traditionalism. The customary practices and values undergirding this normative world formed within the subsistence-oriented economy a survival strategy that was perforce accepted by most community members.[69]

Though differing on the vibrancy and creativity of peasant justice in the village, Worobec and Frank shared a dismissive attitude toward the modernizing rationalism of educated Russian society. In their identification with peasant culture, they resembled the Russian "specialists in ethnography, statistics, jurisprudence and economics" who Cathy Frierson found in her 1993 book made the peasantry a "separate, distinct object of study, more other culture than ever before" by 1890.[70]

In a 1994 essay Frank went beyond his earlier interest in peasant justice and considered precisely the other features of peasant culture that so interested Alchevskaia and the Bunakovs: time sense, attitude toward work, and cleanliness.[71] He argued that by the 1890s, "educated Russians reworked peasant culture in their own minds and in their presentations of village life" (91). "Having created a culture of progress, enlightenment, science, rationality, legality, respectability, good manners and cleanliness," they mounted a new "movement to the people" to "colonize" the rural population through philanthropy, voluntary associations, local government, and schools (91–92). Frank's bill of attainder covers Alchevskaia and the Bunakovs. They share with his "colonizers" the odor of Victorian uplift, and an emphasis on civilizing the masses in order to assure *Russia's* future. And Bunakov, like Frank's "colonizers," resorted to degeneracy theory to explain continuing peasant resistance to acculturation. But close as they were to "colonizers," I do not believe Alchevskaia and the Bunakovs quite fit.

The Bunakovs and Alchevskaia shared Dostoevsky's and Tolstoy's goal of a reunification of society and were prepared to meet the peasants halfway to achieve this dream. They took up the cause of theatre for the people precisely because it stimulated discussion and gave peasants an opportunity to bring their own knowledge and skills to bear in creative endeavor. Drama represented for them the seed of a common culture, and not exploitation or profit.

Frank's theory of cultural colonization, however, comes uncomfortably close to fitting the Bunakovs and Alchevskaia in those moments when they want to deceive themselves about their villagers' closeness to the norms of individualism and impersonal (blind) justice. If we disregard for the moment the testimony of Bunakova from 1910 and 1916 on how the Petino participants in a semiprofessional acting company at the turn of the century changed their lives and habits, it becomes clear that the humanism, individualism, and self-control so fervently desired by Bunakov and Alchevskaia were developing more slowly among the peasants than they wished. Bunakov scrupulously noted the local peasants' ignorance of personal rights and the institutions designed to uphold them. He was more reluctant to acknowledge that the first plays that brought villagers crowding into his school theatre glorified the wisdom of the village collective and the patriarchal extended family rather than the individual. Alchevskaia thought her Alekseev peasants remarkable for their warm feelings and empathy. Her account of her auditors' reaction to Katerina's drowning in *The Storm* at first glance suggests a very highly developed empathic sense. But can it not be more accurately seen as a case of the contagiousness of affect among groups unaccustomed to practicing affect control? As for forward planning, they sympathized with Benevolensky for losing track of time in a tavern and missing the only play he ever planned to attend. One of them emphatically did not want Podkolesin to reflect in solitude, to "think about" getting married. And how far from individualism can the egoism they hated have been? They think it proper for the daughter in *The Poor Bride* to marry a much older man because the interests of the tax-paying household unit seem to them much more important than the interests of the individual. It has been suggested that the auditor who objected on the grounds that such a marriage would be "a sin" was thinking not of the daughter's personal fulfillment but that the groom was probably too old to get a child and continue the family properly. Instead of being moved by the discrepancies revealed in drama to ponder their individual value systems, the Alekseev peasants seemed avid to draw the conventional wisdom of the community from the dramatic situations they encountered. But in the end Alchevskaia and the Bunakovs trusted drama to stimulate an independence and reflectiveness that could overcome rigidities and dogmatisms and enable people to function with satisfaction in increasingly complex social interactions.

The scholarly debate that mirrors the nineteenth-century debate in Russia over the possibility or desirability of harmonizing elite and popular cultures has had the unfortunate consequence of minimizing the neutral ground on which the two cultures could meet. The interchange over peasant justice provides a telling example. In the doctoral dissertation on which her 1993 book was based, Frierson discussed the office and function of justice of the peace, created as one of the new zemstvo institutions of local self-government in 1864. She quoted an early holder of this office in the Volga region, V. N. Nazar'ev, to demonstrate how modern or "official" legal consciousness was taking hold among female villagers, thanks to this new institution: "He found that the *mouzhiks* [male peasants] resented him and the institution he represented because they were the product of those 'New

Laws! and the women thank you for them . . . we never hear the end of their threats to go to the justice of the peace if we beat them.'"[72] This remark exactly confirms the lively interest in individual rights and precocious knowledge of statutory provisions displayed by Alchevskaia's Alekseev auditors.

But when Frierson cited Nazar'ev in her 1986 article it was merely to show how ignorant this educated Russian thought the peasants.[73] Although her subject in this article was the *volost'* court, she discussed the justices of the peace as well.[74] In her consideration of the two forms of peasant legal consciousness she refers to the *volost'* courts' origins in P. D. Kiselev's experiments with state peasants in the 1830s.[75] Her presentation of the justice of the peace system failed to mention that the justices were *elected* by district zemstvos, which were in turn elected by all who met a property requirement, *including* peasants. So concerned was she with showing that the Duma's 1910 reworking of *volost'* courts represented an attempt by the nobility to regain control in the countryside through restoration of compliant judges steeped in customary law, that she failed to note the democratic significance of the Duma's 1907 revival of the justices of the peace.

The potential of this democratic institution for creating a common ground where educated and peasant could work through rights and statutes to resolve disputes fairly did not escape those who participated. The memoirs published in 1912 and 1913 by A. A. Sinitsyn, a rural doctor who had served as an elected justice in Tver province, are a case in point. It seemed to Sinitsyn that before the justices of the peace were established in 1864, the peasants were "without personality" *(bezlichnye).*[76] In these courts, he believed, "the peasant first received full recognition of his personal worth and full equality of rights." They were abolished, in his estimation, only because they aroused the indignation of "the retrograde part of the public [that stood] firmly on the soil of serfdom and estate prejudices" *(soslovnykh predrazsudkov).*[77] He recalled his years as a justice as the best of his life. "In [the social openness of local self-government] began to develop the best forms of civil society *[grazhdanskoi obshchestvennosti]*, which constitute the power of west European governments and in which the free development of the personality goes hand in hand with social progress."[78]

In her 1993 book Frierson devoted a chapter to "The Peasant as Judge." She again quoted V. N. Nazar'ev on the ignorance of the Volga peasants he served as justice of the peace before 1872, but this was the only reference she made to the justice of the peace system. She might contend that because her subject was images of peasants, she was perfectly free to ignore evidence of a developing civil society, no matter how influential. Or perhaps limitations of space obliged her to eliminate consideration of an important institution. She again discussed peasant legal consciousness, but rather more tentatively than in her 1986 article.[79]

The courts of the elected justices of the peace, where A. A. Sinitsyn found the Russian peasant first received full recognition of his personal worth, advanced a sociohistorical process first investigated in detail by Alexis de Tocqueville. Tocqueville's early book on American democracy examined the process whereby individuals in a community internalized restraint as they practiced the pursuit of private interest. In the course of time they learned the "art of associating together."[80] This benefit outweighed the chief disadvantage of an increasingly legal consciousness, which Tocqueville identified as the tendency to regard individuals as abstractions. With community standards commonly rooted in tradition, religion, and a deferential attitude toward authority, people moved cautiously. As they became aware of discrepancies between their needs and their aspirations, they developed resources for altering conditions in order to reconcile them. Where the civilizing process ran unimpeded, they developed skills for working constructively with each other. As they developed the "virtue" of citizens, they extended their art of association to politics and legislation. They created institutions that provided new amenities and new satisfactions.

Tocqueville provided a glimpse of the mental change wrought in the sociohistorical process in a passage in *L'Ançien Régime et la Révolution.*

> That word "individualism," which we have coined for our own requirements, was unknown to our ancestors, for the good reason that in their days every individual necessarily belonged to a group and no one could regard himself as an isolated unit. . . . Each set store on his status as a member of a particular group because he saw others asserting their personalities in this way; yet all were quite ready to sink their differences and to be integrated into a homogenous whole, provided no one was given a privileged position and rose above the common level.[81]

In this book he set out to explain how the natural advance of civic responsibility had miscarried. He found that when people deploying new abstractions about individual equality vented their dissatisfactions on the nobility, they could easily repudiate provincial politics simply because nobles had dominated them. Instead of patiently developing their skills and steadily nurturing their citizenly virtue through participation in local public life, they might choose to resign their community authority to increasingly efficient central bureaucracies. In England, he considered, the process had not been derailed by "democratic despotism."[82]

Stephen Frank invokes a different development in western Europe, one confined wholly to elites, to illuminate what happened in Russia's local communities in the 1890s.

> Russian reformers would attempt to colonize the rural population by means of an enlightened culture that was not yet dominant even in cities. . . . In this

> respect, they closely resembled post-Risorgimento Italian social reformers who saw their national and cultural unity threatened by the "inherited backwardness" and degeneracy of the rural south, or French writers who described rural settlements as colonies "waiting to be 'claimed for civilization.'"[83]

It may just be possible that the *mentalités* approach that Tocqueville favored still has some life left in it, even after the unmasking scholarship of the postmodernist period has done its work on the humanizers and an awareness of hegemonic tendencies has exploded some pretensions of high culture.[84] French historiography again points the way in suggesting how sociohistorical processes have been connected to physiological changes. Surely Alain Corbin is correct to speak of a "perceptual revolution" and "sharply reduced threshold of tolerance" to certain odors. He documents the adjustment in France, where "odors simply began to be more keenly smelled" by those at the top of the social pyramid in the mid-eighteenth century, and the masses first began to lose their indifference to the issue of smell at the end of the century.[85] Something regarded as normal, natural, and ubiquitous came to be perceived with fear and avoided. People found that systematic avoidance could be programmed into their behavior.

Are Alechevskaia and the Bunakovs to be denounced for their cultural imperialism with respect to personal cleanliness? The very first thing Alchevskaia did when she opened her Alekseev village school was to hand out combs and explain the importance of cleanliness. Bunakova writing in 1910 (well after her husband's death) told of how their Petino peasant actors took to carrying handkerchiefs and began to keep their own homes and clothes cleaner. In his memoirs Bunakov described how the 1891 famine and his local relief efforts had made him better acquainted with the "bestiality" and "wretchedness" of the villagers. He understood that malnutrition undermined the peasants' resistance to disease and that they must therefore begin to exercise some care in the disposition of their excrement. The famine and its attendant intervention by outsiders constituted their introduction to "sanitary consciousness."

Without subscribing unreservedly to the proposition that "to understand everything is to forgive everything," it may be useful to note that these three enlighteners never thought—as we might—to ask how their own ancestors' acculturation had reordered certain biological processes. First, fear had attached to specific sensory stimuli. With the mastery of systematic avoidance, the fear evaporated and they were left with a new concept, a rational category, a principle that subsumed various rules: hygiene. The concept could be taught, could be worked into child-rearing strategies, where it would then figure as an aspect of education. A related physiological process that lends itself to evolutionary interpretation is affect management. Donald Nathanson has shown how, when culture gives reasons to control affect, people learn to conceal their surprise, fear, anger, and even enjoyment responses as they come to perceive the advantages of privacy.[86]

To sum up, historians who ignore the fact of a civilizing *process*, or disregard the fact that the process *could* promote the development of civil society in the countryside, make a serious error. The civilizing process has several salient characteristics, besides its physiological dimension. It involves the adoption of language rich in abstract concepts to explore and analyze experience critically, to categorize, to compare and contrast. It is associated with an attitude that detaches the self from its environment. In Europe, religious upheaval advanced the process in many communities. Russia was no exception, for Old Believers, obliged to distinguish themselves from those who remained communicants of the official church, cultivated personal cleanliness and thoughtful management in everyday life.[87] Dignity and self-respect go with the civilizing process, which exalts the ability to make choices, move to the discovery and pursuit of private interests and think in terms of personal rights rather than simple perpetuation of family and community. These habits can lead to new forms of association, which in turn encourage self-scrutiny and reinforce the process.

What needs to be said in conclusion about the experiments and testimony of the Bunakovs and Alchevskaia is that despite their exaggeration of the speed with which peasants adapted to individualism and altered their responses to the world around them, they did respond wholeheartedly to the problematic features of drama. In the public discussion of their findings An-skii continued to emphasize as late as the second edition of his *The People and the Book* (1913) just what a short distance most peasants were prepared to go in the direction of individualism.[88] Still, the Russians, elite and common folk alike, had entered a phase of the Public Sphere when, as Habermas put it, "The prospect of free and open discussion seemed to eliminate the last obstacle to 'the rationality that strove to discover what was at once just and right.'"

Chapter Four

"Even in the Workhouse a Theatre!"

AROUND 1886 documented popular theatres began to spring up in communities ranging from Russia's largest cities to her small provincial towns. By 1903, when an expert conducted a survey for the Ministry of Finance, hundreds existed. Theatre professionals, intelligentsia philanthropists, industrialists, ministers, and officials began to organize and institutionalize theatrical performances. Merchants, soldiers, skilled and unskilled factory workers, artisans, and "common, ordinary people" turned up in their audiences. The central, provincial, and municipal governments involved themselves in providing and regulating theatre for the uneducated.

Mass production drew villagers into cities in this springtime of popular theatre. As money and people circulated ever more freely in the metropolis, visual media assailed potential consumers, raising their awareness of formal entertainments. Certain urban spaces came to be permanently identified with entertainment, thanks to the dialectic of work and leisure. A surprising quantity of the theatrical fare presented could claim to raise public taste or contribute to moral uplift. This was an earnest age for the purveyors of literary theatre, not an age of satire. Drama in the service of social and political struggle was scarcely yet imagined.

While the public for folk theatre grew in cities, thousands of country fairs continued to attract huge crowds—even as railway building eliminated their economic rationale. Puppet booths, *balagany,* delighted crowds with the Russian descendants of characters first brought by visiting commedia dell'arte players in the eighteenth century. Central to the fairground booth's appeal was the irreverent linguistic improvisation so admired by Apollon Grigoriev and Ostrovsky in tavern repartee. A succession of cheap printed editions of *Petrushka* after 1890 testified to the scoundrel's abiding popularity with a public learning to read. Catriona Kelly accounts for his lasting merit: "The best [of the texts] combine lurid abuse and doubles entendres with inspired nonsense, puns and *non sequiturs.*"[1]

Feodor Chaliapin recalled first encountering the power of theatrical spectacle at a fairground booth as a boy of eight at the Easter Fair in Kazan in 1881. The main performer had begun as a cobbler, and first started entertaining with his wife, son, and apprentices. "Yasha knew the man in the street. And how well he had mastered the heavy, coarse humor and wit which to this very day delight us. The weighty jokes, his daring gibes at the public, his thundering, raucous voice, enchanted and at the same time depressed me."[2] *Balagan* was manifestly a folk art, representing "production on demand."[3]

What precisely depressed Chaliapin, he did not say. Perhaps it is noteworthy in his description that the spectators are ridiculed by the presenters. Literary theatre takes a different, dignified, approach to the viewer, challenging by distancing her from choosing individuals making mistakes. With respect to plot, as well, this entertainment differed emphatically from literary theatre. In some printed *Petrushka* versions an integrated story is presented, but some variants are nothing but a succession of beatings.[4] Petrushka was a character identified with carnival, with holiday time. The situations he found himself in were not to be taken as representations of reality.

Though intellectuals after the turn of the century would famously take up and rework the character Petrushka, in the 1886–1903 period he made educated Russians uncomfortable by virtue of his incorrect behavior. This take is reflected in an 1894 characterization of folk theatre generally as "where they throw out their knees, stick out their tongues, pommel each other, and swear."[5] And it is apparent in an 1897 article describing a summer fair in central Russia offering diversions similar to that of "the outdoor pleasure grounds of cities like Moscow."[6] The author of the piece suggested that the Prisursk fair became newsworthy because of the appearance nearby of an amateur theatre playing Gogol and Ostrovsky and attracting more and more townspeople and factory workers bored and exploited by the traditional entertainments.[7]

Tolstoy had experienced a similar aversion to popular amusements. In the early 1880s, after locating permanently in Moscow for the winter season, he became interested in how recently arrived country people adjusted to city life. On his walks he observed where they relaxed and amused themselves, as well as where they worked. One result was his decision to turn his hand to writing a morally instructive play.

He told the widow of the composer Alexander Serov that at these places of public entertainment he "heard and saw all sorts of things. . . . You know, I felt ashamed and sick observing all that disorder. Then and there I promised myself to put together something or other for presentation on the popular stage."[8] In the summer of 1886 a circle that had set out a year before to organize public holiday entertainments for factory workers and their families in Aleksandrovsk village beyond the Nevsky Gate in Saint Petersburg successfully premiered his short play, *The First Distiller.*[9] Based on *The Imp and the Crust,* it starts from the conceit that the Russian peasant has so much common sense and works so hard that the Devil must invent liquor in order to bargain for his soul. The Aleksandrovsk workers, accustomed to seeing one-act vaudevilles, pantomimes, and short comic sketches, discussed this playlet for a long time afterward.

Tolstoy's choice of a temperance theme for his first popular dramatic entertainment demonstrated his usual canny insight. Linking perceived disorder and the temperance idea offered a means of engagement for committed individuals. Social reformers could make common cause with authorities in campaigns for improvement that made use of theatre and designated it worthwhile for the masses.

Tolstoy then proceeded to compose a dramatic text that triggered a chain of consequences ending in the state's regulation of theatre for the people. *The Power of Darkness (Vlast' t'my)* is a naturalist work that demonstrates how the temptations of modernity contribute to the crackup of a traditional peasant family. Cheap consumer goods, money and credit, even the new postemancipation legal institutions that seem to relieve family and village of responsibility for righteous behavior, are shown to undermine peasant morality. A published account of a Tula peasant's confession of infanticide gave Tolstoy his initial inspiration. His play shockingly and relentlessly portrays peasant brutality and amorality. It was as though he situated the abusiveness and violence of Petrushka in a concrete social and historical setting, thus challenging (not insulting) the audience.

Alexander III responded sympathetically to the moral implications of Tolstoy's drama. In 1887 an influential actress secured its performance at the Alexandrinskii Theatre as a benefit, and the tsar heard the play read. He pronounced it "a marvelous thing," and spoke of a staging that would combine the talents of Saint Petersburg and Moscow actors. He may have been particularly impressed by *Power*'s depiction of the catastrophic consequences of sexual license.[10]

The complications began when M. V. Lentovskii, the daring entrepreneur who organized the Skomorokh Theatre in Moscow, asked Tolstoy for a play and was given *The Power of Darkness.* The drama censor refused permission for performance at Skomorokh, which welcomed a "fresh" audience with ample cheap seating. Then K. P. Pobedonostsev, Alexander's former tutor, now procurator of the Holy Synod, wrote the tsar. It was bad enough, he said, that the Posrednik company had published an enormous edition of the play, which it sold for ten kopeks. To let this play of peasant corruption and murder, despite its theme of redemption and reconciliation, be seen by the kind of people in sheepskin coats who crowded into theatres for the general public with seats priced from five to sixty kopeks was impossible. The masses, he contended, behaved instinctively, were highly suggestible, and committed crimes with nonchalance.[11] Other officials agreed. The director of the Main Administration on Publication (Glavnoe Upravlenie po delam Pechati) wrote in his memoirs, "It would have been crazy to approve the play for the stage. . . . Fortunately Pobedonostsev took it upon himself to enlighten the tsar."[12] Alexander changed his mind, and *Power of Darkness* was forbidden performance by *all* Russian theatres during his lifetime. (The ban would be lifted for theatres catering to educated audiences in 1895.)[13] The momentous outcome followed in 1888: a special censorship for popular theatre was created that functioned until 1917.[14]

The state would undertake yet another important popular theatre initiative by making available financial support for temperance theatres all over the empire. The other remarkable government action with respect to popular theatre in this period is attributable to the Saint Petersburg municipal government. The decree creating the national Temperance Trusteeship came late in 1894. Two years later Saint Petersburg's governor-general informed the *balagan* operators that they would be displaced from their central location on Mars Field, just blocks from the Winter Palace. The removal was carried out after Easter 1898, with carnival celebrations henceforth located at Semenevsky parade ground at the city's edge.[15] A contemporary journalist explained that when the educated public patronized the fairgrounds it had made sense to allot space for them on Mars Field, but now that only working classes attended it was pointless to transport them to the center and then back home.[16] The showman Aleksei Alekseev-Iakovlev speculated that the government acted out of concern for possible revolutionary unrest.[17] The government-sponsored temperance theatres would be located mainly in working-class districts at the city perimeter, but they would function daily and year-round. Thus in one sense the fairground entertainment, with its exceptional, carnival tone, lost its desirable central space in the imperial capital as it was eclipsed by permanent theatrical entertainment woven into "the fabric of day-to-day urban life."[18]

By 1903 the audience for popular theatre in Russia already numbered three million, and by 1905 government-subsidized temperance theatres alone numbered 361.[19] Presenters carefully assessed the impact of plays on popular audiences. The government took a remarkably active role in promoting such theatres, even as it filtered the drama the lower orders could see. Though the movement developed haphazardly, it progressed with astonishing speed. As ordinary people demonstrated a lively interest in literary theatre, educated Russians persuaded themselves of the civic and economic benefits of a theatre that could advance the civilizing process.

THE FIRST POPULAR THEATRES

Despite the Russian saying, "A reputable actor doesn't go to a village," six freshly trained professional actors from Moscow did precisely that, settling in the Volga village of Balakovo in the summer of 1886.[20] They went not to make money by presenting plays, but simply to spend the summer in pleasant surroundings. Since they had no money to set up a theatre booth, they threw in with a traveling Swede who had a panorama. With the income from the panorama and mummers' plays they gave on the square, they raised the funds to construct a simple show booth. When the company arrived, the villagers had no idea what an actor was. From their reference point of circuses and *balagan* troupes, they wondered if the performers would do a trapeze act. The village clergy, considering show booths only slightly less sinful than public houses, urged their congregations in their sermons not to attend. (When one member of the company wanted to marry, the priest refused to perform the service and advised him to go to Orenburg.) The local intelligentsia, whom they had counted on to support the theatre, proved not to be numerous enough to provide a sufficient financial base.

At first the company chose the wrong repertory, assuming that the plays popular at Moscow's best private theatre, the Korsh, would succeed in the countryside. From their initial offerings, *Uriel Acosta, The Monster, The Destruction of Pompei,* and *Woe from Wit,* only the Griboedov play drew well—with receipts from the second performance nearly double those of the first. *Uriel Acosta,* with excellent sets and costumes, took in only thirty-six rubles. They moved on after a fortnight, but returned twice during the summer, encouraged by rising attendance. On their first visit they took in 300 rubles; the second, 500; and the third, one thousand. When they returned a following year, they were invited to perform in a newly constructed, and excellently outfitted and decorated, garden theatre, and they stayed two and one-half months. By now they had learned that village audiences generally ignored the Korsh repertory, and so they played Ostrovsky. Uneducated villagers developed the habit of theatregoing and learned the conventions by observing the intelligentsia. At first, if there was any applause, it came from the intelligentsia. When an actor bowed to the audience, most of the audience bowed back. The response gratified the troupe, who were delighted to find that playing in a village could be "incomparably more interesting than in a city, because here you immediately feel some kind of invisible moral connection between . . . the actor and the public, which rarely happens in the city."[21]

Their success in Balakovo and the quickening pace of the nation's economic life encouraged the company to build their own professional theatre. It had not been possible earlier because in the summer peasants were entirely occupied with fieldwork. They chose a village called Dubovka in Saratov province not far from Tsaritsyn because it was a convenient gathering place for an outlying population of fifteen thousand. They dealt with an entrepreneur who had leased a garden from a merchant and constructed a buffet and billiard parlor. He agreed to furnish and light the theatre for 30 percent of the gross receipts on holidays and 10 percent on weekdays. A structure accommodating two hundred was built and fitted out in ten days, at a cost of eighty rubles. They opened on a Sunday evening in May with *Getting Married* and S. Stakhovich's *Pasturing Horses for the Night (Nochnoe),* a vaudeville they had found to be invariably successful. Their dress betrayed the social standing of ticket purchasers on that opening night. Twenty-seven men wore jackets, 52, long-waisted coats, 102 came in the attire of simple workmen and the lower middle class, 10 were in intelligentsia dress, and two in military uniform. Many of them had obviously never been to the theatre before. They interrupted freely during the first scene of *Getting Married* with exclamations like "Good lad!" "Look, look, the matchmaker has got angry!" and "Well, he's a flabby fellow, brother!" and laughed noisily through the second and third scenes. When the curtain fell, they remained in their seats a long time discussing whether Podkolesin would in fact marry.[22] The inexperienced audience had no idea of literary theatre, an "invisible text" with an author behind it. Judging from the conversation, most regarded the play as exclusively the work of the actors. Many commented on the matchmaker's similarity to the local one. They compared Agafia to a local merchant's daughter. For some time after, villagers came up to the actors on the street, addressing them by the names of the characters they had played, to ask whether any marriage had taken place, or just to chat.

The Storm produced an especially deep impression here, because people in this area lived freely and were shocked by the repressive merchant family life represented in the play. The villagers thought no woman could have the influence exercised by old Kobanova. But one was impressed by the "rightness" of the denouement. "What is strange here is for someone to drown herself. Such a sin—for what? But it really is very good. It is as it would happen in reality, as it would always work out in fact."[23] The Dubovka audience continued to mature as theatregoers, applauding for the first time at *Don't Get into Somebody Else's Sleigh.* The actors took heart from their warm reception and began to hope that before long the stigma attached to their profession would disappear, and they would be honored for serving the countryside.[24] Moreover, the healthy environment brought out the best in them. Though they earned little money in a summer season, they lived as a working collective (artel), ate together, didn't squabble over roles, gave no one priviliged treatment, and played well together.

A different kind of acting company began to assemble at the village of Rozhdestveno near the Seversk railroad station in Saint Petersburg province in 1889. Its nucleus was a circle of amateurs that included a female doctor, a female *fel'dsher,* the local teacher and his wife, and neighboring landowners. They raised 150 rubles by subscription, constructed a simple theatre seating one hundred and played *You Can't Live Just As You Please.* The first production pleased the local peasants, who came in greater numbers than the theatre could hold. Four more Ostrovsky plays were presented the following year. In 1891 peasant players joined the intelligentsia amateurs. The village had a troupe of ten peasants who performed the folk plays *Tsar Maksimilian* and *Lodka* in nearby villages, but interest in this repertory had declined over the years. Now they presented a modern Russian play, N. Polevoi's *Ermak Timofeevich,* on the Rozhdestveno stage in an adaptation by one of the peasants and followed it with N. Polushin's popular *The Whirlpool (Omut).* The peasant actors were helped by the director of the local amateur circle, Evtikhii Pavlovich Karpov. A populist who had suffered arrest and six years in exile, Karpov wrote plays on peasant and factory life and would go on to play an important role in the institutionalization of the popular theatre movement. The Rozhdestveno theatre faltered but was revived in 1894 with material support from a local landowner, who redecorated the building and expanded its seating capacity to 285. Now, though the intelligentsia amateurs continued to act, the peasants took the majority of the roles in the amalgamated cast. They presented plays every Sunday afternoon and on certain holidays. A paid provincial actor served as director. When N. F. Bunakov visited late in 1895, he noted that their ticket prices were much higher than in Petino.[25] He found their production of Ostrovsky's *A Warm Heart (Goriachiia serdtsa)* "not bad," but greatly admired the fiery performances of two peasant actresses, who far outperformed all the female players he and his wife had trained. The mixed company, he observed, made it possible to produce a much wider range of plays than in Petino, where the young actors were limited by the fact that they knew only peasant life firsthand. Another difference he commented on was the Voronezh audience's eagerness to see favorite plays again and again. The Rozhdestveno public constantly demanded new plays, which made it difficult to cast the roles and find sufficient rehearsal time. V. S. Serova was sufficiently impressed with the company's performance of an Ostrovsky play, despite a few blunders, to come to work with them to prepare excerpts from her husband's unfinished last opera, *Satan (Vrazh'ia sila),* for a jubilee marking the twenty-fifth anniversary of his death in 1871. The correspondent from *Novoe Vremia* wrote of the performance, "The first scene went smoothly and an unaccompanied peasant sang Dashina's aria with correct intonation and feeling. The public, seeing the free, intelligent movement of the actors on the stage, began to doubt—were these really peasants on their own? But when they heard the peasant speech (with its involuntary emphasis on the letter *o*) and its rather coarse pronunciation, they doubted less and less. . . . After the second act members of the excited audience went over behind the stage in order to get a closer look at the unusual troupe."[26]

Another popular theatre dating from the same time was established in the Ivanovsk textile factory in the Zvenigorodsk district below Moscow. It was founded by S. M. Popov, a university graduate, who ran the factory for his father. Impressed by S. A. Iur'ev's account of peasant response to his Voskresensk village theatre in 1862 (which first appeared in 1889) and Bunakov's success with school theatre at Petino, he instituted performances of plays "in the interests of the struggle against drunkenness and debauchery among workers on holidays."[27] In February 1890 white-collar workers and factory laborers performed *Getting Married*, which drew large crowds of workers and inhabitants of neighboring villages. S. N. Popov took a great interest in the theatre and supervised its activities until 1917. He insisted that the workers from the shop floor not defer to theatrical judgments of the "intelligentsia" office staff. And he brought in his nephew, Nikolai Aleksandrovich Popov, to direct the productions, thus launching the career of an important popular theatre activist. At first the mainly illiterate audience paid more attention to the sets and effects than to the plays. Introductions were thus added before the curtain opened to establish the context and say something of the content of what was about to be seen. Here too Ostrovsky plays were most successful with the audiences, followed by those of Gogol.

A short-lived popular theatre started up in the summer of 1893 at the village of Krivtsovo, deep in the Orel province, some twenty-five miles from Mtsensk. Its origins recall Petino. Here a general's widow had established a school and equipped a medical clinic. Her daughter and close associate in philanthropic cultural activities, E. V. Lavrova, had completed the Higher Courses for Women in Saint Petersburg—the equivalent of a liberal arts education. They built a three-hundred-seat theatre and offered performances free of charge to the public. While they sought to tie the theatrical productions to instruction in their school, they also wished to know just how much peasant audiences understood of the plays they saw and to test their tolerance for a broad range of theatre. At first the audience looked upon the actors as mummers, and made so much noise their words could hardly be heard. Only after some evenings of short sketches and tableaux vivants did the viewers get accustomed to concentrating on the sense of the drama unfolding on stage. Amateurs from the neighborhood and outsiders played the major roles. Peasants took some small parts.

The younger Lavrova invited her friend N. N. Arkhipov, a law student who later became a famous director under the name N. N. Arbatov, to spend the summers of 1895, 1896, and 1897 helping her produce and perform plays at Krivtsovo. He in turn invited two friends from the Society for Culture and Literature, N. A. Popov and G. S. Burdzhalov. The neighbors had misgivings about the activities and informed the local authorities that "the Lavrovs are making bombs." But despite frequent searches, the police found nothing to complain of.[28] Lavrova and her associates introduced demanding plays they had reason to believe popular audiences might like. After a successful production of nine scenes from Pushkin's *Boris Godunov*, they mounted Molière's *George Dandin*. Glikeria Fedotov, widow of the director of the 1872 Polytechnic Exposition theatre, had told Arbatov how well received it had been there. They also premiered works, like Popov's comedy based on Russian folk tales, *Unjust Trial (Shemiakin sud)*.

Once they felt certain that their audiences could follow plays they presented a romantic fantasy, Kh. Herts's *Iolanthe,* about a blind princess and a knight. Reasoning that most plays presented for the people were chosen with a view toward uplifting and enlightening, Lavrova wanted to try something peasants might have selected for themselves, judging from the taste for "absurd novels" and adventure tales of the literate among them. She also knew of the great demand for melodrama at the Vasili Island popular theatre in Saint Petersburg, and probably sought evidence that would enable her to contribute to the debate then raging over whether the genre represented appropriate fare for popular theatre audiences. *Iolanthe* shared billing with *Getting Married* in a theatrical evening that lasted until 2:00 A.M. A week or two later, students in the school were asked to describe their recollections of the play of their choice. Almost twice as many wrote on *Iolanthe.* This production had the most lavish set and costumes yet attempted at Krivtsovo, and the decorations, along with the exotic characters, mysterious atmosphere, and happy ending may have attracted viewers. Lavrova judged from conversations afterward that the illiterate members of the audience probably did not understand it so well as the literate, but that all left with a happy impression. Student accounts of *Getting Married* were much skimpier. She concluded that at least half the peasant audience missed the satirical significance of the play.

> [A]ll the verbiage of Zhevakin, his conversation with Anuchkin, made no impression whatever. And that is completely natural. Their judgments on Sicily and on the French language need not appear comical to the peasants. Iaichinits's desire to acquire a detailed knowledge of the bride's dowry also does not seem strange in the peasants' eyes. They themselves begin the matchmaking process with inquiries on the bride's financial condition, and, like Iaichinits, do not in any case like to spend time to no avail. And the very situation of the bride, in which the matchmaker provides six suitors, is not amusing to a village public. It often happens that a peasant girl who is a good catch receives several proposals at once from suitors she has not even met and chooses among them on the basis of comments about them by the matchmakers and relatives. It is interesting that the very costume and figure of the bride, her exaggerated corpulence do not seem funny to the old women; just the opposite—they said after the play that, "there was great pleasantness in the bride" and "she was nicely dressed." They especially admired the bride's bright green dress and her headdress of crimson paper flowers. Many took the white bed jacket [*kofta*] and petticoat in act 1, scene 2, for a white dress. The procedure of dressing and departure for the groom also failed to arouse laughter from the peasant audience. They go through almost precisely the same business: they take away the bride and withdraw for her presentation to the groom, and etiquette demands that she sit motionless, silent or else speak in empty phrases. The peasant bride puts her hope in bewailing her bitter lot, so that Gogol's Agafia Tikhonovna behaves in accordance with all the rules of art.[29]

Lavrova's analysis has an ethnographic character. She tries to understand how peasants think in their own terms. Her attitude is quite unlike that of Bunakov and Alchevskaia, who were introducing theatre to rural audiences at the same time. Enlightenment did not represent for her the noble calling it seemed to them. She was not of the generation imprinted with Chernyshevsky's asssumptions.

The breakneck pace of her theatrical experiment at Krivtsovo and her failure to impose even a modest fee structure as a means of testing peasant preferences make Lavrova's in some respects the most whimsical of all the important Russian popular theatres. Yet she posed questions of great interest to an educated society suddently fascinated by the peasant mind. She and N. A. Popov edited the large and well-illustrated *Popular Theatre: A Collection* in 1896, which, despite its high price, sold out its first printing almost immediately. Letters and requests concerning popular theatre began to flood in from all corners of Russia. After the 1897 season she decided to terminate the performances at Krivtsovo so that she and Popov could devote their full attention to publishing literature for popular theatres.

Yet another popular theatre sprang up in 1897 in a northern Chernigov province town of nine thousand with a substantial Jewish population. Thanks to the national temperance organization recently funded by the Ministry of Finance, a tea room was built that could accommodate up to two hundred. During the day country people drank tea there, but in the evening young people of both sexes gathered to read magazines, listen to the piano, and nibble sunflower seeds. The establishment attracted mainly artisans, workmen, and petty officials, members of the lower middle class. At an evening of dancing planned for the facility, some gathered to heckle and ridicule the dancers, but the awkwardness gradually wore off and the dancing went so well that it became a regularly scheduled event. On the strength of that achievement someone proposed that they put on a play, and volunteers immediately came forward to act and promised to find women to play the female roles.[30] They selected *You Can't Live Just As You Please,* and a shoemaker directed a tailor, a bricklayer, a roofer, a chambermaid, the daughter of a policeman, and the daughhter of a baker in the leading roles. At a disheartening first reading it became apparent that the actor who was to portray Peter could hardly read at all, and the others read badly. Still, all promised to learn their roles. A man who was a blacksmith agreed to play the part of the blacksmith. Just one member of the local intelligentsia deigned to join the troupe. Employed as a clerk, he later explained that he volunteered only to "let his talent shine" and to show "this shoemaker" how acting should be done. When a housemaid joined, they were at least able to complete the casting.

Some in town feared that the dance evenings and theatre would spoil the shoemakers and cooks and grumbled that they could be in danger of going without boots and having to fire up their own samovars. Others protested that the lowly upstarts profaned art and were thrashing Ostrovsky with *balagan* playing. The actors, especially the women, found themselves objects of ridicule and banter. Parents also disapproved of their children's participation. At dress rehearsal the shoemaker expected his legs to buckle from stage fright; but the players overcame their initial confusion. After the audience applauded the clerk it became easier for the entire company to go on. The second and third acts elicited loud applause. Though the direction and makeup left something to be desired, the audience approved the production and the company played twice more to full houses. The author of the published account of the Chernigov theatre group estimated their achievement as an assertion of abilities: "The successful performance justified the recognition of such talents among the people as were up to this time considered in our town the property of the privileged class alone."[31] The company fared less well with their next Ostrovsky play, *A Much Frequented Spot (Na boikom meste),* because it lay beyond their range of experience. But they triumphed with a Ukrainian operetta. In January 1898 they had a group photo taken, and with great ceremony the troupe installed it in the tea room, under a portrait of Ostrovsky.

A very different tone characterizes the account of a beleaguered enlightener who saw a popular production in 1896. A. Sindeev described the first play presented for the townsfolk by amateurs in the town of Staryi Oskol (between Kursk and Voronezh), in a setting he compared to the Krivtsovo and Rozhdestveno popular theatres. Without providing details of the company's organization, Sindeev explained that it had as its goal "to educate the people in an understanding of art, in the knowledge that it is almost the only path to ennobling the spirit of the people and averting the moral decomposition of the popular mass."[32] Admission prices at five, ten, and twenty kopeks opened the performances to virtually all the townspeople. The first offering combined *Coachmen (Iamshchiki),* a one-act comedy of popular life, and the last two scenes of Ostrovsky's *Slough of Despond (Puchina).* Not everyone in Staryi Oskol liked the idea of theatre for the people. While some local citizens opposed it on grounds that such entertainments would work to the detriment of religious and moral enlightenment, others remained completely indifferent.

The reporter for the newspaper *Kurskii Listok* objected that the first-night audience could not, strictly speaking, be called "popular" because no bast sandals were in evidence on the theatregoers' feet. But Sindeev pointed out that such sandals were rarely worn by anyone in town now. He testified that the first-night audience consisted of workmen of various occupations in the town. Its representative character made its identification with Ostrovsky's malefactors all the more alarming.

> The *narod* of the town, shaky in its own moral values and coarsened in spirit, was on the side of the characters who should have inspired indignation. The *narod* . . . commended Kiselnikov's father-in-law for being able to force him

> to forgive his debt. And then on top of being amused by that, they applauded the lawyer for being able to force Kiselnikov to go through with the forgery. I am certain the people respond this way because they praise any person who looks after his own affairs, even though the business may be dirty: they say "Well done!" and "Yes, he's a clever rascal!" about everyone who steals successfully, deceives, swindles—but all the same, this sympathy shown in the March 31 performance produced a negative impression on me, since in every case it was on the side of the victor, whether he was right or wrong.[33]

For an audience to take the side of injustice in an Ostrovsky play, to identify with submission to temptation and weakness, dismayed enlighteners. Sindeev reacted to rejection of probity and integrity by honestly admitting his personal distaste, and offering a persuasive psychological explanation—that the powerless can cope by identifying with power in whatever form it takes. At this stage in its development public opinion could easily assume the inevitable triumph of individualism and a respect for facts and law. With Western science and technology visibly reshaping the whole world, educated Russians almost automatically assumed their outlook would triumph with the masses.

TWO POPULAR THEATRES IN SAINT PETERSBURG

Two theatres established in the capital in 1886 to serve audiences with a significant working-class component received wide publicity and stimulated both government and enlighteners to take advantage of the potential for changing behavior suggested by their patrons' reactions. Eventually both were reorganized or moved, but each attracted its own following and demonstrated remarkable flexibility in adapting to meet its cultural needs. An early Soviet scholar of worker theatre described the workers as "passive guests in this phase of Russian theatre's development."[34] While he is perfectly correct, it must be added that worker response clearly provided the catalyst that activated the authorities and the intelligentsia committed to acculturation.

The Vasileostrovsk theatre had the more colorful beginnings. Peter the Great selected Vasili Island as the location for his reorganized government departments. But after his death the city's focus shifted across the Neva to the mainland, leaving most of the island a neglected, barren waste until the late nineteenth century, when factories began to spring up there. P. A. Gresser, the city's governor from 1882 to 1892, initiated construction of a cheap wooden theatre to attract workers away from the taverns on the island. Factory owners financed the building, which was located in a large square situated in an uninhabited area on Smolensk Field, open to the wind sweeping in from Galernyi Harbor. The Vasileostrovsk dragged out a miserable existence at first, passing through the hands of several factory-owner entrepreneurs. It had a seating capacity of 765, but few cheap seats. So minor bureaucrats, shop assistants, and clerks outnumbered the working people for whom it was intended. When a member of the Temperance Society took over its management, hired an experienced director and strengthened its troupe, the theatre began to attract workers en masse.[35]

With summer fetes and garden setting, the theatre offered players the advantage of year-round employment and cultivated a measure of ensemble playing. The Vasileostrovsk became known for its escapist fare: bombastic patriotic pieces, and abundant melodrama. Most of the press who reviewed it disparaged the repertory as insufficiently uplifting. But Ivan Shcheglov (Leont'ev), who wrote a book on popular theatre championing melodrama for the masses, pointed out that it was a celebrated French melodrama, A. F. Denneri's *Two Orphans,* that saved the theatre by giving the company a smash hit when it was on the verge of collapse. At one performance, as rising waters disposed the governor to order the building evacuated, the audience refused to leave without learning the orphans' fate.[36] Shcheglov's defense of the genre hinged on his contention that the simple folk had a right to see plays that not only show life as it is but as they expect it must be. He observed that popular audiences liked *The Inspector General* for the same reason they liked melodrama: because the "hand of Providence" is seen at the end. The absence of classic Russian vaudeville from the Vasileostrovsk repertory he attributed to "an empty-headed intelligentsia prejudice against loud and hearty laughter." Shcheglov saw *Othello* played there to the approval of "the popular parterre" in a socially mixed audience. *Hamlet,* he said, delighted audiences in 1899.[37] Though avid for melodrama, open to foreign classics, and well disposed to historical drama, the Vasileostrovsk public preferred anything to Ostrovsky.[38] Yet it matured sufficiently to let the inferior melodramas be weeded out of the repertory and replaced by the best of the genre. The theatre functioned until 1906.

At the opposite end of the city, an attempt by factory owners to provide outdoor recreation for the tens of thousands of workers of the Aleksandrovsk suburb beyond the Nevsky Gate gave rise to the Nevsky Society, which came to operate three theatres. In 1885 a trustee of the Imperial China Factory, M. S. Agafonov, and two brothers who owned a paper factory, V. P. and P. P. Vargunin, formed a group to provide holiday entertainment consisting of one-act vaudeville, short comedy sketches, and pantomimes for thousands of workers with their wives and families.[39] The festival went off agreeably, and in the following year, they expanded the stage and played *Poverty Is No Vice* and *The First Distiller.* The audience especially liked the latter. In 1888 the group moved to a park on the Shlussel'burg Road next to the China Factory, which they leased from a brewery. The enterprise first broke even in 1890. In 1891 a statute authorized transfer of the property to a new Nevsky Society, empowered to construct a popular amusement facility. The document defined the management's goal: "to help supply the local working population with moral, temperate, and inexpensive entertainments," including plays.[40] The lower level of the winter theatre building housed a buffet run by a committee of the Saint Petersburg Temperance Society.

When Shcheglov visited the park's summer theatre in 1893 he found the facilities "tacky" and the play being performed just interesting enough to hold the attention of the most ragged in the audience. But productions soon improved. When his 1898 book came out with his eyewitness account of an unusually attentive audience relishing one of the weaker Ostrovsky plays at the Nevsky, a summer theatre seating 2,000 had just been completed to supplement the original open-air theatre, which seated 351. He found the Nevsky public to be much broader than that of the Vasileostrovsk, comprising unskilled factory workers, skilled factory workers (he overheard a conversation between two who were obviously readers of the *Petersburg Gazette*), soldiers, and "common, ordinary people."[41] The park, with its amusements and dancing, could handle crowds of ten thousand. Another writer on popular theatre, impressed by the high standards of conduct in the park, noted, "No one who has not attended one of the fetes has the right to claim that the Russian people are undeveloped, crude or do not know how to conduct themselves. They are ignorant, yes—they are burdened by want—but they have a sensitive soul, perceptive native intelligence and gumption."[42]

The Nevsky Society's success at providing entertainment to families impressed everyone. Healthy recreation had been one of its primary objectives. One of its committees had described the Shlussel'burg suburb as a place with sixty thousand inhabitants where, during the workday, streets appeared deserted but on holidays people swarmed in such numbers that it became almost impossible to move. "Workers rarely spend their free time at home, which is perfectly understandable: worker apartments are for the most part filthy, stinking, and fearfully overcrowded. In the best case the worker wanders aimlessly in the street, not going to a drinking establishment where his last kopek would disappear."[43] The comportment of crowds in the park must have gratified the founders and confirmed their assumption that decent leisure surroundings would help stabilize the population. Besides providing undemanding recreation like a toboggan ride in carriages on rails (called "American Mountains"), the Society prided itself in catering to the cultural needs of its patrons, as with the "Reading Hall" it constructed with the governor's permission in 1893.

The theatrical component of the amusements grew because it so powerfully attracted the broad public that frequented the park. The family theme was even carried out in the creation of a special children's theatre opened in 1894, where the actors were children. The very first director of the summer theatre had set the tone by presenting plays by the best authors along with light entertainment. Of the thirty plays presented in 1894, fourteen were by Ostrovsky. The Society also had permission to present tableaux vivants from Russian history but limited these performances to twice weekly because each scene had to be approved separately by the authorities. Although the Nevsky Society theatres fell under the jurisdiction of the highly restrictive Popular Theatre Censorship created in 1888, the directors frequently petitioned to perform plays not included on the approved list. The censorship often honored their requests, and they performed a service for popular theatres generally by demonstrating the capacity of mass urban audiences to respond sensitively to a range of plays. Eventually it began to approve plays *exclusively* for the Nevsky Society, though often only after making extensive cuts in the requested dramas, such as *Othello*.[44]

The Society earmarked the theatre for its most ambitious investment for the future. Its winter theatre, in an old building purchased along with the park, seated only 250. By 1897 the Society had collected 40,000 rubles toward the construction of a stone theatre to accommodate two thousand people, which it estimated would cost 200,000 rubles to build.

To get a clearer impression of how well they were serving their public, the Society solicited its patrons to fill out a detailed questionnaire telling whether they understood the plays presented, whether the entertainments satisfied them, and what they considered to be their significance in moral and material terms. They were also asked for their comments on the arrangements to maintain order ("Was any sort of unpleasantness at all caused by the security guards and . . . police?") and on the food. Although the *ankety* (questionnaires) have apparently not survived, extracts were widely published. The most extensive selection appeared in the journal *Russian Wealth*, edited by the populist critic N. K. Mikhailovsky. "The main motifs of all the more interesting respondents," he summarized, "were first an unaffected joy over a corner where one could spend time pleasantly without drink and second, rapture over the theatre."[45]

Of those whose works already figured in the Nevsky Society repertory, the respondents mentioned Gogol, Griboedov, and Ostrovsky as preferred authors. (They also singled out Molière's *Tartuffe* for praise.) A lower-middle-class employee of the Obukhov steelworks recognized the importance of the Ostrovsky plays in his answer to the question on accessibility (while pleading for lighter fare):

> As for whether the plays presented by the Nevsky Society are understood or not, it must be answered that the majority of plays presented belong to Ostrovsky, and such plays do not require an explanation. Their themes are taken from almost the same environment as the environment of the workers, and their language is the native language of every Russian. But it would also be desirable to present plays of lighter content on the open-air stage, so that the cause of recreation might be served in the summer.

Another patron, a peasant working in a cast-iron foundry, had reservations about the food: "Maybe it seems cheap to you, but we don't earn much ourselves. . . . The victuals may be okay, but they taste strange to me and I don't buy them." Much more common in the responses was a note of gratitude, as in this answer from an assistant foreman at the Nevsky machine works to the question about arrangements in the park: "In your garden I did not meet drunkards or heavy drinkers; I never met a group of men hungrily eyeing the women who passed by; I never encountered in the garden or buffet any attempt to fleece the poor; I never witnessed a scabrous scene on leaving the garden."[46] Patrons as well as organizers wanted good order in the newly carved out recreational space.

Manufacturers confronted a peculiar plenitude of holiday time, for the Russian calendar offered a far more generous schedule of religious holidays than any in western Europe. In 1900 average workdays in Russian industry numbered 264. Factories stood idle fully a quarter of the year.[47] This free time magnified the significance of current alcohol consumption patterns. I. I. Ianzhul, who had written on the problem of alcoholism in Russia since 1880, called attention to the atypical nature of Russian holiday drinking. Comparing Russian consumption of spirits to that of Germany, Sweden, Denmark, and Poland, he found it to be much less. "Among [these foreigners] you rarely see drunkenness, but among us, on holidays . . . vodka is drunk recklessly, senselessly."[48] The industrialists who subsidized the Nevsky Society in its early years sought to create a space where the dualistic conventional organization of time could be overcome. Their questionnaire specifically asked whether those who frequented the park appreciated the dignity accorded every individual in this place where norms of decency were enforced. Respondents appreciated the policing, but went beyond what was expected of them. The atmosphere here engendered in some of the patrons an interest in self-development through reading. (A "reading hall" is the last thing Westerners would expect to find in an amusement park!) It also contributed to a voracious interest in literary theatre, where issues of personal values, choice, and commitment could be explored without the mediation of the printed page.

A range of responses reveals the impact of viewing plays upon individuals of different degrees of development. A barely literate worker at the Spasskii spinning mill, impressed by Zhadov's commitment to principles in *A Profitable Post,* attempted to integrate the experience into what must have been a strongly religious outlook:

> Theatrical presentations acquaint [us] with the life and morals of the people we have to work for, correct us, appeal to our taste; they depict the righteous form of life and the unrighteous [and show] which life is easier, which more difficult to live; what kind of work [it is] conducting a righteous life with ardent feeling; who does more on behalf of others—accepting a striving for righteousness.

The respondents' self-images are perhaps the most interesting feature of the documents. A worker at the Thornton textile factory used a nature image typical of peasant expression to represent his situation in this newly created industrial environment. "[The Nevsky entertainments in general are] a rivulet of fresh water in a putrid swamp. . . . The fish from the putrid swamp are being asphyxiated, but they refresh themselves in the fresh stream." Another statement of rejection of the prevailing way of life—from a joiner in a carriage works—explicitly mentions factory discipline, but explains how the theatre offers a sort of alternative by presenting another code of personal conduct.

> Seeing a good play causes one to fall under its spell, to try to imitate the considerateness it reveals, and to try to discuss what remains unclear. The benefit in this is that one releases crude abusiveness less often. . . . Many of the plays were unsatisfactory and even produced sadness and some distressing reflections. Last summer plays were done several times on factory life and occasionally even on peasant life. But these plays were so tedious that the director himself could see whether the public liked them or not. On the stage factory workers' immoral revelry was depicted—very originally, to be sure—but why should a factory worker want to see such prosaic stuff [in the theatre] when it disgusts him in everyday life? How can a man be blamed for being made a little crazy by continuous work? Take a look at how they leave the factories in the evening, how crazed they are from being kept out of God's light. In such a life a man does not even have time to pretend to preserve his morals.[49]

The longest of the published responses was submitted by a woman working at the Pal' weaving mill. She emphasized the theatre's function of suggesting alternatives to what exists and stressed its usefulness in developing one's personality.

> The winter theatre is perfectly satisfactory for people. The worker temporarily forgets his situation in it; he is completely absorbed by what he sees and hears in the theatre. Theatre is relaxation for the people, but not the kind of recreation we have at home. You come to the theatre and attentively watch what is happening on stage. You don't notice anything else going on around you. . . . You escape into what you see and hear and even sort of feel yourself to be a real person.[50] After returning home it takes a long time to fall asleep, and the play you just saw is still rushing around in your imagination. You arrive at work with a clear head and you set to work cheerfully, feeling pleased at how you spent your holiday. A friend comes up and asks, "What did you see at the theatre?" "Very well," I answer, and begin to explain what I saw. I chatter on enthusiastically, and my companions also get enthusiastic, and when I finish they approve or censure all the characters, judging according to the circumstances I have just narrated. Then you go up to somebody who was at the theatre and begin to exchange opinions. . . . The theatre acquaints us with a different, a high class of people, and we see their life, their views of life in re-

> lation to the lower class. And you wonder whether a time will come when all people will resemble, for example, the young man in the play *A Lucrative Position*, who wants to live by his own labor and not by graft. Or whether some day all will be as wise and honorable as Chatsky, so that nobody will laugh at good and clever people. On stage we see people's shortcomings as in a mirror. The theatre helps people correct their defects. A person cannot see his own shortcomings, but in the theatre immediately after watching a play, you see the good and bad sides of real people, and eventually you examine yourself and if you find some shortcoming you try to correct it. I confess that the theatre enabled me to correct one deficiency in myself. Often when I was with my girlfriends I criticized those of our friends who were absent, pointing out their faults while failing to notice my own. But now, thanks to the theatre, I realize how shameful and stupid it is to laugh at one's friends.[51]

This was the sort of response that confirmed enlighteners in their belief that the experience of theatre sparked a self-scrutiny in everyman that could not help advancing the course of civilization. The gratitude frequently expressed by the recipients must have flattered them as well. But a tendency among the folk to see plays as absolutely objective depictions of reality containing lessons that could be mastered by anyone wishing to perfect himself ought to have given the culturists pause. A peasant artisan wrote, "[In the theatre] you can see what's demanded in life and what can smash life, what miserliness, pride and deceit do; you see all this; it is always presented in a lively fashion, where deceit leads to the worst and how you get out of this unhealthy stream." On the other hand, a peasant employed in the Thornton factory evinced an alarmingly low tolerance for the ambiguity normally associated with art.

> Of the productions presented on the stage, very few are comprehensible. So it would not be a bad idea to explain before a presentation what in this play it is necessary to understand, what consequences flow from it—[as, for example] why wicked people corrupt others who are under their power. But it is essential to say before a presentation in what environment the people depicted grew up, what their elders were like and what led them to influence destructively the people dependent on them.

A foreman echoed the assumption that dramatic texts were readily reducible through analysis and explanation: "I think that if the Society would produce a published guide to how to understand the plays, a concise analysis, then surely no one who did not understand the plays would fail to read it and be gratified." If any enlighteners noticed this inclination to regard the theatre as a source of universal lessons and absolute truths, they probably expected it would fade with more experience of playgoing.

In the 1890s the Vasileostrovsk and Nevsky Society theatres were unique in Saint Petersburg. Other quasi-public summer gardens boasted theatres, but at the New Hermitage, Svetlana, Izmailovsk Garden, Amerika, New

Bavaria, and Ekaterinhof Garden the vodka and beer flowed freely, the plays and acting aimed to enhance the usual festival mood. Some factory owners considered the provision of theatrical amusements a wise investment. Owners of the Putilov works beyond the Narva Gate and manufacturers on the Vyborg side joined to form a Society for the Establishment of Popular Amusements (Obshchestvo dlia ustroistva narodnykh razvlechenii) and contributed one ruble per worker to its treasury. Individual factories operated in-house theatres, but these were usually short-lived and the documentation is scanty. Presumably the factory owners had less interest than the enlighteners in the development of personality among the masses and more interest in the obvious capacity of theatre to compete with the taverns and reduce drunkenness on the job and absenteeism. One of them asserted that after the popular theatre had been open a month, drunkenness almost completely ceased among his workers.[52] This phenomenon—when the theatres opened, the taverns emptied—was also noted by A. N. Kremlev, who proposed to the Saint Petersburg City Duma in March 1896 that it underwrite a popular theatre that would serve as "a school of the arts" for the city's masses and play a repertory of Russian and foreign masterpieces (half of which were not yet authorized by the censor for popular production).[53] The Duma had rejected a similar proposal for some kind of social entertainment for the people in 1893 as "inopportune." Property owners and taxpayers frequently argued that before thinking of such cultural refinements it was necessary to concentrate on bridges and gas lighting.[54] In 1896 the Commission on Popular Education supported Kremlev's project and argued that the example of the Vasileostrovsk theatre and the practical experience of the Nevsky Society proved the value of such theatres and that their "social utility" would convince people who studied the matter that they should be built. Even though this particular project to invest in human capital failed to win approval, municipal authorities all over Russia and even the central government were soon erecting such facilities.

POPULAR THEATRE IN MOSCOW

One of the most colorful figures in nineteenth-century Russian theatre, Mikhail V. Lentovskii brought an astonishing range of experience to bear on his Moscow project for popular theatre. His father, a former serf and violinist in a serf theatre, tried desperately to give his children a good education.[55] But at the age of fifteen Mikhail dropped out of school after writing to M. S. Shchepkin in Moscow begging to be taught acting and being welcomed into the old man's home. Working in provincial theatres until he was thirty, Lentovskii began directing with N. N. Diukov in Kharkov, where he also learned theatre management and played leads in Ostrovsky plays. After a stint with the Maly, he joined the Artistic Circle in Moscow, which played summers in a pleasure garden, "L'Hermitage," catering to families. In 1878 he reopened an abandoned theatre on the property as the "Buff." The park he enlivened with entertainments that included aerial acts illuminated by electric light, storytellers on an open-air stage built in the form of Greek ruins, and a gypsy camp by a pond. Years later Stanislavsky recalled the broad popularity of the Hermitage gardens and Lentovskii's determination to maintain good conduct in the precincts.

> Families, commoners, aristocrats, courtesans, wandering young people, businessmen—everyone would run to the Hermitage in the evening, especially on hot summer days when Moscow's oppressive heat made it difficult even to breathe. . . . Courtesans feared [Lentovskii] like hellfire, and so behaved in the garden just like ladies from a high-society boarding school. Anyone who distrupted the public order was permanently banished from the garden.[56]

Having gained a reputation for pleasing crowds with operettas, patriotic skits, fairy plays, and serious drama, he was invited to organize a fair and pageant at Khodynka Field in 1883 for public celebration of Alexander III's coronation. So successful was the elaborate allegorical procession that Lentovskii received a life pension. In 1886 he opened his most ambitious undertaking yet, a people's theatre dedicated to serious drama.

Moscow's Skomorokh (the name recalled medieval traveling minstrels) in many ways resembled Petersburg's Vasileostrovsk and Nevsky. Founded in the same year—on the premises of a former panorama on Sretenskii Boulevard—it also sat in a public garden conceived as an orderly setting for healthy recreation. Lentovskii opened with *Poverty Is No Vice,* playing Liubim Tortsov himself. He told a reporter a few weeks later that Ostrovsky would occupy the chief place in the Skomorokh repertory.[57] The new theatre also found a following for plays about peasant and worker life. A. A. Potekhin's *You Cannot Profit* and *Man's Law* drew well. E. P. Karpov offered Lentovskii *The Workers' Settlement (Rabochaia slobodka),* which also became a hit. But Lentovskii's reputation for variety fare worked against him in this new venture to offer uplifting entertainment to the uneducated. To maintain cash flow to defray development costs he had incurred, while keeping seat prices low, he had to resort to other sorts of entertainment. When he presented patriotic historical skits with his trademark special effects, conservative papers praised him. But when he presented significant plays, they jeered.[58] Lentovskii had a clear vision of how quality theatre could make a civil society out of spectators: "[The theatre] must sometimes fulfil purely civic duties, give a nudge to society, awaken it to active participation in current events, bring it together and direct it toward reasonable solutions."[59] But his financial obligations precluded maintaining a focus on serious people's theatre. In 1891

Lentovskii surrendered control to A. A. Cherepanov, who ran the operation to satisfy creditors and only intermittently uplift the folk.

Skomorokh continued to attract a diverse audience, surely meriting the "general access" designation it received. Signs in the lobby advised "Remove Your Caps" and "While the Music is Playing, Do Not Shout and Make Noise." But Shcheglov, who described it in an 1893 essay, observed soldiers' overcoats, merchants' fur coats, and peasants' cloth coats in the cloakroom, confirming an audience broader than just the simple folk.[60] Now the great disparity between Skomorokh's best and worst offerings impressed everyone who wrote about it. Shcheglov contrasted its *Inspector General,* whose ensemble playing he considered comparable to that of the imperial theatres, to its "infamous" adaption of *Anna Karenina.* It routinely performed patriotic pieces and horror spectacles to overflowing houses. Yet it remained capable of making serious theatre spellbinding and influencing critical opinion.

Skomorokh's production of *The Power of Darkness,* which it mounted in 1895 when the performance ban was lifted and which ran 140 performances, constituted the jewel in its repertory. Tolstoy himself attended and spoke of the pleasure he derived from the simplicity of the principal players' acting. He thought the audience understood the play profoundly and valued it highly. A journalist who regarded the play as among the most harmful in Moscow for the uneducated changed his mind after seeing the Skomorokh production.[61] Claims of the unsuitability of Tolstoy's play for viewing by the *narod* generally took one of two lines. Part of the press represented the folk as children, who needed to ripen in character and could not possibly profit in their present state from viewing a dramatization of their ignorance and criminal tendencies. Others followed Pobedonostsev's criticism, insisting that *The Power of Darkness* instructed peasants in crime and wickedness.

The writer for *New Times* observed that the play's brisk tempo, simplicity, and clarity made it especially attractive to uneducated audiences. At the performance he attended, "Not a single word from the stage was lost: sympathetic situations called forth exclamations of approval, unsympathetic ones, murmurs."[62] He did concede that the unsophisticated viewer had his own way of perceiving: "He lives minute by minute; he laughs at a funny word, and if a sad one follows, he begins to cry." But the play, he found to his surprise, produced precisely the impressions Tolstoy must have intended. "To the dark person [*temnomu-cheloveku*] viewing the play the sin becomes ugly and terrible . . . ; the man who transgresses is seen as an 'unfortunate,' and the desire for repentance as a valuable achievement."

Moscow had hosted Russia's first popular theatre in connection with the 1872 exposition, the city duma subsidizing construction of its building on Varvarskaia Square. The structure passed to S. V. Teneev, who operated a private general-access theatre in it, and eventually was destroyed. A government register of popular theatres in and around Moscow lists fifteen such from 1872 to 1895.[63] One was a railroad theatre. Employees of the Workshop of the Moscow-Kazan Railway presented plays for the entertainment of their families and friends. But most were theatres in factories organized by owners for their employees.[64]

At least one of the factory theatres had a long history.[65] T. V. Prokhorov opened the first factory school in Russia in 1816, and it was still functioning in 1900. His factory, called the Trekhgornaia because of its location near the Trekhgornaia Gate, traced its theatre's beginning to 1820, when students in the school had given the first performance. Prokhorov had been given a rigorously religious upbringing by his mother. According to his biographer, he was sensitive to "the sad state of the moral condition of the lower class of people and especially factory workers." His mother took a personal interest in the theatre, often making costumes for the plays. It ceased to function in the 1840s but was revived in the 1890s by an heir, S. I. Prokhorov, who ran the factory and personally prepared the actors. A worker who acted in *The Minor* recalled being criticized by Prokhorov: "Logic—you have no logic!"[66] After S. I. Prokhorov's death, the Trekhgornaia theatre closed in 1901 or 1902 over some misunderstanding with the Moscow police.

Another Moscow factory listed in the inventory whose theatre came into being in conjunction with a school was the Ramenskaia, owned by the Maliutin brothers. One of its directors, a professor at the Imperial Moscow Technical School, sought ways to improve the lot of workers and in the 1870s persuaded the owners to construct a large school building on the premises with a room for popular readings suitable for theatrical presentations. It remained unused for some years, the readings beginning only in 1883.

The exhibit on popular theatre that opened in December 1895 sponsored by the Committee on Literacy at the Fourth All-Russian Agricultural Exposition in Moscow did much to launch the popular theatre movement in provincial Russia. It featured an 1880 letter from A. F. Fedotov calling for the establishment of a national popular theatre, along with objects and documents relating to his 1872 Polytechnic Exposition theatre. Bunakov and Alchevskaia were on hand to meet visitors, and publications relating to their schools and use of theatre were displayed. E. V. Lavrova donated some of the costumes from the Krivtsovo production of *George Dandin*. The public could examine a fully assembled stage appropriate for rural theatres, complete with curtain and aprons. Detailed construction plans were available, along with an estimate of costs. A map pinpointed the location of Russia's town, village, rural, and factory theatres that presented popular plays and *balagany*.[67]

Several conferences that monitored and shaped the progress of the popular theatre movement met in Moscow. In 1893 and 1896 Congresses on Technical and Professional Education took up the questions of accessible repertory and appropriate ticket prices for workers at city theatres. Between congresses the organization created a permanent department on popular theatre and maintained communication. The 1896 Congress considered various proposals to establish theatres for workers in Moscow. N. A. Popov recommended a Parisian model, with actors performing one play at a time in a series of small theatres scattered throughout the working-class districts. He said the time had come for action because working people had become accustomed to theatre, had defined their tastes for it, and had outgrown amateur performances.[68] Popov considered the state-subsidized theatres of Saint Petersburg unsuitable for emulation in Moscow.

The First All-Russian Congress of Theatre Personnel (S"ezd stsenicheskikh deiatelei) in March 1897 began by charting the recent growth in popular theatre. E. P. Karpov, a well-known director, said in his address that theatres for the working man had been constructed in more than half a dozen cities besides the capitals, including Archangel, Astrakhan, Ufa, Ekaterinburg, and Odessa, so that the whole Russian land could truly be said to participate in the movement.[69] Reports also testified to the expansion of the theatre into district towns, factories, and larger village centers. The congress called for the theatre gradually to be taken out of the hands of commercial interests that operated without regard for aesthetic values. It also expressed a desire to purge the repertory of "pornographic" farces translated from French and German.[70] When it concluded its business, it supplied the Moscow city duma with a copy of its transactions. It endeavored to interest the Moscow province zemstvo in popular theatre in the same way, making known its views on the rights and the financial situation of the enterprise.[71] After the meeting the pace of activity increased, as a society for the organization of general-access amusements was founded in Moscow and societies for the construction of popular theatres in connection with other useful pastimes for the people sprang up in Kharkov, Saratov, Samara, Orel, Tambov, and Penza.[72]

Among those attending the 1897 congress was Anton Pavlovich Chekhov. Though his international reputation at this time rested on his short stories, Russians knew him for the extremely successful farce-vaudevilles, dramatic studies, plays, and monologues he had been writing since 1885.[73] He took his friend A. S. Suvorin, the wealthy publisher, to the meetings. Suvorin had begun as an impecunious liberal journalist in the 1860s (he was arrested in 1866 for an article on Chernyshevsky) but had moved sharply to the right after taking control of the newspaper *New Times* and building it into a mass-circulation daily. As a book publisher, one of whose subsidiaries printed a "Cheap Library" of the classics, he had extensive financial interests in the acculturation of the Russian masses. He was, moreover, a lover and patron of the theatre and had himself written widely performed plays. Chekhov took Suvorin to the congress to persuade him to build a popular theatre in Moscow. Stanislavsky, who had one of his first encounters with

Chekhov at a meeting to discuss a project of F. O. Shekhtel to construct a building for popular theatre (Narodnyi dvorets), later recalled the writer's great pleasure over the project, which he considered "would bring a small ray of light to the ignorant."[74] But Suvorin would not be convinced.

The Moscow Art Theatre, one of the most influential Russian cultural institutions of the century, grew out of the deeply held belief of a few Muscovites that theatre had a powerful role to play in enlightening the masses. Conceived in the famous eighteen-hour conversation between Stanislavsky and V. I. Nemirovich-Danchenko that began at the Slavianskii Bazaar restaurant on 22 June 1897, it was originally envisioned as a *popular* theatre that would approach the goals set by Ostrovsky for a Russian national theatre. In August, Nemirovich-Danchenko wrote to Stanislavsky, "The social, enlightenment side of the matter attracts me . . . and more and more I am inclined to a general-access theatre and not simply an art theatre."[75] That very summer students he instructed in the Moscow Philharmonic Society acting school had given Sunday performances in a large village, with morning shows for peasants at ticket prices ranging from five to twenty kopeks.

After some disappointing attempts at raising capital for the new theatre by selling shares, the two approached the Moscow city duma with a project to create a Moscow general-access theatre and a request for support in the form of an annual subsidy of fifteen thousand rubles. Nemirovich-Danchenko argued that transmitting artistic impressions to the masses was paramount.[76] The repertory, he said, should consist of plays by Ostrovsky, Gogol, Griboedov, Pisemsky, Pushkin, Tolstoy, Shakespeare, and Molière—there was absolutely no need for melodrama, fairy tales, or "tendentious tableaux vivants." The theatre building must not be too large, lest the intimacy required for drama be lost. (He explicitly opposed theatres built to seat thousands so that they could meet expenses by packing in huge crowds on holidays for operas or lighter musical fare.) The theatre must attract as part of its audience those social groups already familiar with serious plays, so that they can help educate the novices from the *narod*. Growing impatient with the duma's inability to reach a decision, Stanislavsky and Nemirovich returned to selling shares in a theatre of their own, and by June 1898 they were able to organize rehearsals of the new company. Eighteen months after the proposal's submission, the Moscow duma declined to support the project.

The new theatre at first called itself the "Moscow Artistic-General-Access Theatre" (Moskovskii Khudozhestvenno-Obshchedostupnyi Teatr). In an 1899 letter of greeting to German dramatist Gerhart Hauptmann, it referred to itself as simply the "Moscow Popular Theatre" (Moskovskii Narodnyi Teatr).[77] To attract Moscow workers it entered into an agreement with the Society for Popular Entertainments. It designated four plays to be performed for workers at reduced prices in December 1898 and January 1899. But only one of the four, Ostrovsky's *Late Love (Pozdniaia liubov')*, received clearance for popular viewing. The Moscow chief of police (an officer of the Ministry of the Interior), General D. F. Trepov, summoned Nemirovich-Danchenko to remind him of the 1888 modification to the censorship statute requiring special approval for plays presented to popular audiences. When Nemirovich objected that their theatre's performances were not popular productions (that is, not presented in factories or in the countryside), Trepov pointed out that they were indeed popular in this case, because the Society for Popular Entertainments was "simply giving half the tickets for these performances to one factory, half to another." The director had a choice: he could halt these performances or be taken to court. Given the Art Theatre's precarious finances, it could not risk a lawsuit. Thus, the theatre ended its agreement with the Society, shelved its goal of bringing quality drama to workers at low prices and dropped "General-Access" from its name.[78] It is noteworthy that when the Moscow Art Theatre nearly collapsed, the two people who saved it—Chekhov by giving it *The Seagull* and then writing new plays for it, and Savva Morozov by spearheading its successful recapitalization—had both already demonstrated their faith in popular theatre as a vehicle of acculturation.

The Moscow city duma, despite its decision to reject Stanislavsky's and Nemirovich-Danchenko's theatre project, soon began to sponsor theatre for the people. Described as "a generally liberal body interested in modernization," the locally elected duma steadily expanded its provision of public services, growing increasingly impatient with the central government's heavy-handedness all the while.[79] In 1904 it opened a People's House, which featured mostly opera but eventually formed an acting company. The results must have been gratifying, because in 1915 it decided to open a network of nineteen such facilities. The war prevented implementation of the plan. But already in 1902 the Moscow Workhouse, which the duma had taken over from the central administration of police in 1893, had its own theatre. Other duma agencies tried to stimulate self-reliance and self-improvement through libraries, public readings, picture shows, and concerts.[80] The Workhouse theatre was too much for the conservative daily *Moscow News*, which called the Workhouse the "favorite child" of the "city duma windbags." The newspaper demanded that it offer more religion and fewer plays: "Theatre, theatre," it grumbled, "everywhere the theatre, even in the Workhouse a theatre!"[81]

THE TRUSTEESHIP FOR POPULAR TEMPERANCE AND THEATRES FOR THE PEOPLE

Many new arrivals to Russian cities found themselves at loose ends absent familiar village routines. Functioning without the customary constraints and adjusting to the vastly larger scale of the urban social organism perplexed the displaced. Theatre presented itself as a means of addressing disorientation.

D. Stepanov, who investigated the attraction of the taverns by asking factory workers and laborers why they went there, received the predictable answers, that it was boring to stay home and there was nowhere else to go. But something else he was told, he thought, better explained their broad appeal: "At the public house you meet Peter, who is always looking to get married, and the gossip Ivan."[82] In other words, the tavern offered a chance to meet unusual, interesting people. Stepanov knew of a tea shop near a textile factory where the management decided to provide newspapers and stereoscopes with an ample supply of pictures for the use of the patrons. They ruined the business by introducing diversions that distracted from the give-and-take, the human interchange that people came in for. He reasoned that theatre for the people could empty the taverns, but only if it offered its own eccentric characters *(chudaki)* and avoided the mistake of offering mere entertainment and diversion.

In an 1898 essay surveying popular amusements, T. Polner asserted that popular theatre had entered a new phase. He quoted an observation from a recent public lecture: "We recognized that distraction from the tavern results in a diminution of absenteeism and that the seed of enlightenment supports the good humor of the worker and thereby increases his productivity."[83] He concluded that the Imperial Technical Society must now approach the question of popular theatre from an economic perspective.

The Ministry of Finance under Sergei Witte had already embarked on such a course. The rationale for this unlikely government activity was to address the "disorder" among urban workers induced by the accelerated pace of Russia's industrialization. Witte's program or "system" called for the ministry to direct massive investment into developing the country's railroad network and steel industry. Low productivity of Russian labor was a concern from the beginning. To augment its resources in order to meet these new responsibilities, the Ministry of Finance, whose budget trebled between 1890 and 1900, turned to the liquor excise. The 20 December 1894 legislation, which restored the government monopoly on the sale of spirits, also created the Trusteeship, or Guardianship, for Popular Temperance. The elimination of the system of tax farmers (who purchased the rights to collect the excise) proceeded gradually. At first the government established its monopoly only in four eastern provinces. As the process was completed, revenues from liquor taxes increased sharply. Income from this source more than doubled between 1890 and 1904, and came to represent 30 percent of total state revenues.

The apparent irrationality of expanding liquor sales in order to finance popular theatres to distract workers from taverns would not pass unremarked. But the trustees' budget, which peaked in 1903 at 4.7 million rubles, accounted for less than one percent of the revenue from spirits. And its funds went to projects besides theatre. The prospect of an economic breakthrough to a higher level of national maturity justified the Witte gamble, and the gamble justified drastic measures to squeeze revenues from the population. While not exactly an afterthought, the trusteeship was conceived as a modest experiment. It was perfectly consonant with the Ministry of Finance's *dirigiste* role, a role the Imperial Government had often assumed in the past.

The activities of the trusteeship began to be organized in 1897. Guidelines issued in January of that year outlined the uses of popular theatre and its presumed advantages for reaching the masses:

> Popular theatres, for their part, may be a good means for drawing the folk away from drinking establishments. Accessible to both the literate and the illiterate, and presenting more varied impressions than are possible at public readings accompanied by lantern slides, they will undoubtedly please the people most of all. The comparative length of their performances is an advantage, in that they fill an evening and leave no time for visiting taverns. At the same time it must be said that popular theatres may serve not only as entertainment but as a means of exercising moral influence on the masses. In particular, the trusteeship, through the responsible selection of plays, can use theatrical presentations . . . for spreading the idea of the dangers of alcohol abuse.[84]

Another proposal in the guidelines—that the trustees involve members of the folk in the theatre by inviting them to assist in productions or casting them in minor parts—remained interested in the trusteeship theatres. A recommendation to include the armed forces by inviting soldier troupes to perform in the trusteeships perished at the hands of the minister of war, A. N. Kuropatkin, who courteously informed Witte that such participation would be unsuitable for the discipline of the forces. Kuropatkin did, however, offer the trusteeship the services of military bands for use in their theatres at minimal cost, and they became permanent fixtures in some of the larger theatres.

A February 1897 decree authorized the minister of finance to establish trusteeship committees in provinces and districts as the treasury implemented its monopoly on the sale of spirits.[85] He could appoint the committees and start funding their work up to six months before tax farming ended. By December new district committees of the trusteeship had been created in Novgorod, Pskov, Olonets, and Kharkov, and a special city trusteeship in Saint Petersburg.[86] Appointments to the district committees remained the prerogative of the Ministry of Finance, with the approval of the Ministry of the Interior and the Ministry of the Imperial Court. Many more district committees would be created in the following years. A January 1900 circular set out instructions for the establishment of trusteeship theatres. It advised that they be opened only where a demand had already ripened. "Thus it is essential for the time being that popular theatres be constructed exclusively in cities and especially important factories and trading settlements."[87]

The Saint Petersburg city trusteeship had the right to create its own departments. Its membership included representatives from the Holy Synod, the Ministry of War, the Ministry of the Navy, the chief of excise collection for Saint Petersburg province, the city's senior factory inspector, the director of public schools for the province, the Saint Petersburg Society for Literacy, the executive board of the Standing Commission to Organize Popular Reading in Saint Petersburg, the inspector of the capital's Medical Administration, the chief of police for the province, the senior inspector overseeing the book trade, the president of the City Administration on Public Education, two members chosen by the Council of Trade and Manufacture, two councillors from the city duma, and up to ten persons appointed by the minister of finance. It is hard to imagine how a committee so rich in upper-middle bureaucrats could find a meeting time, let alone conduct business. Yet in December 1900 this committee opened the doors of the trusteeship's showplace, the Nicholas II House of the People.

The Nicholas II auditorium went up near the Peter and Paul Fortress, across the Neva from the Winter Palace. It boasted fireproof cast-iron construction and seated fifteen hundred, with standing room for fifteen hundred more. At times of peak demand it presented operas, operettas, and ballet. Classics like *Rusalka, Sadko, Prince Igor,* and *A Life for the Tsar* shared the stage with difficult new works. The fare cannot have contributed much to enlightenment, for peasant viewers were seen to strain to get the words and to be confused about the ideas and even the subjects of the operas. Those indifferent to the productions could, for a ten-kopek admission fee, wander the halls and hear a concert by a military band. In a 1903 newspaper article Shcheglov took the trusteeship to task for the "extravagant luxury and tinsel brilliance" of its sets at the expense of the internal side of the business, and failure to trust what Anatole France called the people's special capacity to listen.[88] A few competently performed plays by Ostrovsky and Gogol were presented, but the management scheduled them at times when factories operated, so that workers could not attend. On holidays jugglers, clowns, and animal acts performed. Shcheglov complained that with its better offerings the trusteeship inadvertently attracted an overwhelming crowd of intelligentsia along with their popular audience. The former came not so much to be distracted from drinking as to spare their pocketbooks the expense of drinking in *cafés-chantants* like the Arkadiia, Olimpiia, and Teatr Buff.[89] The censor Pchel'nikov made a similar observation in his report on Moscow popular theatres for the 1902–3 season. "As was the case last year, the productions attracted mainly the middle . . . class. The people, for whom these productions were intended, were present in the most limited minority."[90]

The trusteeship also rented private theatres for operatic and dramatic productions. The director of these theatres, E. E. Kovalevsky, concentrated his energies on melodramas and fairy tales. At a public garden with a new open-air stage and seating built by the trusteeship in 1901, the garden had enormous success, "but drama eke[d] out a most pitiful existence."[91] As it cast about for distracting entertainments, the trusteeship showed little if any faith in the folk's capacity to rise to the challenge of serious drama. Anthony Swift points out that the trusteeship hired fairground showman Aleksei Alekseev-Iakovlev in 1898, immediately after the removal of the *balagany* from Mars Field, to take charge of Tavrida Garden and then the People's House and garden. To draw crowds, the showman aimed to create a festive atmosphere and offer patrons a wide variety of genres.[92]

In its effort to attract large audiences the trusteeship also ignored the special censorship restrictions for popular theatre. In 1901 the Main Administration on Publication informed Witte that 75 of the 190 plays performed under the auspices of the Petersburg trusteeship had never been authorized for presentation to popular audiences. A strong bureaucratic rivalry had developed between the Ministry of the Interior, which included the censorship, and the Ministry of Finance. While the budget of Finance had tripled between 1890 and 1900, Interior's had grown hardly at all. The downturn in the business cycle that began in 1900 undercut Witte's prestige. Personal animosity between him and minister of the interior V. K. Plehve became intense in 1902, and Plehve actually dismissed two provincial governors for cooperating too enthusiastically with Witte's investigation into the causes of peasant disturbances. In a 1901 speech to the presidents of the provincial committees on popular temperance Witte had cautioned that their focus should be the simple folk, and they must not confuse popular theatre with general-access theatre. But by 1903 the censor Pchel'nikov was complaining that the Moscow trusteeship rented the Georgian House of the People for forty performances but refused his requests for a seat at any of them.

Even as the Ministry of Finance declined in imperial favor, the pace of its investment in popular theatre quickened. In 1902 the trusteeship began to publish its own weekly journal. Its first number announced that "People's Houses, auditoriums, libraries, reading rooms, theatres and similar organizations form a dense net covering the enormous territory of the Russian Empire."[93] The trusteeship, with its provincial and district committees, offered strong incentives in the form of subsidies for organizing popular theatres. Moreover, the trusteeship took to heart early criticisms of management and repertory. In 1903 it engaged Shcheglov to prepare a model catalogue of one hundred plays for popular theatres, which it published. (Eight of his choices, including works by Gorky, Tolstoy and Turgenev, still lacked approval from the popular theatre censorship!) Then it commissioned him to visit its theatres all over Russia, report on the quality of their offerings and suggest improvements.

Although the trusteeship's budgets shrank steadily after 1903, the sheer scope of its activities made it a cultural force to be reckoned with. In a 1909 report to a temperance congress, D. N. Borodin called for transfer of the trusteeship's libraries and reading rooms to either the zemstvos or the Ministry of Education.[94] He noted that in 1904 it had 1,786 libraries and 1,067 reading rooms. He recognized that entertainments to distract from drunkenness had taken on a larger scale under the trusteeship, but considered that the resources expended on its theatres could be better managed by some other agency. Yet despite the overall low quality of operations, the trusteeship constructed entertainment facilities for a commonplace public in a country that had very few such amenities. It brought literary theatre to places where the market had just begun to grasp its popular potential.

SHCHEGLOV'S SURVEY OF RUSSIAN POPULAR THEATRES IN 1903

The Ministry of the Treasury department, with jurisdiction over Temperance trusteeship theatres, paid Ivan Shcheglov fifteen hundred rubles to visit popular theatres all over Russia in the summer of 1903 and write a report on their condition. His *tour d'horizon,* which survives in the ministry files, describes a rapidly growing unsophisticated public with a taste for theatre too genuine and compelling to be put off by bureaucratic ineptitude and intelligentsia arrogance. Author of numerous articles on popular theatre, and books on the subject in 1895 and 1898, Shcheglov possessed unimpeachable qualifications as an authority. He had originally come to theatre not as a culturist, but as a craftsman trying to please an audience. After retiring from the army in 1883 with the rank of captain, he wrote stories and plays before establishing himself as an essayist on the burgeoning popular theatre movement. He undertook the survey as an opinionated, cranky, and sarcastic expert.

If the ministry merely sought an endorsement of its initial efforts, then, considering his well-known misgivings about the policies of the Temperance trusteeship theatres, Shcheglov seems an unlikely choice. The commission from the Ministry of Finance may have come because of his feuilleton in the 6 March issue of *New Times,* "Enigmas of the Petersburg Popular Theatre."[95] He argued there that a genuinely popular repertory had never been worked out for the Temperance trusteeship theatres, with the result that they played a "general-access" repertory unsuitable for the masses. He quoted approvingly Witte's warning in a 1901 speech to presidents of the provincial committees on popular temperance that if they were to provide distractions from drinking, they would have to focus exclusively on the simple folk and avoid confusing popular and general-access repertory. Further, he mentioned that in the West popular theatres had always done with minimal sets, and he chided the trusteeship for the extravagant luxury of its stage decoration. He also attacked the practice of presenting opera, which he said remained a mental puzzle even for intellectual audiences; peasant viewers had difficulty following the sung words and so often remained confused as to an opera's subject, let alone its idea.

Shcheglov's report praised Witte, now dismissed from the Treasury, for having shrewdly anticipated the swelling demand for popular theatre and giving it a broad, genuinely Russian scope. He concluded, "Is it his fault . . . if Chichikovs and Manilovs climbed into the . . . nests he built?"[96] Treasury subsidies too often attracted the wrong people to establish theatres. Shcheglov found factory and railroad theatres, which not only lacked treasury subsidies but often the provincial governors' goodwill, superior because they were closer to the people. He reproached the intelligentsia for being too often drawn to popular theatre out of vanity, and for foisting alien and sometimes incomprehensible works on the people. He endorsed Tolstoy's condemnation, in *What Is Art?* (*Chto takoe iskusstvo?* [1898]), of the "decadent" tendencies in Russian art. As he saw it, any service the elite had rendered the masses by bringing them literary theatre was negated by the supposedly perverse fashions that had now overtaken high culture: "[i]n view of the progressive decay of the contemporary art of the upper classes . . . popular theatre assumes an even greater importance, as a symbolic Noah's ark on the flood of contemporary lies and nastiness."

Shcheglov's disdain extended to intelligentsia acting as well, which he claimed was always stuck on one tone. He considered it inferior to that of professionals who, at any one time, played a variety of roles. He conceded that intelligentsia amateurs were ready to go anywhere to act—but vanity could have been their motive here as well. They were preoccupied with themselves. Their other unpardonable fault was their predilection for staging the works of Ostrovsky.

Shcheglov remained keenly interested in the question of repertory, and his 1903 report made no secret of his preferences. Popular audiences, he insisted, deserved to maximize their pleasure from theatre. Melodrama and "jolly plays" could best satisfy this requirement, and he damned intelligentsia organizers for filtering out much of the richness of theatrical literature in their vocation to uplift the folk. Almost everywhere he traveled, he found folly in the pastime's organization, the most common deficiency a disinclination to be guided by the people's tastes. He reserved his bitterest scorn for decadent works, followed by "modish" contemporary plays (among which he included symbolist drama).

He conceded that popular theatre had progressed farthest in Saint Petersburg, though denying that it served as a distraction to licentiousness there. The provinces he compared to "an incorrigible coquette . . . continually gazing into the dull Petersburg mirror." Moscow, in both quantity and quality of popular performances, he found lagging far behind the capital.

Shcheglov calculated a potential Moscow audience of almost half a million for popular theatre—half of them illiterate. These included 120,000 factory laborers, 113,000 skilled workers, 9,000 working at home, 41,000 employed in transport, 32,000 engaged in the iron trade, 34,000 artisan apprentices, 10,000 unskilled day laborers, 40,000 servants and workers in public buildings, and 90,000 domestic servants. The Moscow duma supported construction of a popular theatre on Vvedensk Square. He quoted from a petition signed by seventy-five workers requesting a theatre in this location that would provide healthy diversion for the people: "In Moscow there are many tea shops where workers spend a night. They have everything—accordion music, wine, beer, prostitutes, acrobats, and even places for sexual relations. After eleven the price of everything doubles." He hoped the duma would also implement the proposal of Professor Ger'e to ring the more democratic Moscow suburbs with a network of ten small popular theatres.

For the time being four people's gardens served most of the simple public's needs. The Cherepanov Theatre on the Moscow River catered to the newly arrived. Shcheglov said that to visit it was like being dropped into some unkempt provincial corner. The drawls of the customers and their naive rapture reminded him of Zadonsk or Novorzev. Although impossibly stilted dialogue characterized the unfortunate melodrama he saw there, "To the parterre, these unnatural phrases are like the most natural words of M. Gorky." When he attended a performance there 10 August, he found a solid wall of workers filling the square.

The People's Pleasure Ground (Narodnaia Gulian'ia) in Sokol'niki Park seemed like another planet. The Society for Educational Popular Entertainments, which operated the facility, tolerated no melodrama and no advertising. To Shcheglov everything seemed "proper, a little academic, and a little boring." He thought the Society "soared too high." Besides Ostrovsky, here was the "amateur-intelligentsia" repertory that "had long set the teeth of the capital on edge": Nemirovich-Danchenko's *The New Undertaking (Novoe delo),* Sudermann's *Homeland (Rodina),* and Chernyshev's *A Broken Life (Isporchennaia).* But by a happy coincidence, he happened to see at Sokol'niki Park only the second "genuine popular merry play" of his whole inspection tour. Stanislavsky assisted with a presentation of Beaumarchais's *Barber of Seville,* done with the proper tone and real enthusiasm. The audience expressed delight. One young man Shcheglov spoke with afterward declaimed a line or two of Dr. Bartolo's "calumny rising" speech, and asked where one could get the whole text of the play. When Shcheglov pulled from his pocket a copy of the Cheap Library edition, the lad expressed "boundless gratitude."[97]

Atypical commercial outdoor theatres, the Garden and Theatre Hermitage, advertised in the papers as "specializing in light comedy and attracting the cream of society." Shcheglov encountered whole families, with children and maids, in the lobby when he attended 17 August. The "Summer Review" included a play called *Stylish Lioness.* In the chambers of the "lioness," the women sat on the men's knees drinking champagne, and at the end of the second act they all danced the can-can. At the intermission, a soloist sang something in German, two girls did a frenzied dance, and an orchestra composed entirely of women dressed in nightshirts held forth. The other Moscow summer pleasure parks—the Zoological Garden, the Aquarium Garden/Omon, and the Bauer Garden in the Catherine Park—offered similar frivolous entertainment. He observed that at the Omon the luxurious surroundings and expensive sets did not prevent the "select public" from enjoying fights in the parterre that left dozens of couples with bloody noses and elbows.

The Moscow Temperance trusteeship had but one theatre, and strove to make it as unlike as possible the well-developed Petersburg operation. In Saint Petersburg, for instance, the curtain rose; in Moscow it parted. Like the entrepreneurs of the Moscow pleasure parks, the trustees augmented their theatre offerings with public dances. Shcheglov took a jaundiced view. "Because of unskillful management, the . . . dancing . . . reminds one more of a kind of zealous horse whipping, where dancing cavaliers, with cigarettes in their teeth, using very little space, turn folk dances into an international cake walk." He condemned as well the trusteeship's practice of presenting opera. For one thing, it cost twice as much to produce as drama. More important, he claimed, "in a significant sense, opera kills drama" by destroying the audience's participation in the play.

> Generally, when an opera is presented, one judges the performers more than the subject of the work. With a dramatic presentation, on the other hand, the performers are forgotten for the play, which satisfies as something natural, experienced, true-to-life. Just as drama illustrates life and criticizes it, opera only produces an impression.

The trusteeship claimed that opera had greater success with audiences than drama, but Shcheglov attributed this to its novelty alone. He also faulted the trusteeship for its deployment of resources on holiday matinees at the New Imperial Theatre, which he called "a rollicking parody of popular theatre." "In the audience are the cheerful faces of educated people, the silk blouses of female students and gymnasia students; in the loges, ladies with lorgnettes and men with candy." Since all the Moscow private theatres from the Korsh on down gave matinees at reduced prices on holidays, he wondered what possible purpose such an expenditure of treasury subsidies could serve.

Pushing and jostling with a crushing holiday crowd of workers in a densely populated center like Moscow, Kiev, or Odessa made Shcheglov feel the people's irresistible thirst for affecting and comic theatrical performances. They were better served in Kiev, where the Temperance trusteeship operated the well-designed Lukianovskii People's House, with a spacious tea room, tidy night lodging, well-lighted area for a school, library, and bookshop, and a theatre accommodating up to six hundred. As with most trusteeship theatres, performances at the Lukianovskii began at 8:00 P.M. The actors consisted mainly of gentlemen amateurs, yet some of the performances matched the standards of the finest professionals. The repertory was completely hit-or-miss. Though only in its first season, it had presented some solid fare, like Gorky's *The Petty Bourgeois (Meshchane)*, S. Naidenov's *Vaniushin's Children (Deti Vaniushina)*, and Viktor Krylov's *The Spoilt Girl (Balovnia)*, but the repertory lacked a single historical or classical play. Ukrainian plays enjoyed the greatest sucess, crowding out some interest in Great Russian works. With a larger theatre, the People's House of the Kiev Society for Literacy on Trinity Square chalked up an attendance of twelve thousand for the 1902–3 season. It performed Gorky's *The Lower Depths* no fewer than eleven times.

Shcheglov found the Railroad Theatre, housed in a shed at the depot, more to his taste. The railroad management provided and heated the modest facility. The unsubsidized theatre group installed there, now in its fourth year, appealed more to the simple folk than to the local intelligentsia. Historical, melodramatic, and comic elements predominated in its still haphazard repertory. The enterprise demonstrated, Shcheglov believed, what could be accomplished with little more than keen and energetic private initiative: "They chose to do *Ismail*, and the costumes and playing were far beyond what one would expect from railroad workers. From the parterre, filled to capacity, came a hurricane of cheers and applause after every act."

At Odessa's People's House, the Amateurs of Dramatic Art in May 1903 were playing *Trilby*. Posters also advertised: "Decadent Play. The most carefully selected ultradecadent one-act play. For a limited engagement. *Zaza*, by L. B. Iavorskii." Shcheglov attended a performance of *Trilby*. "Not far from me," he recalled, "sat two common Black Sea sailors with their girlfriends, and on the faces of all four could be seen simultaneously sour disbelief and ill-disguised sorrow that they had not gone instead to the bar next door." Odessa also boasted a highly unusual variety of popular theatre. The Temperance trusteeship ran a "Tearoom by the Sea" in the center of the transient district. It had a temporary collapsible stage that functioned mainly in the winter months: in effect, a theatre especially for tramps.

It distressed Shcheglov that those who arranged recreation for Russian working men lacked any knowledge of native holiday customs. Temperance trusteeship committees in Kiev, Odessa, and Sevastapol sponsored "popular balls," but did not seem to realize that for the faithful it was still quite unacceptable to go dancing directly after vespers. Sunday morning lectures at the People's Houses also disrupted the free day of the Russian working man. Worst of all, Temperance trusteeship theatre performances always started late in the evening. Shcheglov attributed this to the fact that members of the temperance boards liked to dine at seven. He recommended scheduling holiday performances at 5:00 P.M., and sketched the holiday routine of the typical Russian working man to demonstrate why:

> He goes off to early and late Mass. On the way back he stops at the bazaar or the shops to make purchases. Then a hurried dinner, and a nap from three to four. At five he washes, oils his exuberant hair, and soon finds himself on that mysterious Russian crossroads between the tavern and the strict resolution he made earlier, and the Popular Theatre opening late.[98]

As he visited theatres in different towns, Shcheglov scrutinized audiences as well as offerings. On his fourth day in Saratov, for example, he found near the city limits a small theatre of what he called "semipopular" character. The players were amateurs performing in the smallish auditorium of the Saratov Women's Institute. He attended a conscientious performance of Ostrovsky's *The Forest.* Three-quarters of the audience consisted of artisans and craftsmen. They listened to the comedy literally holding their breath, too decorous to unbend at all. Saratov built a popular theatre in 1897, which burned down in 1901. The Department of Popular Entertainments, which had operated in the building, mounted a campaign to raise funds for a new structure to accommodate the well-attested needs of the city's working class and small property holders. Shcheglov generally approved of the plays they had performed, but wondered about the absence of melodrama, and the preference for the "academic" Molière of *Tartuffe* over the more broadly appealing *Doctor in Spite of Himself.*

In Pskov he encountered a genuinely popular audience in the gallery at the Popular Theatre: old women, soldiers, lower-middle-class women in kerchiefs, traders, and mechanics. But the production of Prince Sumbatov's *The Celebrity (Muzh znamenitosti)* left a sour impression. "In this filthy corner of the theatrical world," he remarked, "two representatives of the intelligentsia were prominent on the stage, behaving in such a way as to arouse at the same time complete contempt for the world of theatre and the world of the intelligentsia." The following day, a holiday, he noticed that the pranks and licentiousness in a three-act French play, *At Sixes and Sevens,* affected the audience in ways that showed cultural differences and followed the fault lines of class. The intelligentsia in the parterre smiled at the cackling in the gallery, rather than at the play. In the vaudeville that followed, the gallery was not at all amused and laughed "just after the gentlefolk, in order, so to speak, not to lag behind the intelligentsia." Despite the handsome facility, Shcheglov left Pskov with a bad impression. His experience in the popular theatre had been more encouraging when he visited the city in 1900.

Bustling Rostov-on-Don, however, held out more promise for popular theatre development. He had last passed through fifteen years earlier, when it was a district trading town. Now he found an American-type industrial center with twenty-two thousand factory employees: "a Russian Chicago." A poster at the railroad station announced a free matinee performance of Gogol's *Getting Married* at the dining facility of the Vladikavkaz Works. That night L. I. Antropov's *Van'ka Kliuchnik* would be given at prices ranging from five to seventy kopeks. The Railroad Police Authority guardians sponsored the theatre. The Temperance trusteeship underwrote an "adequate" rendition of Molière's *The Would-Be Gentleman* at the Pioneer Garden. The company, the Rostov Artistic Society, did much better with *A Profitable Post*, even displaying a remarkable comic talent. Shcheglov shuddered to think what would become of intelligentsia amateurs without Ostrovsky, who had written precisely half of the twenty plays performed by the Rostov Society the previous summer. He paused to praise work by a member of the Rostov city duma on a project for construction of a locally supported People's House to be maintained by tax revenues.

Two of the cities included in the inspection tour boasted lavish popular theatres built by wealthy local factory owners. The Alfuzov family of Kazan had constructed on the premises of its sprawling leather factory an enormous castle in the Kazan-Moorish style, a People's Palace with high windows, massive oak doors, and four minarets. An intricate crystal chandalier and dazzling parquet floor graced the foyer, along with a white marble bust of Nicholas II and a portrait of the Tsar Liberator. The theatre had three circles, a parterre with comfortable benches, and a deep plush box for the governor. Two circles were specially designated for "dark" workers, and the inexpensive buffet served no strong drink. Shcheglov deplored the light, amateurish repertory played here and likened the enterprise to a worthless picture in an expensive frame. The Kazan duma had laid the foundations and cornerstone for a People's House named in honor of Pushkin. Construction had been halted, and it was rumored the project had simply been a stratagem to secure a government subsidy. The poor frequented an amusement park nearby in the Nikolaevsk Garden, attracted by a carousel, "Panoptikum," and wax museum. In the evening the regimental band thundered out the Skobelev March.

> One gets a picture of true popular open-air merrymaking from the crush of bodies in bast sandals, red shirts, sarafans, and kerchiefs against the dusty background. Around the bandstand, peasant women stand in tight rows, and if it were not for the meticulous town police, would probably break into country songs and round dances.

People in Kazan could resort to two other spots for amusement. Families often took their samovars and spent the day at "Russian Switzerland" outside the city. Couples favored the music hall offerings in the late evening at the Panaevsk Garden.

The Korzinkinsk Factory near Iaroslavl' sponsored a popular theatre in a grandiose building with seating for a thousand. From what Shcheglov could ascertain, historical drama and melodrama figured prominently in the repertory; the organizers also favored Ostrovsky, because of the familiar picture of life his plays presented. The theatre operated only in the winter. But he was able to attend one of the performances of the popular festival held on the Korzinkinsk premises. He compared it to the evenings at the Vargunin pleasure grounds in Saint Petersburg—with half the starched shirts and ladies' hats, and twice the open space and greenery. A military band provided dance music, and a temperance buffet offered cheap food. The Iaroslavl' Society for Popular Entertainment had constructed "a wretched barracks" in which the city's common people were treated to interminable lectures and opera highlights at Easter. Shcheglov described what he saw here as "a poor imitation of popular theatre." A comic followed a vaudeville entitled "Unhappiness of a Special Kind," with an excellent impression of a dog. Shcheglov lamented that a hundred and fifty years after Volkov had first welcomed the public, "Russia's cradle of popular theatre" could offer so little distraction from boredom.

He had little to say of what would shortly become one of the most notorious People's Houses, the Nizhegorodskii Narodnyi Dom. Built under the patronage of the local marshal of the nobility, its true guiding spirit was Maxim Gorky, Nizhni Novgorod's internationally famous writer, and a man sprung from the people. The architecturally undistinguished building had the customary restaurant, tea room, library, and reading room. Shcheglov found the theatre facilities much inferior to those in Kiev's Lukianovskii People's House and much better than those in Cheliabinsk. A treasury wine depot nearby proposed to present plays with a temperance theme, in contrast to those given at the People's House. It also sponsored dance evenings, gave concerts, and organized penitential singing at Lent. The theatre could not compete, and closed after the second play.

When he revisited Kineshma, Shcheglov discovered a thriving company making admirable progress. In the six years the Musical Dramatic Circle had presented plays for the people in their theatre named for A. N. Ostrovsky, simple folk always packed the gallery. Though he faulted the Circle repertory for its complement of frivolous French farces and trendy Saint Petersburg fare, he recognized it as one of the most conscientious and energetic groups in Russia responding to the swelling demands of the Popular Theatre. If he thought the Circle guilty of trying to raise the people above themselves, he nevertheless had to admit that they showed stunning ingenuity in finding new ways to serve the people. Their playing had improved so much in the four years since he last saw them that he hardly recognized them. They had begun making flying visits with the whole troupe to local factories and villages. Their festivals celebrating famous writers had won wide praise. They had expanded their facilities with the predictable tea room, library, bookstall, and reading room, but they had also added a small garden near the main theatre with a small musical stage where they gave children's festivals. And in the summer, company and buffet repaired to picturesque Mezhakovo Field—a favorite of the town's common folk on holidays—where they set up a wide variety of activities.

Shcheglov's survey, for all his prejudices and idiosyncrasies, reveals the diversity and growing strength of the Russian Popular Theatre movement. What he actually observed on his far-flung travels may even warrant his habit of capitalizing the phrase. If he was too quick to condemn as unsuitable successful contemporary plays on issues he deemed irrelevant to the uneducated, his impatience with overdependence on Ostrovsky's plays in most repertories reflected a growing dissatisfaction with the dramatist's increasingly dated picture of Russian life. Shcheglov reminded the Ministry of Finance of the cultural responsibilities of its Temperance trustees by insisting on a theatre that both illustrates life and criticizes it. And, as much as he despised the intelligentsia in general, he did testify that some of them, at the turn of the century, had found a new way of going to the people.

Shcheglov spoke in his 1903 report of holiday crowds in densely populated centers like Moscow, Kiev, and Odessa as "wretched people ruthlessly cut off from their home on the land." Popular theatre became popular in Russia as markets for labor and goods expanded with unprecedented speed. Newcomers to cities welcomed theatrical entertainment as they set about designing routines, and the Temperance trusteeship employed liquor tax revenues to increase the supply of such entertainment in cities. Literary theatre, which offered consumers a choice of constructed texts in performance, now competed effectively with traditional folk entertainment shaped for audiences on delivery—even at fairs and crossroads. That the newcomers discovering literary theatre for the first time should have struck the already established as "wretched" should not be surprising. In this phase of the popular theatre movement the advancing market seemed to offer its own ordering and stabilizing mechanisms for social interaction.

Precisely this assumption can be seen in the ambitions of the leading citizens of Birmingham in 1774 when they rebuilt the Theatre Royal along grander lines to make it conform to the growing economic and social importance of the town and serve "to improve the morals . . . of the people." In fact the classic enlightener identification of morals and the progress of reason had been enunciated in France at that very moment by L.-S. Mercier, when he called in 1773 and 1778 for plays that would mold the morals of citizens and a popular theatre to "illuminate and arm the people with reason." In Russia from the mid-1880s to 1903 popular theatre was discussed and promoted in the context of its capacity to propagate morality. The acting company that set up in Balakovo in 1886 sensed an "invisible moral connection" between actor and public in the countryside. The 1891 founding statute of the new Nevsky Society called for the delivery of "moral entertainments" to the local working-class population. The questionnaire it distributed to viewers in the mid-1890s specifically requested comment on the significance of the entertainments offered "in moral terms." Respondents made a case for plays exerting a moral influence on their lives. To be sure, one indicated that prevailing working conditions militated against moral deportment, when he said, "In such a life a man does not even have time to pretend to preserve his morals." But the consumers as well as the sponsors of literary drama accepted morality as a dimension of serious theatre. A journalist who doubted that Tolstoy could have made a play that provided moral guidance to the unwashed had to admit after seeing a performance of *The Power of Darkness* at the Skomorokh in Moscow that, as presented, "the sin becomes ugly and terrible." An 1895 article credited the 1891 famine as a wake-up call alerting the educated to the spiritual and moral needs of the people. "Our estrangement from direct concern for their good and [their] enlightenment is a heavy sin, for which Russian society will answer before the court of history."[99] The author of the 1896 account of the first play presented by amateurs native to Staryi Oskol explained that one of its goals was to "avert the moral decomposition of the popular mass." Even the 1897 guidelines of the Temperance trusteeship specified that popular theatres serve "as a means of exercising moral influence on the masses." Habermas succinctly summarizes the certainty of thoughtful people concerning the inevitable triumph of moral sentiments when he remarks that reasoning in the Public Sphere gave rise to "assurance in matters of moral judgment."

Russian observers of literary theatre performances perceived that they promoted the civilizing process in viewers. The Finance Ministry took very seriously evidence that theatre somehow altered workers' sense of themselves and disposed them to behave more responsibly. The government sponsored popular theatre not because it considered the simple folk entitled to high culture, nor because it sought to promote a consciousness of individual rights, but rather because it stood for order and stability. And the Nevsky Society responses indicated that the folk welcomed a well-policed space where they could develop their self-control and work on themselves as discerning, judging, independent persons. Testimony that as a benefit of trying to imitate what one has seen in a good play "one releases crude abusiveness less often" seemed to confirm the theatre's usefulness in the attainment of self-mastery.

Another connection between theatre and the civilizing process that emerged in this period was the theatre's curious relationship to literacy. Evidence from the first popular theatres suggests that prolonged exposure to plays led to awareness of a text behind the action on stage. Balakova first-timers had no inkling of a text, nor did the Staryi Oskol viewers who perversely identified with the victors. But Beaumarchais's *Barber*, we remember, sufficiently dazzled a young man at Moscow's Sokolniki Park that he asked Shcheglov about the availability of a printed text.

Finally, twenty years' reflection on literary theatre and the civilizing process as it affected the simple folk revealed another, unexpected, implication. What if the enlighteners themselves were experiencing an ongoing process? I. I. Ianzhul well understood that the changing perceptions of Westernized Russians had more to do with concern over temperance than any recent change in ritual drinking.

> We ourselves, the middle class, have undoubtedly become more temperate, and therefore sterner with others; drinking among the people and disgraceful behavior ending in public houses and on the street now assault our sensibilities more sharply. One of our best-informed publicists who writes on this issue is perfectly correct when he notes that formerly drunkenness was and was considered to be a sort of right—the only right of a serf. . . . Now it is completely different: we became incomparably more demanding of people once they were declared to be equal; we get annoyed and bitter at their lack of skill . . . in conducting their affairs; we forget the past and regard the present with indignation; and therefore drunkenness strikes us more sharply and seems to be gaining more and more force.[100]

If the cultivated classes' perceptual equipment continued to evolve, it followed that objects of their perception—like morality and order—represented subjective categories.

Other absolutes suddenly became questionable. The early popular theatres clearly affected thinking about Russia's social order. The common folk who dared to perform *You Can't Live . . .* in Chernigov's Ministry of Finance–sponsored temperance tearoom demonstrated an acuity in the people that had formerly been considered an appurtenance of rank. It was a discovery that would be repeated in hundreds of People's Houses all over Russia and warrant second thoughts about a graded society of estates. Reactions to *Woe from Wit* in Saint Petersburg testify to growing interest in social equality and the possibility of progress in standards of judgment and behavior for the nation as a whole ("so that nobody will laugh at good and clever people"). Yet in 1903 the conception of social distinction and hierarchy remained deeply ingrained, so that even the popular theatre expert could find companies "soaring too high" and raising the people "above themselves."

Part Two

Chapter Five

Expansion in Contentious Times

AT THE BEGINNING of the twentieth century the Russian government took several remarkably progressive steps to free the creative forces of society. In January 1902 it initiated consultation with any local figures who cared to testify on the systemic and institutional defects hobbling Russian agriculture. In February 1903 it abandoned its long-standing policy of resorting to beatings to collect taxes from peasants in arrears. In December 1904 an imperial decree effectively abolished the estates system that had proved so detrimental to the development of community action in the countryside. In October 1905 Nicholas II committed to create a democratically elected legislature with a broad franchise.

But all of these momentous reforms were in fact withdrawn completely or else sharply compromised. They were initially granted in an attempt to deal with social tensions and protests that would range from peasant rebellion in 1902 to full-fledged revolution in 1905. In significance they rank with the changes of the Great Reform era. And the last two emerged during a war with Japan, which, like the Crimean War, discredited the government's overall competence in the public's eyes.

Public response differed from that of 1857–63, although the public mood shifted as sharply around 1902 as it had in 1861–62. By 1903 professional identification and self-confidence emboldened specific groups to insist on the right to associate and work constructively on behalf of public education and public health. But the very goals of free association and local community initiative raised the ire of powerful government figures. A list could easily be assembled of arbitrary acts committed by the government in these years as impressive as the list of canceled or vitiated reforms.

An upsurge in teachers' association and internalization of a new professional ethos, "that of confident cultural activists," became evident by 1902.[1] A physicians' conference in January 1904 issued a hundred resolutions assailing current policies on public health and zemstvo restrictions and "erupted with one of the first denunciations of the autocracy."[2] The Ministry of the Interior, responsible for maintaining internal security, noted the challenge posed by freer association. "In 1901 and again in 1904 the [Department of Police] renewed their criticisms of governors for 'frequently' ignoring the . . . rules and maintaining lax supervision over charity benefits and all other activities of private societies."[3] One characteristic of the new public mood was its talk of civil rights. Linda Edmondson found that "even by the end of 1904, before the mass protest movement of the revolution had fully erupted, references to civil rights had become so standard, so ubiquitous, that one might be tempted to dismiss them as rhetorical devices were it not for the fact that they touched the everyday lives of people at all levels of society."[4]

In a letter to Dmitri Miliutin dated 22 December 1904, jurist A. F. Koni remarked how quickly the public mood was changing:

> The current situation in Russia is strange and, I have to say, frightening. Society is bursting out of its swaddling clothes, in which it was forcibly kept and which dulled the mind and atrophied any feelings of self dignity. But it already wants to run, although it doesn't yet know how to walk, and indeed to stand on its own feet.[5]

He added that the masses were "a new factor"—which brings us back to Habermas's explanation of the expansion of the Public Sphere and its loss of prestige.

The changing public mood around 1902 clouded enlighteners' sunny optimism of the previous fifteen years with respect to theatre's potential to civilize the masses and hasten cultural reunification. Habermas had observed, in *Structural Transformation,* that as culture became a commodity, the affairs that it had made public began to elude the intellectual control of a critical public (140).

> The public was expanded, informally at first, by the proliferation of press and propaganda; along with its social exclusiveness it also lost . . . coherence. . . . Conflicts hitherto pushed aside into the private sphere now emerged in public. Group needs that could not expect to be satisfied by a self-regulating market tended to favor regulation by the state. The public sphere, which now had to deal with these demands, became an arena of competing interests fought out in the coarser forms of violent conflict. (131–32)

His theory is helpful in following the Russian developments because it alerts us to (a) the appearance of violence in the cultural arena, (b) grudging acceptance of the state's usefulness as regulator and protector of privileged interests, and (c) the new focus on individualism as an escape from the disharmony of the expanded Public Sphere.

Lower-class rejection of polite society's norms of discipline, cleanliness, and temperance, took a form that demanded attention and required a name. "Hooliganism," Joan Neuberger reports, "occurred in public space. As a public crime, a public exhibition, and usually a public confrontation, it dramatized conflicting values and conventions."[6] Pranks, drunkenness, swearing, and disrespect "served to reinforce the impression that the lower classes were increasingly dangerous, reckless, brazen and hostile" (114, 46). The chronology of the naming established by Neuberger is suggestive.

> As early as 1901 it is clear that when writers used the word *hooliganism* they fully expected their audience to understand it. . . . By 1903 it had developed resonances and an identity of its own, and *hooliganism,* the word, and hooliganism the phenomenon, replaced other labels for and forms of lower-class rowdiness and petty crime in the forefront of public concern. (42)

Her explanation accords with Habermas's account of an exploding Public Sphere. "Publication exposed even the private or distant world of taverns, stairwells, and working-class suburbs to the gaze of the comfortable reader. By publicizing details of life in the slums, the boulevard press broke down barriers that had prevented Petersburg society from becoming familiar with the lives of the poor."[7]

Habermas noted the reactions of J. S. Mill and Tocqueville as unreconciled interests had flooded the Public Sphere in the West. He quoted from *On Liberty* (1859): "the masses do not now take their opinions from dignitaries . . . or from books. Their thinking is done for them by men much like themselves . . . through the newspapers."[8] And he underlined Tocqueville's concern with the "despotism of an increasingly bureaucratized state" as public opinion became merely one power among other powers, quoting from *Democracy in America* on the "immense, protective power" that is "absolute, thoughtful of detail, orderly, provident and gentle" but "only tries to keep [its charges] in perpetual childhood."[9] In Habermas's theory the prestige formerly accorded rational argument now transferred to specialists. The educated began to doubt reunification and consensus.

Russians interested in social change had earlier noticed manifestations of peasant individualism. Kliuchevsky, for example, in a lecture on clothing and manners that he presented in 1897, declared that the contemporary emphasis on dress demonstrated a turning away from religious and community values toward exaltation of the individual and shallow efforts to impress others.[10] But after the turn of the century lower-class resistance caused the educated to ponder the phlegmatic village community and pin their hopes on the exceptional, the individual peasant. "Hooliganism," Stephen Frank finds, "helped to finalize the conclusions of educated reformers: . . . a new, frighteningly independent and degenerate generation of peasants . . . now represented the greatest threat to Enlightenment, progress and order in the countryside."[11] Frank contends that the inability of village elders to halt the growth of hooliganism disposed Russian moral reformers to retreat to a spirited defense of individualism—the fallback position taken by Mill and Tocqueville in the face of an expanded and transformed public sphere.[12]

Popular theatre soon reflected the individualist and radical tendencies emerging after the turn of the century. N. F. Bunakov availed himself of opportunities presented by reform to accuse the regime of criminal bungling. His radical intransigence finished him and his People's House theatre. As for the scope of popular drama in this period, the censors' reports describe offerings authorized and rejected, and clarify the rationale for regulation. Two playwrights wrote vehicles attuned to the new mood equal in importance to Ostrovsky's, Potekhin's and Pisemskii's plays for the Great Reform era. Finally, it will be useful to consider a new institution that delivered challenging drama to popular audiences in Saint Petersburg and facilitated the delivery of quality dramatic productions in the hinterland: the "Wanderers" traveling theatre.

BUNAKOV'S END

As early as 1898 Minister of Finance Witte informed the tsar that peasant backwardness seemed to be impeding his development program. Nicholas appointed a commission the following year, chaired by Witte's deputy, to study the central black earth provinces. It found the commune to be harmful, but inextricably interwoven into the fabric of peasant life. In 1901, another famine year for the region, Nicholas created a second Commission on the Center. The backing of Minister of the Interior D. S. Sipiagin led him to approve in January 1902 Witte's proposed Special Conference for the Clarification of the Needs of Agriculture and Related Branches of the National Economy. To ensure that the conference did not recommend sweeping social reforms, he first created an Editorial Committee for the Drafting of a New Peasant Statute and appointed a reactionary bureaucrat to preside over it. Still, by authorizing Witte to consult local people and publish their recommendations, the tsar unwittingly opened the way to reconsideration of the rights and relations of the most important social groups. As a student of the Russian liberal faction put it, "A paradoxical situation was created whereby Nicholas and Sipiagin, who had used all their powers of repression to suppress public opinion, were instrumental in creating the most extensive sounding-board of public opinion that Russia had ever known."[13]

Witte acknowledged in the program he prepared for the conference that the recent expansion of railways and introduction of market pressures associated with his industrialization drive had "caused a crisis in agriculture and that only areas with western European historical influence were satisfactorily able to adapt."[14] He did not abandon the question of peasant status to the Editorial Committee, and he appeared ready to rethink his well-known opposition to the zemstvos in a bid to build a base of support in society as economic contraction eroded the tsar's confidence in his economic program.

Witte considered several ideas promising for encouraging initiative, and they were widely discussed in the 25,000 meetings held by the 668 local and provincial committees in 1902 and 1903. One called for ending the estates system *(soslovnost')* and putting peasants under the jurisdiction of courts that now served the rest of society. Another envisioned all-class local government in the countryside, so that the gentry could be joined by educated professionals and others of middle-class background in helping the peasantry. Witte favored the encouragement of agricultural societies and cooperatives. Indeed, many committees pointed to the success of cooperatives in the Lithuanian province of Kovno, where the absence of *soslovnost'* enabled educated elements to assist with organization and management tasks.[15]

The crisis in agriculture that motivated Witte to organize the Special Conference erupted in peasant uprisings in Voronezh, Poltava, Kharkov, and other central provinces in 1902.[16] The committees gathering testimony for the Special Conference continued; most district committees completed their work by December 1902, the provincial committees by February 1903. Late in 1902 Witte's ministry lost jurisdiction over the conference committees, but in 1903 Interior published a 58-volume official compilation of their findings.

The government at this time also abruptly reversed its policy on the collection of peasant taxes. An imperial manifesto of February 1903 "concerning plans for perfecting the political order" announced abolition of collective, communal responsibility for direct taxes; a March decree made current taxes and arrears the responsibility of the individual peasant household.[17] This policy shift was closely related to a public campaign waged in the press for the abolition of corporal punishment (for the estates not already exempt), because now-distasteful whipping had routinely figured in the collection process.[18] In western Europe a modern system of internalized discipline had caused punishment to be refocused away from the body early in the nineteenth century.[19] Here again public opinion influenced the Russian government decisively in 1903.[20]

But the autocrat did not like to appear to be controlled by reformers or advanced ideas. Witte fell into disfavor. In February 1903 the Ministry of the Interior announced that it would take charge of rural reform and work within the framework of the commune and the existing estate structure. In August Witte lost his position as minister of finance. The public, however, became increasingly critical of government after the Japanese declared war on Russia in February 1904. So after the assassination of the reactionary V. K. Plehve in July, Nicholas appointed as his successor at the Ministry of the Interior the conciliatory P. D. Sviatopolk-Mirsky, who averred that the government must earn the public's confidence.

The climate of opinion again began to work to Witte's advantage. In November 1904 the conference had its jurisdiction expanded to cover the peasantry's legal status and land tenure. Only now did the debates in the conference begin to take into account the findings published in the voluminous committee reports. In January Witte had written a *Memorandum on Peasant*

Affairs for submission to the Ministry of the Interior in which he called for an end to all limiting aspects of *soslovnost'*. There was scarcely a province that did not have at least one committee urging the creation of a local institution in which all classes could work together on an equal footing.[21]

Witte rode the rising tide of public support for civil equality in December 1904. He probably drafted the imperial decree dated December 12 that embodied his original goals for the committees.[22] It ordered the Ministry of the Interior and the conference to make peasants into "free rural inhabitants enjoying full rights." And it proposed specifically that the empire's court structure be unified so as to secure the equality of all before the law.

But the tsar changed his mind yet again, troubled by what seemed to him an inexorable escalation of demands from the public. In January 1905, *before* the "Bloody Sunday" massacre, Nicholas approved a circular that ordered the governors to disregard the December decree. The peasants were to remain a separate estate. Witte saw all his conference proposals rejected, including abolition of the internal passport system. The conference itself was abruptly closed in March 1905. Thus the government strode into the 1905 revolution not unmindful of public opinion but intermittently attentive to concepts of equality and dignity adumbrated in a public sphere vastly larger than the one that lost bearings when the first *glasnost'* era ended in 1863.

The last years of N. F. Bunakov illustrate the magnetic attraction of the expanded Public Sphere. Entering political life through the Voronezh zemstvo, which had a "liberal" reputation, the educator let his antipathy for bureaucratic authority and the dominion of the noble estate draw him into a confrontation that earned him national and even international attention. The Voronezh committee gave him a platform for a bitter and intemperate attack on imperial educational-cultural policy toward peasants. Witte's "sounding board" brought him Minister of the Interior Plehve's immediate attention. Plehve's arbitrary treatment helped win him a heroic martyr's role at the end, and may have contributed to the destruction of his Petino People's House theatre into the bargain.

His entry into politics followed his forced ejection from teacher-training courses. After 1896 some of the more advanced zemstvos, sharing an interest in putting more resources into education, had convened teacher-training conferences without observing the rather restrictive rules for such meetings laid down by the Ministry of Education in 1875. The Kursk and Tambov zemstvos, for example, encouraged free discussion between instructors and teacher-auditors—in violation of the 1875 statute. While giving a teacher-training course in Kherson Bunakov had shouted down a Ministry of Education inspector who forbade the participants to converse freely with each other.[23] He assured his pupils that they served the people and not the authorities. In 1901 the Ministry of Education ordered him to give no more teacher-training courses.[24] He refused to address the noble chairman of the provincial zemstvo as "Your excellency." The Ministry of the Interior stepped up its monitoring of his activities. The governor of Voronezh received a list of unreliable persons from Saint Petersburg with Bunakov's name at the top.

Bunakov turned over the operation of the Petino school theatre to others and stood for election to both district and provincial zemstvo councils, winning easily. Because of his tireless work on behalf of public education, peasants on the district council listened to him. Although elected unanimously to the zemstvo educational council, Bunakov failed to secure confirmation from the governor. The case went to the Ministry of the Interior, which also declined to confirm him. As originally created in 1864 the elected local governing bodies had been free of any Ministry of the Interior confirmation process, so Bunakov might be forgiven for feeling that reactionary autocratic politics had reversed Russia's progress toward local independent self-government through the zemstvos.

In October 1902 the Voronezh committee met to receive testimony on the needs of agriculture. The local marshal of the nobility was a liberal determined that the committee should deal with politically sensitive issues.[25] Voronezh had an active zemstvo that employed specialists with established reputations in their fields and a taste for political activism. Bunakov in his speech denounced what he saw as decades of disastrous neglect of public education. A mere six months after the peasant uprisings that had roiled the central provinces he denounced "this order . . . characterized by absence of personal rights, class conflict and antagonism, arbitrariness of administration stand[ing] above the law . . . and the horrifying ignorance of the masses." He indicted the government for "the complete suppression of the individual" and equated Russia with Turkey in rural cultural retardation. His flair for the dramatic produced an equally intemperate reaction. Plehve personally commanded that Bunakov be interrogated in Saint Petersburg, then dismissed the governor of Voronezh for failing to repress the speech and testimony supporting it. He had Bunakov and three other zemstvo figures exiled from the province.

The official compilation of the work of the committees, running to more than 25,000 pages, omitted Bunakov's speech entirely. The speech, however, received enormous publicity thanks to Plehve's response. Peter Struve, editor of *Liberation (Osvobozhdenie)*, a paper established by Russian liberals in Stuttgart in January 1902, called Plehve's policy "nothing but a systematic provocation of terror."[26] Struve demanded that Witte bring the matter to Nicholas's attention so that Bunakov's police supervision and three-years' residence restriction could be canceled.

The episode in fact lowered Witte in the tsar's estimation and cast doubt on the wisdom of public discussion of the needs of agriculture, or anything else. In London, *The Times* reported in a 28 February 1903 article detailing the Voronezh crackdown that Plehve had ordered provincial governors to prevent discussion of questions raised by all district committees regarded as "liberal," thereby violating the imperial decree that created the committees in January 1902, and rendering the consultation of the country through them a "ridiculous or rather a melancholy farce."[27]

The authorities confined Bunakov to his Petino estate. Yet he could not return to teaching, for the police made him sign a document promising not to go to the school nor do any "enlightenment" work in the village. The Ministry of the Interior stipulated that he could reside elsewhere only if he sold his Petino property. The Bunakovs stared out their window at the empty new People's House. Early in 1903 they put out a call for actors, as they had done in the past. But no one came forward. It seems plausible that the authorities' campaign of harassment deterred the local youths who had learned to act in the school. But Bunakov's widow, writing fourteen years later, suggested another possibility. The actors, sizing up the new facility and considering their proven ability to draw theatregoers from a wide area, held out for substantially more lucrative terms than they had enjoyed in the old theatre attached to the school building. Offering no explanation, she said that their "dreams were shattered and the Petino People's House stood boarded up.[28]

Bunakov would enjoy the reversal of fortune that restored Witte to influence in 1904. Upon taking over at Interior after Plehve's assassination, Sviatopolk-Mirsky telegraphed the governor of Voronezh to lift the surveillance on Bunakov and restore his right to carry on social activity. Bunakov boarded a train for Saint Petersburg to attend the first All-Russian Zemstvo Congress in November, but suffered a stroke en route and died a few days later.[29] Because he had become a symbol of the late Plehve's brutal opposition to peasant education and equality, his funeral represented an opportunity for significant public protest. Gorky wrote to his wife that "tomorrow at Bunakov's funeral there will probably be a serious demonstration by serious people."[30] And indeed, a student at the graveside called for Russian society to do battle with the autocracy, and the crowd left the Volkov cemetery singing the Marseillaise.

The regime surely deserves censure for Plehve's repressive and illegal acts. Obviously it would have done better to implement Witte's goals and eliminate peasant economic and legal disabilities. But gentry landowners, the regime's mainstay in the countryside, resisted social equality.[31] While landowners participating nationally on committees to examine the needs of agriculture could agree on the need for rapid expansion of educational opportunities, they were far less interested in equalizing peasant and noble tax burdens or even equalizing peasants' rights and the rights of members of other estates.[32] It seems unfortunate that when a narrow stage opened to play out a discussion of reforms, the participants found it so difficult to avoid villainizing each other and adopting overblown gestures to play to the largest possible audience. It is also ironic that as Bunakov chose a role on the national political stage—representing the larger interests of "the people"—his new theatre may have failed because he lacked the flexibility to work with peasant actors who were developing a clearer sense of their personal interests and economic worth.

THE CENSORS ADAPT

The theatre censorship had taken steps in 1901 that suggested concern about a form of communication expanding too rapidly for comfort.[33] A new position was created to monitor audience reactions in private theatres to plays already passed by the censor. E. M. Pchel'nikov commented in his first report on the importance of regulation for the lower orders.

> Only . . . the most attentive control can ensure that the powerful influence of theatre is directed toward a positive effect on the simple folk. Insufficient control—or, worse, none at all—could give rise to the most undesirable and troublesome repercussions, since the unprepared theatre viewer is always inclined to take on faith everything he sees or hears in the theatre. His lower level of development leaves him no means of evaluating his impressions critically.[34]

He also expressed reservations over expansion of Temperance trusteeship theatres. In 1901 the trustees expended 7 percent of their budget in the provinces. He urged that they be opened only where a demand for theatrical entertainment already existed, and that their construction for the time being be limited to "cities, especially important factories and trading settlements."

At about the same time, Minister of the Interior Sipiagin issued a circular tightening supervision of entertainments for workers. According to an *Iskra* editorial published in October 1901, "The . . . circular requires that before giving permission for a theatrical presentation, concert evening or reading, the authorities determine the true goals pursued—that is, investigate the good intentions of the producer."[35] In subsequent issues the Social Democratic paper followed police repression of theatre, which increased, it argued, with the growth of worker unrest.

Just a month after "Bloody Sunday" opened the 1905 revolution, a committee convened to review the theatre censorship. It would include Prince N. V. Shakhovskoi, representing the Ministry of the Interior; O. I. Lamkert, censor at the Main Administration of Post and Telegraph; S. A. Vereshchagin, a censor of dramatic works at the Main Administration on Press Affairs; and jurist A. F. Koni. Participants with theatre backgrounds were A. E. Molchanov, president of the Imperial Theatrical Society, E. P. Karpov, director of the Saint Petersburg Maly Theatre, Suvorin, and Nemirovich-Danchenko. At this first meeting Prince Shakhovskoi enunciated the significance his ministry attached to the regulation of theatre in maintaining social order. "The questions and tendencies stirring contemporary life that are reflected in stage productions can produce unusual social animation and may have innumerable consequences."[36] The committee prepared to review the theatre censorship policies of England, France, Germany, Portugal, and Italy.

The 1905 review concerned itself only with censorship for performance of plays, not their publication. (But because most dramatic compositions at that time still came to less than ten printed pages, they fell under the prior censorship requirement for publication in any case.) Two meetings in May would be devoted to discussion of proposals to change theatre censorship.

At the 5 May meeting of the committee on censorship, Nemirovich-Danchenko proposed that theatrical censorship be abolished altogether. As a playwright, he had struggled with the drama censors for twenty years. "The censorship," he claimed, "has exterminated many talented productions in order to strengthen its influence on the public."[37] It ruled the most important contemporary issues off-limits for treatment on stage. A student could not speak of student demonstrations. No worker could talk about the labor movement, no peasant about the shortage of land. It was absolutely forbidden to speculate about God. Nemirovich did not cite it, but the censor's rejection in 1896 of his application to authorize two of his comedies, *Last Will* and *A Lucky Man*, for popular audiences, neatly illustrated his point: "Both these plays . . . would, I think, be completely undesirable for popular theatres since they not only do not include anything educational for the people, but touch upon various social and moral questions completely incomprehensible to the simple and uneducated public and can only introduce uncertainty into the healthy popular understanding of marriage and conjugal duties."[38]

Suvorin objected that drama censorship existed all over Europe and in England apparently maintained a tougher stance than in Russia. Moreover, he pointed out, men took their families to the theatre with the expectation that the government protected them from exposure to anything unsuitable for wives and children. Prince Shakhovskoi reminded the group that plays and even songs for the general public were forbidden by statute from including indecent words or actions that could be harmful to anyone.

Nemirovich then turned to the arbitrary character of theatrical censorship. One often received notice that one's play had been rejected without the slightest hint of the basis for the decision. And of course when the censor decided to authorize a play with cuts, he had no obligation to explain why he cut particular words and phrases. Karpov agreed that "we have to know what we cannot touch upon," and alluded to the confusion caused by seeing plays like Pisemsky's *A Financial Genius* passed and then suddenly forbidden. Censor Vereshchagin listed some of the burdens he and his colleagues worked under. Too many circulars had piled up; it would be logical to introduce the collegial principle to censoring. In the case of historical plays, they consulted the censor of the imperial court. Thus *The Death of Ivan the Dread* was forbidden in the provinces by imperial command. Similarly, it was forbidden to portray persons of the Romanov house on the stage. Although the decision on each individual play was taken by the censor assigned to read it, the head of the Main Administration received complaints, and sometimes the Council of the Main Administration determined whether to forbid a play.

The committee considered a slightly different form of Nemirovich's proposal. The Society of Dramatic Writers and Opera Composers recommended combining the theatre and general censorship, so that only published plays could be performed and only a court decree could block a play's performance. This seemed undesirable to some because the cost of prior publication would be too great for many theatres to bear. Vereshchagin said that of 2,334 plays submitted to the censorship committee in 1903, some 249 had been forbidden. In 1904, some 266 of 2,360 were denied registration for popular audiences.

Speaking for the Ministry of the Interior, Prince Shakhovskoi noted the recent rapid progress of theatre in Russia.

> Theatre in this country is growing by leaps and bounds. While formerly only the largest provincial cities (besides the capitals) had permanent theatres, today there is hardly a provincial city without one. Theatre has begun to be a necessity for society, and as this happened, its importance for and influence on the public has grown. It is attempting to penetrate the widest possible circles of society, to become available at a cost everyone can afford.

After listening to Karpov argue for abolishing the distinction between popular and general-access theatres, he recommended repeal of the 1888 statute that created a special censorship for popular theatres. Nonetheless, he thought it essential to retain theatre censorship. While he seemed not to fear any philosophical or political impact the theatre might have on the masses, he, like Karpov, worried about malign influence from noisy, vacuous entertainments and "pornographic farces" that had begun to be imported from France and Germany in the 1860s. "The only thing the public needs to be protected from is operettas, comic ditties, satirical songs, and the light productions that develop bad taste and corrupt manners." The worthless offerings had now, he averred, "attained a colossal scale."

The committee discussed decentralization, with a censor's office in each province. I. F. Koni valued the benefits of national uniformity, suggesting that a circle of professors of art or literature take over at the center—credentialed scholars with an interest in the work.[39] His suggestion confirms Habermas's observation that the authority of specialists overtook the authority of the reasoning process as the Public Sphere expanded. But it should be noted that in Russia, where the state had played an exceptionally prominent role in organizing professional education, professionals had long expected the government to recognize their special attainments.[40]

In the end, no formal changes whatever were made in theatre censorship in 1905. The existing structure responded to perceived challenges. The censor charged with monitoring the actual impact of plays on audiences did not fail to notice the sudden expansion of dramatic product available. Pchel'nikov wrote a memo 14 May 1905 noting the heightened theatrical activity brought about by the trusteeships and by private theatres lowering admissions and attracting lower-class audiences. Though February had brought new peasant revolts in the black earth provinces and April, the radical demands of the zemstvos and professional organizations, Pchel'nikov took a calm view of the growth of theatre. In the present season, he observed, amateur theatrical circles had sprung up among workers in printing, in weaving, and in manufacturing (at the Jena works). "To put it briefly, a sort of theatre fever has sprung up."[41] This development, he said, raised a "real need to regulate it, to guide it in a more or less precise channel." To that end, he proposed to divide all theatres into two groups: those serving cities, and rural theatres serving mainly agricultural populations. Special attention could be given to supervising the former, as required by recent developments. He saw no immediate cause for alarm from the "theatre fever," because modern drama was so difficult for audiences to grasp. He had spoken in his report on Moscow private theatres for 1901–2 of the "new direction" taken by the Art Theatre in a season when 37 percent of its performances were of Chekhov and 35 percent of Ibsen and Hauptmann. These plays did not, in his experience, uplift the public's spirits. On the contrary, they carried the viewer "to the limit of his endurance, oppressing his spiritual state." Nothing here to threaten the fabric of society. He called attention to a tendency on the part of directors since the 1897 All-Russian Conference of Theatre Personnel to "exert influence on the insufficiently developed new viewer" by acquainting him with the newest dramatic literature. These plays "analyzed the most delicate fibers of human existence" and "developed their ideas in the thickest fog." He could not consider them dangerous, because he had seen with his own eyes that even the intelligentsia portion of the audience was often far from understanding completely the plays of the classical repertory.[42] In his opinion, no struggle could be successful against the fashionable direction in the contemporary dramatic literature. No defensive measures could be introduced with positive results.

Censors' rulings on specific plays indicated a cognizance of developments in public opinion, but nothing like panic over the possibility that developments in the arts could topple the autocracy. Pchel'nikov noted in his 1904 report that he had had to "tone down" Brutus's monologue in the first act of *Julius Caesar* at the Art Theatre. At the end of March 1905 the popular theatre censorship rejected a request to approve the vaudeville by D. T.

Lenskii, *Lev Gurevich Sinichkin, or The Provincial Debutante.* This work, a particular favorite of Stanislavsky, had only recently been authorized for general audiences.[43] The censor ruled, "The work . . . is hardly suitable for popular theatre, since the author presents the Russian aristocracy in such a caricatured form that it is undesirable for the people."[44] On 23 June the Main Administration ordered the governor of Moscow to reprimand the Zoological Garden theatre management for its provocative staging of a recently authorized dramatization of a Russian fairy tale, *Konek-Gorbunov.* "The tsar is presented as an extremely weak old man, getting tangled up in his purple robes, falling off the throne, receiving blows on the back from Ivanushka the Fool." The presentation, moreover, deviated from the censored text. In view of "the dangerous and divisive influence which it could have, in its present form, on the viewers," the production was to be removed.[45]

Vereshchagin mentioned in the 10 May meeting of the censorship committee that a production of *William Tell* in Odessa recently had precipitated a brawl because it showed a popular uprising on the stage. A month later, the crew of the battleship *Potemkin* mutinied in Odessa and set out to sea, in one of the more colorful events of the revolution. The censorship withdrew authorization for *William Tell*'s production. But local policing, which should have anticipated such an extreme reaction among viewers, had arguably shown itself to be the weak link in the system. The Main Administration sent out a reminder of local responsibilities on 25 January 1906, in the form of circular number 758, emphasizing that "an indispensable obligation of the police [is] steadfast supervision so that dramatic productions presented on stages *are in strict compliance with the censored copies of the texts* of these plays."[46]

Strikes also closed theatres. The 1905–7 period saw four popular theatres shut down in Moscow and the number of productions and size of audience decline steadily.[47] Nevertheless, the authorities' measures to control popular theatre in time of revolution were surprisingly haphazard. One writer in 1905 anticipated that the vigilant eye of the drama censor would probably remain focused on the popular theatre for a long time. "But," he insisted, "a certain weakening with regard to popular theatre is observed all the same."[48] While a few plays were withheld from popular audiences by flustered censors in decisions that strain credulity, the government appears to have continued to support popular theatre as an enterprise to raise the cultural level of the masses. In November 1906, for example, Chekhov's *Uncle Vania* was authorized for popular audiences.

In 1906 the Saint Petersburg theatres began to show more political commitment, except for the Nicholas II People's House, Suvorin's theatre (which played patriotic fare), and the Aleksandrinsky, which tried to steer a middle course. Nevertheless, the censors in reviewing specific plays proposed for popular audiences took a cautiously accommodative stance.

A close reading of the censors' rulings from 1905 through 1907 reveals that the regulators attempted to broaden the range of fare available to popular theatre audiences, while sedulously guarding against incendiary provocation. The "protective power" showed itself to be "thoughtful of detail, orderly, provident, and gentle." In March 1905 censor Mikhail Tolstoi reviewed a request to authorize plays that had been forbidden in 1836 and 1841, when the Third Section censored drama. He could not fathom from Count Benkendorff's resolution what was objectionable about the works. Finding them "extremely patriotic," he lifted the ban.[49] A censor authorizing the heretofore forbidden *Patalen the Lawyer* on 22 March observed, "This comedy in the costumes of the sixteenth–seventeenth century is so naive that it could scarcely arouse anything in the *narod* besides laughter." Censor F. Lashker in December reversed an earlier ruling forbidding *Uriel Acosta;* the ruling alleged the play glorified the Jewish creed and disdained Christianity. Lashker considered that the play did neither, and authorized it for popular theatres. Censor Khereshchagin, also in December, lifted an unfavorable ruling of 1893 on Pisemsky's comedy *The Division* (*Razdel* [1853]). The play portrayed relatives of a recently deceased landlord quarreling over his estate. Judging the types represented to be "rather caricatured," he saw nothing "harmful for the people" in it. At the end of the year Lashker authorized *The Power of Darkness* for popular audiences. In explaining his decision, he said,

> Considering the high moral idea contained in this drama, and also the circumstance that it was banned not so much out of censorship considerations as out of a desire not to popularize Tolstoy's name among the people, I propose that it would be just to permit its presentation in popular theatres—all the more since at the present time it is scarcely necessary to reckon with Tolstoy as a proponent of extreme ideas.[50]

The censors found it possible in 1906 to authorize a number of plays after material deemed offensive or dangerous had been excised. A request was granted to present the opera *Dubrovsky,* with libretto by Modest Tchaikovsky, at the Nicholas II People's House after major revisions. In the new version of Pushkin's account of an idealistic young nobleman turned outlaw by a corruptible legal system, the law clerks were recycled into bailiffs, and Dubrovsky—not his zealous peasants—set fire to his house! When P. P. Gaideburov petitioned to present *Scenes on the Volga,* a play containing references to a "Golden Charter" (a grant from the sovereign of land and freedom to serfs, supposedly suppressed by landlords), he tried to get an unfavorable ruling overturned by adding lines stating categorically that rumors of such a document were manufactured by persons of evil intent. But this attempt to neutralize something objectionable failed. In August a revised adaptation by S. Mel'nikov for the popular stage of Meyerbeer's *John of Ley-*

den recast a peasant movement against landlords into an uprising against occupying Spaniards. Once the opera represented a people striving to throw off a foreign yoke, it became acceptable to the censor. Mussorgsky's opera *Khovanshchina,* found unsuitable for popular theatres in September 1905 because of the dark picture it painted of revolt and civil war in the regency of Sofia Alekseevna, was passed 4 October 1906, after undergoing extensive abridgment.

Later that month Mikhail Tolstoi reversed a censor's rejection in 1899 of *Dzhentelmen,* a play about a new *meshchanin* (petit bourgeois) type appearing in the milieu of Moscow merchants. He could not be sure why the play had been disapproved, but surmised that his predecessor had found its plot "too remote for popular understanding, according to the opinion prevailing at that time." Simultaneously, Khereshchagin honored Nemirovich-Danchenko's request to reconsider his comedy *Last Will* for popular audiences. This time the censor passed it, pointing out that many plays of similar content had been approved for popular audiences. In November S. Naidenov's comedy *A Wealthy Man,* rejected as recently as 1903, was approved by censor Lamkert. He remarked, by way of explanation to his department head, "At that time the prevailing tendency in the drama censorship was to limit the popular repertory as much as possible to plays that were either purely patriotic or moralizing. Plays where types from the higher classes of society and even the merchantry were depicted in anything less than completely attractive form were not permitted at all on the popular stage." Now that it was deemed possible to expand that repertory, he could recommend *A Wealthy Man* because its only fault had been to present a merchant and his subordinate with both good and bad qualities.

Censor Tolstoi revealed something of his agency's view of the Nicholas II People's House when he approved Mel'nikov's version of Rossini's *William Tell* exclusively for that theatre. He said its public consisted mainly of "officers, officials, and people like them or otherwise well-off." Obviously it could not be authorized for the provinces, where audiences might identify themselves with the role of the Swiss. He added that in the rear of the People's House, where simple folk might be able to afford a seat, "it is impossible to make out the words."[51] In May 1907 the Theatrical Society petitioned to secure approval of Chekhov's *The Cherry Orchard* for popular theatres. A similar petition had been rejected 16 January 1906 on grounds that it "depicts the degeneration of the gentry in vivid colors." But it could now be approved, along with *Ivanov,* since it had nothing whatever to say of the relations between landowners and peasants.

Yet even as the censors accommodated an expanded repertory for the popular theatre, they had continued to reject plays for which such authorization was sought. Late in January 1905, Tolstoi reviewed an adaptation by S. A. Iur'ev of Lope de Vega's *Star of Seville.* In the play the king of Spain commands a knight to fight a duel with his sister's fiancé to avenge an insult to his majesty. A court, disregarding the king's command, sentences the knight to death for his role in the fatal duel. The denouement simplified Tolstoi's task: "The outcome is the king's public repentance and gift to the people of the right to participate consultatively in government affairs through estate representation. In view of such a conclusion, I propose that the play not be authorized for the people nor for general audiences." (In a little more than six months the tsar's minister of the interior would propose the creation of a national consultative assembly—only to discover that most Russians considered such an institution to represent an insufficient political concession from the autocracy.)

Other historical plays had similarly uncomfortable resonances. In May 1906 Schiller's *Don Carlos,* in M. M. Dostoevsky's translation, approved for general audiences, failed the test for admission to the popular repertory. "The cruel reign of Philip of Spain and his minion the Duke of Alba discredit the concept of monarchy . . . and the revolt against the king further increases the play's harmful potential for the *narod.*" B. Grinchenko's adaption of Schiller's *William Tell,* proposed for popular audiences 5 February 1907, met rejection on different grounds: "I propose that this play not be approved for the Little Russian stage, all the more because its production could, in my opinion, facilitate the arousal of frontier patriotism and fan the separatist strivings of the Ukrainophiles." By this point in the revolution, Ukrainian nationalism had emerged as a considerable force, along with Polish, Georgian, Baltic, and Muslim nationalism.

Through the whole of the revolutionary period the censors refused to authorize plays for popular audiences that presented the existing relations between social groups in an unfavorable light. If it occurred to them that they thereby deprived theatre of the right to a kind of scrutiny that constituted one of its ancient and original offices, no trace of remorse registers in their reports. On 25 April 1906 *An Easy Raise (Legkaia nadbavka),* a play specifically intended for popular theatres, failed to qualify. The censor summarized its defects: "Basically it is about the exploitation of poor people by kulaks, a foreigner's mockery of the Russian people, and the heartlessness of rich people." Moreover, the play showed aristocratic types behaving offensively and was filled with complaints about the lack of humanity of people of means. A month later a censor refused to reverse the 1891 decision forbidding *A Happy Day* from playing in popular theatres. This farce about a provincial postmaster who takes bribes, beats subordinates, and spends his time reading newspapers he cannot understand was deemed inappropriate because it showed a representative of state power compelling people to commit illegal acts. A second censor reviewing this decision concurred, deploring "the tendency prevailing in our time to discredit indiscriminately the holders of government power, from small to great, in the public's eyes.

Baronessa Fekla, a one-act farce by S. F. Saburov about a down-on-his-luck baron who courts his cook when he believes she holds a winning lottery ticket, was judged "extremely undesirable for popular theatres" in July 1905. D. E. F. Aubert's opera *Fanella,* about the scion of an old family who seduces and abandons a girl who is mute, met rejection because "the depiction of violence practiced illegally by representatives of the highest estates [*sosloviia*] on the lowest classes [*klassy*] and lynch law, to which the *narod* resorts in such cases, can scarcely be desirable on the stages of popular theatres." Also in August 1905, the author of the play *Two Powers* requested that the popular theatre censorship review its 1894 decision to disallow the work. The drama contrasts a well-off kulak who prospers by robbing other peasants with the complicity of the local police, and his philanthropic son, a physician who treats the poor free of charge. The son is assisted by a wealthy count, a man full of humanitarian ideas who opens a tea room. The kulak raises the peasants against his son by giving them drink and persuading them that he is responsible for the appearance of cholera in the district. The peasants head for the tea room to kill the doctor. The censors found the play unsuitable still.

Just a month before the general strike of October 1905, Rossini's version of *William Tell* was again rejected for popular audiences. The censor explained the danger:

> In these perilous times Russia is experiencing, I consider it impossible to present this opera on popular stages. Especially in border regions with foreign populations . . . [where] more or less serious ferment is manifest, . . . this opera . . . could exhibit harmful action to the public and present agitators an additional opportunity and free material for igniting the various tribes and arousing revolt. France offers a historical example of the workings of such theatrical representation on a public already prone to agitation. There the first outburst of the Revolution of 1848 occurred in a theatre as an inflammatory play was being presented. In anticipation of something similar, I would propose that it would not be prudent to permit this [work] on popular stages.

Two weeks later, A. V. Sukhovo-Kobylin's comedy *Raspliuev's Merry Days (Raspliuevskie veselye dni)* failed to pass muster. The censor cautioned,

> Presenting a satire on the administration in general and the police in particular, this play is completely unsuitable for popular theatres. The author . . . underlines the arbitrariness, extortion, and bribery of representatives of government power with a bright red pencil. Such plays discrediting power—it cannot be ignored—are unconditionally harmful for simple folk . . . and I would propose that it . . . not be authorized for popular theatres at all.

In December another Sukhovo-Kobylin play, *Business Matters (Delo),* met a similar fate. About a family ruined by paying bribes to move a lawsuit through the court system, the play was judged by censor Khereshchagin to be artistically constructed but to concentrate on atypical situations. He found it "contains many disturbing truths, and therefore if presented on the stages of popular theatres it would produce an extremely unpropitious impression." One of Ostrovsky's very best plays, *A Ward of the Mistress,* again met rejection for popular audiences. The censorship stood on its 1894 decision that the play presented relationships between the old landlords and their servants from such a negative point of view that to approve it "seems completely impossible."

Several plays rejected in 1906 and 1907 were written around remarkably unpromising subjects, considering the popular theatre censorship's mandate. That they were submitted for consideration at all seems more surprising than that they were rejected. V. Demidov's *The Convict,* set in a prison, centered on a peasant. Exiled to Siberia for robbery, he escaped and returned to his village. Khereshchagin noted, "The incarcerated complain about the arbitrariness of the authorities, who on the one hand sentence people to hard labor for the most trifling crimes while on the other real thieves go scot-free. . . . Portrayal of prisoners' escapes and their grumbling about unjust treatment by the authorities are hardly appropriate on the stages of popular theatres." A comedy called *Batman Dushkin's Day* elicited a terse rejection on 7 August 1907: "A play that dramatizes the intolerable situation of a batman ordered about by numerous members of an officer's family and their spoiled servants is not permissible for the stages of popular theatres." A. Bakhmet'ev, who wrote *A Village Teacher (Friend of the People),* petitioned for its authorization. The censor ruled, "Considering that it presents district authorities in a negative manner, indulging the local kulaks who oppose the enlightening activity of the teacher Laptev and arrest him, I consider it necessary to refuse the author's petition."

Apart from authorization for Halévy's *The Jewess,* which in April 1906 lifted the ban originally motivated by the work's "depiction of Christian oppression of Jews," dramas portraying Jewish life fared badly. Censor Tolstoi observed of Halévy's work, "It is scarcely possible to suppose that the public could find any analogy with the present epoch in a plot treating the persecution of the Jews at the time of the Catholic inquisitions." Khereshchagin rejected three plays set in the present in January and February 1907. He said of S. Al'fredov's *Without a Homeland,*

> The content consists of judgments about the oppression of Jews and limits on their rights imposed by the government. The play is filled with conversations about the horrors of Jewish pogroms and appeals to struggle for Jewish equality. It is permeated with hatred for the peasantry. [It] is extremely tendentious and . . . cannot be allowed on the stage.

Story of a Jew, by Ia. M. Gerkez, merited even more summary dismissal. "In this play the author dramatizes the struggle of the Jews with the Christians and the oppression of the Jews, who groan from injustices. Mindful that this play is extremely tendentious, I propose that it be forbidden." In July the administration of the People's House in Kharkov petitioned to present E. N. Chirikov's *The Jews* (1905). The censor ruled, "Keeping in mind that the depiction of a Jewish pogrom on the popular stage could hardly be considered appropriate, I would advise that the petition be refused."

The popular theatre censors also showed a striking antipathy to antique classics and antique themes. V. Alekseev had translated Sophocles' *Oedipus the King* for popular audiences, but failed to secure authorization for its performance in 1899. The censor turned him down again on 23 November 1906: "Incest is described in the play under review. Oedipus kills his father and marries his own mother, and children are born as a result of this union. Such immoral scenes are completely impermissible in popular theatres." Fedor Sologub's *Gift of the Wise Bee* treated the cult of Dionysus, a theme influential among Russian artists at the beginning of the century. The censor could not countenance it for the folk, even when the subject was the god whose celebration engendered theatre in the first place—as his report of 6 July 1907 shows. "In the second act of this tragedy, whose subject is taken from the time of the Trojan War, the festivals of Dionysus are depicted, in the course of which the actors, inspired by voluptuous dancing, uncover their persons. Recognizing that the depiction of such rites is completely impermissible on the stage, I would propose that this play be forbidden performance."

The censors' efforts to augment the popular theatre repertory reflect a determination to be reasonable and consistent in their rulings. Their reports show that they still considered the simple folk to be excitable and highly suggestible. Still, with the expansion of the public sphere, the imperial bureaucrats' image of the folk lost its capacity to terrify. In place of Pobedonostsev's instinctive, amoral brutes in sheepskins, they saw working people in search of entertainment, with no need to trouble their minds over rigid social distinctions or what the social classes owed to each other.

CHEKHOV AND GORKY

The trying times that culminated in the 1905 revolution presented rich opportunities to playwrights who could ask probing questions and suggest appropriate responses and adjustments. New patterns of scientific explanation and new fashions in literary creation also beckoned to artists keen to correct their predecessors, or just to be right at last. Habermas noted a sharp difference between the relation between writer and audience at the Public Sphere's inception and at the time of the Public Sphere's transformation:

> Of Richardson's *Pamela* it could be said that it was read by the entire public, that is, by "everyone" who read at all. Roughly with the advent of naturalism

> this intimate relationship between artists and men of letters and their public dissipated a bit; at the same time the public that had been "left behind" lost its critical power over the producers.[52]

As it happened, Chekhov and Gorky both constructed plays along new lines thanks to naturalism and symbolism, and they both addressed the problem of the public that had been "left behind." Yet the two playwrights appropriated very different materials from the life around them, spoke to very different audiences, and drew very different conclusions about the way of the world. In examining their importance for popular theatre, we should determine how they respectively defined their audiences and calculated the effects of the theatrical devices they concocted. Little need be said here of Chekhov's texts, because they have triumphed, becoming accessible and available everywhere now in freshly staged and filmed renditions.

Just as the French Impressionists cast off the classical fixation with modeling the figure in isolation in favor of probing the way figures relate to each other and the way their relating charges the space between them, Chekhov concentrated on the intermediate space and its atmosphere. He insisted on his characters' responsiveness to environment in the form of atmospheric conditions and time of day. And he carefully showed their behavioral orientation to the mores of their class. He also indicated, in apparent sympathy with symbolism, a concealed inner reality behind phenomena and manifestations that is accessible only to the most finely attuned perceivers. In the first of his four major plays, *The Seagull,* he had addressed symbolist aesthetics explicitly and ironically. And his professor in *Uncle Vania* is charged by Vanya with having wasted his life "chewing over the thoughts of others on realism, naturalism, and all the other similar rubbish; for twenty-five years he has read and written about what intelligent people have long known and stupid ones have no interest in."[53] But how is this charge to be construed? Is it true that intelligent Russians had long known the ins and outs of the literary "isms"? Or is Vanya just tincturing the atmosphere here? A bit of the nomenclature of contemporary poetics finds its way into the protagonists' talk—a perfectly appropriate and necessary strategy in realist drama. But the procedure is typical: in Chekhov's late plays viewers are constantly called on to discount characters' assertions and assumptions.

What the author achieved was a supremely democratic theatre, in which the viewer must do more work than ever before.[54] Chekhov never tells his viewers what to think, but requires them to become active participants in the drama and decide where their sympathies lie as they choose from equally flawed characters, among whom good and bad qualities are equally distributed. The characters reveal their inner selves in the smallest details of their lives and so require the closest scrutiny. Here is Chekhov's avenue to humanity. But his truth, like Plato's, is difficult. If every personality has an absolute claim to respect, being a real person and expressing an inner unity requires constant work for all. Under such a regime, no concessions can be made to any intelligent human being on account of cultural disadvantage.

One specific example should suffice to indicate how Chekhov drew materials from life to construct his demanding machines. In his last play, *The Cherry Orchard,* he perfectly balances three contemporary outlooks. A feckless family of noble landowners with charm to spare are about to lose their estate. They exude an appealing atmosphere, spun from talk of such unlikely matters as sordid love affairs and family tragedies. But they are simply ludicrous when they try to incorporate philosophy or books in their conversation. A well-read young revolutionary materialist shuns small practical deeds and emotional attachments, waiting instead for a world-historical cataclysm to clear the way for human honesty, intimacy, and communication. The son of a former serf on the estate devotes himself to work and identifies with rising living standards and city people establishing some connection with the land. Yet he is clumsy and tactless, unpleasant when he crows about his money, and depressing when he talks of subdividing the old cherry orchard. Comedy is everywhere in the play: while each of the three approaches to life depicted takes in the world, none of their exponents sees himself with any clarity. Chekhov calls on his viewers to identify with one of these points of view but at the same time recognize the defects of its qualities. Chekhov's legendary tolerance is evident here, as is his ironic appreciation of the limitations imposed by having any definite viewpoint at all. One clear implication of Chekhov's vision is the inappropriateness of rage toward Russia's landed nobility. The cultural baggage that has come with their property has rendered them merely absurd. Tocqueville surely would have applauded the mature individualism at the heart of this vision.

The emergence of an audience sensible to the merit of Chekhov's vision took time. It was as if, like Goethe before him, he had determined to address the loved one hidden in the audience, individual by individual. The impact of Chekhovian drama on, and then through, two influential Russian thespians reveals much about the process of discovery in Chekhov's own lifetime.

P. P. Gaideburov came from an intellectually prominent family deeply involved in the arts. He shared an interest in writing and a social commitment with his father, P. A. Gaideburov, who had worked with Nekrasov when he edited *Sovremennik* and had founded the liberal populist journal *Nedelia (The Week)* with E. Konrad in 1872.[55] His mother had contemplated a professional acting career, but withdrew before making her debut at the Aleksandrinsky Theatre, and never acted professionally. She had gone to school with Fedotova at the Elizabeth Institute in Saint Petersburg. Pavel Pavlovich became habituated to amateur theatricals at home with the younger members of his family.

Expelled from the university for participating in an antigovernment demonstration, in 1899 he joined the company of Mme. Ushakov, an enterprising director in Minsk. A new audience for theatre had begun to emerge in the provinces in the 1890s. Demand for cheap balcony and gallery seats rocketed. After turning business away for a time, impresarios had addressed the shortage of supply and started scheduling one or two performances a week that offered all seats at reduced prices. These they designated as "general-access," in order to circumvent the Popular Theatre Censorship. The performances appealed to the new theatregoers and routinely sold out.[56] Budding provincial theatres demanded more actors and more dramatic vehicles. Gaideburov debuted as Treplev in *The Seagull,* and Mme. Ushakov cast him in no fewer than fifteen major roles. As theatre increasingly absorbed him, he became attracted to an accomplished actress nine years his senior.

N. F. Skarskaia was the daughter of F. P. Komissarzhevskii, a well-known singer who had been a friend of Mussorgsky and Dargomyzhskii and a champion of Mussorgsky's theories of musical truth.[57] Skarskaia made her acting debut in the Railroad Club in Saint Petersburg in 1899, then joined the Moscow Art Theatre, where she played Mrs. Elvsted in *Hedda Gabler* and Shakovskaia in *Tsar Fedor Ivanovich.* Her older sister, Vera Komissarzhevskaia, whom she closely resembled in appearance, formed her own very successful company after leaving the Art Theatre.

Gaideburov had performed as a student actor in Chekhov's beloved vaudeville, *The Bear,* in 1898. He had seen *The Seagull,* the first of the major plays, in its flawed premiere at the Aleksandrinsky Theatre in 1896. Some of the audience there had laughed at points in the play where it was inappropriate. Arguments broke out in the foyer over interpretation of the puzzling work. He had not understood most of it, but later recalled that

> there was something insistently unsettling about it, like a hand unceremoniously laid on [the] spirit, quietly but persistently agitating it. Something was aroused in the ordinary viewer without his volition. The author found something unsatisfactory, and we the viewers had to experience a feeling of dissatisfaction, but about what wasn't precisely explained. And it seemed to me that the viewer became agitated by this very indefiniteness and the persistence of the author's call to interior work, which he, the viewer, had to perform himself.[58]

Skarskaia also saw the Aleksandrinsky premiere: her sister played Nina. When Gaideburov first read "Three Sisters" in *Russkaia Mysl'* (Russian thought) in 1898, he did not understand it and could not imagine how it could be staged. He acted in *Uncle Vania* in Minsk in 1899, the very year the play was completed. N. S. Vasil'eva, who had acted at the Aleksandrinsky, directed him. She attentively studied the work of the Moscow Art Theatre, which had first performed *The Seagull* successfully and had become closely associated with the playwright's late work. Nevertheless, Gaideburov still was not able to play Treplev in a "Chekhovian" fashion.

It was Skarskaia who enlightened him. After her debut, she joined the Moscow Art Theatre in 1899. She played Sonia in *Uncle Vania* and had the opportunity to discuss her role with Chekhov. She left the Art Theatre revering its work, even while regretting some of Stanislavsky's excesses as a director. In 1901 she joined Gaideburov's "artel of dreamers" in Elizavetgrad. There they worked to serve more than just the ticket-buying public, regularly organizing free performances for students in the public and municipal schools. After ending the season with a substantial deficit, they moved their company to the Novgorod municipal theatre, where they found a much more sympathetic public. They proposed to lease the theatre for five years, but the city authorities declined, reasoning that with an avant-garde repertory the house could not generate sufficient revenue.

Gaideburov recalled spending many hours poring over Skarskaia's copy of *Uncle Vania* with Stanislavsky's rehearsal notes penciled in. He said that they drew from her experiences to define their subsequent creative endeavors, and that for a long time Chekhovian drama held a quite unique significance for them.[59] They agreed that most contemporary actors were at too low an intellectual level to play Chekhov and most audiences too philistine to understand him. In Zhitomir, for example, Gaideburov found that his colleagues drank a lot, patronized the brothels after the show, played cards, and devoured novels. One even sniffed cocaine. When Skarskaia insisted on *The Seagull* for her benefit in Nizhni Novgorod in 1900, the director dismissed the company early at only the second rehearsal so that he could adjourn to the baths. Not surprisingly, ensemble playing did not materialize. Still, even in these early years, audience response rewarded imperfect attempts to bring Chekhov to a larger public. Her two benefit performances attracted a full house.

In Elizavetgrad (today Kirovograd) they made major changes in production and management. A directorate of actors was given a measure of control over the way plays were staged. The company kept abreast of the latest innovations of the Moscow Art Theatre as well. In a period of four months, Gaideburov played thirty-seven roles in forty-six productions. Besides *Uncle Vania* and *Three Sisters*, they performed three plays by Gerhart Hauptmann and works by Rostand and D'Annunzio. When they ended the season with a deficit of almost eight thousand rubles, an Odessa newspaper blamed their "attempt to inoculate us with exclusively intelligentsia drama."[60]

Chekhov had elicited sharply mixed responses in Elizavetgrad. Pupils from the local Junker Cavalry School, which "held the town under continual threat of wild terror," nearly ruined a performance of *Three Sisters*. After boozing steadily in the loge, they made their way backstage brandishing weapons. In the intermission before the last act one of them stormed out on stage half-sitting, half-walking in the prop baby carriage. He demanded that the curtain be raised early so that the audience could get a look, but Gaideburov managed to dissuade him. Nevertheless, one Elizavetgrad viewer sent them a note testifying to the powerful impact their performance had on her. "I returned home from the theatre under such a strong impression of your playing that I cannot sleep until I write and thank you for the rapture it produced. You keenly understood Masha, and did not so much act as suffer through this role."

In 1902–3 Gaideburov and Skarskaia took their company to Novgorod. Here too they began the season with *Uncle Vania.* The "box office" public resented the play, and preparations for the production upset the staff as well. The set designer refused to construct a room with working doors and windows for it, because he considered "such realism betrayed the 'theatricality' of the theatre. The doors, he insisted, must be painted on canvas and the two halves open of their own accord when an actor appeared." Overruled, he left town in a rage, and Gaideburov and Skarskaia learned how to build the set themselves. Yet here as well they enjoyed some encouraging responses. The editor of the local newspaper, a former actor well known for his prowess in the Ostrovsky repertory, began the season voicing grave doubts about Chekhov's plays but ended it by praising the actors under Gaideburov's direction for their conscientious playing. The local public too began to accept Chekhov.

When the pogrom in Kishenev in 1903 caused the artel to cancel its engagements, the actors settled in the small town of Prilukakh and gave three performances a week, mainly of Russian classics. The only contemporary playwrights they performed were Chekhov and Gorky. To their surprise, *Uncle Vania* played twice to full houses. Considering the paucity of cultural opportunities in this remote area of Ukraine, Gaideburov was astonished at the warmth with which the townspeople received something so advanced.

It seemed to Gaideburov and Skarskaia that they were living at a historical moment when the oldest and most deeply held assumptions were becoming untenable. In their estimation, "life was catching up with the theatre." Attempting to explain the importance of the Chekhov dramas, Gaideburov referred to the work of two contemporary painters. One Chekhov had known and remained close friends with since youth. "The elegiac order of Levitan Russia freshened itself with a passionate faith in the Russian person and his beautiful future."[61] The other, Ilia Repin, had adopted techniques from the Impressionists. The title of one of his paintings, *What Space!* captivated Gaideburov and Skarskaia. "This was exactly our experience: 'What space! Greetings, new life!' "

The plays of Chekhov and Gorky, so different in their tone, effect, and implication, share a surprisingly wide range of theme and incident. Gorky had been quick to see that *Uncle Vania* represented significant innovation. He wrote Chekhov in 1899 that it was "a completely new form of dramatic art." And Chekhov's symbolist leanings fascinated him.

> Nobody can go farther than you along this path, no one can write so simply and about such simple things as you are able to do. After your most insignificant story everything seems crude, as though written not with a pen but a log. And—the main thing—everything seems not to be simple. . . . It is true. (G, *Ss* 28:113 [17 January 1900])

Gorky's plays followed Chekhov's example in attempting to show life in flux, without the specially constructed dramatic situations that seldom happen in reality.[62] In Gorky's vision, a grossly unjust society determined people's destiny. But that society was changing, and with enough will, its coercive power could be smashed forever. Thus naturalism figures here, with its insistence on the blind forces of the environment bearing down on the individual. But it is mated in the early plays with a rhetorical and pathetic idiom alien to anything in Chekhov, ringing strange and unnatural to late twentieth-century audiences, yet evidently appealing to Russian audiences at the beginning of the century.[63]

In his stories that began to appear in the 1890s he offered up vagabonds and drifters—characters who simply broke away from the structured legal society of estates—as worthy of the highest respect. While admitting that his outsiders were often violent, brutal, and deceitful, he held them to be superior because of their individualism.[64] If Plutarch's history disclosed character as undetermined by status, Gorky described Russians as molded by their group. Society in his view was to blame for many of the defects of its members.[65] Peasants he held in particularly low esteem.[66] One reason that workers so fascinated him was that so many of them had left villages for this alternative life.

Gorky spent the summer of 1897 in the quiet and peaceful village of Manuilovka, in the Ukrainian province of Poltava. There he directed plays and occasionally acted with village amateurs. Manuilovka was atypical, in that its people had never been serfs. He described the villagers as polite, gentle, and literate and said they possessed a clear sense of their own worth and related to the local landlord with dignity (G, *Ss* 30:295). His "troupe" consisted entirely of peasants, except for a female teacher and the sister of a writer who worked for *Russkoe bogatstvo*. The season featured Ostrovsky's *It's a Family Affair . . .* and *You Can't Live Just As You Please*, along with Potekhin's ever-popular *You Cannot Profit from Someone Else's Property*. The villagers also performed a play by the Ukrainian playwright M. P. Staritskii, as well as his dramatization of Gogol's *Taras Bulba*. Gorky had written in the *Samara Gazette* that "the goal of theatre is to agitate the soul," and his choice of plays for Manuilovka suggests an attempt to do this while gauging peasant reactions to popular chestnuts from the middle of the century.

Between his first summer at Manuilovka and 1900, Gorky changed his mind about what was needed in Russian life. In 1898 he remarked that there was "no place for heroes" in contemporary life, but in 1900 he wrote to Chekhov that a time had come that required heroes.

> Really, a time has arrived that needs heroism: everybody wants the bright, the exciting, in order to be, you know, unlike life but above it, better than it, and more beautiful. It is absolutely necessary that contemporary literature decorate life a little, and if it only begins the process life will decorate itself—that is, people will begin to live faster, more brightly.[67]

In the interval he had become rich and famous. The two-volume collection of his sketches and short stories published in 1898 sold a hundred thousand copies in its first year. Within months of its appearance he completed a story called "The Reader" *(Chitatel')*, in which he tried to clarify what he now saw as the writer's responsibilities in Russia.[68] He took the realists to task for describing existing evils—digging in the mire—without offering a way to a better life. His Reader explains that the common folk cannot lead themselves because they have known only violence and have been cowed by power. Therefore the writer-intellectual must use "levers" like anger, hatred, courage, shame, repulsion, and despair to "destroy everything on earth."

Gorky returned to Manuilovka for the summer of 1900, and he and his wife revived their local theatre. This time neither Potekhin's nor Ostrovsky's plays, whose types he had conceded were already quite dated, figured in the repertory. Instead, he turned to foreign material, staging an adaptation of Mark Twain's *Tom Sawyer* and Gerhart Hauptmann's 1898 tragedy *Drayman Henschel.* Through his wife, he tried to secure the notes made by Stanislavsky when he directed the Hauptmann play at the Art Theatre.

The Art Theatre courted Gorky to write for them. In Yalta for his health in the winter of 1900, he corresponded with the admired author of the plays that had enabled the fledgling theatre to establish itself. In March he undertook to interest Chekhov in attending some of the dress rehearsals of the plays the company would be presenting locally in a fortnight: *Uncle Vanya, The Seagull, Hedda Gabler,* and *Lonely People.*[69] Stanislavsky later confided that one of the reasons they went to Yalta was to get Chekhov and Gorky to write new plays for their use.[70] Nemirovich-Danchenko told a well-known critic that as a new theatre trying to say something new, they of course needed to cultivate new authors. Gorky had the opportunity in Yalta to become acquainted with the directors and company over long lunches, and his esteem for them only increased. One measure of his respect was the comparison he later made of the Art Theatre to "the very best Moscow had to offer—the Tretiakov gallery and Saint Basil's Cathedral." He decided it would be "a crime" not to work for it. The theatre also beckoned because his fiction was being adapted for the stage by others. *Foma Gordeev,* his 1899 novel describing the generational conflict engulfing the new middle class, appeared in no fewer than eight different versions by 1903.

Gorky first attempted to write a play at the beginning of 1900. The difficulty he experienced as he tried to move away from the story form reminded him of advice attributed to Shcheglov: "write a five-act tragedy . . . rework it into a three-act drama, then . . . into a one-act vaudeville, wait a year, burn the vaudeville, marry a rich woman—it's in the bag."[71] By July Chekhov was urging him to send his manuscript; the good doctor promised to react to it with perfect candor and underline any words not suitable for the theatre. In October Gorky read a draft of *Scenes from the Bessemenov Household* to Nemirovich, who encouraged him and suggested some rearrangement. Gorky set the work aside for a few months, and though the documentation is inadequate, the first ideas for *Na dne* (literally, "On the Bottom," but translated as "The Lower Depths") apparently came to him at this time. He completed Bessemenov, which was retitled *Meshchane* (variously translated as "The Petty Bourgeois," "Smug Citizens," "The Philistines"), in March and April 1901. In September Nemirovich came to Arzamas, where Gorky had been exiled after arrest and imprisonment in his native Nizhni Novgorod, to hear it read. He pronounced the play a success and told Gorky that it exceeded his expectations. Chekhov judged the play "very good, written in the Gorky manner, original, very interesting."[72] He even offered casting suggestions, fearing that if the production failed Gorky would give up writing for the theatre. He wrote to others of his very high regard for Gorky's talent.

Gorky called his play "noisy and bustling" when he announced its completion to Chekhov. The tone reflects one of the play's central issues: *nekul'turnost'* (lack of manners).[73] In the opening scene, Peter, the bored son of a self-important townsman, articulates his contempt for the meanness, the incessant complaining and *meshchane* bustle of the Bessemenov household. He says he believes only in individuals, free of the demands of society; he attributes his expulsion after three years in the law faculty to his having heeded society's call to be a citizen. Education has shown him what to hate, but not how to live in a constructive, socially committed way. He remains an *individual* aloof, cold, and uncommitted to anything but his private satisfaction.

Gorky chooses the topic of theatre to draw out and clarify the younger characters' attitudes toward social progress. Peter's sister declines an invitation to the theatre, saying she thinks she won't go this season: "I am sick of it. All these plays with pistol shots, sobs, and wailing only annoy and vex me. It is all so untrue. Life crushes noiselessly, without screams or tears, without anybody noticing" (G, *Ss* 6:23). These lines undoubtedly triggered theatre cognoscenti's memories of Chekhov's oft-quoted remark that "on the stage people eat, drink, play cards and meanwhile their lives are being destroyed" and his strictures concerning revolvers that appear on stage without ever firing. Lest the reference pass unnoticed, a character seated at the piano strikes "a deep, mournful note" in the middle of the speech that must resonate to the tone of the plucked string in *The Seagull.*

The lodgers, healthier sorts than the effete young Bessemenovs, are involved in amateur theatricals. Local soldiers also participate. Peter says, "I can't understand what pleasure it gives you to act with these simple folk." The widow tries to explain. "We—don't act. We share what we can with them." The student adds: "It is simply pleasant for us to be with them. They are ingenuous. When you are among them it is like breathing fresh air, as in the forest. Our brother bookworms never pause to refresh themselves" (G, *Ss* 6:28). When he learns that they intend to give a performance or two in the railroad repair shops, Peter warns them that they are wasting their time. Any pleasure to be derived from such association must be fleeting. The structure of the existing society inevitably cancels, in his view, all private efforts to pass along the advantages of cultivation.

> I'm telling you that you deceive yourselves by calling all this fuss and bustle a real occupation. You are truly convinced that it is possible to develop the personality. . . . But you are lying to yourselves. Tomorrow your commissioned officer or foreman will come along and give your individual a kick which knocks out of his head everything you had managed to put in—if you drove anything in at all.

But if the usefulness of their occupation remains questionable, there can be no doubt about the constructiveness of the family's adopted son Nil's work for the railroad, where he is about to be made depot superintendent.

Nil detests the household's constant bickering, being himself full of life and liking people. His manner of relating to others is fundamentally different from theirs. He rhapsodizes about the joys of working well and intelligently and participating in the building of a better world. He ignores Bessemenov's advice to marry a woman with a dowry, and chooses instead a seamstress who shares his enthusiasm for work. And he makes speeches, lest his actions fail to demonstrate his superiority to everyone else in the household.

> I know better than you that life is hard, that it is sickeningly cruel at times, that an untamed, brute force contorts and oppresses man. I know this, and I don't like it. It makes me indignant. I don't want things to be this way. I know that life is a serious business, but disorderly [*neustroennoe*] . . . that to put some order into it will take all my strength and ability. I know I am no dragon slayer—only an honest, healthy man—and still I say, "Why the hell not?" I'll do anything to satisfy my urge to get into the thick of things, to wade in however I can—to get involved—to help. That's where the joy of living lies buried.[74]

The play ends with Nil's abrupt departure in protest over Bessemenov's unforgivable rudeness to a courteous old man. Peter decides to marry, and one of the lodgers predicts that he will perpetuate his father's narrow and selfish style of life. Thus in *Meshchane,* Gorky considers acculturation and social progress and finds education's merit to be void when learning is harnessed to egotism.

Tolstoy, after reading the play in 1902, noted in his diary, "*Meshchane* is completely lacking in interest. The milieu is so mediocre, untypical. All this is completely useless to anybody."[75] "Heroes—," he told Gorky, "that's a lie and invention; there are simply people, and nothing else."[76] His opinion remained unaltered, according to an entry in October 1909, "Yesterday evening I read Gorky's *Meshchane.* Worthless."[77] Gorky very much disliked the play himself, but because it had "no poetry, no fire." He promised Nemirovich to write another the following winter.

The result was *The Lower Depths,* the most successful of all his plays, a popular hit from its very first performance by the Art Theatre in 1902. Its setting is a metropolitan flophouse. The rooms are in a basement, so the title refers to the characters' physical situation as well as their social status. The economic downturn of 1900–1901 naturally increased the difficulties of making a living for those on the bottom. Gorky's play therefore had a strong topical interest. As in his stories, he revealed a subculture not previously exploited by literature. A contemporary critic saw a connection to Chekhov's plays: "Chekhov expressed the aspiration for and emigration to the city, and Gorky continued Chekhov, raising the curtain that concealed this very city, the new factor in the coming period of social life."[78]

The Lower Depths, like its predecessor, is a static play, heavily freighted with speeches. The bickering motif of *Meshchane* is also carried over. This time it denotes not the mores of an estate in crisis, but the modus operandi of a whole society's outcasts. For Gorky imagines a community of marginalized Russians. The characters come from all walks of life, all estates but the clerical (an omission decreed by the censorship rules). They share a background of victimization, having suffered beatings, humiliation, and imprisonment. They quarrel incessantly, apparently deriving much of what little satisfaction they have in life from insulting and belittling each other.

When Gorky read him scenes from the play, Tolstoy clearly disapproved. He thought Luka an unsympathetic character, his goodness unbelievable. While conceding that the actor and prostitute came off well, Tolstoy offered a harsh judgment of Gorky's ability to create convincing characters for the stage: "Most of what you say comes out of yourself, and therefore you have no characters, and all your people have the same face."[79] The great popularity of Gorky's plays would trouble Tolstoy until the end of his days. He often insisted that Gorky's success derived from his discovery of a subgroup never scrutinized before: the down-and-outers, the "barefoot ones," exotic but atypical. But that alone could not account for the abiding popularity of Gorky's plays, especially the first two. He also puzzled over the fact that they were translated and read abroad. In early October 1905 he remarked that someone had helped him understand Gorky's appeal by explaining that he touched on important questions and answered them as the masses would.[80]

As a realist writer, Tolstoy was committed to the depiction of individuals located in the context of a specific society, economy, and time, making choices that represented convincing responses to external stimuli. His objection that *Meshchane* was "completely useless to anyone" clarifies the source of his discomfort with Gorky's art. Tolstoy's realism, focused on the choice-making individual responding to typical pressures, provided viewers or readers enmeshed in different circumstances (but with the same need to act) with material for self-improvement. In other words, his fictions furnished objectively accurate information that expanded and extended private experience. But a younger generation of Russian writers had appeared that shifted the focus of literature away from the individual's private concerns and independent growth. Tolstoy agreed with critic G. S. Petrov, who said that this new generation, and Gorky especially, completely evaded the high moral concerns that had been central to Russian literature.[81] While Tolstoy considered that Gorky himself led "a pure, moral life," he deeply regretted that he put his characters into "exceptionally immoral" and atypical surroundings. He could not entertain the possibility that meaningful individual growth had to wait for a transformation of the social system.

Tolstoy's most successful play, *The Power of Darkness*, enjoys its classification as naturalist drama by virtue of a gritty peasant-household setting and the shocking brutalities committed on (or just off) stage. But its central characters' identities are not determined, or even strongly conditioned by, membership in a social or economic caste. They confront temptations, but freely make believable, motivated choices, based on their own unique experiences. Gorky's characters are to a much greater extent prisoners of their status. He asks his viewers to stand back, behold the panorama of society, economy, the times, and commit first of all to actions directed toward abolishing the present unjust order of things. Such a viewpoint was irreconcilable with Tolstoy's conception of individual psychology, responsibility, and behavior.

But Tolstoy was an old man who had survived into a new era. Gorky well understood that the definition of private morality stood at the center of his differences with Tolstoy. In 1929 he wrote to Stefan Zweig, who had published an essay on Tolstoy and praised his *Reminiscences:* "In the end the moralizing ruined [Tolstoy's] life and work."[82] A few years later Thomas Mann would look back with appreciation for Gorky's attempt to present the panorama and raise the call for social justice. "Gorky's *Lower Depths*, a . . . fine play, full of the lofty humanitarianism of Naturalism. My own native element, my own era. It was greater and better, of that there can be no question."[83]

The potency of Gorky's first two plays, like that of cheap music, is not to be doubted.[84] They were seen by the authorities to represent a threat to public order. In October 1902 the Main Administration of the censorship called the attention of the governor of Nizhni Novgorod province to the fact that neither play was approved for viewing by the lower orders and that even the Moscow Art Theatre had to secure permission for each performance when it gave *Meshchane.*[85] He was requested to use his police power to make sure that *Meshchane* be permitted presentation only from copies with cuts made by the censor, and that no announcement of a production of *The Lower Depths* be permitted before censored copies became available. *Meshchane* had already played four times to full houses in the Nizhni Novgorod city theatre. The following month, local authorities in Rostov-on-Don forbade its performance, fearing that it might exacerbate tensions between workers and employers. A disturbance did break out when a Belostock theatre presented it the following February.[86] The "stormy scuffle" spilled into the street, and the police were summoned. They arrested up to thirty workers, gymnasium students, and students from a commercial school. Workers from all the factories joined the demonstration, which continued the following day. When a traveling company played *The Lower Depths* in one of the Riga theatres in March, a disturbance broke out in the gallery. In the prolonged applause after the final curtain, shouts of "Down with the autocracy!" and "Long live political freedom!" rang out. Most of the perpetrators eluded police, and the following day a crowd of around 250 demonstrators marched to police headquarters to taunt the gendarmes. Even when the plays were performed with cuts, literate audiences knew the excised lines. Handmade copies circulated widely. In 1949 a worker recalled having become acquainted with *Meshchane* in 1903 or 1904:

> A comrade from the factory gave me this book. When I came home from work I would lock myself in my room and read the play without interruption. It gave me indescribable joy. Nil became my favorite hero! And not only mine, but all the conscious workers' of that time. Gorky's *Meshchane* opened my eyes to what was going on around me.[87]

Before writing his third play, Gorky again turned his attention to the delivery of theatre to the public. But now he served the vital civic art he deemed best able to stir reason and emotion and rouse people to struggle in a *city,* Nizhni Novgorod. In 1900 he had joined a committee to build a People's House there because he saw the facility as a vehicle for popular theatre. The original plan for the People's House called for a room large enough to accommodate five hundred with a bare concrete floor for dancing.[88] Provision was made for a small stage, but none for dressing rooms or the storage of scenery. Gorky went on the construction committee in 1902 and played a role in expanding the project to a theatre seating fifteen hundred with an inclined parquet floor, a larger stage, and space for actors and sets. When funds ran out and construction halted, Gorky brought Fedor Chaliapin from

Moscow to give a concert that raised the money to finish the roof. When the building was ready in mid-1903, and it was decided to lease the theatre for a year to an impresario, Gorky intervened with a proposal to assemble a group of shareholders, organize an artel of actors, and run the theatre himself. The Society for the Propagation of Primary Education in Nizhegorod province unanimously supported his plan, and agreed to a three-year lease. Gorky raised fifteen thousand rubles by selling shares, as the Art Theatre had done. A group of actors, the first class to graduate from the Art Theatre's school, came to Nizhni Novgorod to participate. Stanislavsky and Nemirovich loaned sets for *Uncle Vanya, A Warm Heart,* and other productions.

Gorky wanted active participation by amateurs, and amateurs played leading roles in the first production, L. A. Mei's *The Tsar's Bride.* One metropolitan reviewer reported the rumor that this theatre would become a second Moscow Art Theatre. But the reactionary *Svet* (Light) said: "If such plays as *The Lower Depths* and the like can be considered among the exemplary productions facilitating the development of the masses and desirable for the softening of manners among the uneducated masses, then it can be asked, what kind of commotion will result from moving in this direction?"[89] Of course neither of Gorky's plays was authorized for production in a theatre under the jurisdiction of the popular theatre censorship. The provincial governor declined the theatre's request in 1904 that he use his authority to grant permission to present plays not on the approved list. An effort also failed to change the name of the People's House so that a "general-access" designation could be secured.

The theatre closed in May 1904. It had given 40 showings of 22 plays (half of them classics) in five months and had played new works secured by Gorky. Though some evenings sold out, the audience was not large enough to support a serious theatre restricted to the popular theatre repertory. N. A. Savin wrote in his memoir of the theatre that Gorky was not to blame: "They were difficult times."[90]

Gorky wrote his third play, *Dachniki* (Summerfolk) in 1904. Because it never attained the popularity with worker audiences that his first two plays enjoyed, little needs to be said of it here. But an aspect of its dialogic relation to Chekhov's *The Cherry Orchard,* written in 1903, deserves mention. At the beginning of act 2 of Chekhov's play, a former serf on Madame Ranevskaia's estate who has become a successful merchant describes a scheme that will enable her family to save their property from bankruptcy by leasing plots in the eponymous orchard to summerfolk. She finds the idea repugnant, and replies, "Dachas and summerfolk—it is so vulgar, if you'll forgive my saying so." She has already established her ability to create a charming, almost magical connection with her environment. She has spoken of the orchard's renown, her son's drowning in the river, her decision to return from France to her own country. She has addressed her bookcase affectionately. And she has so far maintained a kindly tone toward the peasant-turned-merchant, demonstrating the skill one would expect of a gentlewoman in dealing effectively with other ranks. But her persona slips momentarily when Lopakhin sings a line from a vaudeville ditty and confides that he has been to see "a really funny play" the night before. The idea of someone who has not mastered the code of refined manners consuming entertainments above his station is an enormity sufficient to break her composure. Her aristocratic aura vanishes, and she fires back: "You people shouldn't go and see plays. You should try watching your own performance instead. What drab lives you lead and what a lot of rubbish you talk" (C, *Ss* 10:630). It is a hilarious moment in Chekhov's last comedy, given the account she has just volunteered of her ill-fated romances, and the rubbish she herself has been talking.

In *Summerfolk* Gorky sets himself the task of imagining the cherry orchard subdivided and fitted out with villas. He advances his inquiry into contemporary social history by further presuming that the summer homes are occupied by "the children of cooks and laundresses" who have acquired education, money, and leisure. And how do they live now? They are still bickering! The positive hero is a female doctor, who tells the others they have no right to poison the air with their groans. She herself serves the people, and she begs the others to end their social isolation and work to improve the lives of their kin who still sweat in darkness. Most of the summerfolk, however, live frivolously. They rehearse sporadically for an amateur theatrical while they gossip, drink, quarrel, and conduct their love affairs. *Summerfolk* represents a modest retreat from the intransigence of Gorky's first two plays because it suggests that the masses, when they acquire education, have a responsibility to work actively on others' behalf even before attacking the flawed social system.

Summerfolk saw no abatement of Gorky's rather crass proclivity for affect manipulation in the theatre. When he read it to the Art Theatre company in April 1904 it provoked a scathing critique in a letter from Nemirovich, who called the play shapeless, formless, plotless—little more than raw material.[91] Nemirovich particularly objected to the lack of respect Gorky showed in it for the Russian intelligentsia. The director's letter so incensed Gorky that he refused henceforth to let any company associated with Nemirovich perform his works. The Art Theatre's most important financial backer, Savva Morozov, angrily resigned from the board over Nemirovich's disparaging assault.

Gorky was in Saint Petersburg when a confrontation between workers and the government threatened to turn violent if a march to the Winter Palace planned for Sunday, 9 January 1905 could not be either tolerated or canceled. It seemed clear to informed observers that irate workers were about to collide with the police and military. A group of prominent men of letters asked the editor of *Pravo* to intercede with his friend Witte to forestall bloodshed. They then appointed a delegation, consisting of Gorky and another writer, two publicists, two historians, the editor, a lawyer, and an associate of Gapon to see both Witte and Mirsky.[92] Witte pleaded helplessness, but agreed to telephone Mirsky to ask him to receive the delegation. Nonetheless, they were escorted from Mirsky's residence to the police station without seeing the minister, who declined to speak with them.

The march went forward as planned, and police action in various parts of the city resulted in more than a hundred deaths. Gapon escaped, shaved his beard, and wound up in Gorky's apartment. That afternoon, Gorky gave a speech at the public library. In the evening he spoke at a meeting of the Free Economic Society and introduced the disguised Gapon as a worker. Samuel Harper, an American fluent in Russian who happened to be in the city at the time, recorded some gossip about the event from an interview with a Tatar school teacher: "Only a few recognized [Gapon]. Gorky was not ultimately in with him . . . but only kind of literary sympathy. No truth in rumor that he and Gapon were working on a republic."[93] The government, ever jealous of its authority, nonetheless arrested the delegation that had tried to see Mirsky, on the charge that they had declared themselves to be a "provisional government." Gorky repaired to Riga, where he was arrested. In his enthusiasm, he had cabled the Hearst newspapers in New York: "The Russian Revolution has begun!" On 11 January he was imprisoned in the Peter and Paul fortress.

While in prison Gorky wrote his fourth play, *Children of the Sun (Deti solntsa).* If he had loudly criticized Russia's intelligentsia since his emergence as a best-selling author and had cruelly caricatured the figure of the revered writer-*intelligent* in *Summerfolk,* he now reconsidered. Looking back years later he recalled his frame of mind after "Bloody Sunday." "An uneasy sense of the spiritual isolation of the intelligentsia . . . from the popular mood pursued me more or less insistently all my life. . . . If the dissociation of will and intellect is a serious calamity in the life of an individual, this rupture is a tragedy in the life of a people."[94] In this new play he imagined a sympathetic family of educated Russians who lived a lofty and generous version of the life of the mind. The Protasovs' disinterested dedication to science and culture confers an undeniable nobility, but is responsible for their ineptitude as well. The play describes their confrontation with ignorance and an explosion of elemental mass violence. It can be seen as a reflection on the practical limits to the expansion of the public sphere, the intractability of the masses, and their resistance to enlightenment.

The contemporary theme of light's fundamental, almost magical powers —so pervasive in European letters of the turn of the century, and already prominent in Russian poetry—became the governing metaphor in Gorky's play. Max Plank had discovered in 1900 that sunlight and other electromagnetic radiation come in discrete units or packets rather than waves; Einstein's landmark 1905 paper on the special theory of relativity, in which he announced that light is propagated through space in units that move without dividing, built on this breakthrough. *Children of the Sun* concerned itself with the propagation of light as cultural enlightenment in Russia's bifurcated society.

The idea that the sun is a great healer, and that the ruling classes had conspired to impose the disastrous custom of concealing the body from it, made headway in Germany in the 1890s as part of Lebensreform (life-reform movement) and Jugendbewegung (youth movement).[95] German thinkers' appreciation of the sun's role in the development of life on earth exercised a powerful influence on Russian writers through works like science popularizer G. Klein's *Astronomical Evenings* (3d Russian ed., 1900).[96] In Hauptmann's play *The Sunken Bell,* translated into Russian by Konstantin Bal'mont in 1900, the hero abandons his Christian faith, which he finds isolates man from nature, and becomes a worshiper of the sun, which he identifies as the single source of life. The sun as a symbol of eminence and independence began to appear frequently in Russian poetry. The Russian translator of *Cyrano de Bergerac* (1897), which Gorky saw in Nizhni Novgorod in 1900 and much admired, *added* these lines to Rostand's text:

> To the road, to the road, Gascons!
> We are sons of a southern land.
> We are all under a sun that shines all day
> And we are born with sun in our blood!

Bal'mont saw the beginning of the century as an age of victory and healing, a period of new flowering of personality.[97] Gorky agreed, but rejected Bal'mont's notion that the masses were necessarily exempt from these possibilities of personality development. He constructed his play around Bal'mont's distinction between the children of the sun (the intelligentsia) and the children of the earth *(narod).*

Gorky put into the mouth of his central character, an amateur scientist, the precise words of Klein: "we, people, are children of the sun, the luminous source of life; born of the sun we shall conquer the dark fear of death. We are children of the sun! This burns in our blood, engenders proud, fiery thoughts lighting the gloom of our ignorance. It is an ocean of energy, beauty and of the intoxicating spirit of joy" (G, *Ss* 6:326). On another occasion, Protasov says "You should call your picture 'To the sun!' The source of life" (G, *Ss* 6:321). In the final scene he remarks of a peasant who has betrayed his trust, "He angered me. There is something repulsive about him. . . . People should be bright and clear . . . like the sun."[98]

Protasov, the scientist, is a general's son. His family embody the best features of the cultivated classes, behaving toward each other and the village people they encounter with perfect courtesy and attentiveness. The tone of this work differs sharply from that of Gorky's earlier plays, because in the intelligentsia surroundings, everyone is addressed respectfully. The bickering has disappeared. An old servant even chides Protasov for "talking to the *narod* as if to gentlefolk." Honest and high-minded in all their dealings, the gentry family are impractical financially and too cerebral to act decisively in their romantic relationships.

Protasov has engaged the village locksmith to construct scientific apparatus for him. The peasant builds it marvelously from his sketches and always understands just what is required. But they are miles apart in outlook. The locksmith often gets drunk and beats his wife. Protasov tries to persuade him to stop the practice, but the mechanic vows to continue until she is as humble before him as grass to the wind. He adds, by way of defense, that life has been cruel to him as well. Protasov gets further evidence of his family's distance from the people when he hires a girl fresh from the village to work for them as a maid. She drinks a whole urn full of tea and is seen to eat soap. Peasant women are depicted as especially abused here. The house porter remarks at one point, "Women cry a lot for no reason. Give her something across the back of the head and she howls."

The play's final act climaxes with the release of the full fury of the peasants' savagery. As a cholera epidemic begins to take its toll, the villagers surmise that the doctors have spread the disease to increase their business.[99] They riot and destroy the hospital barracks and break through the estate gates to confront Protasov. The locksmith denounces Protasov to the mob as "chief of the witch doctors [*Glavnyi morila*]." Gorky concludes the play quite unconvincingly by showing the mob quickly coming to its senses. The apologetic locksmith claims not to know why he lied about Protasov.

The mob scene produced tumultuous reactions when the play was performed late in 1905. At the Moscow Art Theatre the curtain came down so that the audience could calm itself. A performance in Nizhni Novgorod on 21 November 1905 produced a similar reaction.[100] It was not the allusion to revolution, but the graphic depiction of the differences in aspiration, comportment, and personality dividing intelligentsia and people that touched a raw nerve.[101] Gorky seems to confront the idea that political violence is counterproductive—and incommensurate with rational discourse. This bleak reconsideration may owe something to the circumstances under which Gorky wrote it.

Gorky's prison cell in an outward projection of the fortress was a damp, cold room with a stone floor, into which almost no daylight penetrated. As he wrote *Children of the Sun* he developed a very heavy cough and began to spit blood again. An international campaign supported by leading writers deplored the barbarity of such treatment for a consumptive and secured his release after just over a month of incarceration. Savva Morozov, the textile manufacturer who had refinanced the Art Theatre, bought shares in Gorky's Nizhni Novgorod theatre and put up his bail. Gorky joined his second wife, actress M. F. Andreeva, near Riga, and immediately began a new play, *Enemies (Vragi).*

This time a strike by textile workers gave him his subject. His factory owners, themselves no strangers to the theatre, repeatedly employ the metaphor of spectacle played before an audience hungry for entertainment as they discuss the survival of their class privileges. As one character puts it: "The people considered us interesting as long as we seemed to stand above the boredom of everyday life. But now everyday life is becoming more dramatic. And you hear shouts of: 'Hey, you clowns and comedians! Get off the stage!'" (G, *Ss* 6:509). The society depicted in *Enemies* is experiencing transformation at breakneck speed. There are said to be more lovers of art in every town. "People are becoming more cultivated." The work reflected Gorky's fervent hope that the concerted mass action he had himself observed could finally be harnessed to overthrow the old order. Unfortunately, his play failed as art, unable to render psychologically convincing the strike mentality it sought to dramatize.

In October, when the general strike in Petersburg wrested from Nicholas his pledge to establish an elected duma, Gorky and Andreeva were in Moscow working with the Art Theatre. Gorky of course wanted workers to fight on to end the autocracy, and he took heart from the courageous resistance of workers in Moscow at the end of the year. He and Andreeva proceeded to New York on a campaign to raise funds for the Bolsheviks. While summering in a lodge in the Adirondacks he wrote a novel about Russian workers achieving political maturity and organizing a strike, *The Mother (Mat').* He also finished *Enemies* there. Thus his strike fictions coincided with the Russian government's containment of the last of the revolutionary violence and dismissal of the First Duma.

Gorky's early plays examined the relations of Russia's cultural "possessors" with the rising individuals from the *narod,* who were for the first time becoming literate and claiming their right to hold opinions. They are important in the development of the popular theatre movement because of the ecstatic response they elicited from members of audiences who recognized their own predicament in them. L. N. Kleinbort, the early Soviet authority on worker theatres, found their attraction unmatched: "The workers' favorite playwright was of course Gorky."[102]

Gorky's work was remarkable for its sensitivity to the shifting popular mood as the reading public expanded and more and more people assumed the right to hold opinions. His élan, his boldness in pressing a point of view to its logical extreme, also ingratiated him to this new public. His appetite for large ideas never remained satisfied for long. Thanks to a 1913 survey by Kleinbort of his standing with peasants and workers, it is possible to form some impression of the nature of his appeal to this particular audience. Despite the title, "Maxim Gorky and the Reader from Below," the article considers the impact of Gorky's early plays and emphasizes as well the importance of Gorky's stories as vehicles for reading aloud and discussion by worker circles. [103]

Kleinbort consulted more than two hundred articles and published and unpublished letters from workers and peasants about Gorky. He found Gorky at the top of all workers' lists of favorite writers, ranked above Tolstoy and Chekhov. Peasants identified with him because he had sprung from the people and had "a good heart." One peasant mentioned his unique ability to "infect the dark, inexperienced reader with sincere love through his works." A worker wrote, "I liked Gorky because he was the first who was able to look at the life of inhabitants of night lodgings and cellars, was able to penetrate the wall concealing from us . . . the life of creatures that once were men and show us that in them there tingled the spark of God, which we deny them." They praised him for representing the masses as composed of individuals with diverse characters and opinions. A letter writer compared Gorky favorably to writers who "only fornicate with the language of the people and do not speak with it." Kleinbort found that Gorky's sermonizing appealed to popular audiences, who regarded it as a convenient avenue to instruction.[104] Gorky also mirrored his audiences in that he tended not to be analytical; the responses of those who praised him demonstrated the same characteristic.

Perhaps the most interesting aspect of these responses is their misgivings concerning Gorky's output at the end of the 1904–7 revolution. They recognized *Enemies* and *The Mother* as failures. One worker regretted that Gorky had been cut off from healthy Russian people and speculated that but for this isolation, he would have gone on to create "more multifaceted [resourceful outsiders like] Chelkash, and not holy Pavels [as in *The Mother*]."

Yet these perceived lapses neither detracted from the popularity of Gorky's plays nor diminished the desire of worker drama groups to consult him about repertory. One of Kleinbort's manuscript sources gave the following judgment on Gorky's later works: "Did Gorky stray far from the people, or did his talent begin to fail? I don't know, but I incline to the former proposition." Kleinbort himself concluded: "Was it all the same to the worker if Gorky was a Tolstoyan or a Nietzschean, or traveled in the company of Lunacharsky or Chernov? Yes, because he always had his own anger and flame."

K. V. Skorobogatov, a worker in the Obukhov factory in Saint Petersburg, recalled playing the locksmith in the factory dramatic circle's production of *The Lower Depths* on the eve of the 1905 revolution. The police had prevented them from raising the curtain on Chirikov's *The Jews.* But he considered that play "was not such a strong protest or deep analysis of the social causes of poverty as [*The Lower Depths*], which excited from the first words, awakening revolutionary emotions."[105] In his memoirs he tried to explain why working on Gorky's plays gave so much pleasure. "They always contain a deep and precisely articulated idea, masterfully fashioned characters. And what language! I always hear a powerful force in his fresh and robust words, so dynamic, so strongly connected to physical action." *The Lower Depths* made a tremendous impression on the Obukhov circle, and they knew the text so well that they dispensed with the usual prompting.

Gorky's early plays could be said to be "about" the times in which they were written as truly as Ostrovsky's. But if Gorky's work was topical, his procedures were radically antirealist. While Ostrovsky benefitted as an artist from government patronage under Alexander II, Gorky the artist defied the government and played a role in high politics himself. Gorky's plays, with their preachiness, their speechifying, their arcane references to other plays, and their quest for the heroic are far more remote from us today than the works of Ostrovsky.

PANINA'S *NARDOM*

The people's needs first came to Countess Sofia Vladimirovna Panina's attention when she was in her late teens, during a national emergency. Heiress to one of the largest family fortunes in Russia, she was approached by a schoolteacher during the famine of 1891 who apprised her of the fact that many children were arriving at the Ligovsk primary school on the outskirts of Saint Petersburg without even having had a piece of bread for breakfast. Panina agreed to set up a facility where children could eat free, and on 1 November 1891 opened a dining room accommodating fifty in a building on Ligovsk Street.[106] When the operation moved to a larger structure, she added a well-lighted reading room for the children. Lantern slides were shown in the evening. She took an interest in meeting and talking with the families of the children, and began to provide services for them as well.

Exceptional for her wealth and influence, the countess was no less remarkable for her liberal conviction in a country where faith in the people had usually taken a utopian bent in the nineteenth century. Her father died before her first birthday. Her mother, whom she described as "distinguished for her intellect and education," personally taught Sofia at home until she was ten. Several years after her father's death, her mother married I. I. Petrunkevich, a landowner and liberal constitutionalist long active in the zemstvo movement. She later credited both Petrunkevich and her mother with exercising great influence in her intellectual and moral development.[107] She completed her education in the Historical Faculty of the Petersburg Higher Women's Courses.

Panina communicated directly with the working-class people whose interests she determined to advance. Guided by their wishes and goals, she never hesitated to exploit her connections to provide what her clients requested. The success of the evening reading program suggested the need for a library. In order to secure the required authorization, she agreed to put the facility under the nominal supervision of the district inspector. The adults' enthusiasm for the readings and the library indicated a demand for more formal education. They moved quarters again, and in 1900 Panina secured permission to establish evening classes for workers, this time under the auspices of the Imperial Russian Technical Society. They circumvented the prohibition on teaching the Russian language by introducing it under the guise of Sunday school instruction. The Sunday reading gradually turned into lecture demonstrations with pictures and visual aids.

According to an anonymous typescript history in the People's House archive, interest in theatre sprang up quite spontaneously among the Ligovsk students themselves:

> The students wanted entertainment and began to put on plays, beginning with invited artists, but later performed by the students and teachers themselves. And everyone was happy to make the sets, run the lights, and come to rehearsals. Our Ligovsk audiences attended free, and although they sat on kegs, they were satisfied, even though it was crowded and stuffy.[108]

The countess decided to look for a piece of ground and build a structure specifically designed to suit their developing wants and needs. She found the site for her Nardom (People's House) near the Obvodnyi Canal, in an area crowded with factories and inhabited by workers and tradespeople. The new building was begun in June 1901. Besides the theatre, the structure included a library, kindergarten, tea room, and people's dining facility. As more popular needs were identified the complex expanded to include classrooms equipped for teaching chemistry, physics, woodworking and metalworking, an observatory (1905), and a savings-bank branch (1910). (It would even offer a legal counseling service.) Officially known as the Ligovsk People's House, it was more often referred to as Panina's People's House by those who frequented it.

The Nardom's amenities attracted a clientele from other neighborhoods. A tram line put it just half an hour from the city center. Workers came from the Narva, Moscow, and Nevsky gate areas, from the Saint Petersburg and Vyborg sides to avail themselves of its services. Some people walked ten versts and more to see the plays. The doors were open to all, and patrons came in a variety of garb, from worker smocks and peasant homespun to "German" suits and flashy uniforms.[109]

Panina invited proposals for organizing a popular theatre that would respond to genuine cultural needs, with a serious repertory. She selected the project submitted by Skarskaia and Gaideburov for inaugurating such a theatre and hired them to direct it. They opened the new Nardom theatre with *The Storm.* Skarskaia played Katerina and Gaideburov her husband. Tchaikovsky's overture preceded the play, executed on two pianos because the budget did not allow for an orchestra. The audience response shattered any illusions the couple might have had that building a public for serious theatre in a worker district would be easy. A reviewer for *Teatr i iskusstvo* sniffed that the "working" public applauded very loudly and continued applauding as they left the balcony by the stairs. "The *narod* laughs in the noisiest places. Why it laughs, and which vaudevilles 'suit' the people here are unanswered questions, despite the experience of popular theatres and all the work of those who participate in them."[110]

When Gaideburov began his duties as director of the new theatre in October 1903, he had to cope with two limitations. One was its official designation as "popular," which put them under the jurisdiction of the Popular Theatre Censorship. This obliged them to choose their plays from an authorized list that omitted most Russian and foreign classics. The other was an audience containing elements with no experience of theatregoing. Gaideburov recalled one of their first productions, *Vasilissa Melent'eva,* when not only applause and deafening whistles reached the actors, but empty vodka bottles fell at their feet. "In the scenes where Vasilissa flirts with Groznyi, or where he admires her beauty, the performers had to listen to instruction and intimate advice from experienced Don Juans from the Obvodnyi Canal. Kisses on stage were taken up with a friendly smacking of lips in the auditorium."[111] Panina herself came out to explain how much effort had been expended on the production and how many people had been involved. But she and Gaideburov would not set down strict rules of conduct for behavior in the auditorium, because they did not want to kill the spontaneity of the audience.

> The countess regarded the mission of the theatre as no less significant than the evening classes. They viewed its task as not just one of enrichment, but also of conveying . . . the bright joy of living that we call culture. Elements of artistic education are necessary for the complete development of the personality. And for this it is necessary not only to teach our viewers to think, but to observe, listen, and feel. Although it seems strange, this is often more difficult and inaccessible than the most abstract mathematical formula.[112]

They continued to insist on presenting works of artistic merit and refused to play the melodramas that drew so well at established popular theatres in the city. Gaideburov and Skarskaia agreed with Panina that the activities of existing popular theatres were haphazard and uncoordinated. They rejected Shcheglov's case for melodrama, finding a nonliterary repertory too impoverished in ideas and artistic content to be worthwhile. Three criteria governed their choice of plays: clearly delineated psychology, literary quality, and absence of hopeless pessimism.

They forged a highly dedicated company, and Gaideburov gave careful attention to casting. They presented one play a week, usually on Sunday, but occasionally on Saturday. Rehearsals lasted from two to four weeks. In the early years the audiences had no interest in seeing a play repeated during the season, so the troupe labored mightily to mount sufficient productions. Actors received between fifty and a hundred rubles a month, but could eat for almost nothing in the subsidized dining room. (Provincial actors at the time earned between four and five hundred rubles a month.)[113] But the players enjoyed working for this rough, though attentive audience. A member of the company writing after the revolution attested to the bonds between actors and audience:

> The public of the People's House, which we loved very much, was surprisingly spontaneous and effusive in its reception of plays. If they liked something they expressed themselves loudly. At intense comic moments the audience clapped, cried out, whistled and stamped their feet. . . . When lyric or dramatic scenes were being played our audience observed with quiet trepidation. And never once did I hear a cough or a chair scraping during a performance.[114]

It was the insistence on the highest standards that established the theatre's reputation. Panina had too high an opinion of the *narod*'s potential to condescend in her educational and cultural work. After favorable reviews of the General-Access Theatre appeared in the press, members of the intelligentsia began to come out to the productions.[115] They in turn helped school the locals in theatregoing. This mixed audience served as the basis for their claim for "general-access" status, which, once obtained, removed them from the jurisdiction of the Popular Theatre Censorship.

One thing that would make the Nardom theatre unique was its management's decision to continue working in the provinces cultivating audiences for the most demanding contemporary European drama. Within a few months of opening the general-access theatre Gaideburov and Skarskaia were at work on a plan that would let them resume touring in the provinces. In March 1904 they began two months of engagements that took them to more than thirty cities and towns. They performed a single play, Ibsen's *Ghosts.*[116] It was painstakingly rehearsed, and they devoted close attention to production values. At a time when traveling companies customarily cobbled together whatever sets they could find at their destination, they transported elaborate sets specifically prepared for their play.

With this solid success, Gaideburov and Skarskaia determined to form a permanent summer touring company from their general-access professionals. One of their avowed aims was to break down the cultural barriers between the Russian capitals and the provinces. In an article in the 12 February 1905 issue of *Slovo,* Gaideburov described a new touring company that would communicate the most recent developments in theatre art and demonstrate the innovations in acting and production being pioneered by the Moscow Art Theatre. It was to be called "the Wanderers" (Peredvizhniki),

> wandering because it must not belong either to the capital or to a particular corner of the provinces. Having business with an unlimited audience, freed from slavish devotion to a particular public, it can courageously embody only the forms and ideas that the theatre deems to have value.

Its purpose was to reach the growing intelligentsia employed in the countryside. Its name was the very one taken by a group of painters in 1863 who had protested government restriction and organized local exhibitions to display their realist landscapes and pictures with a social message. (The Ligovsk People's House had hosted an exhibition of Wanderers' paintings in 1904.)

Bloody Sunday marked the beginning of a revolutionary struggle that would last from January 1905 until the summer of 1906, but its immediate impact on metropolitan theatrical life was slight. The General-Access Theatre was the only one in Saint Petersburg to abort its 9 January performance—the house had sold out—and go into mourning with its audience. The massacre intensified the campaign to secure greater freedom of expression and civil liberties. Skarskaia and Gaideburov joined others signing a note "On the Needs of Russian Theatre," also printed in the 12 February issue of *Slovo,* which decried the oppression experienced by the Russian theatre and called special attention to the disabilities of popular and provincial theatre. "In the present conditions theatre drags out a wretched existence. It does not respond to the needs of society, does not meet the material needs of those working in it, and oppresses the free spirit of the artist with the dismal contradictions of reality." The theatrical profession in Russia, for the most part skittish toward revolution in 1905, hardly threatened to manipulate the *narod* from the stage. This petition comparing the yoke of censorship to the constraints imposed by inadequate material support, was the first public utterance of a political character by Russian actors. And it had been prepared under the supervision of a professor of the Mining Institute![117] Even the more freedom-minded actors followed the course of events cautiously and attempted to steer clear of the revolutionary movement. When the touring company of the Aleksandrinsky Theatre found themselves in Odessa at the time of the Potemkin mutiny, most of the actors dashed home without pausing to observe the circumstances or impact of the revolt.

In 1905 it was committed directors, like Vera Kommissarzhevskaia, who spoke out on behalf of the theatre's independence. Stanislavsky delivered a report on 2 April to the Moscow Literary-Artistic Circle blasting the theatre censorship and comparing its procedures to Dante's circles of hell in the *Divine Comedy.* He considered theatre censorship more burdensome than censorship of the other branches of art and literature in Russia precisely because theatre was the art form that acted most directly on the intellect and emotions of the masses.[118] As someone who had been effectively prevented by the government from addressing workers in mixed audiences through serious theatre, he took advantage of the more open climate for criticism to try to draw attention to the costs of such regimentation for the development of the public.

Gaideburov too believed that theatre censorship impeded the normal development of critical thinking among the newly literate. Educated Russia had long ago learned to decipher and communicate in Aesopian language, but this very language presented a barrier to newcomers. In his view the drama censors had done an effective job of insulating uneducated audiences from challenging plays. "After Ostrovsky, in this desert only flowers that germinated at moments of weakness in the regime of play censorship saw the light of the stage."[119] He had in mind plays of Tolstoy, of Hauptmann and Ibsen in translation, and above all Chekhov. The ideas of these playwrights, he said, had become familiar to all who had encountered them. But they had yet to become the everyday property of society.

The Wanderers Theatre opened 7 March 1905 with the first Russian performance of Ibsen's *Little Eyolf* (which had its very first performance in 1904) in the hall of the Tenishev School. An emblem designed for the new venture featured a griffin against an outline that suggested dressed stones or a grille, and the date 1905. In the revolutionary atmosphere it was sometimes interpreted as a symbol of rebellion. Authorities in some cities where the company toured took violent objection to the colophon displayed on posters, surmising that it represented an eagle caged and specified the year of the bird's entrapment.[120]

The actors, from the general-access company, functioned as a cooperative when they traveled. Members of the artel referred to themselves as "associates of the theatre." They toured with from four to twelve plays each season, which started usually in the spring and lasted four or five months. Each play would be performed from twenty to forty times. The Itinerant Theatre went everywhere, from Vologda to Tiflis, from Warsaw to Vladivostok. They took advantage of the expanding railway net to connect that segment of the nation's population interested in new plays and the new methods of production. Everything was lavishly rehearsed in advance; they used no prompter. Above all they honored the Moscow Art Theatre principles of ensemble playing and painstaking preparation.

Besides the Ibsen play, the Wanderers presented in their first season Arthur Schnitzler's *The Pharisee,* S. Rafalovich's *The River Flowing (Reka Idet)* and O. Dymov's *Cain (Kain).* Their audiences demonstrated little interest in these works during the first two or three seasons. Disappointingly low attendance devastated the fledgling company's finances. Countess Panina's small stipend disappeared quickly. Attempts to find subscribers for "shares" failed, for the most part, although Stanislavsky sent warm words of encouragement and five hundred rubles. It took a few years and Gaideburov's concession to importing tried-and-true classics from the Ligovsk repertory to make the new enterprise a success.

The Nardom audience had not advanced very far by the time of Bloody Sunday. Its reactions were boisterous and raucous. The best that could be said for them was that they had a respectful attitude toward the classics. At this time Gaideburov never dreamed they would develop to the point where they would want to see certain plays repeatedly. They had a great advantage—yet to be realized—in their core of workers (numbering between 500 and 1000 each year) who took night and Sunday classes in all manner of subjects. Some of them served on the Repertory Committee headed by Panina that chose the plays for the General-Access Theatre. When disagreements arose, all the actors joined in to reach a final decision. Gaideburov changed the troupe's name and took it to tour the provinces two-thirds of each year, in part because he needed the more sophisticated audiences he found there to justify polished ensemble playing and the rehearsal time the repertoire he preferred required. It remained to be seen who would be proved right, the censor or Panina and her directors. Would demanding contemporary drama fail to penetrate the masses' skulls—or would the people grow into it and, changing their view of themselves, finally demand a less regulated society?

Popular theatre expanded ever more rapidly in the contentious, argumentative times that began around 1902. Dramatic texts emerged from these new conditions that encouraged radical individualism and radical political action. These texts confirmed theatre activists in their belief that the art they served retained its exceptional importance and was on the cutting edge, delineating radical interior and exterior work that put social justice within reach at last.

The two boldest playwrights of the second *glasnost'* era both banked on individualism. Chekhov recommended interior work on the self and offered some solace for the high cost of discipline in the comic aspect of colliding identities and miscommunication. Gorky demanded exterior work, the forcible rearrangement of a society that prevented personality development of particular groups while facilitating egotistical, antisocial individualism among others. Nothing funny turned up in his plays, but like Chekhov, he called for action. For him, making plays out of current events, snatches of popular science, and philosophy represented committed social action. He engaged his own energies delivering theatre to the people, hoping that if they could be brought to see their disadvantages in a true light they would overturn an unjust society. Chekhov did not live to see the 1905 revolution, but Gorky participated in revolutionary events. The failure of crucial groups to see beyond their own narrow interests and change the social order disappointed him and changed his dramatic viewpoint.[121]

Dramatic texts not only changed minds, they gave rise to institution building. The prevailing order in Russia made it difficult to create responsive public institutions without state initiative. (The drama censors surely did their best to keep common folk "in perpetual childhood.") Yet Panina's Nardom theatre, however exceptional for Russia, was a grander enterprise than Emma Cons's contemporary "people's palace" in London. Though one of the Nardom actresses later referred to its Wanderers touring company as "a completely atypical cultural-educational institution for Russia in these years," it represented a reasonable gamble on the rapid expansion of audiences for serious drama beyond the capitals.[122] The old and new dramatic texts and the Russian theatrical traditions that had developed over a century could be trusted to determine whether a larger public took up theatre as a forum for considering their aspirations and needs. The Wanderers, hoping to rise above "a particular public" by criss-crossing the provinces, might be vulnerable to accusations of cultural imperialism, but they can equally well be seen as coming into existence thanks to the expanded Public Sphere.

Witte had tried and failed to make grassroots institution building easier in the countryside. The 1905 revolution itself produced changes that vastly simplified the process whereby audiences could experience dramatic texts and put them to use for their own purposes.

Chapter Six

New Initiatives, 1907–1914

"THE HISTORY of Russian popular theatre is undoubtedly entering into a new creative phase of development," declared the poet Alexander Blok in "About Theatre," a lecture delivered to the Theatre Club in April 1908.[1] In less than forty years, he said, theatre for the people had demonstrated that peasants and workers want "a higher culture" from plays, and not mere amusement. Popular audiences had proved immune to passing fashions that had so recently enchanted the intelligentsia. The people insisted on "grandly active characters, which modern European drama—and to some extent Russian—is unable to find in contemporary reality on account of its narrow horizons." The popular audience seemed to him "the most open to the content of ideas." "This public, and no other, enables the actors to feel the real life in their work and gives them real wings" (273–74).

Blok spoke hopefully of "seeds scattered on the ground and already sprouting," and "new growths struggling for air and light." He recalled how *The Storm* had transfixed the masses when they first tasted literary theatre on rickety stages under the stars. They, like Katerina Kobanova, had now stopped dreaming of "heavenly trees and mountains" and begun to dream of freedom.

> It is our springtime—a late spring, and there are already threatening clouds in the sky. The words of the heroine of Ostrovsky's great symbolic drama are coming true, for a storm is bearing down upon us. It . . . makes us feel suffocated and terrified. Any day now the banging on the doors of our theatres will come not from the sated body of our contemporary intelligentsia, but from a new one—lively, demanding and audacious. We shall be ready to meet this *youth*. It will resolve our contradictions; it will lift the burden from tired shoulders; it will inspire or it will destroy everything. And we shall eternally remember the prophetic words of the creator of Solness, penetratingly prophetic, frighteningly menacing: "Youth is retribution."[2]

He envisioned a new, healthy intelligentsia, enriched by energetic recruits from the folk, boldly creating a high theatre with a new repertory, once "thousands of eyes beyond our footlights begin to glow with satisfaction *and self-consciousness*" (274–75; emphasis added).

It seemed to Blok that Russia was on the threshold of a new inclusive culture. Youth would topple the old high culture, which had been created through the instrumentality of "the helpers and servers" but without regard for their needs. While he was writing "About Theatre," Blok corresponded with the young peasant poet Nikolai Klyuev. They shared an interest in the problem of communication between artist and audience, and Blok helped get his poems published. But the peasant's rage over the inequality of their positions brought home to Blok Russia's acute need for a common culture within which all could work freely. Blok published part of a letter from Klyuev that testified to the persistence and depth of social alienation.[3] It is noteworthy that Blok identified theatre as the art that had now reached the point where popular support and participation approached a critical mass that made something new possible.

Blok's choice of theatre as the locus for a breakthrough to a new common culture had a solid basis in developments after 1905, for theatre was now penetrating the countryside as never before. Gaideburov's and Skarskaia's Wanderers company had finally found a supportive audience for their mobile productions.[4] Blok remarked in a November 1908 speech to the Religious-Philosophical Society in Saint Petersburg that "it pleased Gogol and many Russian writers to picture Russia as the very embodiment of quiet and sleep; but this sleep is ending; the quiet is being replaced by a distant and growing roar quite unlike the cacophonous roar of the town."[5]

Confirmation of rapid changes in outlook and self-image of peasants after 1905 is to be found in the personal observations of Samuel Harper. In 1906 he covered the Duma as an accredited press representative. There he systematically interviewed peasant deputies, with the long-range objective of writing an article on peasant psychology. When the Duma adjourned, he traveled widely in the provinces, meeting Russians from all walks of life. With the paralysis of the zemstvos, many hospitals were closed; nonetheless, he found on a visit to the Torzh'ak district that the old peasant distrust of hospitals was rapidly disappearing.[6] The wife of a gentry landlord told him that the peasants had never used the term *pomeshchik* (landlord) as a term of abuse until this year. She recounted an incident of a man in a crowd, rebuked for ignorance by a gentry speaker, shouting back, "Why have you not then been educating us?"[7] Such an attribution of blame would have been unthinkable ten years earlier. Harper jotted a note on a conversation in which a Tver landowner summarized the rapid maturation of the peasantry: "Is sure peasants are greatly gaining in real intelligence and v[ery] fast."[8] These two impressions from rural nobles suggest a new peasant activism that resembles the demanding creativity Blok saw in popular audiences. Harper also described the scheme of an American called Flint to invest in the new peasant activism through loans made available through the zemstvos. Flint's high hopes for the Russian peasantry rested on his knowledge that the

Singer Sewing Machine Company had experienced less loss on the installment system in Russia than in any other country where it operated.[9] Economic initiative would figure in the rise of rural cultural initiative.

Important legal changes contributed to the folk's newly expanded range of action. Paragraph 1 of Nicholas's October Manifesto of 1905 had promised freedom of speech to the population. On 4 March 1906, two decrees on associations were issued to move toward fulfilling that promise. A regulation on societies and unions specified that associations could henceforth, in principle, be organized without any prior permission.[10] Public gatherings in closed quarters fell under police supervision, but groups sponsoring such gatherings usually had only to register an application to secure recognition "as a juridical person." This law, which made it easier for workers to meet, also facilitated the organization of amateur theatrical societies wishing to offer public performances indoors.

Middle-class professionals found it easier to meet. In her book on liberal reformers and their discourse on sexual morality and public health, Laura Engelstein discusses no fewer than eleven conferences or congresses between 1906 and 1914, devoted to subjects ranging from educational psychology to criminology.[11] Because papers given at such conferences were normally published, the views of the professionally oriented are well understood. (Proceedings of various conferences on popular theatre are discussed in Chapter 7.) But more important to the burgeoning popular theatre movement was the unaccustomed ease with which, after 1906, amateurs in the countryside could decide to put on a play and proceed to do so unencumbered by a need for authorizations and supervision.

Equally important for the new energy that went into popular theatre was the failure of an attempt to abolish the estates, or even create a local administration that peasants could dominate by way of gaining practical political experience. The campaign against estates began in the First Duma with the very first address to the throne after its convocation and ended with a formal proposal to abolish the *sosloviia* (estates) filed 2 June 1907. P. A. Stolypin continued to target the rigid estates structure when he took up his appointment as prime minister after the dissolution of the First Duma. To replace the existing *volost'* zemstvo (a purely peasant jurisdiction), he proposed a political entity that would incorporate all estates. This would have given peasant-dominated local institutions broad powers, including taxation, over all local inhabitants.[12] The state would transfer central administrative and police powers to all three zemstvo jurisdictions. Frank Wcislo finds that ministerial bureaucrats, including reformists in the Ministry of the Interior under Stolypin, sought to supplant particularism "with an evolving civil society, with its values of property and personal merit, its language of class status, and even its validation of the rule of law, which alone might guarantee the legitimacy of an autocracy forced to exist in this civic universe."[13] But in

1907 Stolypin lost to the gentry the battle to restructure the *volost'* zemstvos, and in 1908 his proposals to reorganize the zemstvos to establish political democracy went down to defeat.

Finally accepting gentry-dominated politics in the countryside, Stolypin rescinded Witte's policy opposing government subsidy to agriculture. Between 1906 and 1913 the state would channel 93 million rubles to the zemstvos (with most of the subsidy allocated after 1909). It was by these means that the unreconstructed zemstvos, after ostracizing their liberal members and purging their bureaucracies, were able to expand their services in the countryside at an unprecedented rate. Among the new services was the financing of community centers, where peasants could meet to organize economic and cultural pursuits—employing energies that might otherwise have gone into grassroots politics.

The central government's tutelary role with respect to popular theatre declined somewhat after the 1905 revolution. In the early stages of the revolution, when cultural activities seemed to offer a peaceful alternative to political engagement, more employers provided theatrical entertainments for their workers than ever before. But strikes had brought these productions to a halt. In the opinion of one authority on Russian popular theatre, after the revolution, "the era of philanthropy was over."[14]

Government support for the Temperance trusteeships declined steadily. In 1907 thirty-nine members of the Council of State introduced a plan to abolish the trusteeships. The trusteeships survived, but their budget fell to 2 million rubles in 1909, less than half the 1903 allotment. Even at that, a speaker at the All-Russian Congress on the Struggle with Alcoholism in 1909 observed that although more entertainments had been organized as a distraction from drunkenness, their significance scarcely corresponded to the means expended on them.[15] And Senator Koni complained late in 1909 that the trusteeship betrayed its responsibility. Referring to a published account of a diversion between acts of an opera at a Moscow trusteeship theatre, where singers dressed as hooligans and sang "hooligan songs," he wondered what such an "apotheosis of drunkenness" could have to do with distracting people from drunkenness.[16] The committee investigating decided to ban songs from the entertainments, finding it impossible to censor them.

But, often as not, diminution of central support meant reduced supervision of provincial trusteeships. Local enforcement of ministry policy on popular theatres sometimes failed completely. When a Saint Petersburg paper alleged that a dramatization of a scandalous decadent novel, Artsybashev's *Sanin* (published 1907), had been staged in the Sevastapol People's House, an investigation was ordered.[17] The resulting report revealed that the Sevastapol trustees leased the theatre to an entrepreneur franchised to make a profit.[18] A Special Committee worked with the management to assure that only plays approved by the drama censor for popular audiences were presented. In this case, the resourceful lessee had put up posters announcing that a play entitled *How to Live* was based on *Sanin.* The advertising had been in error, rather than the production. But the report revealed that neither the chief of police nor the administrator of the People's House possessed a current list of plays authorized by the censorship for popular theatres!

The special censorship for popular theatre, like the *soslovie* system, continued until 1917. Paradoxically, as the zemstvos became active in popular theatre, they particularly pressed for its abolition. After the 1905 revolution the censors remained reluctant to authorize plays critical of the existing social order. But here too, enforcement continued to be spotty. Early in 1913 the Oberprokurator of the Holy Synod complained to the minister of the interior that the popular theatre of one Kuznetsk in Saratov province was performing plays harmful to the religious-moral climate influencing people. An investigation determined that of 245 plays performed in his theatre, only 58 were approved for popular audiences. The correspondence between the synod and the ministry suggests that violation of the popular theatre censorship's restrictions was fairly common at this time.[19]

In the years between the 1905 revolution and the war, community theatre became possible in Russia for the first time. As zemstvos began to spend significant sums on popular theatre and subsidize construction of People's Houses with theatres, the cooperative movement discovered theatre as a means for proselytizing. The virtues of local initiative found embodiment in widely presented plays. Increased circulation of money and goods in the countryside contributed to creation of a Public Sphere in many localities. Young people assembled into theatre groups and considered themselves participants in the civilizing process. A new agency established by Moscow theatre devotees with the objective of facilitating the production of community theatre supported both rural and factory companies with technical assistance.

POPULAR THEATRE AND THE RISE OF INDEPENDENT ACTION

A. K. Klepikov, in an unpublished memoir, recalled the advance of popular theatre in the decade from 1907 as a breakthrough for independent action.[20] "Just as grass breaks through stones," he claimed, "so did independent theatre break paths for its own development."[21] In fact, he organized his memoir around the theme of the spontaneous emergence of grassroots popular theatre. With respect to the forerunner of the Section to Promote Village, Factory, and School Theatre, which appeared in 1909, he said "the intelligentsia agents of popular theatre understood that the moment had arrived when new popular concerns required something different from them: not presentation of prepared plays utilizing someone else's forces, but a combination of local initiative [*initsiativa*] and local forces." It was his conviction that community theatre generated all kinds of local cultural activity and that after 1905 theatre groups "of the people" enjoyed an unprecedented opportunity to carry on independent creative activity.[22] A brief digression will introduce this prominent figure in popular theatre and describe the development of an influential theatre structured to serve working-class viewers in a nonurban venue.

After he studied natural science at Moscow University, the Kokhma spinning factory near Ivanovo-Voznesensk gave Klepikov his first job in 1891. The several brothers who owned the facility had higher technical educations and "were far more cultivated than the vast majority of factory owners with whom we later had to do business." They began to provide services for their workers, permitting themselves to be guided to some extent by the specialists. First they built a new hospital with the most modern equipment. Then a consumers society appeared. A library for workers opened, and finally, through Klepikov's efforts, a theatre.

One of the brothers, an engineer, habitually repaired to Klepikov's laboratory to smoke and chat. Klepikov tentatively unfurled his dream of a theatre for workers, and to his great surprise, found himself given a free hand to organize one. Space was available on the top floor of a newly constructed dormitory for workers. The lower floor had small apartments for salaried employees. Above lived workers with their families, and above them resided workers living alone. The empty upper floor made a fine theatre, with a broad and deep auditorium large enough to accommodate four hundred viewers. Kerosene lamps illuminated the stage; the factory itself did not yet have electricity. The employers provided whatever furniture was required, along with occasional costumes, from their homes. They ordered props and decorations from Moscow, sparing no expense, and brought a hairdresser from Ivanovo. They also handled ticket distribution. Klepikov chose the plays, directed, and had free rein in making theatrical decisions.

The factory employees had no theatre experience that Klepikov could build on. None had acted, and the majority had never been inside a theatre. All the foremen, stewards, and clerks were local people, and almost none of them had ever traveled any farther than Ivanovo. They worked thirteen hours a day, and most carried on some agricultural activities at home besides. Nevertheless, Klepikov was able to find performers among them. He chose *It's a Family Affair* for the first production because of its small cast and assigned roles to an equipment steward, a draftsman, a clerk, and a clerk's wife. "And thus began both my torments and my joys," he recalled.

Rehearsals took place after a hastily eaten evening meal and lasted until midnight. From the very first blocking, tired workers began to gather in the hall to observe, curious and puzzled by the proceedings. When the play was ready, difficulties arose with the local authorities. Though admission was to be free—as if the play were being performed in a home—the district police superintendent identified the enterprise as a popular theatre, and pointed out that *It's a Family Affair* did not appear on the authorized list. The factory director and Klepikov visited the superintendent, but it took a telegram from the governor to persuade him to permit the performance. The play proved more successful than anyone had anticipated. All the theatre buffs from Ivanovo came to see it and expressed their complete approval.

In the winter of 1893–94 Klepikov presented four more plays. The number of employees wanting to act grew and grew. A newly arrived specialist in mechanics, technically trained, with secondary education, played the lead in I. V. Shpazhinskii's *Prakhom poshlo* (It has gone the way of the dust) (1883). Klepikov tapped a worker from the boiler room to play the policeman in *The Inspector General.* Besides possessing a beautiful voice, this muscular former guardsman had a military bearing. "It is indisputable that there was never in any theatre as magnificent a performer of the role. . . . [H]e delivered his rejoinders with such intonation that you saw a genuine Nikolaevan gendarme." Klepikov found the plays made a tremendous impression on the workers, who were for the most part illiterate, had never read anything and had never in their lives seen anything beyond the factory and the hut. They carried on endless conversations about what they had seen on the stage. They sometimes expressed their satisfaction by quoting Ostrovsky lines to him when they met on the road outside the factory.

His theatre work, on top of his twelve-hour days in the factory, drove Klepikov to the point of exhaustion. So when the opportunity arose to become a factory inspector, he took it, assuming his new position in June 1894. Proud of his organizational efforts, he wrote an account of his theatre for workers for the trade and industry congress at the All-Russian Exposition of 1896. Strikes in Saint Petersburg factories caused the central government to cancel the reading of reports relating to the workers' question. But he took solace from the fact that the theatre he had instituted continued to flourish after his departure. When the Kokhma factory constructed new workers' dormitories in 1896, a whole wing was set aside for a theatre. Soon the owners hired a professional director, along with several actors, and the institution became a permanent fixture.

Hired by the Ministry of Trade and Industry to help enforce the factory regulations that had just been introduced to govern relations between employers and workers, Klepikov served as a factory inspector for thirteen years. He again devoted his free time to the advancement of amateur theatre for all walks of society. He chose to reside in Kineshma, a Kostroma province town of between six and seven thousand inhabitants situated on the high bank of the Volga 110 miles northwest of Nizhni Novgorod. When he arrived a mass of factories ringing nearby Saint Vichuga employed sixteen thousand workers. When he left in 1907, more than thirty-five thousand labored there. Kineshma in 1894 knew almost nothing of theatre. He arranged for an amateur company from Kostroma to come with a portable stage and present a play in the zemstvo headquarters. This turn sparked some local amateur activity. But some more civic-minded townspeople, led by the president of the zemstvo board and an engineer who directed a chemical plant, determined the town needed a permanent theatre and set out to raise funds to construct one.

The town council, dominated by merchants who had little interest either in theatre or enlightenment, provided no money, but did turn over a decaying former warehouse on the outskirts of town. After the organizers had secured pledges from local people of from five to one hundred rubles toward its renovation, the local clergy lay siege to the project. Rumors began to fly among the *meshchanstvo* and merchantry that demons had initiated the venture, and local churches resounded with sermons on this theme. In hopes of saving the project, the organizers wrote to Father John of Kronstadt, the Saint Petersburg priest whose followers considered him a miracle worker. They asked him to bless the good work of the struggle against ignorance by means of a theatre. Father John sent them a hundred rubles for the theatre, and local opposition evaporated. The zemstvo contributed 1500 rubles, and its chief raised 7000 more from the local factory owners by reminding them of what they had received from him. It was decided to name the theatre in honor of Ostrovsky, who had close associations with the town and whose ashes were interred some ten miles away. The Maly accordingly gave a special benefit in Moscow for the theatre and raised an additional 1300 rubles.

Construction began in 1897, incorporating the shell of the old warehouse. The Kineshma Musical-Dramatic Circle in honor of A. N. Ostrovsky received a charter and permission to operate the theatre. Some members of the group wanted to run it as a profit-making enterprise, but they were defeated by others who preferred to function as an enlightening society. Before construction was quite finished, a Trusteeship for Popular Temperance organized in Kineshma and secured a subsidy of 10,000 rubles. These funds went immediately into the expansion of the theatre facilities. The stage and dressing rooms were enlarged, and an ample foyer and a room for a buffet added. Special areas were provided for a library–reading room, a tea room, and a large space for set construction. The latter would become the home of the town's first workers' club. The theatre had 450 seats, 180 of them cheap places in the gallery. The dedication took place in late September 1897, when the modifications were nearly complete.

The circle mounted ten productions in its 1897–98 season, despite its lack of experienced amateurs trained to play women's dramatic parts and heroic roles. They hired several professional actresses at the beginning of the following season. A visit by the Maly company, which was touring the Volga region in the summer of 1898, gave them expert performances of

Wolves and Sheep, Talents and Admirers, and *The Forest.* They engaged four Maly actors at very modest salaries to join the company for the season. In the first year a number of amateurs joined the circle, but none of them proved particularly gifted. The following year, a talented amateur with much experience moved to town and joined with his wife, an excellent musician and singer who also played ingenue roles. The theatre attracted people with a strong desire to work and engendered enthusiasm. Klepikov recalled receiving a letter from a young typesetter whose acting experience had been limited to playing military heroes. He begged Klepikov to "make an actor of him" since he had "storm and spirit."

Klepikov took responsibility for coordinating the professional actors and amateurs, and he acted in almost every play. This was true in the first year, when they performed one play a week, and in the later years, when they did two or three a week, rarely repeating themselves. He learned parts while riding to and from work, and in bed, "when I should have been sleeping." He also directed, and helped their lone stagehand rearrange the set during intermissions. In the early years they depended on a single set and a modest suite of furniture. Lighting was primitive; the theatre used kerosene lamps until acquiring a generator after Klepikov's departure. Yet the public responded warmly.

As director of the circle, Klepikov aimed to serve the widest possible audience. The gallery seats, priced from 17 to 25 kopeks, attracted workers from the nearby factories and always sold out. In 1899 the circle distributed questionnaires to the gallery patrons. They revealed that the majority were factory workers and artisans, and that they attended the theatre assiduously. "Many did not miss a single play, and strong drama was surest to please them." To take the theatre even closer to the workers, the circle inaugurated extramural performances in 1899. They began with a trip to the Krasil' brothers' factory in the Iur'evtsk district, about two hours by train and ten by horse from Kineshma. There, in a huge dining hall in the workers' barracks, they had a stage constructed, with electric lights. After curtaining off half the room, they still had space for a thousand viewers. They played the shows that had been most successful with workers in Kineshma, and began to make the trip five or six times a season. When the Konovalov factory went up eighteen miles from Kineshma by rail, it was fitted out with an equipped theatre. But the auditorium accommodated significantly fewer viewers than the Krasil' brothers' dining room, and the viewing public did not consist exclusively of workers. Besides these factory visits, the circle added a trip to a tea room in the village of Vichuga, where a factory was located.

Klepikov tried to persuade the factory owners to create a permanent theatre to serve their workers. As a factory inspector, he was aware from his very first year in Kineshma of activity by factory owners of the Vichugsk district to construct a central People's House possessing a permanent stage.

> I attempted to persuade the factory owners that it was in their interests, since such a people's house would distract the workers from drunkenness, which they were constantly complaining about. These gentlemen expressed complete agreement with this idea; but the matter never got beyond discussion. The great majority of them were in fact generally opposed to any enlightenment of workers, and they were absolutely unable to take joint action in such a matter. Thus the zemstvo created the tea room in Vichuga, not the factory owners.[23]

This Vichuga tea room—which would eventually get a permanent stage—was the work of the zemstvo official who had been so energetic in raising funds for the Kineshma theatre. He envisioned a network of modest People's Houses covering the district, each with tea room, library, and stage. But besides Vichuga, he had only been able to build one other. It went up in Esipiev, eight miles from Kineshma, which was not yet a factory area. The Ostrovsky circle took a play there once. They also went once on horseback to Semenovskoe-Lapotnoe, a village in a purely agricultural area twenty-seven miles from Kineshma. In its first ten years the company gave 337 productions in the Kineshma theatre and 63 in other places.

The theatre circle launched other enlightening activities. The town had no public library, and its reading room was the first source of books for the masses. It enrolled almost a thousand readers—half of them from factories—and made nearly a hundred thousand loans in its first ten years. Unpaid volunteers supported the facility from the beginning, and a paid librarian directed them. Although censorship restrictions strictly limited what books could be offered, the staff chose carefully and were able to stock significant titles in the sciences as well as classic artistic literature. Eventually they added a nonprofit shop where patrons could purchase books cheaply. Sunday readings of stories from famous authors and brochures on geography and natural science were begun in 1898–99. They proved relatively unsuccessful, because the children who attended were noisy and adults stayed away. The circle's tea room, however, served roughly half again as many as its library. The group also organized outdoor summer festivals.

Thus a community of interest emerged around a facility, an entertainment, and a commitment to advancing the cause of enlightenment. Apart from the noisy children, no resistance from below appeared to impede the progress of this common interest group before 1905. Klepikov said that although it contained "almost no active revolutionary forces," the vast majority of the circle's members opposed the existing order and harbored revolutionary sympathies. It included officials, zemstvo employees, people in trade and industry, and the progressive segment of the merchant youth. While the theatre's governing board included some of the local gentry, they constituted an insignificant minority. It was between the circle and its governing board that a rift opened after the 1905 revolution began.

The 1905–6 theatrical season proceeded with difficulty as political debate engaged the townspeople. With the board's permission, party workers' organizations held endless meetings in the theatre, which was the only large hall in town. Meetings were also held there in preparation for elections to the new state Duma. Party organizations rapidly gained followings, and the Bolsheviks opened a workers' club in the theatre in the winter of 1905–6. Besides endless arguments in the nightly meetings on the correct revolutionary course, reports were read on specific topics. Klepikov remembered listening with special interest to one concerning industrial accidents. The popular readings, dance evenings, and outdoor festivals ceased abruptly in 1905, because they seemed so out of tune with the concerns and aspirations of the public opinion the revolution had made possible. The circle's free library expanded its activities. Disregarding the list of approved books, it added works on politics and economics to satisfy the borrowers' requests. The theatre circle attempted to revolutionize its repertory. The concert evenings, with rousing songs like "We Sing Glory to Reckless Bravery," particularly infuriated the police chief. But he could only suffer in silence, lacking the resources to restore "order."

The revolutionary movement in Kineshma achieved its apogee in February 1907, when a sharp rise in the price of bread sparked a worker uprising. Thousands streamed out of factories to attend a meeting on Bazaar Square, which created a Shops Commission, soon to be the de facto government of the town. It moved into the premises of the town governing board—which went into hiding—and began enforcing controlled prices for flour. The police chief went to the commission for instructions, and the governor himself came from Kostroma to confer with its members. But after two weeks, the army arrived, and the commission members found themselves under arrest. The governor ordered the activity of the Ostrovsky Circle terminated, and soldiers were stationed in the theatre. Klepikov had to be present for a search of the library. Then the governor "proposed" that he leave the jurisdiction immediately. The theatre would survive, but stripped of all the other enlightening activities it had engendered. It beat back an attempt by the town to convert its premises into a barracks. Professional companies now presented the plays. It was effectively disabled as a center of cultural initiative.

Klepikov went on to take a position as a chemical and technical adviser at a plant below Moscow, under an arrangement that left him the time and means to continue his theatrical activity. He found amateur theatre in Moscow immeasurably strengthened since his student days in the city. A member of the elected executive board of the Moscow city duma invited him to organize the amateurs at an unusual institution, the Building of Rent-Free Apartments at the Krestovsk Gate. A gift to the city from a philanthropist, the building had several hundred rooms, which were occupied by the most diverse elements of the Moscow poor—from "dark" (common, coarse) workers to intelligentsia. It had a library–reading room, a dining facility, and a playground where free shows were presented for the inhabitants. It was served by a great many local amateurs, whom Klepikov agreed to train and direct. He maintained this association until the beginning of the war, when conscription drained away the performers.

THE GOLITSYN CIRCLE AND THE COMMISSION ON VILLAGE THEATRE

If the Kineshma theatre had become the nucleus of a community center during the 1905 revolution, the restored authorities in the province brutally stripped away all its nontheatrical services in 1907. But memories of community action were not easily suppressed, and participants in the Kineshma venture went on to work elsewhere to establish community theatre. A spark from the Ostrovsky drama circle of Kineshma burst into flame in the village of Bol'shie Viazemy in 1907 or 1908. A. A. Popov, a member of the Ostrovsky board, had retired from his position as tax inspector and was spending the summer in a dacha there before moving to Moscow. He noticed that the young people of the village seemed interested in theatre and so he organized two or three plays with them over the summer. The village had a hospital and a school, and most of the peasants living there were literate. It also happened to be the home of a famous craft artel that produced wickerwork, some of which was exported abroad. The artel took an interest in Popov's work and rented a building near the station of the Golitsyno Aleksandrovsk railway not far from the village for use as a theatre. Thus was born the Golitsyn Musical Dramatic Circle. A charter was written, and after repeated petitions, the government finally granted the group legal status. Plays began to be presented on a more or less regular basis to audiences of up to 250. The guiding forces locally were V. S. Solov'ev, son of the village teacher and a former medical student, and M. D. Shishkin, a remarkable young peasant who was a student in the juridical faculty at Moscow University. Popov told Shishkin about Klepikov, and Shishkin tracked him down and persuaded him to direct the Golitsyn circle in a play. Klepikov chose *Getting Married.*

Something of the participants' attitude toward the circle is known thanks to conversations Shishkin had with Tolstoy on 14 September 1909.[24] Learning that Tolstoy was a guest for two weeks at the Chertkov family estate just three miles from Viazemy, Shishkin hastened to call on him. In spite of his life as a university student, he had not broken his ties with the peasants or the countryside. He was proud of his peasant speech, and fiercely patriotic to his village. Shishkin described to Tolstoy the initial resistance encountered by the circle. Some, he said, had feared such an organization might become a vehicle for revolutionary propaganda, and local peasants were highly suspicious of it.

> Now the circle was exerting influence on the village youth in a way that was commonly agreed to be positive. Instead of the empty-headed time-wasting, mischief and hooliganism so prevalent recently—drinking, etc.—young kids were busy with rehearsals and performances, which contributed mightily to their intellectual and spiritual development. Participants enjoyed a good reputation. . . . Kids known for their bad behavior avoided the circle; they warned their friends, "Go with Shishkin, and you'll stop making mischief."[25]

Tolstoy asked whether the vanity that afflicts all actors, the conceit and pride that take hold when a person begins to make a public mark, could not be expected to damage peasant youths acting on stage. Shishkin replied that arrogance and conceit before peasants was not something his group went in for.

> The members conduct themselves with moderation and modesty to the highest degree. Moving among intelligent people, professional actors, and directors, they only became less shy and timid in their manner among themselves than they were formerly. Before intelligent people, peasants customarily consider themselves to exist at a level that is somehow inferior. But even when youths conduct themselves freely with intellectuals, there is nothing wrong with this.

Tolstoy asked what if he wrote a play for them? The bearded peasant who accompanied Shishkin and had remained silent until then answered, "Write it and we will program it all over Russia!" This evidently troubled Tolstoy, but he asked if he could see the circle perform. The state of his health precluded his setting a date. But three days later, he rode to Viazemy with V. G. Chertkov and Chertkov's son Dima. Shishkin, unfortunately, was in Moscow, and none of the peasant actors could be found.

Dima Chertkov, however, would observe one of the Golitsyn productions, and when he moved to an allotment near Iasnaia Poliana in 1910 to engage in agriculture and associate with young peasants, he decided to establish a peasant drama circle modeled on Shishkin's. They performed *The First Distilling* in late April. Afterward Tolstoy said his author's self-respect was stung: he would have to write a new play.[26] He invited the internationally famous actor P. N. Orlenev to present the result, *Ot nei vse kachestva* (The cause of it all), which he finished in June.

It was Orlenev's obsession with free theatre for the people and his performance in the theatre of the Golitsyn circle that brought this erratic personality into Tolstoy's orbit.[27] Orlenev had already toured widely in Russia when he prepared in 1908 to play *Hamlet.* To escape from the distraction of lucrative tour offers, he went to Geneva, where he met radical Russian students and had long talks with G. V. Plekhanov about art. After a successful provincial tour with *Hamlet,* he performed the play in Saint Petersburg, then in Siberia and the Far East. While in Vladivostok, he happened on an article by N. V. Skorodumov, director of the Burmakino People's House of Iaroslav province, who had been lecturing and writing on peasant and village theatre. With thirty thousand rubles in his pocket from his tours, Orlenev determined to present free performances for peasants with his troupe. He sought out Skorodumov, who advised him to start in the theatre of the Golitsyn circle. Orlenev and his company presented two performances of *The Inspector General* and a vaudeville, *Nevpopad* (*Out of place*), there in the spring of 1910. The audience was very attentive, and after the evening performance it sent a delegation to Orlenev proposing to take up a collection to compensate him. They understood that a community necessarily provides material support for the services it chooses to receive. Orlenev's account in his memoirs indicates a failure to grasp their point.

> They said that they were in a position to pay and that our free productions could undermine their own amateur productions. To this I answered that I would not take money but would allow them to put some kind of dish in the foyer with a sign saying something like: "Payment will be accepted for the playing of the visiting actors in the form of produce for the free peasant productions to come."[28]

The elder Chertkov attended one of Orlenev's Golitsyn performances and took a poster to Tolstoy. He mentioned that he had met Orlenev in London a few years before, when the actor stopped there on his return from an American tour. He had learned then of Orlenev's dream to establish a traveling popular theatre in Russia that would give performances in granaries and under the stars. Chertkov invited Orlenev to meet Tolstoy to discuss performances for peasants. Orlenev professed reluctance, "not wanting to be a pilgrim to any god." But he appeared at Iasnaia Poliana 8 June, in a shirt open to the navel, and practically played out the vaudeville when Tolstoy asked him how the peasants had listened and understood.

Orlenev and Tolstoy met once again for a vegetarian breakfast at Chertkov's on 21 June. Tolstoy criticized him for performing for nothing. He said that if he set a price of only five kopeks the peasants would see this as the goal of his work and take it seriously, whereas without any charge they would look on the business as a florid old-fashioned gesture, a gentry conceit. Orlenev replied that he regarded his talent as a calling, a gift that he wished to play with—"tossing it like a golden ball"—rather than exploit. To Tolstoy's question how he would support himself and his troupe, he answered, "With the help of my best friend, fate." Tolstoy regretted Orlenev's eccentricity.[29]

A few months later, Klepikov accepted the Golitsyn circle's invitation to write a play responsive to local interests that would strengthen the cooperative idea and work in some facts about the Viazemsk artel. He wrote *V "nizinakh"* (In the low places) and directed several performances of it at the Golitsyn theatre. It generated a great deal of discussion in Viazemy and was published by Tsentrosoiuz, the executive agency of Russia's federated cooperatives. He accepted invitations from the drama circles of Moscow consumer societies to present it and participated in a production for the delegates of a congress of Tsentrosoiuz that was warmly applauded. Soon the play began to appear everywhere. It went through four editions.

The Golitsyn circle quickly attracted fame for its ensemble playing. In 1911 a group of visiting English schoolteachers was brought to Viazemy after seeing the sights of Moscow. The circle presented a scene from *Boris Godunov* especially for them. Klepikov was on the train with them as they departed, repeatedly shouting "Hip, hip, hip, hooray!" with great enthusiasm. After they returned home, laudatory articles on the Golitsyn theatre appeared in an English magazine.

In the fall of 1909 Klepikov joined a newly created Commission on Village Theatre. N. V. Skorodumov also belonged, and M. D. Shishkin served as secretary. The organization grew steadily in influence, undergoing several changes of name and affiliation before its restructuring in 1922. It would be best known as the Section to Promote Village, Factory, and School Theatre. For some years, Klepikov headed the subcommission on repertory. His group classified and ranked all serious Russian plays according to difficulty of content (understanding), complexity of staging (sets and costumes), and difficulty of production (formidable roles, crowd scenes, and so forth). They also produced detailed reviews of each play, which were collected and published and widely used by fledgling theatre groups choosing vehicles to match their resources.[30] For two or three years Klepikov worked closely in the subsection with Z. S. Sokolova (Stanislavsky's sister), who had experience of popular theatre through one she created with her husband that functioned for many years in Voronezh province. The organization also considered the preparation and publication of directors' commentaries to be one of its greatest responsibilities; however, it managed to produce only around twenty of these. Klepikov was able to spend even more time on the Section's work after he resigned his factory position and moved into the city to take a post as secretary to a scientific-technical institution.

From its earliest beginnings, the Section sought to simplify staging and costuming as much as possible to bring costs within the budgets of the most impecunious amateurs. The commission, in its quarters in the Arbat, began assembling complete "mountings" for rent. Besides providing scripts and a director's commentary, they made available sets, costumes, and props. Demand was so great that a department was set up to register requests. Skorodumov worked out a method for simplified staging, which involved a painted backdrop with flanking panels of gray cloth. Well-known painter V. D. Polenov, came to the work of the commission challenged by the possibilities in the painted backdrops. When the commission decided to test the stage on a play about everyday life, it asked Klepikov to prepare an experimental production of *Poverty Is No Vice* in an extremely confined space. To his surprise, it worked rather well. At the demonstration he met D. A. Tolbuzin, a jurist active in the Moscow Society for Enlightened Entertainments. Tolbuzin would become the organization's leader and guiding force in its period of rapid expansion.

The Section moved often because of its growth and the difficulty of finding spaces large enough for its sprawling construction departments. When it relocated in a new building on Novoslobodskaia Street, it built a stage comparable in size to that of the average dramatic circle's. There it experimented with various methods for changing sets and hanging flies. It offered demonstration performances to interested groups to show that the physical demands of starting a theatre need not be insurmountable. In 1913 it gave a production for public school teachers from the provinces who were attending a conference in Moscow. Events like this helped spread word of the Section's services in remote areas. But it also had a program of traveling plays to help it raise money with which to spread its message in the interior. Klepikov took part in four such tours.

The first traveling play went out in 1911, when he took *Poverty Is No Vice* to S. V. Panina's estate, Marfino. After going there to make the arrangements, he came back charmed "with the magnificent park and streams and with the hostess herself." They decided to present the play in an enormous threshing barn, a structure large enough to accommodate eight hundred to one thousand people. The countess had a temporary stage constructed in the facility, along with dressing rooms for the performers. On the holiday chosen for the presentation, the barn filled with peasants in festive garb from all the neighboring villages. Panina treated the troupe cordially, paid all their expenses, and contributed three hundred rubles to the Section.

Two or three years later he took *Even a Cat Has Lean Times* to the estate of the late Savva Morozov's son near Voskresensk in the Zvenigorod district. The Section took the initiative, hoping to interest the young millionaire in its undertakings. The play was given on the premises of the industrial school T. S. Morozov maintained near his home. Morozov left the company to build its own stage and the local peasants to feed them. The makeshift auditorium overflowed with locals who had never seen theatre before, and they gave Ostrovsky's play a magnificent reception. Hushed silence alternated with "Homeric laughter" in the appropriate places. "Morozov himself ran to the stage at every intermission and, choking, expressed his complete rapture." He paid the bill for expenses, but neglected to include anything for the Section. Klepikov also took plays to two permanent theatres where the audiences consisted entirely of workers. One performance took place at the Rublevsk waterworks, and the other at the Ivanovsk textile factory of the Popovs.

The Section eventually set out to raise funds for an 80,000-ruble building of its own, which it constructed near the Zoological Garden with the help of a mortgage from the Moscow Narodnyi Bank. The building had an auditorium that seated 250, where plays were given on a regular basis. It housed all the workshops of the Section, its rental collection, library, meeting rooms, residence quarters for some of the personnel, and space for the beginnings of a museum displaying props, construction techniques, costumes, and devices for producing sound effects. Construction was under way at the beginning of the war, and although a dedication ceremony was held in the winter of 1914–15, the "Polenov Building" was only ready for occupancy in the summer of 1915. The Section crusaded for popular theatre, goaded other organizations to take it up, and brought diverse groups of theatre people together to coordinate support for amateur companies as the war altered the conditions under which private initiative operated in Russia.

THE RISE OF COOPERATIVE SOCIETIES

The explosion of rural cooperatives between 1907 and 1914 also opened powerful new sources of support for local theatrical initiatives. In 1900 there were only 1,625 individual cooperatives in Russia, but after the 1905 revolution their numbers grew rapidly. The period from 1906 to 1909 saw a crackdown on consumer societies that had sympathized with revolution. Catherine Salzman attributes this in part to the regime's "distrust of all forms of popular initiative."[31] Yet new cooperatives were formed with increasing frequency from 1905 on. Their growth became even more rapid after the outbreak of war in 1914.

The country's cooperative organizations took several forms, but the two most important types were the credit co-op and the consumer *(potrebitel'noe)* society. The credit cooperative, which employed trained bookkeepers, was more businesslike than the consumer society in its operation. The credit co-ops catered to the better-off peasants, those best able to borrow and repay, and they showed little interest in promoting expanded participation in local decision-making. They sometimes squabbled with consumer societies in the villages. In 1911 Kiev province had the largest number of credit cooperatives, followed by Podolsk, Perm, and Poltava provinces. The number of credit societies in Russia grew from 1,270 in 1904 to 12,000 in 1917.

Consumer societies organized to enable villagers to purchase commodities like salt, sugar, and flour at reasonable prices. They ran shops not unlike the one that Gorky and his employer were burned out of in 1888. The stores threatened retailers who sold on credit, enjoyed monopolies, and priced accordingly. When a consumer society opened in Olenets province in the summer of 1909, for example, retail prices of foodstuffs in the vicinity immediately dropped between 15 and 20 percent.[32] The consumer societies, which existed in city, factory, railroad, village, and worker variants, sprang up much more rapidly than credit co-ops. This was especially true of the village form, which, along with the worker type, had fewer members than the railway and factory societies.

Both credit and consumer cooperatives became interested in practical local education. Two speakers at the First All-Russian Congress on People's Universities, held in January 1908, called attention to sources of support for informal schooling abroad. P. G. Mizhuev pointed out that in England and the United States, where schooling was compulsory, the state actively patronized and encouraged extracurricular education, instead of putting obstacles in its path.[33] V. F. Totomiants, in a paper entitled "Cooperation and Public Education," observed that in England, which had formerly shown little interest in public education, schools established by the consumer societies were now performing a great service to society.[34] He reported that the Milan Cooperative Union had opened free courses for employees in 1906. The Turin Cooperative Alliance had recently started courses to train salesmen. The French union of consumer cooperatives was at present creating a "league for cooperative education" with local sections. In Denmark the government subsidized courses for young male and female peasants who also participated in temperance and gymnastic societies. The main thrust of credit society education was to train employees in credit societies, to transmit a marketable skill.

Education for the consumer societies entailed broader cultural activity. It meant explaining the advantages of membership in cooperatives to a larger public that would serve in such mutual support societies on a voluntary basis. Before the war, consumers' organizations donated around 100,000 rubles in annual grants for educational and cultural activities, while the credit cooperatives gave around 40,000. Salzman found that the workers' consumer societies, which experienced a spurt of growth in 1907–8, stopped growing after 1911. But her calculations show that their expenditures for culture increased substantially between 1911 and 1914, and that the more democratically organized societies allocated more than the less democratically organized.[35] Russian consumer societies generally still spent less than their Western counterparts on cultural and enlightening work in 1917, but they functioned at a lower level of prosperity.

Besides the funds cooperatives began to channel into publishing, reading rooms, and grassroots theatres, the societies contributed to cultural change by promoting association. Regional congresses and conferences were called freely and frequently, especially after 1911. From 1905 through 1911, some 105 such congresses met. In 1912 there were 71; in 1913, some 81. In 1914 the number came to well over one hundred.[36] Contemporaries were struck by the short notice given between announcement and meeting, the vagueness of programs' objectives and the poor organization of the reporting. They attributed some of the ineptness to the fact that more and more peasant delegates and members of the rural intelligentsia were attending these conferences as time went on. Perhaps more impressive than the congresses' shortcomings is their eloquent confirmation of the beginning of a real civil society that reached into rural Russia and saw villagers arranging meetings with their counterparts from other villages and exchanging ideas on matters of mutual interest.[37]

Plays represented an important means of communicating the theory and advantages of cooperation to villagers. Educational and cultural expenditures that went into theatre supported amateurs who developed desirable skills through playing, and entertainment where it was in short supply. But they also constituted an investment in self-advertisement. Klepikov wrote *V "Nizinakh"* in 1911. It became widely popular for presentation by newly organized drama circles, and performances continued to be requested from established circles. The Golitsyn circle, for example, which often received invitations to appear in neighboring provinces, honored requests in the spring of 1914 to present the play to peasant audiences in Moscow and Smolensk provinces. Other plays on cooperatives included M. Shishkin's *Kulak* and A. S. Florinskii's *Two Powers: Scenes from Siberian Cooperative Life*. (Theatrical circles allied to cooperatives were especially common in western Siberia, where they worked under the guidance of the Zakupsbyt federation.)

Klepikov's play rose well above the level of propaganda. It sustains tension and suspense from beginning to end, while incorporating comic moments and violent ones. The central Russian village called "The Low Places" stands in marked contrast to villages depicted in nineteenth-century plays of everyday life. It is connected to the outside world and lies open to influences from that world that promise to transform the conduct and quality of rural life. The play's popularity and its service to the cooperative movement before the war make its content especially noteworthy.

The four acts span the growing season from May to August. It is the fifth year of the schoolmaster's tenure. In his third he persuaded the villagers to establish a basket-making artel so as to retain more of the benefits from the sale of their handicrafts. This summer he is encouraging them to open a consumer's shop to lower the prices of necessities and to free themselves from indebtedness to private traders. The artel has grown rapidly and accumulated a capital of twenty thousand rubles, on which it pays an annual dividend. As one of the delighted craftsmen whose work always meets the artel's high quality standards puts it, "The main thing is, you always get cash. You know, you live like a lord."[38] The money income and increased independence won the simple folk's respect and affection for the pedagogue with the secondhand bicycle. ("Since when have they valued this kind of person?" a member of the artel board asks.)

The loser in all this is the merchant Akindimov. Even his twenty-year-old daughter agrees that he is obsessed with money. Her friend objects that the old man's wealth enables him to keep company with the well-born. The clergy, she adds, also call regularly, and the police officer is deferential. The daughter replies that her father is really just a peasant, and that the only thing that can possibly ennoble a person is education.

Akindimov goes to the teacher to persuade him to abandon the idea of an artel-sponsored shop. First he speaks as a friend.

> To trade requires savvy. You have to know where to buy, how to preserve the goods. It is necessary to put considerable credit into the business. We have been at it for a hundred years, and believe me, we have nothing but losses. I only keep the shop because I feel sorry for the people: there wouldn't be anywhere for them to get provisions without it.

He ends by offering the teacher a bribe, "only kill this business with the peasants." The schoolmaster has taken pains not to run the artel himself. He cheerfully advises when asked, but often avoids attending meetings. "I am very much an outsider. Here today, and gone tomorrow. You have to conduct the whole affair yourselves. It can only be secure when the forces come from inside, from the organization itself, when the spontaneity of the society guides all the work." He does not idealize the organization. When there are rumors of nepotism and corruption within the leadership, he counsels that in time the principled behavior of some of the most committed craftsmen will serve as an example that inspires broad emulation. "It will not happen instantly. People are not transformed suddenly. But the spirit of solidarity, recognition of a communality of interests must unite all conscious elements in friendly work for the common good."[39] He does advise those favoring creation of an artel shop to overcome their instinct to present the proposal as "a most humble request" and act forcefully.

For many peasant craftsmen, the cooperative artel represents an evolved form of the village commune. (The bookkeeper, in his cups, says "Mir, obshchestvo, artel! [Commune, society, artel!] Can you understand this?") Akindimov settles on a tactic legendary in the annals of the *mir*, whereby interests with a proposition to push through "treated" the membership to buckets of vodka on the understanding that those partaking would vote the host's way. He fails in this, because the Nizina drinkers linger in the woods, send for more vodka, and miss the meeting altogether. The committed fear that they will lose, because although they know people are gradually growing wiser, they recognize that "people are still awfully keen for free vodka."

Akindimov avenges himself on the teacher. He brings an oily character in a bowler hat from the city to write a denunciation of the schoolmaster to the authorities. The teacher chooses not to dispute his resulting reassignment.[40] Does he think the authorities believed the charges contained in the denunciation? He answers the question for a member of the artel board: "Who knows them! Probably they did not believe it. Well, for the sake of order they decided nevertheless to propose another school to me." This shrug of resignation recalls Klepikov's response to his own dismissal from government service and ejection from Kineshma in the wake of the 1905 revolution.

The teacher receives a warm send-off from the villagers. He modestly tells them that when they created the artel they recognized their own vital interests, and he contributed only a small push to something that was about to happen anyway. "The artel you organized represents just one of the rivulets that are gradually uniting with each other and must finally form a powerful stream, a mighty river, lifting the well-being of the *narod* on their waves." The local artel has now demonstrated its fundamental health by auditing its accounts and dismissing its errant bookkeeper. It elected *not* to press charges when it learned that he had taken two hundred rubles from the society's cash to complete a house he was building. The schoolmaster would have preferred stronger punishment. "This," he observed to friends on the board when they told him of it later, "is what's remarkable about us: when private interests are involved, nobody ever gives up a single kopek or overlooks anything. But when it comes to public funds, our people are surprisingly easygoing."[41]

Klepikov's schoolmaster leaves the villagers of Nizina more prosperous, but not noticeably happier than when he arrived. A few of them are taking control of their lives: one by giving up drinking after studying its physical impact and observing the grief it causes, another by assuming responsibilities for guiding the artel's new work in an area where costly mistakes can easily be made. The individualism and integrity he espouses do not promote utopian outcomes, but this personal distancing does emerge as a plausible choice in the "low place" near the railway line.

This play's appealing, if low-key, presentation of the cooperative idea and its warm reception represent one small factor in the Russian cooperatives' move to fund cultural enlightening activities. At the beginning of the year in which it was written, only fifteen of some five thousand cooperatives made special allocations for this kind of work. Of course drama circles could be useful for more than performing plays about cooperation. The very individualism that *V "Nizinakh"* illustrated could be cultivated through voluntary participation in local theatre. As Shishkin put it in an article published as an afterward to the play,

> The cultural significance of theatre, when it is properly organized on cooperative principles, is not that it is a rostrum from which much good may be spoken. Participation itself in the life of such a theatre necessarily serves cultural enrichment: participation in the study (sometimes line by line) of artistic literature of all sorts is undoubtedly conducive to broadening and deepening knowledge and develops a range of intellectual interests. Participation in . . .

> production . . . serves to develop innate natural abilities and talents. Participation in the meetings to work out a collective plan to direct and govern, and the necessity then to subordinate oneself to it and help it exist, all this disciplines, accustoms one to social life.[42]

The Golitsyn circle illustrated how a dramatic society could vivify its members and the community. G. Nikiforov, a peasant member, wrote a poem that summed up what the theatre offered. Addressed to "those among us who are dying of boredom," it concluded:

> There burns a light
> Simply come to us, to our theatre
> And heed our advice!
> Forget hatred, enmity
> Make peace with all your enemies
> Believe in truth and goodness.[43]

A certain Kirpichnikov, who was personally familiar with the company's playing, noted that the peasant artists worked together in a happy and friendly way. He happened to be present on occasions when some gymnasium student from town or some amateur was on stage, and he saw a sharp contrast between the "self-centeredness" of these outsiders and the collegiality of the members, whose "concern was for the success of the whole enterprise."[44] From a charter membership of twenty-nine, the Golitsyn circle grew to two hundred in 1912. From 1909 to 1912 it gave 55 performances (38 paid and 17 free), with a total attendance of twelve thousand. It expended twelve hundred rubles a year and took in nine hundred from the sale of tickets.

In 1911 or 1912 the Viazemsk consumer society took the Golitsyn Dramatic Circle into membership and provided an annual subsidy of two hundred rubles. Now the circle set its sights on securing its own theatre large enough to seat 350. The clearest path to this goal seemed to be through a general-purpose structure that would serve the whole community. The first general zemstvo congress on public education in 1911 recognized the People's House as "the basic cell of local extracurricular education." The Perm, Ufimsk, Novgorod, and Olonets zemstvos quickly developed plans to support construction of People's Houses. But not all the provincial zemstvos were so quick to embrace the concept. The Golitsyn circle allied itself in 1913 with the two-year-old Viazemsk Credit Brotherhood and formed a commission to study the feasibility of building a People's House. The rapidly expanding credit brotherhood needed its own space for offices and was very receptive to the idea of a People's House. The credit brotherhood at Marfino, near Moscow, had obtained a twenty-year loan from the state bank at 5 percent interest to build a People's House there.

V. S. Solov'ev addressed the Second Congress on Cooperation, held in Kiev in 1913, with a report on the Golitsyn circle's needs and aspirations. He noted that Russia's rural cultural life was in flux. "In many places, fist fighting has already retreated into tradition, *igrishcha* [the practice of young women and men singing and dancing for recreation in the evening] is also beginning to lose its former popularity, and even *balagan* presentations become more and more infrequent. A demand is being born among the people for more cultured, more intelligent amusements, and the People's House must move to meet this demand."[45] The institution Solov'ev had in mind differed from the structures built around the turn of the century by philanthropists and the Treasury's Temperance trusteeships. The facilities he envisioned would be organized by local people to meet needs that they themselves identified.[46] He insisted that the population must have an *economic* interest in the entities as well. "It should . . . shelter useful local amenities: consumer shops, cooperative offices, artel depots and stores, professional schools and studios, bakeries, laundries, baths, hotels, and even fire protection associations."[47] He defined a People's House as a place where all inhabitants could meet and interact for social and cultural stimulation, "an all-class club, where peasants, workers, and intelligentsia circles alike are welcome," a place where "the social instincts lying in every person can be awakened and developed." He thought the zemstvos should be building not hospitals and primary schools, but People's Houses with theatres. For a People's House to be viable, it would have to be freely initiated by the local population. In areas where people had not yet manifested their "social independence," the time was not yet ripe; but where people had the experience of cooperative endeavor, People's Houses could come into being in the most natural fashion.

The precocious Golitsyn circle rebuffed the Section to Promote Village, Factory, and School Theatre's attempt to include it in its unification program. Instead, it appealed to the Moscow Consumers' Union, which formed its own commission on the creation of musical-dramatic circles in consumer societies. From 26 March to 4 June 1913, eighteen consumer societies were formed, three musical dramatic circles, and one agricultural society. In the area around Moscow, which along with western Siberia was farthest advanced in co-op related theatres, nineteen consumer societies had drama circles in 1913—some created, some adopted. By June 1914, there were thirteen circles with cooperative affiliation, two of which were chartered. Despite the natural affinity between local theatre and cooperation, independently organized theatre groups sprang up more often without co-op support. Many of these looked to the Section for help.

THE SECTION TO PROMOTE VILLAGE, FACTORY, AND SCHOOL THEATRE

In a 1916 report V. D. Polenov explained, "In our Section there arose the idea of using the school for popular theatre, but it remained to figure out how to get it going."[48] Indeed, an educational movement that arose after 1905 for People's Universities anchored this association of theatre-smitten artists determined to advance the amateur production of plays. The Section aimed to support independent theatre groups that operated on a shoestring and most often found space to perform in zemstvo and Ministry of Education schools. It worked out plans for small stages expressly to serve companies playing in village schools. Although they also welcomed requests from circles in People's Houses, the clientele they targeted differed from that of the Moscow Consumers' Union Commission in that they were usually small unaffiliated companies getting by on ticket receipts and members' contributions.

Strictly speaking, the Section was born 9 December 1912. But although the group found a new organizational sponsor and took a new name at that moment, its key personnel and philosophy had been in place since late 1909. Its impetus came from a proposal made by a speaker at the Second All-Russian Congress of Directors in Moscow. At his suggestion the Union of Theatre Personnel agreed to assemble a commission on village theatre, and Klepikov served on the organizing committee. V. N. Bobrinskaia, a philanthropist and social activist, took the leading role. She personally bore all the expenses, and it was she who engaged the commission's comfortable quarters in the Arbat. "Tall, full-figured, of courageous mien, powerful character, enormous energy, she was," as Klepikov remembered, "undoubtedly very liberal in her outlook and had the capacity to achieve her goals. . . . She spoke without any inhibition, . . . with an authority that could decide things one way or another."[49] M. L. Shishkin became the secretary. Subcommittees were formed on repertory, direction, and technical matters, and quickly attracted new volunteers. From the very beginning, the group took an experimental approach to popular theatre, responding to requests, and attempting to relieve bottlenecks that impeded fledgling companies.

N. V. Skorodumov presided over the artistic technical subcommittee, which developed a method for simplified staging.[50] This intrigued Polenov, the famous painter, who joined in 1910. He had first become involved in stage design in Paris, where he worked with A. P. Bogoliubov on tableaux vivants.[51] Polenov had continued in this activity at Savva Mamontov's theatre. He worked as either actor or decorator in ten Mamontov theatre presentations and operas. There he triumphantly introduced open-air effects into scenery painting.

An early effort of the commission was a traveling dramatic production of Lermontov's narrative poem, *The Song of the Merchant Kalashnikov.* It represented an attempt to respond to specific requests from peasant viewers: "You showed us how common people are; now show us how lords are, good or bad. . . . We ourselves know how we live. . . . Show us how other people live. . . . Bring us a play from the tsars."[52] The Lermontov work described the unquenchable love of Ivan IV's favorite bodyguard for the beautiful wife of a merchant. It particularly recommended itself because of the author's authentic imitation of oral folk tradition. But despite a good production, Polenov's stunning sets, and the folk language, the play did not meet its presenters' objectives. Peasants who saw it readily forgave the tsar all his cruelty and bullying. They could not comprehend Kalashnikov's chivalrous conduct, nor quite believe his wife's sincerity. Still, they were glad to watch it, and it was presented at least a dozen times in different places, mostly around Moscow. But peasant audiences much preferred the commission's traveling production of Pushkin's *Rusalka,* which moved women to tears and brought requests for repeat performances.

The commission lost its sponsor when the Union of Theatre Personnel was liquidated at the beginning of 1911. "In the year and a half of its existence," as Klepikov recalled, "the Commission for Rural Theatre established contacts with a number of localities and served both organized dramatic circles and individual productions in the countryside and in factories."[53] Its work was not even interrupted, however, for Bobrinskaia persuaded the president of the Moscow branch of the Imperial Russian Technical Society to take the commission under its wing as a department. It dropped "rural theatre" from its title and replaced it with "factory theatre," without altering its personnel or modus operandi. This arrangement too proved short-lived, and eighteen months later the Technical Society closed its theatre division. The Society's charter, which authorized it to engage in social activity in areas having to do with technology, simply could not be stretched to cover the theatre group's work.

A new sponsor was found in the form of the Moscow Society of People's Universities. Under its aegis the Section grew and expanded its services to local theatre circles. The idea of an organization to disseminate university-style teaching to the masses originated in England in the 1870s and spread to Belgium, Switzerland, Norway, Denmark, France, and Austria. The first Russian attempt at such instruction came in 1897, with the founding of the Saint Petersburg Pedagogical Society of Mutual Help. The demand for places proved so great that hundreds of auditors had to be turned away. Then the Ministry of the Interior quickly closed the Society down. The 1905 revolution stimulated discussion of a national institution to take university courses to the people. In February 1906 a group assembled calling itself the Saint Petersburg Division of the All-Russian Society of People's Universities. But the government balked at the idea of a national organization. In October 1906 the Society dropped "All-Russian" from its title and renounced any connection to other organizations. The Moscow Society of People's Universities was founded at the same time. The 4 March law on associations made it relatively simple for people's universities to form in other cities, and by 1909 they were operating successfully in Kazan, Samara, Voronezh, Smolensk, the Kuban, Pskov, Ufa, Tiflis, and Harbin.

Numerous enlightening societies continued to press for a national organization to unify and coordinate the work of those universities. The minister of the interior did not rule out the possibility of such a body in the future, and he approved the Saint Petersburg Society's request to hold a meeting that called itself the All-Russian Congress of Agents of Societies of People's Universities and other Privately Initiated Organizations. Delegates came from Moscow, Saratov, Kharkov, and Voronezh, but 341 of the 478 in attendance were from Saint Petersburg. Three speakers attempted to put Russia's educational development in historical perspective. One remarked on the need to recognize that "of all the cultured peoples, we are the most uncultured." Another, who had traveled in England, concluded a lecture on informal education there by saying, "In this tragic moment in history, when the old structure is collapsing, threatening to crush the best forces of newly revived Russia under its wreckage, everyone . . . must unite against the common enemy . . . absence of education." The speaker at the fourth session, held at the Saint Petersburg city duma, argued that it was in the governing classes' interest to revise their position on educating the masses:

> The possessing classes in Russia did very little for popular enlightenment, fearing that the ability to read and write, if it penetrated the masses, would educate them for class struggle. [But] . . . social struggle was not related to the development of literacy and understanding among the population. Enlightenment makes it possible for the class struggle to lose its extreme sharpness. Therefore it is in the interest of the governing classes and the whole country to cooperate in all measures that lift the intellectual development of the people.[54]

Even without a national clearinghouse, both the Saint Petersburg and Moscow Popular Universities expanded rapidly. They sponsored individual lectures on all kinds of subjects, established systematic courses of lectures, and arranged excursions. They opened their own libraries and museums and started publishing ventures. Both boasted successful popular conservatories. The Section to Promote Village, Factory, and School Theatre could have found no better home than the Moscow Society.

Where a place was available to function as a cultural center, people could often be found to promote a broad range of cultural activities. A speaker at a conference on temperance gave an account of how the Samara People's University prospered in its first year:

> Though the town was provincial and sleepy, it threw all its energies into this People's University. At first the lecturers were experienced locals, but soon they were joined by lecturers from Moscow, Petersburg, Kiev, and Kazan. All the lectures drew good crowds—sometimes upward of two thousand. Everybody talked about the lectures: the simple masses, workers, *meshchane,* and intelligentsia. . . . Soon systematic cycles of courses were born. Lectures on music, a library, an observatory were organized. The People's House, to which

> the activity of the University largely accommodated itself, now took on the character of an active center of broad popular enlightenment. The Temperance trusteeships . . . created People's Houses in many places in the period of their intensive activity. Now these People's Houses should be considered transformed into People's Universities.[55]

With People's Houses all over Russia becoming centers of locally initiated cultural activity, it was natural that the Section would also offer its services to theatre groups making their home in People's Houses.

When the Section started work under the Moscow Society, it expanded its programs and added staff. V. D. Polenov became president of the board. D. A. Tolbuzin carried over as vice president. He had brought his friends M. V. and N. F. Shemshurin into the department. A couple totally devoted to theatre, they contributed both their time and personal resources to the Section. Shemshurina specialized in costume, and gathered a huge library on the subject. She took charge of the Section's collection of costumes and props available for loan to theatre groups. To keep costs minimal, these costumes were stitched together from the cheapest calico, or even sacks, which were then stenciled. They could be rented or made by a drama group. The Society supplied patterns, stencils, and instructions. (A boyar's costume could be assembled for one ruble seventy kopeks.) Shemshurin specialized in sets, props, and sound effects. Besides designing and constructing simple and versatile furniture, he devised effective props from the simplest materials. His chain mail began as fishnet, knightly headgear as towrope. The Section's museum illustrating the craft of theatrical production also grew out of his work.

The Section simplified set construction too. A method was worked out for painting sets on calico, then applying sketches with glue. The sketches made possible special lighting effects. Designers came up with a system of flies in conjunction with a basic set that made it possible to change quickly from a poor room to a luxurious one, from a hut to a forest dwelling, from a forest to a garden.

Besides set design, Polenov took a personal interest in children's theatre. He wrote *Anne of Brittany*, a children's play, and composed the music and painted the sets for it. For this illustrious painter, the theatre represented elevated, beautiful spectacle. He rarely made sets for realist drama. He considered raising the spirits to be theatre's purpose. Romantic works particularly attracted him. This taste carried into the new building he designed for the Section, "a small palace with turrets," which he characterized as "a theatrical laboratory for all Russia." It was inspired by the fourteenth-century Redon castle of Anne of Brittany.

The building was said to have been well designed to meet the Section's requirements. Its location, however, far from the center, at the corner of Medynka and Kabanikhin Pereulok, made the expensive structure an unattractive place to present plays for general Moscow audiences. Polenov, who was sixty-eight when he took charge of the Section in 1912, had the prestige to attract young artists to its work. He thought the government held him in low esteem, and attributed the Section's difficulty in securing permission to offer courses to that mistrust. "Courses were forbidden in the Section in the beginning . . . , then severely limited. It seemed that . . . I did not enjoy the sympathy of the government."[56] The government's slowness to authorize the Section's foray into courses for theatre personnel before the war probably had more to do with its cautious attitude toward popular theatre than any lack of sympathy for its aged president.

In 1912 the Section had 157 members. They served in six divisions. The first concerned itself with repertory and the library, the second with directors and the realization of texts, the third with artistic-technical aspects of production, and the sixth with school theatre. The fifth was devoted to developing worker theatre in Moscow. The fourth, or Unification division, tried to bring independent circles into association with each other and the Section. Only twelve circles did unify, and most of them were workers' circles.

From the opening of its doors on 19 December 1912, to the beginning of September 1913, the Section received 211 inquiries. Fifty-two percent were from theatrical circles composed predominantly of peasants or workers. They requested costumes, sets, props, plays, directors' commentaries, guidance in set building, sketches, play recommendations, and collections of reviews. Seventy percent of the requests came from the countryside, and only 30 percent from cities. Eleven percent came from Asiatic Russia. The Section's income for these months amounted to twenty-five hundred rubles, half of it from contributors—mainly members. Rentals and admissions brought in six hundred rubles. The balance came from loans from members. The clientele served by the Section grew very rapidly after 1913.

In the spring of 1914 the Section distributed a questionnaire to one hundred circles in order to get some idea of their composition and reception in their communities and to learn what they needed. Of the twenty-six responding, all but two were rural. Twenty-one of the circles were in the central and Volga provinces, three in the south, two in the north. The respondents generally did not have charters and were not legally recognized. If this deficiency was typical of popular circles in cities as well it might account for the relatively poor rate of response. Many circles probably preferred not to put their names on any list if it meant risking attention from government officials.

Predominant among those circles responding were groups in villages miles from the nearest railroad station; seventeen lay between three and ten miles away. The reports the Section received demonstrate the extent to which the urban pastimes were penetrating the countryside by the summer of 1914. In September V. V. Tikhonovich, who had belonged to the Section from its earliest days, published an analysis of the returns in an article entitled "Popular Theatre According to Information Gathered Locally."[57] His data offer a snapshot of rural circles on the eve of the war.

Of the circles reporting, seven had organized in the years 1906–10, and fourteen during the 1911–13 period. The younger circles were the most important ones. Membership in the unchartered groups was smaller—in the teens and twenties—than in those legally recognized, where it ran as high as fifty. The circles and troupes varied considerably in composition. The most common combination included peasants, workers, and intelligentsia.

At least some of the participants in most of the circles boasted formal education. A Saint Petersburg province circle consisted of local male peasants aged 15 to 32 and female peasants aged 18 to 23. All had studied in the one-room zemstvo village school, and some had completed the elementary course. Some now worked in neighboring factories. "When they acted for the first time," the completed questionnaire stated, "some of them had never seen a stage production." Performers in one of the Moscow province circles had all finished the six-year course in the local zemstvo school. The majority were adults from 16 to 25 years old. Here it was customary to withdraw from the players upon marrying. Members of another Moscow province circle, young and old, were all employees of the Aleksandrovsk railroad. None had less than a railroad school education, and some had secondary and higher education. Participants in the Kazan province circle were local peasants, aged between 20 and 40, engaged in agriculture. All had had primary schooling. Amateurs in a Vladimir province circle ranged in age from 16 to 30. They worked in three local spinning and weaving factories. The majority had finished primary school. Many were taking evening classes. There were only three women among them, which greatly limited their choice of plays. The questionnaire returned by the small Simbirsk province circle came back with a precise listing of personnel. Among the men were an official aged 22; a teacher, 26; an office clerk, 20; and an assembler for the Singer Company aged 23. The women included a domestic servant aged 20; the wife of a switchman, 28; a dressmaker (daughter of an inspector of railway cars), 19; and a high school girl, 18.

Besides school rooms, the circles performed in *volost'* headquarters, a firehouse, a credit society, a public house, a warehouse, an inn, a grain barn, a threshing barn, open fields, and a tree-lined street. When a circle in Nizhni Novgorod province was forced to stop using school facilities, it reorganized and made construction of its own village theatre its first priority. It is hardly surprising that these circles possessed little in the way of props, wigs, and furniture. They averaged no more than three productions per year. Audiences ranged from 100 to 400, with 250 the average. Ticket sales furnished most of the circles' incomes, but a few had additional support from school funds, the zemstvo, private contributions, and local manufacturers. Average receipts for a performance were seventy-five rubles, but ran as high as three hundred rubles at the Riazan province circle, which had its own permanent stage graced by an orchestra playing military tunes at every performance and charged up to five rubles per seat.

The circles' fare was dominated by Ostrovsky, and plays were chosen that described the life of various social groups in Russia. The majority of the responses said that local audiences received the productions positively. The Riazan group thought the relationship between audience and circle could hardly have been better. The Nizhni Novgorod circle recalled that the rural viewers had trouble understanding their first performance, but concluded they had little difficulty thereafter. Similarly, the Simbirsk province circle said local peasants had only been acquainted with *balagan* theatre like *Petrushka,* but that they approved of dramatic acting when they saw it. One of the Moscow province circles reported that sometimes the audience approved of the play, and sometimes it did not. The Samara province circle noted that in its audience, the general mass was impassive, "but the youth are interested." Another Moscow province circle said they had little positive response from their audience, but that grumbling was heard locally after ten months had passed with no more plays presented. Some of the old people complained that the plays cost them money, because the young people liked to play the dandy and had felt they had to dress up to attend. Some circles complained of their audiences' passivity, but others noted a willingness to take part, even to keep order in the auditorium. Respondents generally commented on the younger generation's superior receptivity.

Asked about community support from specific social groups, respondents singled out the clergy for negativism. The Perm province circle reply said, "the clergy for some reason have very little sympathy for this business and try to do a lot of harm when the opportunity presents itself." The response from Tambov province explained, "The priest says openly that the plays corrupt the people." Some circles complained that they had little support from the local intelligentsia. The Simbirsk circle's report said the teachers and doctors stayed away because they feared clerical and landlord disapproval would cost them their livelihood. Several replies indicated that the circles' most consistently positive supporter was the *zemskii nachal'nik* (land captain). The Vladimir province circle said, "We don't have a doctor or landowners, the clergy are indifferent, the female teacher is negative; we get sympathy only from the *zemskii nachal'nik.*"

Asked to articulate their goals in the Section's questionnaire, the circles mentioned a civilizing mission far more often than the pursuit of aesthetic satisfaction, regardless of province or region. They routinely perceived themselves as engaged in social action, transmitting something valuable to needy audiences poorly prepared to receive it. Some of the phrases penned in reply to the question concerning objectives suggest the new, rigorously democratic circles to have been as socially conscious as the philanthropists who organized the earliest theatres for the people. Perm: "To give rational, helpful and educational entertainment to the people [and] . . . to divert youth from debauchery." Simbirsk: "To struggle against evil among the people—darkness and ignorance." Vologda: "To satisfy the spiritual concerns of the countryside insofar as we are able." Iaroslavl': "To aid in the moral development of society." Whoever filled out the questionnaire returned by the Kazan peasant circle admitted a variety of motives: "Some are drawn to a mission, others by the goal of self-development and presenting intelligent and useful entertainment to the people." The only reply that cited an exclusively aesthetic motivation came from the president of a worker circle in Moscow province: "From the love of art."

The circles' responses to the question concerning their needs also offer some insight into their view of themselves and their tasks. Assistance with direction and help choosing plays were most frequently mentioned. The directors came from varied backgrounds. Most often they were male teachers. *Volost'* clerks were the second most common group attempting to fill this role. Others included an insurance agent, a visiting student, and some workers and peasants. Sometimes a collective undertook the job, but this evidently did not work very well. Six circles said they needed costumes; four mentioned wigs and help building scenery. Three specified help painting scenery and organizational assistance. The most touching request came from a circle in Petrograd province:

> We need leaders. . . . We are always thinking that this theatrical work we have begun will die. Teach us how to create a formal circle, and how to choose a charter and in what form—otherwise everything will disintegrate. We have here in the countryside only circles of peasant youth. So teach us to operate in a more organized way. The kind of man who takes over everything concerning the presentation of a play is not going to appear suddenly in the country.[58]

In the period after 1905 grassroots organizations became possible in Russia for the first time, and participants quickly preceived the importance of organization.

AN AUDIENCE COMES OF AGE

Back in the capital, the philanthropist's Nardom delivered plays and developed an appreciative audience with strong opinions. Panina and Gaideburov sought the aesthetic cultivation of their clients, a motivation that drew Polenov and others together in Moscow at the Section. The Nardom theatre also took up outreach to factory workers' circles, which themselves grappled with the need for and potential of organization.

Gaideburov could claim the General-Access Theatre a success by a number of measures. The audience for plays had grown steadily. In the theatre's first ten years 145,605 spectators attended 260 performances. An excellent rapport developed between audience and actors. Audiences eventually wanted to see certain plays again and again. More productions sold out as time went on. Viewers' beliefs that they had been changed as members of the audience at the Nardom deserve serious consideration.

In February 1909 students completing the evening courses expressed their gratitude to Gaideburov in an address.

> The dead weight of mass existence presses continually on the life of the worker—which increases the significance of the theatre [for him]. . . . It is almost the only place where one can happily get up to join the battle against the worker's spiritual poverty and renew the struggle with evil forces for a bright and intelligent [*razumnyi*] life. But this maturing demand was left unsatisfied. The intelligentsia theatres were not accessible to him, and the so-called popular theatres pleased only the baser instincts of the crowd. The General-Access Theatre was the first to set out courageously on the road to meeting these demands. Listening to its audience attentively, conforming continually to their level of education, striving with all their strength to communicate in clear, understandable form . . . they raise the audience to a higher and higher level of consciousness. This work is difficult—difficult, but great, necessary, and gratefully received.[59]

The personal statements that survive from the tenth anniversary jubilee testify to the audience's pride in the theatre, and a consciousness that the folk had come a long way. A student who successfully completed the Ligovsk evening classes credited the awakening of the peasants to village schools, popular readings, and popular theatre and argued that a new kind of popular poetry, in the form of *chastushkii* (chastushka: a two-line or four-line folk verse, usually humorous and topical, sung in a lively manner), testified to the changing nature of folk creativity.[60] The jubilee responses suggest an increasingly informed critical attitude toward productions. A mechanic who had attended for six years wrote:

> I saw many plays—dramas, tragedies, comedies. I found them all comprehensible and good. . . . Simple folk come here every so often and say, "What bad actors [they have] here! They can't do anything. Over at the Marinsky Theatre they really know how to act, but here nothing is worth a damn. I could act that well." I've had to talk to such people—even come to the point of having a row—but I always have been a defender of your theatre.[61]

A writer said "Thank you to P. P. Gaideburov for his productions, which are never empty, though there have been times when they were very sad." An official on the court for the affairs of minors praised the productions he had seen of *Hamlet, The Lower Depths,* and *The Cherry Orchard,* but complained that many of the sets had been inadequate. A cobbler observed that Ostrovsky's *The Forest* had been better acted in 1903 than subsequently and had had better staging and sets then as well. A schoolboy who acknowledged his debt to the Ligovsk theatre for his own aesthetic development offered suggestions: "It would be helpful if a definite system could be adopted for selecting plays for performance: a strict program and unified action would show results in a hurry."

An artisan found rather too much spontaneity in the audience: "It would be a big improvement if you could put an end to the commotion caused by the young people in front of the stage after every act." Another worker offered a suggestion that often came up in responses to questionnaires asking how popular theatre could be improved:

> It would be highly desirable if a short paper were read before certain plays—especially plays by foreign authors which most of your audience are encountering for the first time. Constantly keeping in mind the composition of your audience, it would be desirable at the end of each season to produce a questionnaire posing two or three questions to the public, on the basis of which it would be possible to clarify what your audience would like to see on your stage the following season.

These worker comments recall the Nevskii Society respondents' endorsement of good order and concern to establish a play's context.

Responses to Chekhov plays suggest that the Nardom audience had grown to like them. In 1907 *The Cherry Orchard* played at the Ligovsk People's House. In 1910 the General-Access Theatre introduced popular dramatizations of Chekhov tales. In a review of the 1909–10 season, Gaideburov noted that *Ivanov* now invariably played to a full house at the General-Access Theatre. He took this as proof that the appeal of Chekhov's plays was not limited to the intelligentsia. Ivanov's psyche had originally been unacceptable to the General-Access audience. But the distance that had formerly alienated them from the Chekhovian heroes, he concluded, had vanished.[62] The last of the Chekhov plays, *The Cherry Orchard* was the last to become popular with the General-Access audience. A student wrote in connection with the General-Access Theatre's tenth anniversary jubilee that "the workings of *The Cherry Orchard* seem a little strange to me, affected, unnatural." Someone in government service had more serious reservations: "I saw *The Cherry Orchard* and the production of the thing was incomprehensible to me. In my opinion a situation belonging in a children's room should not be [performed as a play]." According to evidence published in the same year, the Ligovsk audience exuberantly chose the point of view of the former peasant: "Lopakhin, cutting down the manor house orchard for future house lots, sets off an explosion of enthusiasm."[63] The observer who reported this preference explained it by saying that the heroic element was what the popular audience loved most. But one might as easily infer that the audience liked to see a commoner rising in the world. At the very least it must be said that Chekhovian tolerance was lost on this audience.

According to Gaideburov, *Uncle Vania* and Hauptmann's *Lonely People* became the favorite plays of the General-Access audience. How illuminating it would be to know whether they identified with Dr. Astrov's environmental concerns (or whether they appreciated the superb theatricality with which Chekhov communicates them through his local historical maps) and whether they saw the point of Vania's absurdly comical assertion, in his rage, that he could have been another Dostoevsky but for his self-sacrifice in staying to manage the estate. The central character in *Lonely People* ignores social convention as well as the mundane concerns of work and family in order to devote his energies to thought about the great issues of the day. But could it be that the play intrigued the General-Access audience because the German's family life was derailed by a young Russian studying in Switzerland who has a distinctly revolutionary background?

The audience undeniably had its likes and dislikes. The first Russian production of Bjørnstjerne Bjørnson's *Beyond Human Might*, which attacks all striving and aspiration that run counter to the limited character of human nature, failed dismally in the 1909–10 season. It would be tempting to conclude that the play's antiheroic bias offended the Ligovsk audience. But Gaideburov said that his coworkers simply "considered it strange and incomprehensible for our audience." Symbolist works never caught on, as the remark from a trader at the jubilee may indicate: "I would like to see a little more reality and actuality, and not fantastic comedies." Yet that audience had a mind of its own, as its desire to contemplate *Antigone* attests. The first performance interested a very modest number of viewers. When it was repeated the following year, a few more people came. In the third year it usually played to full houses. But then it played to overflow crowds, which Gaideburov said "followed it with concentration and fascination." In later years it was given repeatedly each season, and from 1908 to 1914 it was performed more than a hundred times at the General-Access Theatre and by the Wanderers in the provinces. Yet neither the imperial theatres nor Stanislavsky could overcome their audiences' indifference to the work. Petr explained that "The people believed in old gods, but did not rise as far as the new contemplation of the conscious world and sought answers in antique tragedy."[64]

Another source reveals something of the maturation of a particular segment of the Ligovsk audience. In 1958 elderly Leningrad residents with fond memories of the role of the Nardom in shaping their lives met to recall their experiences in the General-Access Theatre.[65] Several were printers and metalworkers who had taken courses there. V. A. Levantsov, who had worked at the Westinghouse factory ten to twelve hours a day and studied every evening in the Ligovsk general education classes, paid the theatre a tribute that must have warmed the aged Gaideburov's heart: "I know for myself that if for some reason I was not able to be present at our theatre, it would be difficult to work all week without the moral recharging that Gaideburov's plays gave." A. Ia. Shakhanov, as a young typesetter, had heard that the theatre presented "plays that talked about life," and so had become a member of its audience. He said that in those days "it was not so easy for the younger generation of workers to understand the 'vexed' questions as it has now become for every komsomol lad, and it was necessary to expend a little effort to penetrate the cunning mechanism of capitalist exploitation." His short memoir nicely illustrates the dangers of relying very heavily on this testimony about the development of an intellectual point of view fifty to sixty years earlier. He especially recalled three plays of Gorky among those that impressed him on the stage of the General-Access Theatre. But the performance records, which are quite complete, indicate that the General-Access performed only two Gorky plays. Still, there is no reason to doubt his assertion that the working-class youth of the city considered it "their theatre."

Countess Panina insisted that her People's House be a place where common people could encounter the achievements of high culture freely, and she used her considerable influence to keep government security agents out. Shakhanov testified that "the Ligovsk People's House was unsurpassed in its convenience and security. . . . For police agents the People's House was a forbidden zone. You could always meet friends or communicate without fear inside the walls of the People's House." A young worker who had taken the two-year evening technical course and courses on history, natural science, and the history of literature, recalled years later that several literary circles sprang up in the Nardom, each with its own handwritten journal. He remembered the names of more than six and noted that they represented Socialist Revolutionary as well as Bolshevik and Menshevik viewpoints.[66] In fact several Bolshevik party members who would become prominent took advantage of this protected environment to carry on political work.[67] Among them were the future commissar and ambassador, A. M. Kołłontai, and Lenin's personal secretary, V. M. Bonch-Bruevich. For a time an illegal paper, *Golos rabochego,* was produced on a hectograph there. And persons wanted by the authorities sometimes slept there. Mashirov-Samobytnik said, "Living in 1912 illegally behind the flies of the Nardom in a specially constructed . . . box, at night we made use of the stage for ourselves."

Several of the 1913 responses indicate a rising class consciousness among the viewers. To the question "Did you understand everything that you saw?" a watchmaker answered, "Yes, but these things that are completely new to me are difficult to take in, and so they don't leave much of an impression. I would like to see vital plays, that is, that speak more directly to workers." A lathe operator agreed: "I would like to see plays where the poor and the humble are treated more truly and with more sympathy, where the author is not afraid of capitalism or the power of property." The Bolshevik party newspapers covered the General-Access productions attentively. *Pravda* in its 20 April 1914 issue probably gave a fair estimate of the theatre's role in the party's scheme of things: "The Gaideburov theatre is far from being a proletarian theatre, but it is perhaps uniquely of its kind an intellectual [*ideinyi*] theatre, and on account of its too courageous intellectualism suffers every possible oppression."[68] Even in the provinces, party members followed the performances of the Wanderers. S. M. Kirov, the future Leningrad party chief, reviewed their *Lonely People* of May 1912 in Vladikavkaz: "They say that this is a drama from German life, but how close it is to us. . . . It is safe to say, without shouting, that it depicts our life, that it shows us as in a mirror, a living mirror—that is what the company of the Wanderers is striving for."[69]

Gaideburov apparently did not expect his audience to refrain from developing political consciousness, but he chose plays that presented a variety of viewpoints. *Pravda* took him to task for producing F. Langmann's *Bartel Tulazer,* a play about a strike in which the leader betrays his followers. Evidently Gaideburov had nothing against the Bolsheviks, for he was known to respond generously to their requests for entertainments outside the theatre to raise money for the families of workers on strike or under arrest.[70] Yet he was cautious to protect his theatre's independence by avoiding its politicization. The General-Access waited until 1913 to present *The Lower Depths.* Gaideburov noted as a sign of his audience's maturity that they received it "quietly, reverently, almost liturgically."

When the time came to celebrate the tenth anniversary of the theatre in 1913, Gaideburov took pains to see that the jubilee program did not become political. A number of representatives of worker organizations were not permitted to appear. The 27 November 1913 issue of *Pravda* carried this complaint:

> Not a single word about the connection between art in general and of healthy realistic and social art with life, not one word about the difference between the Gaideburov theatre and its service to art from the service of the rest of the "geniuses" of the stage. Not a single word about the future of the theatre in connection with the future of the proletarian movement. . . . The general impression was one of some sort of deficiency, concealed in a cowardly fashion from being spoken. It was not necessary to honor the Gaideburov theatre in this way. The proletariat must wait, evidently, to say its word, wait for the next jubilee. We are waiting.[71]

A woman who worked in his company with her husband and later joined the Party was probably correct in saying that even after the war began Gaideburov's own political outlook "did not rise above the level of the consciousness of the petit bourgeois intelligentsia."[72] Nor were his audiences in the main inclined to a Marxist point of view: "Doctor Stockman, an inveterate individualist . . . the seeming antithesis of a social democrat, evokes tears of tender emotion and sighs of joy, and people applaud *An Enemy of the People* . . . feeling the high truth reigning over life and drama."[73]

The celebration of the tenth anniversary of the Ligovsk House of the People encouraged the patron and administrators of their institution to change their focus and consider an "All-Russian field of action." As Countess Panina explained, "The need for People's Houses was felt more sharply as social life in Russia became more complex, not only in big cities and industrial centers with large working-class populations, but much more in the countryside, where the cooperative movement was developing and the population up to that time had been deprived of any assistance because of the sheer magnitude of its responsible and most honorable civic and cultural concerns."[74] Gaideburov wrote on the function of theatre in the People's House for the book Panina planned in 1913 to draw together information on Russia's new community centers. He argued that serious theatre gradually alters the naive viewer's way of seeing.[75] The rising tide of interest in theatre in Russia and the rapid spread of People's Houses, he felt confident, would so stimulate demand for playbooks that a special press like Tolstoy's Posrednik could be organized to print large, cheap editions of them. He observed that the simple folk in Russia were learning how to look at pictures and learning how to concentrate on and learn from serious theatre. For theatres to succeed in People's Houses, he concluded, "The audience has to have a critical orientation to the theatre with an understanding that there must be aesthetic criteria in order to make judgments." He recommended a regular sampling of audience opinion through questionnaires, and, even better, ongoing discussion with members of the audience about the plays they had seen.

WORKER THEATRE

Urban drama circles consisting entirely of workers began to form before the war, but did not establish sufficiently stable foundations to augment the available supply of popular performances significantly. Two conditions apparently had to be met before worker circles were possible. Factory hours had to be reduced to the point where employment left workers some leisure time and energy. And a cadre of workers had to become sufficiently literate and bookish to possess the inclination and skills to select and prepare plays for presentation. The first requirement was met by the decline in average daily hours worked in Russia from ten and a half in the early 1900s to nine to ten hours in 1913. Further, in 1914 the average factory worker worked 22 percent fewer hours per year than his counterpart one year earlier.[76] L. N. Kleinbort, who wrote on worker theatre both before and after the revolution, noted that the first cadres of the "worker intelligentsia" were pushed forward in 1904–5.[77] Anna Brenko, who had opened the first private theatre in Russia for the general public in 1881, started to instruct Moscow working-class amateurs in 1904. When they performed *The Storm* in 1905, workers played all the roles except old Kabanova, which Brenko herself took. They toured the Moscow area, appearing in factories and mills.[78] The emergence of the worker *intelligent,* essential to the creation of a purely worker troupe, can be glimpsed in a 1904 essay discussing a feuilleton published in a local Kiev newspaper. A certain Bulgakova collected questionnaires from worker theatregoers and found that she could easily distinguish replies from "conscious workers." Two such workers she quoted mentioned books in explaining why they were attracted to theatre:[79]

> Formerly I went to the theatre to laugh a little, but most often they served up the kind of play where you have to cry. These plays flew in the face of my disposition to laugh, and I recognized that the theatre is nothing other than a reflection of life, according to the times and customs, that it represents those types that you don't understand so precisely in the books you've read—no matter how artfully the author may have expressed them.
>
> Theatre is nothing other than a temple of knowledge. . . . A person can't get what one gets in the theatre by reading books.

Kleinbort recalled how Gleb Uspenskii had anticipated with pride the "mass of future readers" that would come from the *narod.* They were now a reality, and the worker actor was just as inexorably making his way into existence.[80] In an essay published a year before the war began Kleinbort observed that "the worker intelligentsia . . . is still weak and uncertain—but the work has begun to boil." Nonetheless, he admitted, "As quickly as the [worker dramatic circles] spring up and spread wider and wider, they just as quickly disband after presenting two or three plays."[81] He used virtually identical language in an essay published in 1923, but followed it with the statement "Then the movement went forward, standing on its own feet."[82] Worker theatre unquestionably stirred before the war, but the getting to its feet came after the revolution and under state auspices rather than through spontaneous action from below.

Kleinbort considered Moscow to have been ahead of Saint Petersburg in the development of worker theatres. The initiative to create a bureau in Moscow to support worker theatre came from workers in the Presnensk district (north of the Zoological Garden), who united with an Over-the-River workers' drama circle. They approached the Technical Society, which formed a commission on worker theatre. This became the Section's fifth division. Klepikov thought it "curious" that the workers wrote Gorky a letter asking him to endorse their idea of a worker theatre and advise them on how to proceed.[83] But Kleinbort well knew the unique appeal of Gorky's early plays for workers, having written that "when a worker troupe is assembled, it begins with *Meshchane* or *The Lower Depths.*"[84] Gorky responded with a warm reply and suggested that they turn to Stanislavsky for help. Stanislavsky assigned six actors from the Art Theatre to instruct the workers in declamation and diction. In 1912 there were four groups studying the former and two the latter. A study group discussed *Boris Godunov, The Forest, The Inspector General, The Storm,* and *The Power of Darkness,* using the Art Theatre's method. The courses were reorganized in the summer of 1913. Under D. A. Tolbuzin's direction, the Section trained an all-worker traveling troupe. Its casts presented *The Power of Darkness,* with sets painted especially for them by Polenov, and Nikolai Popov's one-act *An Unjust Trial.* Klepikov said that a number of very able performers came out of this company.

Some of the questionnaires returned to the Section in 1914 came from circles composed exclusively of workers. Tikhonovich found their preferences in repertory to be less impressive than those of purely peasant circles replying.[85] He did note that younger workers wanted to see plays about the everyday life of working people but were no longer satisfied with older efforts in this genre like E. Karpov's *Rabochaia slobodka* (The workers' settlement [1891]) and *Zhite privol'noe* (Free life [1892]). They expressed a keen desire to see Hauptmann's *The Weavers.* They also professed a strong interest in historical plays. They preferred drama to comedy. Foreign plays were of interest only when they depicted an environment close to the workers' own. These worker circles had no interest in the fantastic.

In Saint Petersburg planning was under way before the war to create an organization analogous to the Section to nurture and sustain worker dramatic circles. Several such circles had come and gone. One called "Art and Life" had mounted five productions before disbanding. Enlightening societies spawned worker dramatic circles. The "Cultural-Educational Society Named in Honor of M. M. Stasiulevich" had one for a time, as did the "Source of Light and Knowledge" Society. The Kolomenskoe and Ligovsk Society aided a workers' circle by providing a piano. The workers themselves arranged a series of literary evenings, mornings, concerts, and plays. The mornings proved especially successful, because "then the workers had more energy for concerts, and plays." They readily attracted audiences that were willing to contribute generously.[86]

But even with some institutional support, worker circles broke up quickly. It seemed that professional training and specialized assistance might provide what they needed in order to survive. In 1913 the Vasili Island drama circle approached the General-Access Theatre in Panina's People's House for help. The General-Access had done more for worker theatre than any other institution in the city. It had taken ten workers' cooperatives under its wing. It had a "workers' studio." And students in its evening course had presented *The Lower Depths* and *Meshchane.* Now it sent P. P. Sazonov, a member of the Gaideburov-Skarskaia company, to direct plays for the Vasili Island circle. The organizers were committed to the independence of workers in all fields of endeavor, and the business of the circle was conducted democratically in meetings of the general membership. The circle presented successful productions of *Getting Married, Sin and Sadness are Common to*

All, Hauptmann's *Before Sunrise,* and a Gorky work. Gradually the membership became divided into two contending factions.[87] The majority, under Sazonov's leadership, defined itself by its commitment to "pure, nontendentious, holy art, standing above matters of class." The Marxist minority claimed that because art manifests real life, it necessarily demonstrates how class underlies everything. After many disagreements, they warned that if the company chose to abandon the principles of worker theatre, they would have to change their name to the "art standing above class" ensemble and become like a hundred other companies operating in Saint Petersburg. The dissidents remained committed to the proposition that theatre should illuminate the situation of the working class and indicate a way out of it. The circle disbanded.

A signed article in the Marxist newspaper that printed an account of the schism in the Vasili Island circle noted "the ever-growing demand among workers for aesthetic enrichment."[88] It said that the artistic circles in clubs carried the germ of proletarian creativity in embryo and promised a true proletarian theatre in the future, in which the working class would create something of its own in art. A student in the two-year evening theatrical course at Dom Panina wrote after the revolution that the worker theatrical movement in Saint Petersburg had arisen there. He recalled that the chief of police had authorized the "first worker theatre" in 1913, and that it had rented a building on the Obvodnyi Canal and presented an Ostrovsky play, only to be disbursed after a right-wing newspaper complained.[89] According to Mashirov-Samobytnik, "The Bolsheviks dominated the advanced workers connected with the Panin People's House. From 1908 to 1914 the Panin Nardom was a Bolshevik stronghold." Though his claim should be accepted with caution, it does confirm that the idea of tendentious worker theatre exercised considerable appeal among young, literate, "conscious" workers before the war. Its author also recalled how these worker-students at Dom Panina formed literary circles and arranged a meeting with Gorky in 1913 through the assistance of the secretary of *Pravda.*

A review of a 1914 worker production of Pisemsky's *A Bitter Fate* also testifies to the continuing enthusiasm for the possibility of worker theatre completely emancipated from bourgeois theatre, capable of refreshing an audience, inspiring it, and sending it away instructed.[90] Its author took heart from the astonishingly improved acting of the worker company he was reviewing. When they performed *Meshchane* earlier, the actors had played themselves. Now they had attained "great and noble self-control and ripeness and harmony of acting." They now created living characters, psychologically motivated and interacting convincingly. The audience were enthralled, forgot they were viewers, and believed themselves participants in this unfolding rural drama. The crowd scenes came across powerfully. There were "blunders," to be sure, but not even professional actors were immune to blunders. On the strength of what he saw at the 11 May performance, the reviewer concluded that "'worker theatre' has almost been realized. . . . Yes, the beginning of this beautiful future is almost here; worker theatre almost exists already."

In the years between the 1905 revolution and the beginning of the war, significant numbers of popular theatres sprang up for the first time. Institutions developed that provided assistance to these fledgling popular drama groups by responding to their particular requests and needs. The growth of some of these agencies is well documented; that of others (like the "Moscow League of Amateurs of Theatre Art") is not. The government disliked initiative from below and remained generally unsupportive. Polenov commented on its restrictive policies with regard to the Section's courses for theatre organizers. And Tikhii noted in June 1914 that "in recent times administrations have begun to look askance at popular theatre, and permission to present plays is given very unwillingly."[91]

After repeated attempts to establish civil equality in the countryside had failed, the now richly subsidized zemstvos promoted theatre. The countryside came to life with local community centers where plays stimulated discussion. The ideal of a respected public forum where the nation's conditions and social arrangements underwent informal critical examination was rarely attained. Nevertheless, some of the educated could still hope for cultural unification based on the individualism supported for the first time at the community level.

Klepikov's *In the Low Places* eschewed the cosmic perspective that Chekhov and Gorky had employed with such success just a few years earlier. Although its central character spoke of the distinction between the public and the private and called for higher standards of public behavior in village life, the play dwelled on mundane matters like the value of a work ethic, assertiveness, and a community life based on an equality of interests. Yet there was something refreshing about the pragmatism of this work that examined the nuts-and-bolts requirements of harmonizing interests in a progressive rural community.

Audiences for popular theatre became more demanding in this period. The author of a 1909 survey of Moscow city and temperance theatres for the people printed in the new popular *Penny Newspaper (Gazeta Kopeika)* observed that disappointed viewers were wandering off to sample the work of "clumsy club productions."[92] Panina's mixed audience matured and warmed to difficult works, but the groups who took advantage of the protection her theatre offered may not have developed the political outlook she expected. She cited the increasing complexity of social life in Russia when she turned her attention to the countryside and threw herself into the cause of establishing People's Houses.

By the eve of the war, with the help of supporting agencies independent of the government, the quality of performance in grassroots theatres was becoming passable. Rural theatregoers in huge numbers saw plays that presented individualism, civic responsibility, economic independence, long-range calculation, and intellectual curiosity in the most attractive light possible. The youths all over Russia who participated in productions as actors were permanently changed by the experience. The Viazemsk players, for example, developed a sense of community lacking in "self-centered" outsiders. In the remote countryside, play production obliterated social distinctions for participants in amateur circles, and they felt exalted by the humanizing enterprise that brought them together. In the cities, where the public sphere had been transformed, matters were more complicated. Blok perhaps had reason to think that the distant and growing roar from the hinterland was quite unlike "the cacophonous roar of the town."

Chapter Seven

The Popular Theatre Unbound

WITH THE COMING of the war centrifugal forces giving rise to talk of revolution in April 1914 subsided, and the new common goal of victory made it possible for the members of the disparate estates to forget temporarily what divided them. The central government altered its stance toward society, attending now to public opinion and disencumbering both local government and private agencies engaged in social activities, like the Section and the cooperatives.

In February 1914 Nicholas had spoken in ukase against the Treasury's dependence on the intemperance of the people. The war brought the closing of the vodka shops as a temporary measure. The newspapers clamored for the policy to be made permanent, reasoning that the nation's gain would far outweigh the Treasury's revenue loss. This reform had major implications for the expansion of local popular theatre, as activists in the area of community development asserted at the time in books and pamphlets. A docent at Kharkov University noted that Nizhni Novgorod province alone saved three million rubles in the year following the introduction of prohibition.

> We know that in many places the former alcohol-induced intoxication gave way to intoxication generated by the heat of play. And it is perfectly understandable why in many villages, especially where cooperatives are operating, the idea sprang up of constructing People's Houses as soon as possible. We deeply believe that to defeat the enemy we must not only escape from the economic, but also the spiritual enslavement of the nation.[1]

A professor who had written as early as 1898 of the need to decentralize the organization of enlightened popular entertainments and extend them into every corner of the provinces now wrote:

> In the great historical moment we are now living through, when fate has sent our fatherland a hard test, our cultural shortcomings, our defects in public education, in social initiative and self-help, are clearer than ever. And the weakness of our organization of social forces is also clearly revealed, as are the shortcomings of our intellectual and social development.[2]

The experience of prohibition at a time of national emergency suggested expanded scope for individual self-reliance and social integration. The author of a pamphlet recommending People's Houses as community centers for adult spiritual development stressed the opportunity presented by the new perspective the war opened.

> The war with Germany showed how much drunkenness harmed us and how beneficial temperance is. People's Houses are like beacons to the health and joy of life, like hearths of culture and enlightenment, to reinforce popular temperance and to enlighten the popular mind. We must hurry![3]

In March 1914 the Wanderers and Ligovsk General-Access theatres began publishing a new journal on contemporary drama in hopes of somehow unifying urban audiences dominated by working people and "the Russian working intelligentsia, born in the . . . provinces and residing there."[4] This new venture was a response in part to requests from Wanderers' patrons, "scattered far from each other across the wide open spaces of Russia," who wanted to feel closer to the country's unfolding artistic life. The Section also began publishing a journal, *Narodnyi Teatr* (People's theatre). Additionally, the numbers of professionals engaged in theatre grew rapidly after 1902 (nearly doubling by early 1917). The Russian Theatrical Society (RTO) continued to provide a forum for discussion of the condition and needs of popular theatre. As people began to seek something special from theatre, actors had begun to think of themselves as professionals.[5]

The war quickly created opportunities that let independent agencies broaden the scope of their work. In August 1914 the zemstvos undertook to furnish medical facilities and services. Representatives of provincial zemstvo boards convened in Moscow to consider forming a national union of zemstvos. In September the union received official imperial sanction. The Section soon became the first body to provide entertainment to soldiers in infirmaries.

The war stimulated popular theatre, an obvious solution to the need to fill "temperate spare time."[6] But V. V. Tikhonovich insisted that escapism also fostered the growth of theatrical circles that contributed to "the general victory of self-organization and spontaneous action." Some of the new members attracted to art during the war viewed it as a refuge from the horrors of life. After the war Zviagintsev continued to stress the community-building function of theatre circles in People's Houses. "The circles . . . are very pleasant for their members: they train them for general activity, for harmony in behavior, and social education is very precious. Plays . . . not only contribute to the artistic or aesthetic enjoyment of the audience—they introduce a spirit of community to the members of the circle."[7] In 1915 Tikhonovich assessed the impact of theatre on both viewer and amateur actor. "Theatre," he said, "opens up before us the depths of the human soul and exposes the nerves of social life, . . . makes social classes that are strange to us seem close,

. . . awakens inquisitiveness, expands mental horizons, develops imagination, enriches the viewer with feelings and desires."[8] To participate in its creation was even more beneficial than to view it. He reported the observation that performers from the *narod* were distinguished by greater spiritual integrity and strength, more moral temperance and steadiness than intelligentsia amateurs. Various classes and nationalities, he hoped, could each contribute something of their own to the forging of a new democratic theatrical culture.

The war encouraged the government to remove some of the restrictions the practitioners of popular theatre had worked under and stimulated demand for organized entertainment. While it was being fought, theatre's promise of self-awareness for the masses seemed less a threat—despite the medium's habit of fixing attention on social distinctions and gradations—than it had been before national trial by combat.

THEATRE ACTIVISTS CONFER

By the time the war began, enough specialists committed to popular theatre existed in Russia to form the nucleus of a national movement. They came from the theatre, professional eduction, the zemstvos, the co-ops. When the government dropped its opposition to social activity, they found themselves free to meet and coordinate a national campaign to identify the obstacles to the formation of grassroots popular theatres and take action to eliminate them. The medium of the national congress presented itself as a forum for discussion and planning. The law on associations of 4 March 1906 had not altered the legal status of congresses; under section III, paragraph 17, they had to be sanctioned in advance by the minister of the interior in agreement with other appropriate ministers. Nevertheless, even before the war, the authorities granted such authorization much more freely than they had prior to 1905.[9]

Organizers of cultural enlightenment activities in the countryside met in the summer, fall, and winter of 1915 to bring the thoughts of national experts to bear on regional projects. Each of the conferences reviewed recent gains and considered concrete proposals to capitalize on new conditions and encourage local popular theatres. The Christmas gathering, a conclave devoted exclusively to popular theatre, summed up the movement's progress over the years and mustered an impressive battery of ideas on how it could finally facilitate the *narod*'s preparation for life in the modern world.

The Kharkov Society for Literacy met in June to consider a range of educational activities for Kharkov province. In his welcoming address the Society's president, Sergei Aleksandrovich Raevskii, greeted several of the nation's most active and knowledgeable authorities on popular theatre. Eight of the presentations dealt with popular theatre. The Society published the proceedings before the year was out.[10]

A striking feature of the reports is their authors' common assumption that a new level of cultural development has just been attained in the countryside. E. N. Medynskii in "The Next Tasks in Establishing Enlightened Entertainments for the Population" noted the critical confluence of rising literacy and "the struggle with hooliganism and the sobering-up of the countryside" (*TsK* 138). V. V. Tikhonovich, in a paper on societies of People's Houses, observed that local factories and railroads had produced a middle class in the towns, which figured in the appearance of "cultural cells" like library societies, sanitary trusteeships, trusteeships for the poor, fire protection societies, agricultural societies and cooperatives (*TsK* 99). He acknowledged that rural development remained uneven, and conceded that "in the remotest corners," where social life remained undeveloped or "where they are just beginning to wake up," unified management was appropriate in any people's houses that might be established. In the majority of localities, where social life was developed, but comparatively few people were active culturally, it was appropriate for the community centers to be dominated by larger bodies like the cooperatives. But in areas where social life was developed to a high degree and where culturally active people were numerous—like parts of Moscow province—"decentralization of direction" was now possible. People's houses there could be operated by separate circles and commissions freely accessible to all who might care to participate (*TsK* 107). Ia. A. Grinenko, in "The Next Steps in Developing Popular Theatre," observed that theatre had been the first enlightened entertainment available in the countryside. It had become important in some villages and district towns, but still was not solidly organized. Formerly, local "landowners, wives of land captains and various other female guardians" threw themselves into the work and invited some of the village intelligentsia to participate. Now students in the village school took part, along with the teacher, the fel'dsher (surgeon's assistant), the sexton, the doctor, the clerk, and the agronomist. "A new type of literate village population appeared in the countryside—this is the youth of the most recent times" (*TsK* 415). The increase in village drunkenness and hooliganism, along with the great desire of villagers to see plays, combined to give the "new village intelligentsia" a social cause. Tikhonovich, speaking on the significance, tasks, needs, and organization of popular theatre, proclaimed that "the initiative [*samodeiatel'nost'*] of local drama circles now forms the foundation of popular theatre's development" (*TsK* 373).

The speakers at the Kharkov conference agreed on the importance of the People's House in unifying local social life. Medynskii insisted that it must become for adults what the school is for children. Tikhonovich quoted approvingly from the "Cooperative Desk Calendar for 1915" that the People's House needed to provide space not just for official meetings, but for "regular private meetings and private conversations of members with each other."

There was less agreement on the credit to be given the zemstvos for their work on behalf of People's Houses.[11] Tikhonovich praised the recent zemstvo tendency to stop giving everything from the center of the province or district and to make localities depend on "locally organized social forces" for support. The Kharkov district zemstvo had recently decided to give material support to existing groups in the district to present plays. Medynskii chided the zemstvos for being so slow to move from sponsoring the expansion of rural literacy to supporting rural aesthetic and moral development by supporting theatre, choruses, art exhibits, and the like. After twenty-five years of zemstvo work on behalf of literacy, Russia now had twenty thousand people's libraries. But Medynskii considered that the people needed moral and artistic development far more than they needed the ability to read and write, and the zemstvos that had built collections of lantern slides and museums devoted to textbook materials had not yet got around to building collections of props, sets, and books on theatre.

He called attention to the natural bridge connecting basic literacy and the development of moral faculties through artistic activities like theatre. He faulted the zemstvos in general for regarding the folk as objects, characterizing their present mind set as "I give out the books, they read them! I read, they listen!" Judging theatre a more influential art than literature, he reasoned that it creates an especially potent worldview and outlook. Its value lay in the obligation it imposes to reconcile different values and systems rather than to any "moral tendencies fastened to plays." Tikhonovich was interested not just in "theatre for the people" but in "theatre through the people." Spectators gained from their experience in the theatre, but rural amateurs presenting just two or three plays a season had even more to gain.

> To be an actor means to educate the will, to discipline oneself in self-awareness and self-control [*priuchat' sebia k samonabliudeniiu i k samoobladaniiu*]; to be an actor means to bring beauty to one's speech, movements, words, to one's whole body. This cannot be overvalued.

The Section was well represented at the Kharkov conference by members reporting on concrete steps it was taking to strengthen popular theatre in the countryside. Klepikov noted that rural expansion could cause the demand for printed plays to grow "by a factor of several tens." It was already beginning to bring down the selling price of playbooks. But he feared to leave the matter to the market alone, and spoke of the advantages of creating a community press to publish plays at cheap prices. N. N. Golovanov reported on the Section's plans to organize a cadre of directors of plays suitable for rural theatres "from among the youth devoted to the business of rural theatre." It had its demonstration plays for the annual summer teacher-training courses in Moscow and was planning special courses covering all aspects of rural theatre to be given at Shaniavskii University. D. A. Tolbuzin cautioned that the work of a rural *rezhisser* (producer) of necessity remained much broader than that of his urban counterpart, who had the luxury of concentrating on deepening the psychic action of the characters, establishing proper relationships among them, and revealing the author's intentions. "The *rezhisser* in the countryside is administrator, psychologist, producer, set designer, and make-up artist."

In the autumn of 1915 another conference met to discuss means of satisfying the people's craving for art. The Iaroslavl General Zemstvo Conference on Cultural Activities (Iaroslavskoe obshchezemskoe soveshchanie o prosvetitel'nykh meropriiatiiakh) accorded special significance to theatre in an array of cultural undertakings that included concerts, vocal, instrumental, and dance evenings and mornings, educational, scientific, artistic, and sports circles and societies.[12] A program of instruction introduced to prepare workers in adult education included a course on principles and methods of organizing performances under rural conditions. Advanced zemstvos like those in Perm and Viatka provinces already had systems for supporting theatres. At the *volost'* level popular theatre circles financed themselves by collecting dues for their presentations. The district zemstvo maintained a theatrical library for the circles, rented props and costumes to them, took responsibility for printing posters and tickets, and arranged annual meetings for the participants. The provincial zemstvo engaged a director, who served in all the districts. The Iaroslavl conference endorsed the idea of establishing a stage in every district.

The last—and most important—of the 1915 conferences brought together 365 participants in Moscow in December to review the enormous recent gains made by popular theatre in the provinces and "clarify the tasks, needs and organization of popular theatres in Russia." Those attending hailed it as "the beginning of a great popular movement" and "the first swallow of a new life." Some of the participants saw the conference as a direct descendant of the 1897 First All-Russian Congress of Theatre Personnel. Most preferred to regard it as a harbinger of popular theatre's brilliant prospects in a social order now ready for fundamental change. It was the first of all the Russian conferences on theatre to form separate national sections uniting the representatives of theatres of the national minorities.

The Moscow conference may have had its origins in two debates on amateur theatre held in the winter of 1913–14 in the museum of the Moscow Polytechnic. The initiative for organizing such a meeting was taken by the playwright V. V. Protopopov, who proposed in November 1914 to the Council of the Imperial Russian Theatrical Society that it undertake the creation of an extensive network of "rural theatres" across Russia. His memorandum suggested that they inquire of the provincial governors where such rural theatres already existed. (Klepikov considered that this recommendation betrayed the "astonishing naïveté of a man completely uninformed about what is really going on in life.") After five meetings to discuss the project, the council decided to convene a conference. A. N. Lenkovskaia, president of the Section on Rural, Factory, and School Theatre, indicated that group's desire to take a leading role in the work of organizing such a conference. A bureau was set up that included representatives of the All-Russian Union of Cities and the All-Russian Zemstvo Union. A number of city and zemstvo jurisdictions asked to be assigned delegates to the congress and contributed financially to the meeting.

The Ministry of the Interior, though long reluctant to encourage the formation of common-interest groups in Russia, smiled on the council's request. The routing of its petition, to the Division of Public Health in the ministry's Main Administration on Matters of Local Economy, suggests that the authorities were considering the gathering's potential contribution to the supply of village distractions rather than an implicit endorsement of the profession of cultural activists. Indeed, the grant of approval specifically mentioned the propitiousness of such a meeting in view of the measures pending to strengthen popular temperance. In June 1915 the governor of Moscow authorized a meeting to be held in Moscow, on condition that (1) "persons of the Judaic faith not maintaining a right to permanent residence in Moscow not be permitted to participate, (2) the governor receive in ample time for perusal a list of all participants, a detailed program of activities, and also the theses of any papers proposed for delivery to the conference, (3) all participants be provided with badges and then no one without such a badge be admitted.[13] In July the ministry consulted the Department of General Affairs on a request from the committee organizing the conference for support in opening popular theatres. The department responded that while the temperance value of such action was clear, it was necessary for the Council of Ministers to "weigh the matter with other activities of a cultural, educational, and economic character" and that the question was now receiving special attention. Permission for a meeting stood. Originally planned for November, the congress was rescheduled to the Christmas–New Year's holiday for the convenience of those coming from a distance.

Delegates to the First All-Russian Congress on Popular Theatre meeting at the Shaniavskii City University represented diverse tendencies, including populist, cooperative, and Marxist. Klepikov thought it remarkable that they were able to find a more or less common language and agree on resolutions. "One idea connected everyone here: the necessity of political revolution and the realization of the *narod*'s eternal aspiration—the opening to it of the broad path of initiative."[14] The organizers sent questionnaires to eight hundred popular theatre circles and societies. Unfortunately, the responses they received were never tabulated. But the proceedings of the congress were published in 1919, with the help of subsidies from both the Provisional Government and Soviet ministers of education.[15] The proceedings contain reports on their activities from some circles and the discussion that followed their reading. So while they do not provide a comprehensive analysis, they do document the rapid expansion of rural popular theatre after the war began and indicate areas of disagreement over what was needed next.

At the opening meeting representatives of several groups reading greetings pointed to sharp differences over what course the popular theatre movement should take. The delegate from the Moscow Society of People's Universities called on the congress to reject the idea of a special theatre for the people and begged it to return to the unfinished task of creating a general-access theatre as a means of democratizing the highest cultural values. A representative from the Tomsk Society of Popular Education and the Tomsk Society of Popular Entertainments reported that both groups had dramatic commissions that presented plays regularly. He said that dramatic societies and circles were scattered all over Siberia, but that they were isolated and lacked a general plan. One delegate favored a centralized union to coordinate the work of the grassroots theatres, which would leave the theatres sponsored by cooperatives to their own devices. Another objected to creation of a centralized popular theatre organization, preferring instead a loose union of private popular theatres. The delegate from the Surikov circle insisted that popular theatre should be as it was with them, a local phenomenon reflecting the collective—but as one of the highest expressions of human art, not an entertainment designed to amuse the crowd, like bourgeois theatre. Prolonged applause greeted the peasant E. A. Adamov, from the Pokrovo-Rogul'skii People's House, who said,

> We, peasants from a circle of amateurs of dramatic art, especially welcome this meeting because we, peasants, have long dreamed of healthy and rational entertainments, and we came here to learn [how to] give our peasant neighbors some small understanding of theatre. And I see that many here want to help us succeed in this sacred goal. (*TV* 23)

He had the opportunity at the conference to hear the reports from other circles on what plays and techniques worked well for them. Otherwise, the most informative reports came from officers of the Section on new plans to assist circles and by affiliates of the cooperative movement on the potential they identified in popular theatre.

Reports on recent experiences of a zemstvo and of a cooperative theatre organizing group showed how radically receptiveness to theatre in the countryside had changed. In 1914 the Kamyshlovsk Uezd Zemstvo Board of Perm province earmarked three hundred rubles for the support of popular theatre. In 1913, eighty-two performances had been given in its jurisdiction by mixed companies of intelligentsia and peasant performers. Usually they were given in school buildings, which necessitated negotiation with the *volost'* administration. Audiences proved receptive, once they became familiar with the conventions. At one early performance an audience new to theatre concentrated on the costumes and makeup, were restless at first, then cried. But after this awkward introduction, it had no difficulty focusing on the plays. The board determined that more popular theatre was needed, as long as the casts included peasant amateurs. They declared theatre to be as important as Sunday schools and public readings. In their 1915 report they called it "incomparably more powerful than reading; it has, however, additional significance, since theatrical circles with popular participation are excellent schools of social life for young peasants." They hired a director-instructor at twelve hundred rubles per annum and increased their subsidy to nineteen hundred rubles in 1915.

Objections were raised after this report on the Perm zemstvo had been read. One discussant remarked that the Kamyshlovsk experience could not be taken as the norm, because in the majority of zemstvos, people from the lowest levels of society did not respond to zemstvo leadership. It was suggested that the cooperative movement might prove more effective than the zemstvos in propagating theatre, because the cooperative organization was closer to the people. Someone else observed that the Kamyshlovsk zemstvo was just "a drop in the ocean" compared to what could be done.

A. I. Shestova described the Vologodsk Agricultural Society's Cultural Enlightenment Commission, which had been founded in 1914 to coordinate the cultural efforts of cooperatives in the northern region (*TV* 81–84). The commission encouraged small amateur groups to perform in village schools until new People's Houses could be built. It established a library of a thousand scripts and set up facilities to provide costumes, makeup, wigs, and even sets. In 1915 four new People's Houses were completed, and thirty plays presented. But the new circles lacked knowledge of the theatre, and many of the productions proved unsatisfactory. Overall, players succeeded well with Ostrovsky and Chekhov, less well with "cooperative" works, like those of Klepikov, and not at all with Gogol's *Getting Married* and Tolstoy's *The Cause of It All.*[16]

The conference also heard from well-established groups that performed for urban audiences. S. A. Raevskii reported on the theatrical work of the Kharkov Society for Literacy (*TV* 217–19). It had built a modest theatre seating twelve hundred, which was used by two amateur companies—one Russian and the other Ukrainian. An engineer and his wife headed the Russian troupe, whose members came from the intelligentsia and the working class. In ten years it had performed 149 plays; 20 percent of their performances were of Ostrovsky works. The Ukrainian ensemble was headed by an *intelligent* who came from the peasantry and maintained his peasant ties. Working-class members predominated in it. They had performed ninety plays in ten years. Ostrovsky's merchant plays were difficult for them, because that characteristic type was exceptional in Kharkov. Raevskii confessed that the acting of both groups was uneven. They presented more plays written by foreigners than most popular companies attempted. And foreign plays were among the audience favorites. Kharkov audiences did not especially like Gorky's *The Lower Depths,* and they liked *Meshchane* even less.

The boldest proposals made at the conference came from the champions of the cooperatives and from representatives of the Section. Cooperative membership was growing exponentially. In January 1914, one percent of the Russian population belonged to cooperatives; by late 1917, eight percent would belong.[17] Lydia Armand, the most optimistic of the cooperative spokespeople, insisted that popular theatre must be organized from the periphery to the center, and not from the top down—as one speaker she characterized as "utopian" suggested (*TV* 163). Nonetheless, she was certain that cooperatives in fact held the key to transforming people. E. D. Kuskova's paper, "Popular Theatre and the Cultural-Enlightening Activities of Cooperatives in Russia and Abroad," averred that "while pursuing material goods, cooperatives at the same time create a 'new' man and require for this all possible means of cultural action upon the spiritual constitution of their members. Popular theatre is a powerful means of educating the mass" (*TV* 69). Armand herself asked why the Russian people, after hundreds of years of domination by secular and spiritual authority, had not created a popular theatre of their own as these pressures had been reduced.[18] She answered that "until fairly recently" the *narod's* favored creative genre had been song, and that that choice bespoke its attitude toward the world: "It did not breathe its spirit into theatre. Is this not because song reflects . . . an external-passive acceptance of life, while theatre engenders a real beginning? Theatre is born from a surplus of action, and it affects life as a striving for action." She insisted that from well before the time of Peter, the *narod* had practiced evasion and perpetual withdrawal. "And I think it is a continuation of the very same line in our time—a withdrawal from political struggle into boycotts of all kinds." In Armand's view even the events of 1905–7 failed to penetrate the masses. "The slogans were true, but never caught the imagination of the people." She offered as evidence for this that the epoch was reflected "only very weakly, very insipidly" in popular songs.

But she identified a critical turning point in the booming of cooperatives after 1907. Without speaking of any new *man,* she asked whether the rapid change in the conception of *personality* was not obvious: "Is not the idea of personality advancing everywhere? In propaganda as a stimulus to activity? In management, as a criterion for the selection of personnel? In economic life, as the principle for distributing advantage as credit-worthiness is measured?" The cooperatives, she asserted, had attracted millions of people who decided they would not merely suffer life, but create it for themselves. These people were imperceptibly becoming accustomed to the idea of self-government and independence, to the essence of democracy. "But theatre will be needed in the struggle against the traditional worldview—or, more accurately, the worldview of meek submissiveness—in battle with the jealous [patriarchal] family and with inertia itself." The material side of cooperatives could not, she believed, attract the idealistic segment of the young. They could, however, be attracted to participation in theatrical activity. "And this could be their first school of public affairs."

But Armand was describing an opportunity within reach and not an accomplished fact. One delegate noted that in Saratov province popular theatre had already attained a high level, while cooperatives were little developed. Chairman Karpov opined that the cooperatives had so far accomplished very little in the field of popular theatre. (Nevertheless, the central government must have feared the cooperatives' moves in this direction, for in a few months it would crack down on them. Its repression aimed squarely at the consumer societies' cultural work.)[19]

Section representatives delivered several reports at the conference. Like Armand, they were most impressed by the pace of rural popular theatre's growth. As Academician Polenov put it, "interest in rural theatre is growing not day by day, but hour by hour." The fullest expression of their shared assumptions aired in D. A. Tolbuzin's paper on existing rural theatres run by peasant theatrical circles, "The Organization of Rural Theatre" (*TV* 141–48). Indifferent to whether the local circle's support came from the zemstvo or a cooperative, Tolbuzin reasoned that "rural circles exist: it is necessary to help them organize themselves." To exert leadership, one member of the circle needed authority. But amateurs were often unwilling to acknowledge personal authority in a cohort of equals. Companies often disbanded after a production or two for lack of experienced leaders. Even where such leadership seemed solid, it could vanish overnight. Tolbuzin recalled a village that had put on plays successfully year after year. When the schoolmaster moved away, the circle suddenly expired; though remaining members had knowledge and experience, none could exercise authority.

He offered a simple solution. Organize individual circles into unions (which could also be formed on the basis of the 4 March 1906 legislation), and train leaders to assist the circles and coordinate their efforts. One union could maintain collections of costumes and sets large enough to support ten productions at a time. The Section proposed to begin training such leaders as soon as its headquarters building in Moscow was completed. It would offer short-term courses for those interested in making a hobby of this work, and long-term courses for those preparing themselves exclusively for careers in popular theatre (*TV* 229). A union of circles could afford to pay a leader. Besides his responsibilities for guiding productions, the leader could undertake to widen the intellectual horizons of circle members by means of readings, conversations, and the planning of "evenings." It seemed desirable that the leaders be of the same social stratum as the circles' participants and audiences.

In a speech he gave later in the year to the instructors assembled to train leaders, Tolbuzin stressed that the goal of institutions such as the Section was not to govern, but to guide the local circles and help them get started. The Section had, for example, developed a method for making cheap costumes, but it had no intention of forcing this method on circles that sought its help. The Kharkov Society for Literacy's drama group had built an excellent costume collection by asking for donations of old clothes. The work of the Unions, the Section proposed, "must rest on the initiative [*samodeiatel'nosti*] of every [circle] and every single member."[20] The organization of circles into unions would mean greater independence for the circles.

The Moscow Conference aired a wide range of views on the direction popular theatre could take. S. A. An-skii, who gave one of the closing speeches, alluded once more to the gulf that still separated the culturists and the people they wished to serve.

> We recognize [the people] as our equal. And when we say the people don't understand . . . we don't want to say that they are beneath us. We are saying that the psychology of the people is the psychology of another class. Its psychology, its understanding of truth, and especially beauty are completely other than what townspeople have worked out and the requirements of the people in this are completely different. (*TV* 445)

And he concluded by warning that cultivated society at large could still fail in the mission to welcome the *narod.* He predicted that if the intelligentsia helped the people to "find the door and discover all the paths and possibilities," then when the people found itself and found its own theatre, the intelligentsia could learn from the people. "If it opens the doors the intelligentsia will be saved. If it does not—it will be drowned in its present civilization." His tone was much like Blok's in 1908.

PEOPLE'S HOUSES

The Golitsyn People's House constructed by the Viazemsk consumer cooperative society represented a signal advance in the evolution of Russian community centers. Its impetus came from the local musical-dramatic circle, which afforded young people a creative outlet for their spare time and furnished an entertainment the rural public found appealing. Where such people's houses were organized, behavior patterns often changed markedly. In the village of Sednev, for example, three taverns closed in 1913 because of the influence of the People's House.[21] These new grassroots People's Houses did not always spring from the dreams of a drama circle, but where they appeared, space for dramatic presentation usually figured in the planners' objectives. A Chernigov province agricultural society formed in 1912 set the beams for its Rylovichakh village People's House late in 1914. The secretary of the society said that its hall, designed to accommodate two hundred, "should make it possible to organize other societies that are necessary—a volunteer fire brigade, dramatic circle, popular chorus and so forth."[22] Where drama circles appeared, playgoing became a regular pastime. In the Volokolamsk district of Moscow province, for example, "plays ceased to be a rarity." In 1915–16 ninety-one performances were given in twenty-seven villages there.[23] Panina and her associates were especially interested in the potential the cooperative movement offered for rural cultural development. At the end of 1913 they decided to publish a compendium of information pertaining to these new institutions created by communities to meet their own needs.

The compilers of *Narodnyi Dom* (The people's house) began by attempting to gather complete data on all the People's Houses functioning in Russia. A committee assembled lists of rural and urban People's Houses by querying the zemstvos. In provinces lacking zemstvos, inquiries were made of Temperance trusteeships, local cultural societies, land captains, and private individuals. Early in 1914 a questionnaire of thirty-two paragraphs was mailed to all the known People's Houses. In the middle of the year those that had not responded received fresh forms. The last mailing went out in 1915, and the collection of data ended in the second half of that year. Results were tabulated for 65 percent of all the rural districts of Russia and 69 percent of all cities and large towns. The research produced complete information on village and town People's Houses for only thirteen provinces.

The war greatly altered the circumstances under which rural People's Houses operated, and so quickly rendered the questionnaire obsolete. The data did show the facilities sponsored by cooperatives to be growing faster than any other sort.[24] In addition to 88 functioning rural People's Houses, the committee identified 61 "in the process of organization and construction." In the towns and cities it surveyed it found 134 functioning and 23 under construction.

Ninety of the People's Houses responding provided information on theatrical productions. Amateur circles presented plays at forty of them, but groups assembled for a single production were more common, presenting in sixty-one People's Houses. Data collected by the committee were gathered too soon to reflect the importance of the theatrical impulse that would figure so prominently in the grassroots People's Houses built during the war years. But Gaideburov noted in his essay "The Theatre of the People's House" that the Okhansk zemstvo's provision of a permanent special instructor "established the beginning of serious popular theatre [in rural People's Houses]" (*ND* 198–99). V. Charnoliuskii called attention in the book's opening section to the war's impact in altering villagers' mental horizons. "The war interrupted every facet of the customary flow of life and furnished graphic proof of what was not clear to [villagers] before: the connection between the life of each personality and the life of the state, other states and all humanity" (*ND* 5). The committee did its work too soon to disclose theatre's contribution to the establishment of grassroots People's Houses in places like Vol'sk early in the war. This city of forty thousand had an ineffectual Temperance trusteeship and lacked a theatre. The city duma there had created a committee to look into constructing a People's House, but became absorbed in matters raised by the war. In 1915 it was the local dramatic circle that led the drive to build the People's House and began collecting contributions for it.[25]

E. N. Medynskii, for *Narodnyi Dom,* surveyed zemstvo efforts from 1911 to 1915 to encourage construction of People's Houses. By 1916 fully half of the provincial zemstvos had discussed subsidizing such construction. Medynskii thought it remarkable that in just five years so many zemstvos had recognized the possibilities opened by community centers. At the time of his writing it remained unclear whether the zemstvos would institute centralized networks of People's Houses or whether they would achieve more solid results by supporting local groups that organized themselves to raise funds for construction. The Perm province zemstvo determined to make People's Houses the center of local social life and devised incentives to stimulate local initiative and independence. In 1911 it created a fund of 10,000 rubles to be used for construction. The allocation jumped to 20,000 in 1912 and 25,000 in 1913. In 1914 it was decided to add 100,000 rubles a year to the fund for ten years. The provincial zemstvo offered to cover one-third of the cost of each People's House (later one-half)—not to exceed 5,000 rubles for any one project. Before 1914 the Perm zemstvo reviewed petitions from forty-eight local social organizations and funded thirteen proposals to build. It set no preconditions on how large an area a community center should serve—a *volost',* a group of villages, or a single village—leaving that determination to the local organizers. It required only that the facilities be open to young people for recreation, and families for reading and conversation, and to local credit societies, agricultural societies, and cultural groups like drama circles. Medynskii judged that the Perm project produced disappointing results. The cooperative movement was well developed in the province, but many highly motivated cooperatives found it impossible to raise even half the money necessary to construct a local People's House. And the project actually did little to arouse local initiative in the poorer parts of the province: "in areas where the population was still unorganized and dark, it went unnoticed" (*ND* 36, 27).

Ufa province, south of Perm province, opted for a three-tiered organization of People's Houses. It proceeded without regard to any local initiative. (It elected, for example, to put a school in every canton with forty to fifty children, whether the local population recognized the need for a school or not.) A central People's House erected for the province was intended to unify and direct the enlightening activity of the district and *volost'* People's

Houses. It helped organize popular theatres at the district level. Each district was to build a people's house, and these district facilities in turn were to oversee construction of *volost'* People's Houses with theatres and other facilities to serve the locality. The project moved forward very slowly. In 1916 Ufa's provincial zemstvo authorized only two People's Houses for construction. Medynskii found that Ufa's centralizing approach actually served to impede such construction. The zemstvo dropped the program and turned instead to local organizations to erect small People's Houses. "They are still springing up by the dozen," he noted (*ND* 42). And at an average cost of 7,500 to 10,000 rubles, they were cheaper to build than similar structures going up in other provinces.[26]

Medynskii found loans to local cooperatives to have been one of the most effective zemstvo strategies for stimulating People's House construction. Only four provinces pursued this course. Kostroma province cooperatives that raised one-third of the construction cost could borrow the balance (not to exceed 5,000 rubles) for ten years at 4 percent interest. Ekaterinoslav cooperatives could borrow up to 5,000 rubles. The Iaroslavl province zemstvo recognized the urgency of building People's Houses in 1914. In 1915 it implemented a plan that offered subsidies of 2,000 rubles for a wooden structure and 3,000 for one built of stone. Localities that raised some money toward the cost could borrow the balance interest-free if they agreed to repay the sum over five years. The Viatka province zemstvo, which allocated 105,000 rubles to construct twenty-two People's Houses in commemoration of the fiftieth anniversary of its founding, also made loans available. The Penza province zemstvo devised creative financing when it designated 100,000 rubles for disbursal from the capital accumulated in its insurance fund in order to stimulate People's House construction in 1916. The Tambov province zemstvo also began to allocate funds for this purpose from its insurance capital.[27]

The city dumas of Saint Petersburg and Moscow too developed plans for networks of smaller popular theatres in 1914. The Saint Petersburg committee planned special facilities with auditoria big enough to seat 150 to 200 people for plays. The facilities were to be located in the suburbs as well as densely populated areas, with space to be rented until the first twenty could be constructed. The Moscow project called for twenty-one district People's Houses with stages suitable for theatre and opera to be built over four years. In 1916 the Moscow duma expended eighteen thousand rubles to construct two People's Houses—instead of the twelve planned before the war. Although the Saint Petersburg project underlined the enormous significance of local groups' defining what they needed in community center facilities, Medynskii found that rural localities did far better than urban ones at exercising this kind of initiative. This he attributed to the fact that rural people could feel at home belonging to a congenial People's House where the audience always included the same people—and of "being the host" there (*ND* 42).

Meanwhile, the Section implemented its plan to provide formal training for instructors or directors of theatres in People's Houses. The Tolbuzin collection contains a printed schedule for a series of lectures given from 20 May to 18 June 1916 at Shaniavskii University. The first week, a session was devoted to plans and architecture of People's Houses. In June, six consecutive days were devoted to popular theatre. V. V. Tikhonovich lectured 10–12 June; Klepikov joined him on the fourteenth. V. D. Polenov and N. N. Golovanov spoke on the sixteenth and Tolbuzin on the eighteenth. A session scheduled for the last day was entitled "The Organization of the Rural Theatre, the Circle, and its Troupes."[28]

And even as the war ground on, amateur circles continued to spring up and present plays in the countryside. On 13 December 1916 six inexperienced amateurs gave their first performance of S. T. Semenev's *The Spoiled One* (*Porchenyi* [1901]) at the Kraevsk People's House in the Aleksandrovsk district of Vladimir province. They chose the play themselves and produced it without any help from specialists. Of the four who performed, one was an old man who had never seen a theatre performance before. The set painting and carpentry were done by two students, the local teacher, the bookkeeper for the credit brotherhood, and the zemstvo agronomist. Pupils from several nearby schools attended the dress rehearsal. On the day of the performance people started arriving three hours before curtain time, despite extremely cold weather.

> The hall nearly filled, with 350 in attendance. Many of the audience had never seen a play before. When the curtain went up, the setting produced a stunning impression. It was not the sort of thing to be expected 130 miles from Moscow; but it was easy to explain the make-up of the public. Under wartime conditions, women, children and old people predominated. Adult males . . . were few. The play animated the viewers, who responded warmly. As soon as outbursts and laughter began to interfere with the audience's hearing, people shushed their neighbors, and order was restored. After the curtain fell there was noisy rapture; many in the audience shouted "Thanks!" to the actors.[29]

This reaction is not unlike that recorded by S. A. Iur'ev, the landowner who in the summer of 1862 built a theatre on his estate and presented a play to local peasants. The difference lies in the fact that this drama was performed in premises constructed by local people for their own use and that local amateurs were able to mount the play successfully drawing entirely on their own resources at a time of extreme national hardship. The author of the account quoted added, "The same thing, on a larger or smaller scale, is being observed in other places. Plays are important and necessary."

And at one of those other places the observing was being done by an American. Ernest Poole, who had met Gorky in New York in 1905, covered the war as a journalist. His travels took him to London, Berlin, the Western Front, and, in 1917, Petrograd. After some months in the restive capital he felt a need to escape from the shouting crowds, street parades, and political rhetoric. To get to the heart of the real revolution in Russia he determined to observe the life of the people themselves. And since nine-tenths of the population were peasant villagers, this required a journey to the countryside. In August 1917 he went with Tarasov, a man of mixed peasant and gentry stock who had studied chemical engineering and translated foreign books into Russian, to his native village.[30]

When Poole and Tarasov arrived, they found the villagers debating land reform and the possibility of a radical revolution that would abolish private property altogether. Poole conscientiously noted these concerns, but was more interested in ascertaining how far the village had already progressed on the course of modernization. He found civic initiative flourishing and influential institutions in place training villagers to function in an interdependent market economy with literacy, numeracy, a scientific outlook, and a knowledge of the outside world.

The teacher explained to Poole that the 1905 revolution had contributed significantly to improving the peasant attitude toward education. Elections to the state Duma gave peasants a voice in the national discussion of land reform. The experience of their representatives presenting legislation that favored their interests made peasants look on books with more respect (though only on books that dealt with the land). The village sorcerer, whom Poole also interviewed at length, attested as well to the impact of education in transforming the outlook of Russia's young people: "They are taught so much in their foolish little colleges, and they read so much in newspapers and books, that their souls grow hard and dry and become like crowded little rooms" (*V* 189).

The economic impact of the war was clearly visible when Poole arrived in the village. Local people told him they had more money in their pockets than ever before but were experiencing increasing difficulty buying manufactured goods. Flax and wool were still produced here, and he found villagers repairing their old looms and spinning wheels, which they had not used for years. He saw one Singer sewing machine. The cooperative store still had a stock of goods, but was beginning to run low on seeds and agricultural implements. Six thousand new members from the area had paid five rubles each to join the cooperative in 1916 and gain access to preferential pricing. The hospital the cooperative had built in 1911 had been taken over by the central government for military casualties. The doctor had left, and now the village had fallen back on the services of a midwife. But the cooperative was expanding rather than curtailing its activities. When the time had come in 1916 to pay a dividend, its honorary chairman, Prince C., decided instead to begin construction of a People's House. The facility would be, Poole informed his readers, "a real community center, owned and run by the people themselves, part of a vast and intricate system of such centers all over the land" (*V* 126).

Young villagers had already organized an amateur drama circle and were giving plays at the local school. Their most recent production had netted seven hundred rubles, which was to be used to buy a new pump and hose line for the village fire brigade. The midwife's son, an active participant, told Poole of their plans to give a score of plays during the coming winter months. Proceeds would go to the People's House building fund. The construction, which was scheduled to begin soon, would provide steady work and wages all through the fall and winter. "He kept on talking all the while of what they would do in the People's House. He pointed out of the window to the vacant lot nearby, where the foundations were already laid. 'As soon as we build the first floor,' he said, 'we shall turn it into a theatre'" (*V* 132). Poole met two young women in the village who had some personal experience of plays elsewhere. The eldest daughter of a self-made mill-owner had gone to boarding school in the district town, where she had taken part in plays (and learned new dances that came all the way from America). A young Finnish woman of eighteen employed to care for an elderly invalid had actually worked for a time in a theatre in Finland. Poole attended a performance of an Ostrovsky play in the school and was deeply moved by what he saw:

> In deepening surprise I watched these village players and the spell that they were casting. Like most amateurs, they dragged their lines; but it was just this leisurely art, this lack of all impatience for having anything happen, this deep and delighted absorption in the characters themselves, which was creating this atmosphere, holding this peasant audience, of which the players were a part. There would be a tense silence, then a quick laugh. (*V* 140)

These firsthand observations of an inquisitive and enthusiastic foreign journalist confirm in a forceful way the rather dry reports by specialists of the monumental social changes that accompanied and facilitated the widespread advance of popular theatre in Russia during the war. What could be expected to come of this spontaneous cultural movement?

AT THE FRONT

In the summer of 1915 Samuel Harper visited two of the Russian armies on the Western Front during a lull in the fighting. Cordially received at headquarters in a village some sixty miles behind the line, he talked with officers, accompanied some of them to a moving-picture show, and visited a hospital before leaving for the front itself. Based on what he saw he declared, "in the Russian regiments there was the atmosphere of village life from which the soldiers came. They play or sing when they are not working or fighting; ten hours out of the trenches and they are normal once more."[31] He continued to follow closely the fortunes of the peasants. The following summer he noted the incipient breakdown of economic exchange between city and countryside. This retreat from money did not hurt the producer: the village, he learned, had never been so prosperous. Peasants now served their guests not vodka, but candy and meat. They dressed in city clothes and wore boots.[32]

The February 1917 revolution that terminated the autocracy led to an arrangement whereby a Provisional Government shared power with *soviets*, the councils elected by soldiers, workers, and peasants. The new liberal regime labored to keep Russia in the war—the one policy almost all the nation's diverse political factions could agree on—while it planned a major land reform program and prepared for the democratic election of a Constituent Assembly. The three institutions that succored popular theatre did not fare equally well during the Provisional Government's tenure.

For the Section, old constraints vanished with the old regime. Courses for local theatre coordinators could now be expanded. The Zoogarden administration invited the Section to set up a summer theatrical division, and Polenov considered mounting a version of Jules Verne's *Around the World in Eighty Days*—a spectacular production of which had run for decades in Paris. Polenov registered his reaction to the revolution and optimistically assessed its importance for the cultural development of the people in a letter dated 16 March.

> Yes, I am unspeakably happy that I lived to see these days, only they won't change the darkness that was before. . . . What the best people of many generations dreamed, what they went into exile for, suffered under the knout, to death, has come to an end. Russia at the present moment is overcome by the joy of resurrection. Such bright, happy days have rarely come her way. For us everything is peaceful for a little while, and everyone will again go back to work and, one hopes, to great and constructive work. You write that the old regime was good manure for the new shoots. That is hardly so: the old bureaucracy, with its stupefied official brain, did not fertilize but ruined the soil. And you will have to work hard to cleanse the land. . . . But let art shine in the clean, free air.[33]

The cooperatives also gained certain advantages. The Imperial Government's crackdown on their cultural activities led to fines and closing of cooperative newspapers and curtailed public lectures. The Provincial Government enacted legislation introduced in the Duma in 1915 to reduce interference in the cooperative movement.

For the zemstvos it was another story. From one angle, it might appear that the Provisional Government finally implemented Stolypin's scheme to establish a floor of democratic village units with independent authority under the structure of indirectly elected district and provincial zemstvos. On 21 May it created the *volost'* zemstvo, and elections were held in August to staff the new jurisdiction.[34] In the autumn a new zemstvo act transferred control of police in the provinces from the Ministry of the Interior to the zemstvos, though they would continue to be funded from the state treasury.

The new act also initiated a restructuring of the zemstvos' taxing authority and provided for the creation of zemstvos in those provinces that had none. But these gains came as the soviets were laying siege to the zemstvos. New soviets created in the countryside added their own members to the zemstvo assemblies, leaving the Provisional Government no choice but to confirm their action. By the end of May these soviet members outnumbered the experienced elected incumbents, and soon the entire system of local self-government was paralyzed.

In the summer and autumn of 1917 the institutional structures of Russian life took on a wavy, mirage-like quality. The public in the countryside and the cities felt the foundations heaving beneath their feet. Mobilization had profoundly altered social relations, tearing millions of peasants from the fabric of their villages and putting them under military discipline. Keeping Russia in the war finally became a hotly debated political issue. The upcoming elections to the Constituent Assembly and the scope of land reform claimed the attention of the peasants in uniform. Even at the front the changing thoughts and attitudes of the folk were briefly subject to inscription, thanks to the traditions of Russian popular theatre.

During the summer P. P. Gaideburov approached the Cultural Enlightenment Department of the Political Direction of the War Ministry about a theatre/concert tour of the Northwest Front. The enthusiastic department sought to give the tour an agitational character, but the Wanderers categorically refused to take any political literature. Gaideburov chose a repertory of three plays: *Getting Married*, Ostrovsky's *Even a Cat Has Lean Times*, and *Tell*, by Swiss dramatist René Morax. The company left Petrograd 21 September and returned 16 November.[35] In fifty-six days it presented plays and concerts forty-four times. The performances were estimated to have been seen by 27,000 viewers. After every performance the audience was invited to fill out questionnaires. The company collected 4,400 responses, of which 4,000 were collated and 2,000 preserved.[36]

The tour began inauspiciously in Revel. The company played there to a "socially diverse" audience at the sailors' club. The sailors were gracious, but the audience did not behave well during the first concert. Audience reception of *Getting Married* on 25 September left the players with the impression that the sailors were satiated with amusements. Only 13 percent of the viewers filled out questionnaires, and only eight respondents said they found the play interesting. The players presented *Even a Cat* to a more appreciative audience of twenty-five hundred in a barracks. *Tell* they gave in the Revel Russian Theatre. For open performances with admission fees they offered Shaw's *Candida* and Bjørnson's *Beyond Human Might*. The concerts featured a singer, an accompanied dancer, a piano soloist, and occasionally Gaideburov supplementing the music with readings from stories by Chekhov.

Unable to secure transportation to the front, they went on to Pskov on 4 October, to comfortable and secure surroundings. The responses to the questionnaires filled out here were less direct and sharp than those written elsewhere. At one performance, young people in the balcony made so much noise cracking nuts that Gaideburov had to come out and ask them to stop. From Pskov the Wanderers went to Polotsk, but on 18 October they were at last taken near the front—to the village of Brussa, near Lake Naroch.

Their appearance provoked a few protest meetings. Some individuals warned the crowd not to trust them, calling them "provocateurs" and accusing them of having been sent specifically to distract soldiers from fundamental and important issues. Two responses to questionnaires echoed the warnings. "Your work is interesting for many, but others suspect something. I would advise you to explain." "We ask you to explain about the questionnaire. Many have troubling suspicions" (*Tz* 26, 28).

The Soviet author who analyzed the responses divided them into three categories. The first he called "literate." They were filled out by clerks, officers, and quartermasters. Flourishes and rhetorical decorations were typical in this group. The second he labeled "semiliterate." Clumsy handwriting and style, uneven letters, and "nonexistent orthography" characterized these appraisals. "But the specific gravity of such pages," he averred, "was undoubtedly higher than those of the first group" (*Tz* 40). The largest category ("illiterate") papers were marked with crosses and zeros. (The questionnaires offered some alternatives. Under the item asking about what the viewer got from the acting were listed "satisfaction, benefit, rest, fatigue, dissatisfaction." Under "What kinds of plays would you like?" followed "long, short, sad, funny, serious, light.")

Respondents with a revolutionary viewpoint expressed themselves clearly and often. Gaideburov first met this attitude in Revel. When he read from Chekhov in concert the audience of sailors had been convulsed with laughter and thanked him with powerful applause. Then one member detached himself from the audience and took Gaideburov aside. Instead of delivering the expected compliments, he excoriated the actor for his reading. "He demanded a delivery of the Chekhov stories such that from the externally funny text there would emerge clearly a picture of life that would penetrate the consciousness of the viewers and arouse protest and condemnation in them and at the same time plant in them the certainty that the life that Chekhov depicted must be swept from the face of the Russian land and that it would certainly be swept away by social revolution."[37] Some of the replies to questionnaires took the line that the actors, who are bourgeois, came to distract soldiers from the main task, which is revolution. Some disgruntled souls rejected the idea of amusements at the front. One said, "[Better than providing entertainments would be] to end the war and lead Russia quickly to the Constituent Assembly and all power to the Soviets."[38] Another answered in the same vein: "We don't need plays; we need land and liberty and peace. I'll always agree with Comrade Lenin and the soviet of workers [and] soldiers' deputies." Often respondents who accepted the value of plays at the front answered "revolutionary" or "socialist" to the question asking about the content of plays they would like to see. One recommended: "To make your activity more valuable it would be better to present plays that clearly convey an understanding of class distinctions—that is, class interests; in a word, convey class consciousness to the heart of every viewer" (*Tz* 61).

The army intelligentsia often showed a low opinion of the common soldier and questioned his capacity to understand plays. This response was typical: "People who are slightly literate and don't know literature will never be able to interest themselves in such serious things" (*Tz* 56). The rank and file were not unaware of such opinions. One respondent said, "It's too bad that the masses are considered to be unintelligent children. . . . There are among the uncultivated keen and great souls, and they value talent." Those who argued the peasant viewers' immaturity often pointed to their talking during performances. But two responses asked the company not to be put off by coughing at the most intimate moments, explaining that it came from living in the trenches. Questionnaires filled out after concerts often alluded to the inaccessibility of high culture to the folk. But this was "almost never" mentioned after dramatic productions (*Tz* 52).

While lauding the dissemination of theatre, numerous responses revealed something of their authors' self-image, as these samples indicate:

> Very few of us have seen anything learned. We grew up in the country, in the wilderness, and would have died there, but the war snatched us out of there. Now we are all in a small group—don't lose a minute, and do everything possible for us: you know, they want to destroy all of us. Rescue us.
>
> I wish the artists success in the development of the simple folk, for darkness is ruining Russia.
>
> It is necessary to show in a play just how nasty the countryside is and the way to make it good.
>
> In order to improve our life it is necessary that many know—that is, have understanding of, how other people live, or stated more simply, comprehend the life of other people and then we will know which rules (laws) we require for a just life for the people.
>
> Your play was a joy. I had never gone to see contemporary acting on the stage, so I did not have much sympathy for the theatre, but now I love it. I think there are many happy people like me, who value the theatre after seeing you perform: it teaches us how to live in the light. I hope you persist in this difficult work. . . . I like best dramas which reveal on the stage all our incorrect actions.
>
> Continue your work with diligence, and especially at the front, to bring pleasure to the gray multitude, which defends our homeland with a sad heart.

> The war is winding down. Save your strength and health, so that you may teach us and rouse our trampled feelings in peacetime. Awaken beauty in us. Make genuine citizens of former slaves. (*Tz* 44, 45, 60, 46, 47, 49, 50).

The company found sharply different responses to plays from settled civilians and soldiers at the front. Not all of its performances were well received. *Getting Married* proved popular in the cities. Audiences in Pskov and Revel found it funny and enjoyable. But soldiers who had come from the trenches considered it "a bewitchment," and reacted very negatively in the questionnaires. At Brussa the actors were impressed by the soldiers' rapt attention to the play. The rejection of some of the responses shocked them. One read,

> Comrades, answer in writing whether there are in these programs of presentations, the faintest resemblances to life in Russia. If there are, then they should be clarified, because the stage has only left a fog in [my] brain. And if they are only for pleasure, we don't need them at all.

Another said, "Continue, but present serious plays, not rubbish." The players had arrived at Brussa while a meeting was under way in connection with elections to the Constituent Assembly. Their performance caused the meeting to be cut short, and the most violent and abusive of the responses show how the intensity of the political discussion must have put most of the soldiers in the worst possible frame of mind for Gogol's jest.

> Not at such a time: the country is on the verge of destruction, we need bread, peace and freedom. . . . Good advice for you would be to go to the trenches and struggle with us: after a few minutes you would be screaming about peace.
>
> This is our advice—finish and don't seek your crust of bread in our blood. We are sympathetic to those actors who do not distract us from genuine work and still show us the way, and to those who perform plays against the war and for the peace which is at hand.
>
> I agree with the Bolsheviks . . . peace is necessary as soon as possible; we don't want to shed any more blood.
>
> Our dear guests. We received literally nothing from you. We need peace and not your plays. Only little comes from them. We ask you to leave for good. It will be ill if you ever again stop our meeting.

A few viewers maintained their equanimity and were able to comment on the play's message. One respondent said, "We are all more shy than we need to be." Another was able to find some common ground between the play and the concerns of the day: "We are all wearily awaiting the Constituent Assembly. And if your government also jumps out the window the same day?" (*Tz* 77, 89, 77, 90).

The production of *Tell* proved to be unpopular with the middle-class audiences in the towns, but wildly appealing to the soldiers at the front. Morax's drama on the subject of Schiller's 1804 *William Tell* had its premiere in Mézières, Switzerland in May 1914. Gaideburov had arranged for a Russian translation.[39] Inspired by the theatre of classical antiquity, Morax presented the revolt of the league of the founding cantons of the world's oldest continuing democracy as a drama with chorus in which "the unanimous action of the crowd" reflected "the role of the people." The three cantons that formed an Everlasting League in 1291 had arranged for protection from the German Empire, but when an Austrian duke became German Emperor seven years later he sent bailiffs to take over the courts and rule the land. The play's antibourgeois tone is established in the opening scene, when Tell observes that now "everyone is for himself" (25). Patriots become rebels when they discover "the law is nothing" for the foreign landlords. The question is, "Will the bourgeois, the merchants, the money changers, the rich tavern-owners follow the villains?" (87) A peasant whose absentee landlord has confiscated his cattle and blinded his father doubts it: "They say that the rich love the money that frees them and which is their country more than life." Tell's grandfather, who has taught his daughter about "the people, our rights . . . our charters, our franchises," assures him that he will see peasants marching together: "Each one will speak his wishes at the assembly." The assembly finally meets, convoked by Tell after he has killed the bailiff Gessler. They agree that the land belongs to them, not the lords, and pledge to form a single free people. The play ends with their victory in battle. Tell's grandfather announces, "All of us, with a common accord, will write the Law."

Tell elicited almost no negative responses at the front and engaged the soldiers as no other play the Wanderers performed there. For one thing, many viewers identified with the situation described in Morax's play. For some, the experience of overthrowing a hated regime was the principal point of contact. "After such a long damned tsarist oppression," said one, "it seems to me that I could see and hear [such] touching plays day and night without getting tired." Another expressed "joy and anger toward the past." Yet another wrote, "Hatred for the former tyranny, and I am ready to fight against anything that resembles it." The play's depiction of peasant life attracted others, like the author of this: "[I am] with the tillers of the soil, who play the main role in life and who stand so low in humanity."

Some questionnaires spoke of the play's revolutionary content. One expressed, "my complete gratitude for raising the revolutionary spirit. I consider . . . that it is perfectly correct that such theatres unite the general mass, which in the present case is necessary for the hope of the native land; and such organization leads us to the general construction of a new life." Approbation for the play's antibourgeois tenor was recorded: "In this, autocratic pressure on the *narod* is understood by everybody; the executioners and bourgeois be damned. Long live the International." Another respondent asked, "Why is only patriotism spoken of and not a word about internationalism?" An "intelligentsia response" warned of Russian political immaturity: "It would be good if people here understood what they need. Unfortunately, this is not as it was in Switzerland."

Nevertheless, viewers commented frequently on the play's morale-boosting and educational impact. "Before the play I was defeated by life, now I am strengthened," confided one. "I myself was in the paws of these enemies of Russia, so I couldn't see the crowd for my tears," testified another. "Such plays are desirable which make our hearts tremble, like *Tell,* so that we can see with our own eyes how dark and wild we are; such plays aroused our conscience, diverted our enmity, and lack of faith in each other. You awaken the human in us, and for this we are deeply grateful." Nor did the play's implications for citizenship go unremarked: "This play got me thinking about how citizens of a free country, like ourselves, are obligated, and what I must do in order to be useful to my native land" (*Tz* 96–102).

On 27 October the company received a telegram saying that the Provisional Government had been arrested and the Bolsheviks had taken power. By evening the new government announced an armistice on all fronts. In the general collapse, the players found it impossible to perform. They went to Minsk on 30 October and returned to Petrograd on 16 November. Their concert soloist, A. D. Aleksandrovich, wrote that everyone he met "said they wouldn't last more than a week. They are called adventurers; bloodshed is expected" (*Tz* 24).

CLOSURE

After issuing its decrees on peace, land, and bread, the new government abolished the *soslovie* system. (The Provisional Government had taken the decisive step in this direction when it established the equality of all citizens before the law.) Within months it had dissolved all the zemstvos in the areas it controlled. In provinces like Perm, where local peasant identification with the works of resourceful zemstvos was strong, armed detachments of Red Guards had to be called in to effect the liquidation.[40]

Little time was lost snuffing out local cultural initiative that had developed around the People's Houses. The emphasis in official talk about peasant acculturation now was on the very long time that would be required to educate "them." In the summer of 1918 Ernest Poole, traveling in the central provinces, had the new paradigm from someone in the Commissariat of Supply:

> The revolution has shown to us that the layer of civilization here is about one thousandth of an inch thick. . . . For the bulk of the population, peasants who for centuries have been living in the dark, long years of education and patient

> teaching are required—teaching of a practical kind. . . . How to handle these 160,000,000 peasants, it is hard to tell. Again and again I have seen the agents of our government, young schoolteachers with high ideals, go out among the "dark people" and there soon lose all faith in their work on account of the utter lack of response that they found in the villages. For the average peasant's vision is as cramped and dim as the hut where he lives. . . . The people are still in darkness.[41]

By May 1919 precisely this dark appraisal of peasant potential for acculturation divided the ranks of the theatre section (TEO) of the Commissariat of Education, where important writers like Blok had found employment. V. V. Tikhonovich, newly appointed leader of TEO's subsection for worker and peasant theatre, wrote the convocation for the First Congress of Worker and Peasant Theatre, scheduled for late February; he spoke of theatre as "the people's self-education," and neglected to mention either proletariat or workers.[42] But at the Congress for Adult Education held in May, P. Kogan bitterly attacked popular theatre as alien to the proletariat.[43]

The class composition of grassroots cultural societies posed a huge theoretical problem for the national leadership of Proletkul't, an organization founded by A. A. Bogdanov and A. V. Lunacharsky, to develop a distinctly proletarian literature and art and promote specifically proletarian artistic creativity. Theses of the February 1918 Moscow All-City Conference of Proletkul't proposed that "for the development of independent action [*samodeiatel'nost'*] among the worker mass through popular theatre it is necessary to create people's dramatic studios—with committed, progressive, experienced specialists—and not dilettante circles."[44] Lynn Mally found that because the first national congress of Proletkul't, held in September 1918 received extensive coverage in the national press, hundreds of groups appeared seeking Proletkul't affiliation.[45] Funding may have been a motive, but Proletkul't's cardinal principles of autonomy and independent action exerted great attraction. Groups writing the leadership received back issues of *Proletarian Culture,* the Proletkul't organizational plan and the printed protocols of the first conference. They organized neighborhood clubs, factory theatre circles, choirs, clubs offering literacy classes, and community centers determined to continue the People's House tradition. The problem was that the leadership defined proletarian very narrowly, as industrial workers with political consciousness. "Local groups that welcomed toilers," Mally notes, often "used the word 'proletariat' as a synonym for . . . *narod.*"[46]

The disparity between leadership's intentions and popular response did not keep Proletkul't ideologists from battling for control of the Commissariat of Education. TEO published a new edition of the 1910 translation of Romain Rolland's *Théâtre du peuple,* which apparently appealed to the Proletkul'tists because of its exhortation to restore the proper connection between theatre and the people by reviving mass festivals from the French

Revolution. At the First Congress for Worker and Peasant Theatre reports were read from across the country indicating that mass dramas, often organized under Proletkul't supervision, had become "a central element in public life."[47] Nevertheless, the Proletkul'tists failed to win the conference to their viewpoint. P. Kerzhentsev, a prominent advocate of mass festivals, consoled himself by publishing an account of the conference debate that unmasked the majority. "He pointed out the 'opportunism' of the congress and its organizers and stressed that the majority . . . were 'representatives of cooperative organizations, trade unions, and delegates from the provinces', i.e. presumably cadres from the prerevolutionary popular theatre movement."[48] These groups would soon be brought into line, but by the commissariat.

In September 1919 a decree was signed by Lunacharsky as commissar of education, and by Lenin's personal secretary on behalf of the Council of People's Commissars, entitled "Unification of Theatrical Work."[49] A Central Committee to "regularize" all theatrical activity was established in Lunacharsky's ministry. The higher leadership of state theatres and others, including those affiliated with cooperatives, were to be unified in the executive body of this committee. The theatrical property—from buildings to costumes—of societies, associations, and circles desiring to operate theatres or maintain acting companies on a regular basis was transferred to this committee. In the copy of the decree preserved in the Section's files, one paragraph is marked by a penciled exclamation point in the margin. It reads: "[The committee] has the right to give autonomous theatres information guiding the character of repertory, with a view to bringing theatre closer to the popular mass and their socialist ideals."[50] In other words, independent troupes forfeited any right to determine what plays they would perform. It was a fairly short step from here to the nationalization of all theatres. The Section was informed of this decision by letter:

> The Theatre Division of the Ministry of Education announces the nationalization of the Section. Sale of theatre supplies and books is to end 10 February 1920. A special committee is named to receive the property and financial assets (V. V. Tikhonovich, P. A. Tamm, three members of [the executive committee of the Theatre Division] to be chosen later). The transfer will be made—the new commission will start work—at noon on February 1.[51]

According to M. D. Shishkin, the decision to nationalize was made by O. D. Kameneva when she became commissar of theatres. Despite the concerted efforts of Gorky and assembled artists representing Moscow theatres and People's Houses, the commissar had her way:

> The next morning Red Army soldiers were blocking the approaches to the theatres and the theatres were padlocked. The Commissar defeated not only those of us who represented the cooperatives and proponents of independent theatre. With us were [Lenin's wife] Krupskaia, Tomskii of the professional

> unions, Stanislavsky, Gorky, and Tsentrosoiuz, as well as the professional unions and other worker organizations.[52]

All the private support systems for independent theatre had now been swept away.[53]

Some individuals who had done excellent work in the realm of popular theatre adapted to the new dispensation and continued to work in Russian theatre. Some figures who had been prominent in the popular theatre movement in Russia, like Shishkin, emigrated. The Moscow city encyclopedia writes a poignant epitaph for the urban People's Houses, and perhaps the movement itself:

> After the victory of the Great October revolution, the People's Houses, along with the first worker clubs, became political-education centers for cultural mass work. Lenin spoke more than once in the Aleksandreevsk and Vvedensk People's Houses. In the 1920s they were converted to clubs or palaces of culture.[54]

Lenin's Party never established a comprehensive policy on popular theatre. Rather, bedrock Bolshevik antipathy toward local and professional independence determined its fate under Soviet power. As soon as the civil war was won, Lenin moved to strip Proletkul't of the autonomy it had enjoyed since 1917. A letter in *Pravda* 1 December 1920 sealed its fate. For one thing, the Workers' Opposition demands were sounding very much like Proletkul't's, especially the call for the state "to allow more room for workers' independent action."[55] Even local government bodies' initiative became unwelcome. In 1919 and 1920 localities built dozens of new power stations. But the diversion of resources from the well-advertised national electrification program caused the center to discourage and even forbid such local undertakings.[56]

In fact Lenin acted decisively in 1922, before the first attack of the illness that ended his life, to prevent the revival of prerevolutionary public activity in Russia. It may have been the Third Congress of Agronomists, held in March 1922, that first gave cause for alarm. There the most prominent Russian economists spoke against government interference in agriculture and argued for the development of private initiative.[57] Dmitri Volkogonov recounts how an All-Russian Congress of Physicians in Moscow in May 1922 scandalized the Party leadership. Commissar of Health Nikolai Somashko reported to the Politburo: "The recent Congress of Physicians revealed such important and dangerous trends in our lives that I believe it essential not to leave members of the Politburo in further ignorance. . . . A campaign was waged at the congress against Soviet medicine, while local government medicine and health insurance were eulogized." Lenin wrote to Stalin that the report should be shown to Felix Dzerzhinskii, chief of state security, "*in strictest secrecy* and without making copies."[58] Lenin himself ordered Dzherzhinskii to start preparations for the exile of "professors and writers."[59] In June the Politburo met twice, at Lenin's behest, on "anti-Soviet groups among the intelligentsia" and ruled:

> All printed publications were to be carefully vetted, "no congress or All-Russian meeting of specialists (doctors, agronomists, engineers, lawyers, and so on) may be convened without NKVD permission," while local meetings would require the authorization of the equivalent local organs, and "existing specialist sections of trade unions should be specially registered and put under special observation."[60]

Thus was the 1906 right to assembly overturned and the way prepared for the restoration of tutelage.

Specialists who were sufficiently pragmatic could still trim their sails and adjust to the new winds. V. V. Tikhonovich, long a champion of popular theatre as a means to local initiative, made a rather staggering adjustment to the official repudiation of initiative from below. In his 1922 book entitled *Independent Theatre* he now found a justification for theatre (for workers!) in science, hygiene, and productivity:

> The working man, undoubtedly trying to restore the upset balance of his organism, resorts to art and unhealthy stimulants [like] alcohol and . . . gambling. But rational entertainments, which are capable of stimulating the brain . . . , arouse impressions that . . . are more natural and healthy means to these ends. Here physical labor gives way to activity of the brain and nervous system, here the tired body receives its rightful rest, here the pleasures of art banish the boredom of work that gets on the nerves and the humdrum cares of life. That is why theatre in the hygienic sense, according to Professor V. Ia. Danilevskii, is capable of preserving the nervous and psychological health of the population—and in the economic, according to professor A. I. Chuprov, by raising the capacity for work, increasing the intensity and adroitness of work and reducing absenteeism.[61]

It could be assumed that the state as employer would want from theatre exactly what manufacturers had wanted from it in the 1890s.

The fact remained that the loss for independent community exploration through theatre art in Russia was irreparable. Gorky acknowledged as much in a letter written to Romain Rolland in the month of Lenin's death:

> At the beginning of 1918 I understood that no other power was possible in Russia. . . . However, that does not mean that I was completely sympathetic to Lenin. During those four years I argued with him, pointing out that his struggle against Russian anarchism was taking on, had taken on, the character of a struggle against culture.[62]

The development of grassroots associations in the countryside during the war confirms Norman Stone's account of the Russian economy in these years. Government spending stimulated commerce, labor mobility, investment, and employment and brought as much change as the whole previous generation beginning with Witte's vast expansion of the railroads and steel industry. "It was, indeed, the economic 'takeoff' that men had been predicting for Russia; that had, in a sense, caused the First World War, since German apprehensions of it had led Germany's leaders into provoking a preventive war."[63] The number of savings banks doubled, and more bank branches were opened between 1914 and 1917 than in the whole of Russia's past.[64] Removal of excess human population and the end of grain exports caused the cattle population to rise 25 percent and the sheep and goat population still more.[65] The impact of this "wealth effect" on the outlook of villagers cannot be overestimated.

Stone argues that the wartime crisis that is the stock theme of the historical literature, starting with collapse of the rail system, fuel and metals shortages, and the food crisis that produced revolution, resulted from unmanageably fast growth and resultant bottlenecks. The tsarist regime simply could not cope with the growth, could not coordinate a society already marked by extremely divisive tensions.[66] "The system did not break down because of Bolshevik agitation alone," Stone finds. "Russia . . . went Bolshevik because the old order collapsed, more or less as Lenin—uniquely—had foretold it would."[67] Of course the rapid expansion of private wealth accompanying the dislocation seemed to offer irrefutable confirmation for an ideology that neatly explained the nation's suffering.

Focusing on the same period, Thomas Porter and William Gleason describe a parallel development to the associations that sprang up around People's Houses in the countryside. In 1914 the central government chartered an All-Russian Zemstvo Union for the duration of the war that would finance and equip hospital units, run evacuation trains, provide refugee assistance, food, and vaccinations.

> From 1914 to 1917 thousands of doctors, nurses, statisticians, lawyers and engineers worked for the union developing associations with rural and urban Russia that went far beyond the purely functional capacities they fulfilled. From this perspective, the story of the *zemstva* unions demonstrates the continued development of public initiative in Russia; it also illustrates the beginning of a civil society and a coherent set of ideas and practices that might have served to guide the political and economic growth of the country.[68]

Porter and Gleason insist on a vital link connecting the Crimean War, Russo-Japanese War and World War I as accelerators of change in Russia, as has the present study.

The point, then, is not to vilify Lenin, but to note a historical irony: it took a moral absolutist, an incarnate Chatsky, to dissolve the new associations of 1914–19 and recentralize Russia in the name of social justice. For given the man's biting, critical, compelling, endless utterance, he is surely more the being imagined by Griboedov than the "Pugachev d'université" prophesied by Joseph de Maistre.

Conclusion

POPULAR THEATRE in western Europe resigned its Enlightenment commission to develop *sensibilité* in its viewers, mold the manners and morals of citizens, and reunify high and popular culture. By the later nineteenth century it contented itself with more modest aims, like advancing temperance and raising class or national consciousness. On the eve of the Great War it attracted larger audiences than ever before. Despite high-sounding proposals and hard-fought campaigns to capitalize on the theatre's potential for serving burgeoning nationalism, and despite continuing evidence of its civilizing capacity and conduciveness to good deportment, the state—in Britain, in Germany, and in France—declined to take it over.

Norbert Elias argued that the distinguishing features of French, German, and English society could actually be explained by studying civilization as a process embracing many generations.[1] In the first phase of the process as he described it, court aristocracies of the sixteenth and seventeenth centuries established rules of *courtoisie.* "In court circles . . . the growing compulsion to be restrained and self-controlled, becomes a 'mark of distinction' that is immediately imitated below and disseminated with the rise of broader classes" (*CP* 1:159). Toward the end of the eighteenth century *civilité* replaced *courtoisie;* after the first third of the seventeenth century *civilité* "began to sink," its content taken up and extended in a new concept, *civilisation.* "The concept of *civilisation* indicates quite clearly in its nineteenth century usage that the *process* of civilization—or more strictly speaking, a phase of this process—has been completed and forgotten. People only want to accomplish this process for *other* nations, and also, for a period, for the lower classes of their own society" (*CP* 1:104).

Over time, Elias found, Europeans relied less and less on physical force in their dealings with peers; the "spontaneity of affective action" diminished as new forms of dependency led to increasing regulation of affects in the form of self-control (*CP* 1:258, 186). Increasing division of labor lengthened and strengthened the bonds of dependency. "What changes is the way in which people are bonded to each other. This is why their behavior changes, and why their consciousness and their drive economy, and, in fact, their personality structure as a whole, change" (*CP* 2:276). What Elias called an "armor-plating of self-constraint" will increasingly "distance people from each other."[2] The long-term mental change, the altered look and feel of the world resulting from rising self-control, is prodigious:

> From the end of the Middle Ages on we can observe a strong shift towards the idea that objects can possess an identity, an effective reality, independently of the affect-charged ideas associated with them here and now by the groups concerned through their traditions and situation. This shift towards an increased consciousness of the autonomy of what is experienced in relation to the person who experiences, toward a greater autonomy of "objects" in the experience of "subjects," is closely related to the thickening armor that is being interposed between affective impulses and the objects at which they are directed, in the form of ingrained self-control. This shift makes it possible for people, in their search for wider knowledge of their world, to attain greater certainty of knowledge, a better approximation of concepts to their objects and so a greater degree of control over these objects, in certain areas of their lives.[3]

And one result of the process of distancing is a vantage point that discloses humanity. "The view that one commands from a particular plateau of detachment reached through a particular process of distancing—a plateau the temporal conditions of which can be very exactly explored and explained empirically—is interpreted as an eternal, timeless, immutable 'human condition'" (*CS* 243).

The fashion for self-control and restraint in manners could sweep through a society in short order. Edward Gibbon—to give an example not cited by Elias—was struck by the spread of what he called urbanity ("which from the court has diffused its gentle influence to the shop, the cottage and the schools") when he returned to France in 1763, after a mere five years' absence.[4] In Russia the period from 1913 to 1917 would prove equally favorable for the lengthening of the bonds of interdependence, increasing choice in association, autonomy.

The Russian educated classes had probably completed the process of civilization by the mid-nineteenth century. But the walls of traditional village culture had to be breached before the overwhelming majority of the population could take the all-important first step toward autonomy, broad choice in their associations and economic behavior. The *narod* had to undergo the process that lengthened the chains of interdependence before they could construct a civil society founded on mutual respect and promoting reciprocal integrity and the pursuit of private interests.

Literacy shook the bastions of an oral culture that had constantly adjusted its lessons to fit the perspective of the present.[5] Jack Goody and Ian Watt found that literacy contributes to an "awareness of individual differences in behavior and the personality which lies behind them" and gives the impression that the individual creates his own personality "by selecting, rejecting or accommodating to the conflicting attitudes in his culture."[6] Instead of embracing "the right thing to do," an individual with access to written accounts could develop an autonomous moral value system.

But literacy alone made little difference in villagers' and workers' conception of selfhood. It was extremely rare, if not unheard of, for peasants to acquire the habit of rapid and extensive reading that leads to reorganizing experience around logical categories. It took them a long time to learn to read well enough to acquire the impression that they had the capacity to create their own personalities. Thus theatre assumed the utmost importance in the *narod*'s transition to individual autonomy and a civil society. This was due in part to opportunities it presented for participation and organization—individual *initiative*—in production and acting from 1906 on. But equally important was its impact on habitual viewers. Like readers capable of reading widely, theatregoers entered a world where highly diverse characters were juxtaposed and contrasted. By stimulating the empathic sense, drama magnified the province of perceived choice in life and disclosed the possibility of self-creation.

The distancing Elias found central to the civilizing process may not be unrelated to the distancing produced in the theatre of the Greeks or to the appearance of silent reading itself in classical antiquity. Jesper Svenbro rejects the notion that the Greeks graduated from rendering written texts orally to silent, extensive reading simply because the quantity of texts multiplied. He reasons instead that certain distinctive traits of theatrical representation structured the new practice of silent reading. He begins with the distancing of the audience from the stage.

> This separation delimits the fictional game played out on the stage and constitutes in a certain fashion the very originality of the theatre: the public cannot intervene in this game. It is not possible, for example, to tell a character on the stage what one already knows about his destiny. One cannot stop the course of events to tell the characters what they should do. One must "contemplate" them *(theâsthai)* as they go to their own destruction. The tension created by this situation renders the action on stage even more fascinating: the theatrical spectacle gives itself over to an *auto-nomie* [self-government] that the public cannot interfere with, which was the rule of this game *(paidiá)* which Thespis spoke of in the mid sixth century, when he developed his new art against Solon's indignant criticism.[7]

Actors play a vital role in the passage to silent reading because they do not simply reactivate a text, but rather produce a "vocal copy" of the text. Therefore the audience hears a dramatic text that speaks with complete autonomy. Svenbro reasons that the text which comes to be recognized in a visual fashion seems to possess the same *auto-nomie* as the theatre spectacle. The reading voice finds itself interiorized.

One might well ask whether the distancing required by the theatrical game really is anything out of the ordinary. Recorded instances of the difficulty it presented to Russian folk audiences as they first encountered literary theatre suggest that it is. According to Vladimir Filippov,

> In the Moscow People's House when [Ostrovsky's and N. Y. Solov'ev's] *Belugin's Marriage* was played a box of chocolates, placed on a table, gave off a sound that clearly revealed it to be empty. Which led someone in the audience to cry out: "How do you like that? The swindler gave her an empty box."[8]

In his remarks to the commission considering changes in the popular theatre censorship in 1905, E. P. Karpov recalled,

> *The Russians in 1812* was given in Tula. In one scene Napoleon orders that the Russian prisoners be shot. This was sufficient to make the audience shout: "Down with him!" "Fight him!" However, the director, who was playing the role of one of the adjutants quickly found the right thing to say. He turned to Napoleon and said, "Your Majesty! Show mercy and free them!" and this quieted the crowd at once.[9]

Konstantin Paustovsky remembered an aunt who visited his family in Kiev every winter when he was a boy. His mother loved to take her to the theatre, and they went chiefly to plays in Ukrainian.

> Once in the middle of a play Aunt Dosia jumped up and yelled at the villain on the stage in Ukrainian, "What are you up to, you scoundrel, you and your shameless eyes!" The audience roared with laughter. The curtain came down. Aunt Dosia cried all the next day out of shame, and begged my father's pardon, and we didn't know how to reassure her.[10]

While the first instance might be taken as a comment to fellow viewers rather than a violation of the separation of audience from the stage, it seems clear that to some at least the autonomy rule of this new theatre game had to be learned.

Elias pointed out that for people embarked on the civilizing process a self-control mechanism establishes itself, blocking spontaneous action, which creates a new level of consciousness. There is evidence to suggest that Russian peasants who determined to pursue enlightenment experienced this kind of change in their own mental processes. Ernest Poole met a remarkable peasant woman in a benighted central Russian village in 1918 whose horizons had been broadened by travel. She told him,

> I have to hunt in my mind for my thoughts as though they were lost in the dark, I work on the fields and I know I am thinking, but nothing seems clear to me. Sometimes I am not even sure what I am thinking about, and so I go on with my work. But then suddenly, like a flash of lightening in the night that shows you just for a moment every house in the village, so my whole mind is lighted up.[11]

The same observation is to be heard in Semën Kanatchikov's memoir in his recollection of his mental processes as he struggled on the path to "become fully conscious" at the turn of the century.

> In those days I still had trouble making sense of people, of my environment, of events that were sometimes very significant; yet, under the influence of my own bitter experience, I was beginning to develop a certain "feel" for things. Thus, for example, I was unable to explain, to demonstrate logically, the injustice of a particular wrongdoing, but I immediately and definitely felt antipathy and disgust toward the person who'd done the deed.[12]

His years in the village school had not prepared him to read widely. It took him a full month of evenings to plod through an article larded with abstract concepts and foreign words. He would welcome a prison sentence because it gave him more time to "work on" himself. In fact, it would take him enormous effort and many years to build up his store of general knowledge and become fluent in articulating his thoughts before strangers. He revealed that one reason workers hated liberal professionals was because of their easily attained cultural advantages, the ability to speak unself-consciously, to generalize and summarize from wide reading.

There is no reason to suppose that texts delivered in the theatre and on the printed page to the uncultivated could not in time have sparked the transition to autonomy and broadened scope for individual decision among enough of Russia's population to make civil society a reality. When the Bolsheviks came to power they appeared to endorse progress toward this end when they formally abolished the estates.[13] Their action against initiative from below in the theatre movement can be seen in part as arising from centralizers' antipathy to spontaneous cultural decentralization.

Here it becomes necessary to recall the conditions under which the Greeks invented theatre. Enlightenment thinkers who insisted theatre could yield far more than entertainment invariably invoked the role of publicly performed plays in reordering the community life of classical antiquity. They apprehended a major difference between modern drama, which pitted the individual against social forces, and the constraints depicted in antique drama—as exemplified by an Oedipus pursued by destiny or Orestes by the Furies. As Benjamin Constant put it in 1829, "The social order, this network of institutions and conventions that envelops us from the day of our birth and whose impact on the individual we do not fully comprehend—this is the equivalent of the *fatalité* of the ancients."[14] But recent scholarship downplays this distinction, stressing precisely the function of rapid social change and heightened social tensions in the creation of drama (characterized by the opposition of roles and parts) out of fertility rite. Theatre's birth was thus the direct result, in Oddone Longo's formulation, of "the more pluralistic system of the *polis,* where division of labor, social stratification and class struggle reduce precisely the area of unanimity in the community."[15] As Richard Seaford puts it, "the major genre produced by the polis [was shaped by] the needs of the developing polis."[16]

In Seaford's view, procession evolved into performance at the very moment the polis became a new kind of community, comprising city and clearly demarcated outlying territory. City Dionysia helped the Greeks break traditional associations "by generally arranging things so that everybody consorts with each other as much as possible" (*RR* 247). Tragedy brought non-kin together "around a single focus of emotion," and demonstrated how order and cult could resolve crisis and confusion (*RR* 398). "Dionysus is the *civic* god who in tragedy after tragedy presides over the self-destruction of the ruling families of the mythical past, to the benefit of the polis, the god who has thereby indeed put an end to that introversion and autonomy of the family which gave rise to tragic conflict" (*RR* 367). Like the laws of the new courts, the dramas are written down, and inscription confers "authority, consensus and a lasting identity" on the performance of cult and on the administration of justice (*RR* 219). Theatre and justice are, moreover, additionally connected by the idea that order and lawfulness depend on the people themselves and their understanding of measure (*RR* 228).

Bernard Williams concludes that "the real difference" between the outlook of most Greeks and modern political ideas is the notion that a higher political entity than the polis could somehow correct for the attenuating impact of necessity and luck on justice. The modern outlook "has given itself the task of constructing a framework of social justice to control necessity and chance, in the sense both of mitigating their effects on the individual and of showing that what cannot be mitigated is not unjust" (*SN* 128). He contends that today "we are, in our ethical situation, more like human beings in antiquity than any Western people have been in the meantime" (*SN* 166). Our ideas of action and responsibility are close to the Greek ideas expressed in ancient tragedy, which "precisely refuses to present human beings who are in harmony with their world, and has no room for a world that, if it were understood well enough, could instruct us how to be in harmony with it" (*SN* 16, 163). This assessment enables us to gauge the significance of Lenin's decision to nationalize Russian popular theatre.

The enlighteners who first took literary theatre to the *narod* dreamed of a common culture for all Russians.[17] They at first had to supply the performances, but from the beginning took a keen interest in the medium's capacity to activate the viewer. They discovered theatre's power to challenge its audience to work on the self. They noted its ability to stimulate an interest in reading and the adoption of a new relation to the world that entailed a respect and thirst for knowledge.

After decades of extremely rapid population growth in the countryside (the result of "death control without birth control") and a burst of conservative gentry political activity at the center to block all avenues leading to peasant participation in politics at any level, the People's House sprang up as a new kind of space for community action. Like the Masonic lodges of an earlier century, *narodnye doma* opened a common ground where persons from different estates could relate to each other as equals. The theatres within their walls might seem a thin reed to support such weighty developments as deliberate, concerted local action to identify new sources of satisfaction and facilitate the creation of new amenities. But the complex texts that "speak themselves" stimulated a critical attitude; viewers were challenged to consider their individual needs and invited to reach for higher aspirations. Theatre invited its audience to dream. Grassroots theatre in Russia gave its participants invaluable experience in planning, coordination, and execution, with locally attainable rewards in self-satisfaction and self-esteem and the completion of meaningful work that gave pleasure to neighbors while challenging them to better themselves. Left to itself, it could have done much to foster civic responsibility harnessed to individual initiative.

Even as the new regime liquidated the support systems for rural amateur circles built up by the zemstvos, the cooperatives, and the Section to Promote Village, Factory, and School Theatre, it encouraged participatory large-scale urban theatrical events built around scenarios rather than dramatic texts.[18] The object appeared to be the development of political consciousness among the people rather than a more basic self-consciousness. It seems significant as an attempt to change the theatre game by *eliminating* the separation between drama and audience. In time the authorities took custody of popular theatre, certified its specialists, and oversaw its delivery to recipients looked after by their cultural superiors. When the new government established its theatrical monopoly, trusteeship returned with a vengeance. The *narod* became "the masses."[19] The popular theatre movement, after beginning to make a significant contribution to the civilizing process among the *narod* in Russia, was diverted to other ends.

Lenin's personal responsibility is clear here. Ken Jowitt, a political scientist intrigued by the way traditional eastern European peasant societies maintained their traditions and cohesiveness under Leninist regimes, noted the failure to develop "a way of life based on the individual, impersonalism, association, and tolerance."[20] With some justice, he claimed that Leninist regimes fostered the outcomes of centralized despotism famously listed by Tocqueville: "depriving the governed of any sense of solidarity and interdependence, of good-neighborly feeling and [identification with] the welfare of the community" (290–91). Perhaps the last word on this matter should be left to Habermas, who, when asked in the course of a discussion of the attainment of radical democracy through a perfected Public Sphere, replied, "I don't think that we can ever again, or that we should ever again, bridge the institutional differentiation between the science system and political agitation and political organization and political action. That is what Lenin tried to do. And I think that it's a part of the past that we don't want to retrieve."[21]

The destruction of grassroots popular theatre as a focus for community activity and an arena for local initiative ended an institution of inestimable value for inculcating the habits of self-discipline and self-control, cooperation and compromise so essential for establishing a civil society.[22] Once theatre returned to being just another uplifting entertainment delivered by professionals and guardians to that segment of the population categorized as disadvantaged, it ceased to be very helpful at advancing for individuals the process of interiorization, privatization, and expansion of the inner space of the self.

Soviet Russia of course provided unparalleled management opportunities for persons from the lower orders who happened to possess self-discipline and a breadth of horizon. Klepikov recalled in his memoirs traveling through Kineshma in 1928 with his wife for the first time in twenty-one years. A middle-aged man who had been in his teens when Klepikov had worked in the theatre there recognized them immediately. "Now he occupies a very important place in the factory," Klepikov wrote, "and remembers the circle of this long-ago time with great gratitude and warmth."[23] Other avenues to social mobility, like formal education, remained and even expanded after independent local theatre ceased to exist. But the rate at which those people formerly called "dark" became complex, modern people continued to disappoint. Russia remained a highly stratified, compartmentalized society, as sociologist Tatiana Zaslavskaia dared to say in print in the 1980s.[24] Even in that decade Basile Kerblay could insist that features of Soviet urban culture commonly attributed to "national temperament" ought in fact to be traced to peasant survivals. He mentioned "the need of a sense of belonging, which makes people both more dependent and vulnerable, but also warmer hearted," desire for identification with the community, and "a lower degree of self-control, a kind of impulsiveness in which depression and exaltation alternate, coupled with greater indulgence of other people's weaknesses" (which he related to "the individual's sense of affective frustration").[25] Perhaps even the larger process by which literacy achieved dominion in civilized societies by crowding out other forms of remembering and communicating failed to achieve completion in Soviet Russia. Eric Havelock commented on the continued importance and prestige of poetry there in this context.

> The role of poetry in literate societies . . . is narrower, because literacy, by entrusting the storage function to documented prose, has gradually stripped poetry and poetic experience of their dominant position in the culture and emptied them of their complexity. In Western culture, and in the twentieth century, this process seems to have completed itself everywhere except in Russia.[26]

The campaign begun by educated Russians in the middle of the nineteenth century to breach the folkways of the simple with literary theatre and present their values produced impressive results. A remarkably energetic and widespread movement of local people emerged to take possession of theatre and establish a society that balanced public and private interests in a small-scale community. But it perished in the wake of the recentralization of the Russian Empire.

Notes

INTRODUCTION

1. Eugen Weber, *Peasants into Frenchmen* (Stanford, Calif., 1967), 495.

2. Loren Kruger, *The National Stage* (Chicago, 1992), 22.

3. Zygmunt Hubner, *Theater and Politics* (Evanston, Ill., 1992), 181.

4. "J. J. Rousseau à M. d'Alembert sur son article GENEVE, dans le VIIe volume de *l'Encyclopédie* sur le projet d'établir un théâtre de comédie en cette ville," in *Oeuvres complètes* (Paris, 1791), 16:48.

5. Emmet Kennedy, *A Cultural History of the French Revolution* (New Haven, Conn., 1989), 112.

6. *Du théâtre* (Amsterdam, 1773), v.

7. Kennedy, *Cultural History*, 171.

8. Frederick Brown, *Theater and Revolution* (New York, 1980), 68.

9. John McCormick, *Popular Theatres of Nineteenth Century France* (London, 1993), 8, 4. "Before the revolution, the notion of a mass audience was more an abstract idea . . . than . . . a regular theatre-going public."

10. Ibid., 19.

11. F. W. J. Hemmings, *The Theatre Industry in Nineteenth-Century France* (Cambridge, 1993), 132, 100.

12. F. W. J. Hemmings, *Theatre and State in France: 1760–1905* (Cambridge, 1994), 242.

13. See David Fisher, *Romain Rolland and the Politics of Engagement* (Berkeley and Los Angeles, 1988), and Kruger, *National Stage*, 47ff.

14. Romain Rolland, *Le Théâtre du peuple* (Paris, 1926) 85–86. The Russian edition appeared in 1910, and an American edition in 1918.

15. See David J. Fisher, "The Origins of the French Popular Theatre," *Journal of Contemporary History* 12 (1977), and Helen W. Machan, "The Popular-Theatre Movement in France" (Ph.D. diss., University of Illinois, 1950).

16. Maurice Pottécher, *Théâtre du peuple à Bussang* (Paris, 1913), 10–11.

17. Kruger, *National Stage*, 44.

18. See Hemmings, *Theatre Industry*, 132.

19. Nicholas Boyle, *Goethe: The Poet and the Age* (Oxford, 1991), 21.

20. Ibid., 403.

21. Robert Sackett, *Popular Entertainment, Class, and Politics in Munich, 1900–1923* (Cambridge, Mass., 1982), 10–11.

22. See Vernon Lidtke, "Nationalism and Socialism in Germany," *American Historical Review* 79, no. 1 (1974).

23. Cecil W. Davies, *Theatre for the People* (Austin, Tex., 1977), 24.

24. Quoted from *The Manuscripts of the Earl of Dartmouth* by Douglas A. Reid, "Popular Theatre in Victorian Birmingham," in David Bradby, Louis James, and Bernard Sharratt, eds., *Performance and Politics in Popular Drama* (Cambridge, 1980), 66.

25. Ibid., 74.

26. Peter Bailey, *Leisure and Class in Victorian England: Rational Recreation and the Contest for Control, 1830–1885* (London, 1978), 165.

27. Bailey characterizes the Old Vic as a "counter Music hall"—kept afloat only "through the generous subventions of Samuel Morley." Ibid., 163.

28. George Rowell, *The Old Vic Theatre* (Cambridge, 1993), 56.

29. David Bradby and John McCormick, *People's Theatre* (London, 1978), 35.

30. Rowell, *Old Vic,* 59.

31. Quoted ibid., 84. In Finland, where plays had been written in the native language only since the 1830s, the temperance movement—along with the labor movement and youth movement—stimulated rural and urban popular theatre across the country by the turn of the century. See Pekka Lounela, "Theatre by the People for the People: Amateur Theatre in Finland," *Cultures* 2, no. 3 (1976).

32. Nicholas Tomalin and John Elsom, *History of the National Theatre* (London, 1978), 25.

33. Quoted in Rowell, *Old Vic,* 76.

34. For Tomalin and Elsom (26), "The Old Vic was the only theatre in London, other than some music halls, which could truly claim to be a people's theatre." But see Kruger (211 n. 51): "The Old Vic's character as a philanthropic institution does not confirm claims that it was a people's theatre as suggested by David Bradby and John McCormick."

35. Janet Minihan, *The Nationalization of Culture* (New York, 1977), 142–43.

36. James Woodfield, *English Theatre in Transition, 1886–1914* (Beckenham, Kent, 1984), 101–4.

37. They followed in the footsteps of their Western counterparts. F. W. J. Hemmings estimates that well over a hundred private home theatres existed in France before the Revolution. "Many of the nobles attached to the court had incorporated in their private mansions studio theatres of quite extraordinary splendour and luxury; they used them occasionally for private perfor-

mances, but would also engage senior [actors from the Comédie-Française] to enact plays for the pleasure of their high-born guests." *Theatre and State in France*, 229, 72.

38. *Polnoe sobranie sochinenii v tridsati tomakh* (Leningrad, 1972), 4:19.

39. Priscilla Roosevelt devotes a chapter to estate theatres in *Life on the Russian Country Estate* (New Haven, Conn., 1995), 129–53.

40. T. M. Akimova furnishes a useful survey of the secondary literature on popular folk theatre: "Russkii narodnyi teatr v issledovaniiakh poslevoennykh let," *Sovetskaia etnografiia* 5 (1976). See I. I. Savushkina, *Russkii narodnyi teatr* (Moscow, 1976); and V. E. Gusev, ed., *Narodnyi teatr: sbornik statei* (Leningrad, 1974). Also Elizabeth A. Warner, *The Russian Folk Theatre* (The Hague, 1977); and Russell Zguta, *Russian Minstrels: A History of the Skomorokhi* (Philadelphia, 1978). The festival character of traditional Russian folk culture is discussed in A. I. Mazaev, *Prazdnik kak sotsial'no-khudozhestvennoe iavlenie* (Moscow, 1978). See also A. F. Nekrylova, *Russkie narodnye gorodskie prazdniki, uveseleniia i zvelishcha: konets xviii–nachalo xx veka* (Leningrad, 1984) and A. M. Konechnyi, "Peterburgskie narodnye gulian'ia na maslenoi i paskhal'noi nedeliakh," in *Peterburg i guberniia: Istoriko-etnograficheskie issledovaniia* (Leningrad, 1988).

41. Anthony Swift, "Theater for the People: The Politics of Popular Culture in Urban Russia, 1861–1917" (Ph.D. diss., University of California, Berkeley, 1992), 261, 276, 280–81.

42. A. A. Bardovskii, *Teatral'nyi zritel' na fronte v kanun oktiabria* (Leningrad, 1928).

43. "The decree 'On the Unification of Theater Work' (1919) . . . put all Soviet theaters under the political control of the Central Theater Committee, a special section instituted by Narkompros, the People's Commissariat for Education. Theaters 'whose cultural value' was recognized by the Central Theater Committee were given some autonomy, but the state retained for itself 'the right to give the autonomous theaters certain indications of a repertorial nature in order to link them with the popular masses and their socialistic ideal.'" Hubner, *Theater and Politics*, 72.

44. Thomas Burger, trans., *The Structural Transformation of the Public Sphere: An Inquiry into a Category of Bourgeois Society* (Cambridge, Mass., 1991).

45. See Joan Neuberger, *Hooliganism* (Berkeley and Los Angeles, 1993), 46ff. and Louise McReynolds, *The News Under Russia's Old Regime* (Princeton, N.J., 1991), 12, 288–89. It may be appropriate to note here that Roy Robson utilizes Habermas's later communications theory in *Old Believers in Modern Russia* (DeKalb, Ill., 1995); see 140 n. 47.

46. Daniel Brower, *The Russian City between Tradition and Modernity, 1850–1900* (Berkeley and Los Angeles, 1990), 94ff.

47. Burger, *Structural Transformation of the Public Sphere*, 9–10.

48. Roger Chartier, in one of the most telling recent applications of Habermas's theory to French history, goes so far as to speak of "the Kant-Habermas model" because of the "text that served Habermas as the matrix of his demonstration: Kant's . . . 'What is Enlightenment?' which appeared . . . in the *Berlinische Monatsschrift* in 1784." Lydia Cochrane, trans., *The Cultural Origins of the French Revolution* (Durham, N.C., 1991), 16, 23.

49. Quoted Habermas, *Structural Transformation*, 110, from I. Kant, "On the Common Saying: 'This May Be True in Theory, but Does Not Apply in Practice.'"

50. Craig Calhoun, ed., *Habermas and the Public Sphere* (Cambridge, Mass., 1992).

51. "To establish its supremacy, in Gramsci's view, a dominant class . . . must demonstrate its claims to 'intellectual and moral leadership' and this requires the arts of persuasion, a continuous labor of ideological intervention." Geoff Ely, "Nations, Publics and Political Cultures: Placing Habermas in the Nineteenth Century," in Calhoun, ed. *Habermas and the Public Sphere*, 294, 323.

52. Francisco Adrados, *Festival, Comedy and Tragedy* (Leiden, 1975), 435. See also François de Polignac, *Cults, Territory, and the Origins of the Greek City-State* (Chicago, 1995), 40, 60, 84.

53. Bruno Snell, *The Discovery of Mind: The Greek Origins of European Thought* (Cambridge, Mass., 1953), 95.

54. John J. Winkler and Froma Zeitlin, eds., *Nothing to Do with Dionysos? Athenian Drama in Its Social Context* (Princeton, N.J., 1989), 1.

55. G. E. R. Lloyd, *Demystifying Mentalities* (Cambridge, 1990), 8, 36.

56. Paul Veyne, *Did the Greeks Believe in Their Myths?* (Chicago, 1988), 42.

57. Ibid., 31.

58. Eric Havelock, *The Muse Learns to Write* (New Haven, Conn., 1986), 69.

59. Eric Havelock, *The Literate Revolution in Greece and Its Cultural Consequences* (Princeton, N.J., 1982), 8 (emphasis added).

60. Adrados, *Festival*, 435.

61. Oddone Longo, "The Theater of the *Polis*," repr. in *Nothing to do with Dionysos?* 16.

62. Rosalind Thomas, *Literacy and Orality in Ancient Greece* (Cambridge, 1992), 108.

63. Longo, "Theater of the *Polis*," 10.

64. Thomas, *Literacy and Orality*, 48.

65. Alfred Burns, "Athenian Literacy in the Fifth Century B.C.," *Journal of the History of Ideas* 42, no. 3 (July–September 1981), 376–77, 386.

66. Charles Segal, "Tragedy, Orality, Literacy." in *Oralità: Cultura, Letteratura, Discorso: Atti del Convegno Internazionale a cura di Bruno Gentili e Giuseppi Paioni* (Rome, 1986), 226.

67. Paul Fussell, *The Great War and Modern Memory* (New York, 1975), ix.

68. See, for example, John Elsom (*History of the National Theatre,* 330): "[A national theatre is needed] to provide a flowing repertoire of the world's best plays, in good productions, so that those living in Britain would have a better chance than before of forming their theatrical tastes by experiencing a wide range of what (for want of a better word) we might call masterpieces." See also Kruger (*National Stage,* 16–17 [paraphrasing Herbert Marcuse]): "'[A]ffirmative culture' (the realm of the beautiful that purports to transcend opposition in the world) 'cancels social antagonism in an abstract internal community,' offering solace rather than resolution of that antagonism."

69. Daniel Lerner, *The Passing of Traditional Society* (Glencoe, Ill. 1964), 73.

70. Francis Fergusson, *The Idea of a Theatre* (Princeton, N.J., 1949), 236–38.

71. Eugen Weber, "Who Sang the Marseillaise?" in *My France* (Cambridge, Mass., 1991), 98.

72. See Bailey, *Leisure and Class,* 176, 178.

73. Ely, "Nations, Publics," 325.

CHAPTER ONE

1. Quoted in S. M. Solov'ev, *Istoriia Rossii s drevneishikh vremen* (Moscow, 1961) *Kniga VI, (Toma 11–12),* 545.

2. Quoted in Nikolai Tolstoy, *The Tolstoys* (New York, 1983), 52. For a full translation of the diary, exhaustively annotated, see Max Okenfuss, trans., *The Travel Diary of Peter Tolstoi* (DeKalb, Ill., 1987). On Venetian drinking habits and opera, see esp. 149–54.

3. A. A. Kizevetter, *Pervyi obshchedostupnyi teatr v rossii* (Moscow, 1904), 8.

4. "His journal of his foreign trip notes his activities day by day. . . . They went to the theatre." V. O. Kliuchevskii, *Kurs russkoi istorii* (Moscow, 1958), 4:17.

5. Quoted in Kizevetter, 10. *Temnie liudi* presents difficulties for translators. Its literal rendering, "dark people," rings alarm bells for American readers, who cannot help thinking of negro slavery and thus assume racist overtones. The term was widely used in Russia (and not unknown in the Soviet period) to refer to the unenlightened, uneducated, and uncivilized masses. The Russian serfs did not, of course, differ ethnically from their more or less Westernized masters. The phrase can be translated simply as "ignorant," but I usually prefer "simple folk," since the Russian indicates more than a lack of knowledge or information.

6. Simon Karlinsky, *Russian Drama from Its Beginnings to the Age of Pushkin* (Berkeley and Los Angeles, 1985), 47–48.

7. "A . . . novel feature of Renaissance individualism . . . lies . . . in the emergence of men who are able to imagine themselves in more than one role; who stand as it were outside or above their own personalities." Paul Delany, *British Autobiography in the Seventeenth Century* (New York, 1969), 11.

8. Friedhelm Kaiser, "Der europäische Anteil an der russischen Rechtsterminologie der petrinischen Zeit," *Forschungen zur osteuropäischen Geschicht* (1965), 10:317–26.

9. Quoted in Evgenii Anisimov, *The Reforms of Peter the Great* (Armonk, N.Y., 1993), 34.

10. Quoted ibid., 223.

11. N. V. [Osten-] Drizen, "Vliianie teatra na detei i iunoshei shkol'nogo vozrasta," *Russkaia shkola,* no. 1 (1911), 39.

12. See Karlinsky, *Russian Drama,* 50 n. 21.

13. Aleksei Iartsev, "Pervyi fabrichnye teatry v Rossii," *Istoricheskii vestnik* (May 1900), 648..

14. ("Teatr est' shkola narodnaia, a ia v nei pervyi uchitel'.")

15. Isabel de Madariaga, *Russia in the Age of Catherine the Great* (New Haven, Conn., 1981), 327.

16. Priscilla Roosevelt, "Emerald Thrones and Living Statues," *Russian Review* 50 (January 1991), 5.

17. I. I. Podol'skaia, ed., *Russkie memuary: izbrannye stranitsy xviii vek* (Moscow, 1988), 157.

18. It has been shown that the book's sections on table manners and social behavior were borrowed from Erasmus's *De civilitate morum puerilium* (1530), which had been far and away the most important guide for the diffusion of courtly manners in western Europe. See Max Okenfuss, *The Discovery of Childhood in Russia* (Newtonville, Mass., 1980), 45–48. Norbert Elias charted the origin of the European concept of *civilité* from the unprecedented attention accorded to this short treatise of Erasmus; *The Civilizing Process* (New York, 1978), 53–60. See also, Jacques Revel, "The Uses of Civility," in *A History of Private Life* (Cambridge, Mass., 1989), 3:168–78.

19. Iu. M. Lotman, "Bytovoe povedenie i tipologiia kul'tury v Rossii xviii v.," in *Kul'turnoe nasledie drevnei rusi* (Moscow, 1976), 22.

20. Iu. M. Lotman, "Teatr i teatral'nost v stroe kultury nachala xix veka," in *Stat'i po tipologii kul'tury,* (Tartu, 1973), 2:47.

21. "As early as 1765 the *St. Petersburg News* wrote an awed account of amateur theatricals in the Count's recently enlarged house in St. Petersburg." Bertha Malnick, "Russian Serf Theatres," *Slavonic and East European Review* 30, no. 75 (June 1952), 396.

22. On Kuskovo and Ostankino, see Priscilla Roosevelt, *Russian Country Estate,* 59–66.

23. Tat'iana Dynnik, *Krepostnoi teatr* (Moscow, 1933), 243–355. But see Malnick on Dynnik's numbers (393): "there must have been more." Dynnik tabulates the published theatres by city and province, giving the name of the proprietor and time of existence, when known.

24. Malnick, "Russian Serf Theatres," 395.

25. Lotman, "Teatr i teatral'nost," 73.

26. The Marchioness of Londonderry and H. Montgomery Hyde, eds., *The Russian Journals of Martha and Catherine Wilmot* (New York, 1971), 237. (To Harriet Wilmot, 21 October 1806.)

27. Laurence Senelick, "The Erotic Bondage of Serf Theatre" *Russian Review* 50 (January 1991), 29.

28. For an analysis of authority patterns in texts of some Russian operas of the day, see Marshall Shatz, "The Noble Landowner in Russian Comic Operas of the Time of Catherine the Great: The Patriarchal Image," *Canadian Slavic Studies* 3, no. 1 (Spring 1969).

29. Richard Wortman, "Theatricality, Myth, and Authority," *Russian Review* 50 (January 1991), 49. He suggests that organizing a serf theatre may have offered a way of compensating for a sense of personal insecurity in the Catherinian order: "The nobility's displays of grandeur may have conceled a lack of real power in a system where every benefit and privilege was sought from above."

30. I. S. Zhirkevich, "Zapiski" *Russkaia starina,* Vol. 13 (1875). (He wrote his recollections of the theatre in 1847.) Subsequent citations are from this source.

31. A. S. Griboedov, *Gore ot uma* (Moscow, 1984), 49, 134–35: "A nashe solnyshko? nash klad? / Na lbu napisano: Teatr i Maskerad"

32. "Zapiski L. P. Nikulinoi-Kositskoi, artistki Imperatorskikh Moskovskikh Teatrov," *Russkaia starina* 21 (1878), 302.

33. N. S. Leskov, "Tupeinyi khudozhnik," in *Sobranie sochinenii* (Moscow, 1958), 7:220–42.

34. Quoted in Laurence Senelick, *Serf Actor: The Life and Art of Mikhail Shchepkin* (Westport, Conn., 1984), 49.

35. A. A. Kizevetter, *M. S. Shchepkin* (Moscow, 1917), 16.

36. Nikolai Efros, *M. S. Shchepkin* (Saint Petersburg, 1920), 21.

37. See, for example, "O vospitanii i nastavlenii detei," translated by V. Snow in *Russian Intellectual History,* ed. Marc Raeff, (New York, 1966), 68–86.

38. Quoted in Malnick, "Russian Serf Theatres," 400. If landowners responded to the Pugachev jacquerie by regarding peasants as children, unable to think for themselves, requiring guidance and supervision, it follows that at least some landowners persuaded by new theories of child-rearing later in the century would extend their practices to peasants in their care.

39. Senelick, *Serf Actor,* 61.

40. Donald Fanger, *The Creation of Nikolai Gogol* (Cambridge, Mass., 1979), 82. Gogol's essay, "Peterburgskaia stsena v 1835–36 g.," can be found in *Sobranie sochinenii v semi tomakh* (Moscow, 1978), 6:455–65.

41. "The novel and short story were beginning to teem with them: the heroes of Pushkin's tales, Gogol's 'little men' in the Petersburg stories, the insulted and injured of Dostoevsky's early works." Senelick, *Serf Actor,* 135.

42. Vissarion Belinskii, *Polnoe sobranie sochinenii* (Moscow, 1956), 12:433.

43. V. I. Kuleslov and A. A. Gozenpud, "Provintsial'nye gastroli M. S. Shchepkina," in *Teatral'noe nasledstvo* (Moscow, 1956), 276.

44. M. S. Shchepkin, *Zapiski, pis'ma. Sovremenniki o M. S. Shchepkine,* ed. A. P. Klinchin and S. N. Durylin (Moscow, 1952), 243.

45. Kizevetter, *M. S. Shchepkin,* 9.

46. Ibid., 51.

47. Quoted ibid., 35 (italics in original). Kizevetter adds: "He was dedicated to his art and considered it a vehicle for bringing people moments of great happiness. Yet he saw theatre not as escape, but a great, serious business."

48. Quoted in Vladimir Filippov, *M. S. Shchepkin i ego rol' v istorii russkogo teatra* (Moscow and Leningrad, 1938), 55. Nikolai Efros considered that it was Shchepkin's "reverential attitude toward his art—'Theatre as Temple'" that gave him "the very highest place in Russia's theatre history." *M. S. Shchepkin,* 11.

49. Senelick points out some difficulties with a celebrated passage in Shchepkin's memoirs where he tells of the profound impression made upon him by the acting of Prince A. A. Meshchersky, who spoke his lines quietly, simply, and naturally but managed to create the illusion of living the part. *Serf Actor,* 26–29.

50. Ibid., 145.

51. She was a teacher of Stanislavsky, and her confidence in and sympathy for him were a factor in Vladimir Nemirovich-Danchenko's desire to meet him—a meeting that led directly to their collaboration in the Moscow Art Theatre. See Nemirovich-Danchenko, *My Life in the Russian Theatre* (New York, 1936), 75.

52. On "enlightened bureaucrats," see W. Bruce Lincoln, *The Great Reforms* (DeKalb, Ill., 1990), 52.

53. Ian Hacking, *The Taming of Chance* (Cambridge, 1990), 26.

54. On *glasnost',* see W. Bruce Lincoln, *In the Vanguard of Reform* (DeKalb, Ill., 1982), 184–88, and *Great Reforms,* 50–56. See also Terence Emmons, "The Tsar's Reforms," *Times Literary Supplement,* 27 December 1991, 19: "the word took on at that time its present meaning, having before the 1860s been a technical term in the lexicon of jurisprudence."

55. *Structural Transformation*, 19.

56. See my "Alexis de Tocqueville in Russia," *Journal of the History of Ideas* 37, no. 2 (April–June, 1976), 289.

57. P. V. Dolgorukov, *Des réformes en Russie* (Paris, 1862), 117–18.

58. William Woehrlin, *Chernyshevsky, The Man and the Journalist* (Cambridge, Mass., 1971), 95.

59. Chernyshevsky may have been recommended for the editorship by Dmitri Miliutin, who would serve as war minister in the 1860s and 1870s and who believed officers needed to begin with a well-rounded general education and go on from there to study military science. E. Willis Brooks, "The Improbable Connection: D. A. Miljutin and N. G. Ĉernyŝevskij, 1848–1862," *Jahrbücher für Geschichte Osteuropas* 37 (1989), 33 n. 42.

60. Irina Paperno Gasparov, "The Individual in Culture: N. G. Chernyshevsky. A Study in the Semiotics of Behavior" (Ph.D. diss., Stanford University, 1984), 247.

61. Irina Paperno quotes from diaries and memoirs on the influence of his *Contemporary* writings, concluding that "the influence of his writings on society and its ways of thinking . . . was mistaken by contemporary readers and governmental officials alike for political influence achieved through organized underground political activities." *Chernyshevsky and the Age of Realism* (Stanford, Calif., 1988), 23, 30.

62. Quoted in Woehrlin, *Chernyshevsky*, 117.

63. Reginald Zelnik, "The Sunday School Movement in Russia, 1859–1862," *Journal of Modern History* 27 (June 1965).

64. For a foreigner's assessment of the impact of free public discussion up to January 1862, see Charles de Mazade, *La Russie sous l'Empereur Alexandre II: La crise de l'autocratie et la société Russe* (Paris, 1862).

65. N. N. Strakhov in O. F. Miller, *Materialy dlia zhizneopisaniia F. M. Dostoevskago* (Saint Petersburg, 1883), 233. On Pavlov's speech: M. K. Lemke, *Ocherki osvoboditel'nogo dvizheniia 'shestidesiatykh godov'* (Saint Petersburg, 1908), 10. On the rise of student militancy: Abbott Gleason, *Young Russia* (New York, 1980), 127–59.

66. "As the stern regime that Russia imposed on her reconquered Polish lands took shape, numbers of lucrative government positions helped to entice that recently alienated portion of [educated society] away from radical idealism into the imperial establishment by the promise of political prestige and material rewards . . . [and] a larger portion of [educated society] began to hope for a better opportunity for positive action within the framework of the established order." *Great Reforms*, 168.

67. S. S. Danilov, "Materialy po istorii russkogo zakonodatel'stva o teatre," *O teatre. Sbornik statei.* (Moscow and Leningrad, 1940), 180.

68. "Vasilii Sleptsov: Neizvestnyi stranitsy," *Literaturnoe nasledstvo* (March 1963), 71:127. Subsequent Sleptsov quotations are from this volume.

69. G. A. Khaichenko, *Russkii narodnyi teatr kontsa xix—nachala xx veka* (Moscow, 1975), 20.

70. It is possible, but unlikely, that his main concern was peasants who happened to find themselves in the city. The census did not distinguish workers from peasants, and he probably considered workers to be peasants *au fond.*

71. *O repertuare narodnago teatra, razrabotannom komissiei Komiteta gramotnosti* (Moscow, 1870).

72. "Nashy Manilovy i narodnyi teatr," *Russkaia letopis,* no. 9 (2 March 1870), 330. M. O. Shchepkin was the nephew of M. S. Shchepkin.

73. See Joseph Frank, *Dostoevsky: The Stir of Liberation, 1860–1865* (Princeton, N.J., 1986), 38.

74. Ibid., 199.

75. F. M. Dostoevskii, *Polnoe sobranie sochinenii v tridtsati tomakh* (Leningrad, 1972), 4:198–99.

76. Ibid., 19. The actual prison performances witnessed by Dostoevsky in Omsk took place in November 1851.

77. Ibid., 130. Robert Louis Jackson sees Dostoevsky's faith in theatre as part of a larger European project: "The long and detailed theatrical scenes in *House of the Dead* give expression to Dostoevsky's belief—formulated earlier by Friedrich Schiller in his letters *On the Aesthetic Education of Man*—in the possibility of the aesthetic humanization of man." *Art of Dostoevsky* (Princeton, N.J., 1981), 111.

78. Quoted in Ruth Meyer Guffee, *"The Yasnaya Polyana School 1859–1862: Its Place in Leo Tolstoy's Development as a Thinker"* (Ph.D. diss., Yale University, 1982), 291.

79. Victor Lucas, *Tolstoy in London* (London, 1979), 49.

80. Boris Eikhenbaum, *Lev Tolstoi* (3 vols.; Leningrad 1928, 1931, 1960), 1:369–71.

81. See Adir Cohen, "The Educational Philosophy of Tolstoy," *Oxford Review of Education* 7, no. 3 (1981), 247.

82. His list of titles and brief comments can be found in L. N. Tolstoi, *Polnoe sobranie sochinenie* (90 vols; Moscow, 1928–58), 8:395–98.

83. Ibid., 48:82.

84. Guffee, "Yasnaya Polyana School," 143.

85. Alan Pinch and Michael Armstrong, eds., *Tolstoy on Education: Tolstoy's Educational Writings, 1861–62* (Rutherford, N.J., 1982), 249.

86. In later years he credited a German novel with having inspired him to become a teacher. In Berthold Auerbach's *A New Life,* a count, Eugene Baumann, poses as a peasant and discovers himself by becoming a dedicated and undogmatic teacher of peasant children in a rustic village. Auerbach, born in Württemberg in 1812, was reared in a European backwater where primitive manners survived almost intact. Much of his work revolved around the theme of the gulf between the cultivated and the uncultivated, and he

was the much-imitated originator of the peasant-story genre in German. He recalled his childhood in *Schwarzwälder Dorfgeschichten* (Stuttgart, 1843–53). When Tolstoy called on Auerbach in Berlin in 1861, he introduced himself by announcing, "I am Eugene Baumann!" See Dominique Maroger, *Les idées pédagogiques de Tolstoi* (Lausanne, 1974), 103.

87. Eric Havelock's description of Robinson Crusoe as "an epic of survival of a literate European under strictly oral conditions" suggests an unconscious motive; *The Muse Learns to Write* (New Haven, Conn., 1986), 35.

88. Ian Watt, *The Rise of the Novel* (London, 1957), 76.

89. He included a narration of the novel by the peasant children in his first printed collection of school reading material. Chernyshevsky found it to be "devoid of all sense." But the rector of Saint Petersburg University wrote Tolstoy to say that his eight-year-old son had read all the versions of the book available in Russian and found this one to be the best. Guffee, "Yasnaya Polyana School," 159.

90. Maroger, *Idées pédagogiques*, 164.

91. On Tolstoy's editing of student writing, see Andrew Donskov, "L. N. Tolstoy as an Editor of Literature by Peasant Writers" in *Crisis and Commitment: Studies in German and Russian Literature in Honour of J. W. Dyck*, ed. John Whiton (Waterloo, 1983), 41–47.

92. Andrew Donskov, "The Peasant in Tolstoi's Thought and Writings," *Canadian Slavonic Papers* 21, no. 2 (1979), 186. Even the issue of the impact of literacy received attention in his last novel. James M. Holquist has demonstrated the dichotomy in *Resurrection* [*Voskresenie*, 1899] between the literate individual's constant need to reconcile his experience to written texts, and the illiterate's relative freedom, given his collective, nonunique sense of himself. He indeed finds that "the primary metaphorical structure of the novel . . . is defined by the symbolic attributes of illiteracy versus literacy." "The Metaphor of Literacy in Late Tolstoi," *Canadian-American Slavic Studies* 12, no. 4 (Winter 1978), 560.

93. *Polnoe sobranie sochinenii*, 61:23.

94. Anthony Swift, "Theater for the People," 56–57.

95. Ibid., 63.

96. According to one source, a group responsible to the Saint Petersburg Committee on Literacy had Hartman design two theatres, one for Saint Petersburg and the other for Moscow, which could serve as models for future provincial theatres. "They embodied the latest technical means for protecting from the danger of fire and also met the requirements of sanitation and economy." V. P. Ostrogorskii, "Dobryi pochin. K voprosy o narodnom teatre," *Obrazovanie*, no. 3 (March 1892), 70.

97. Quoted in Khaichenko, *Russkii narodnyi teatr*, 32.

98. K. S. Stanislavskii, *Sobranie sochinenii v vos'mi tomakh* (Moscow, 1954), 1:134.

99. Fedotov, describing the history of this theatre in 1886 in the journal *Alarmclock* [*Budil'nik*] said "The goal of the theatre's presentations was acquainting the viewers with the play and the possibility of its correct and appropriately artistic production—not showing off actors, as is the general practice of most impresarios. Thanks to this the theatre remained independent of its own troupe: actors got sick, left service, were replaced by others, and the play went on entertaining the public and the viewer received the undiluted impression of the ensemble, which was the main task of the production." *Predislovie k knige: D. I. Fonvizin. Nedorosl'* (Moscow, 1886), v.

100. A. P. Klinchin, "Narodnyi teatr na politekhnicheskoi vystavke v Moskve," *Teatral'noe nasledstvo* (Moscow, 1956), 350.

101. Fedotov, *Predislovie k knige,* vi. Fedotov's comment illustrates the common prejudice prevailing among educated Russians against folk presentations that amused the uncouth by pandering to their cynicism and endemic suspicion of "the other." He assumes that complex dramatic texts, faithfully enacted, somehow disclose humanity; that is, how civilized people comport themselves as they go about in the world. Physical self-control seemed at this point in history to offer a certain index to distinguish the hoi polloi from "society." See S. L. L'vov's account of a Shrovetide visit to a cheap comedy narrated to Prince P. A. Viazemskii and first published in 1866: "A policeman came up to him and said, 'If you please, your excellency, don't sit so close. . . . When the clown gets very excited, he begins to spit on the people.'" Quoted in V. V. Kallash, *Stranichka iz istorii russkago narodnago teatra* (Moscow, 1903), 18. (See also Chapter 4, note 1 below on physical comedy in "Petrushka.")

102. Quoted in Khaichenko, *Russkii narodnyi teatr,* 36.

103. G. A. Khaichenko, "Narodnyi teatr," in *Russkaia khudozhestvennaia kul'tura kontsa XIX—nachala XX veka,* ed. A. D. Alekseev (Moscow, 1968), 1:219.

104. Henry Morley, ed., *The Earlier Life and the Chief Earlier Works of Daniel Defoe* (London, 1889), 40.

105. Ibid., 45, 42. See also Wilhelm Henis, "Goethe, Goya and the Threat of Modernity," *Times Literary Supplement,* 11 November 1994, 15–16.

106. Gary Marker, *Publishing, Printing and the Origins of Intellectual Life in Russia, 1700–1800* (Princeton, N.J., 1985), 195–210.

107. Senelick, *Serf Actor,* 217.

108. Quoted in Richard Robbins, *The Tsar's Viceroys* (Ithaca, N.Y., 1987), 177–78, from the Central State Historical Archive, Saint Petersburg (Fond Troinskogo).

CHAPTER TWO

1. "There is no doubt that all intellectuals, all those who took part in literary, artistic, religious, scientific and academic life, whether inside the

establishment or outside, felt that they were being watched, oppressed, and persecuted. . . . Paradoxically, though, these constraints seem to have stimulated creativity and imagination in the arts and did not prevent the golden age of Russian literature from taking place—quite the contrary." Marc Raeff, *Understanding Imperial Russia* (New York, 1984), 149.

2. Boris Pasternak, "Okhrannaia gramota" (1931), in *Proza, 1915–1958* (Ann Arbor, Mich., 1961), 241.

3. Iuri Lotman, "Concerning Khlestakov," in *The Semiotics of Russian Cultural History*, ed. A. D. Nakhimovsky and A. S. Nakhimovsky (Ithaca, N.Y., 1985), 160.

4. See David Ingram, *Habermas and the Dialectic of Reason* (New Haven, Conn., 1987), 78–80.

5. Ibid., 79.

6. Henning Beck, *When Men Meet* (Chicago, 1997), 74.

7. On the transition from Romanticism to realism, see Lydia Ginzburg, *On Psychological Prose*, trans. Judson Rosengrant (Princeton, N.J., 1991).

8. Quoted in Margaret Wettlin, "Alexander Ostrovsky and the Russian Theatre before Stanislavsky," in *Alexander Ostrovsky. Plays.* (Moscow, 1974), 10.

9. Quoted in J. Patouillet, *Ostrovsky et son théâtre de moeurs russes* (Paris, 1912), 35. The second time he brought his wife and the tsarevich. Altogether he saw the play four times.

10. On the circle and its formation, see Wayne Dowler, *An Unnecessary Man: The Life of Apollon Grigor'ev* (Toronto, 1995), 73–75.

11. Ibid., 70.

12. Sonia Ketchian, "The Plays of Alexsej Potexin" (Ph.D. diss., Harvard University, 1974), 90. Had English contemporaries embraced a similar conceit, they too need have looked no further back than the sixteenth century for a time when proverbial wisdom figured prominently in the common culture. "The speeches of Elizabethan MPs were interlarded with proverbs, indeed sometimes consisted of nothing else. It was only in the later seventeenth century that polite society discarded them." Keith Thomas, "The Meaning of Literacy in Early Modern England," in *The Written Word: Literacy in Transition*, ed. G. Baumann (Oxford, 1986), 108.

13. Vladimir Filippov argued that the Russian merchants, "thanks to the modesty of their lives, were less superficial and had borrowed less; because of the absence of all enlightenment in them, they were less alien and cultivated, and more sharply expressed the moral and cultural legacy transmitted from generation to generation [from the times of Old Muscovy]." He added that Ostrovsky showed all the causes for the inhibited development of the Russian people. *Zadachi narodnogo teatra i ego proshloe v Rossii* (Moscow, 1918), 43.

14. In the twentieth century Russian Formalists explained literature's need to refresh itself constantly by appropriating linguistic conventions from nonliterary spheres. As examples of material appropriated into literature at various times they mentioned journalistic diction, the verbal play customary in the salon, and the declamation routine for ceremonial occasions. Iurii Tynianov, "O literaturnoi evoliutsii," in his *Arkhaisty i novatory* (Leningrad, 1929), 43. Ostrovsky's practice freshened Russian literature yet again, but his ambitions went well beyond literary craftsmanship.

15. Quoted in Wettlin, "Alexander Ostrovsky," 42.

16. Patouillet, *Ostrovsky et son théâtre*, 18.

17. Perhaps the best place to begin with this line of thought is a well-known essay by Georges Florovsky, "The Problem of Old Russian Culture," *Slavic Review* 21, no. 1 (March 1962).

18. Dowler, *Unnecessary Man*, 77.

19. A. A. Kizevetter, *Teatr i Ocherki. Razmyshleniia. Zametki.* (Moscow, 1922), 100.

20. V. G. Sakhnovskii, *Teatr A. N. Ostrovskogo* (Moscow, 1919), 21. Sakhnovskii found that Ostrovsky regarded these community sanctioned ways as precious, yet "misproportioned."

21. Patouillet, *Ostrovskii et son théâtre*, 409.

22. S. V. Kastorskii, "Pisatel'-dramaturg A. A. Potekhin," in *Iz istorii russkikh literaturnykh otnoshenii xviii–xx vekov* (Moscow, 1959), 180. Ketchian, "Plays of Alexsej Potexin," 34.

23. A. L. Volynskii [A. L. Flekser], "Staryi i novyi repertuar," in *Kniga velikogo gneva* (Saint Petersburg, 1904), 225.

24. N. P. Barsukov, *Zhizn' i trudy M. P. Pogodina* (Saint Petersburg, 1898), 12:287.

25. Dowler, *Unnecessary Man*, 84–88.

26. A. Grigorev, "O natsional'nom znachenii tvorchestve A. N. Ostrovskago," in *Sobranie Sochinenii* (Moscow, 1915), 11:13.

27. The censors suppressed this second article. See Dowler, *Unnecessary Man*, 88–89.

28. "They therefore stood for re-establishment of links between the present and the past." Dowler, *Unnecessary Man*, 88.

29. Laurence Senelick contrasts Ostrovsky's realism with the realism usually attributed to Shchepkin. The latter, he explains, "was less concerned with the 'individual characteristic' than with the 'genus and species.'" *Serf Actor*, 131, 26–29.

30. Police surveillance on him was lifted at Alexander II's accession. The inspector who came to compliment him on his new freedom remarked, "You have not given us much trouble. We have identified you as a well-bred man." Quoted in I. Ivanov, *A. N. Ostrovskii* (Saint Petersburg, 1900), 32–33.

31. Ketchian, "Plays," 14.

32. A. N. Ostrovskii, *Sobranie sochinenii v desiati tomakh* (Moscow, 1959), 2:67.

33. *Polnoe sobranie sochinenii*, 60:158.

34. Ibid., 156.

35. Kh. D. Alchevskaia, *Dramaticheskiia proizvedeniia: Ostrovskii v primenenii k chteniiu v narode* (Saint Petersburg, 1887), 48. Alchevskaia's teaching through plays is discussed at length in the following chapter.

36. B. V. Varnike, *Zametki ob Ostrovskom* (Odessa, 1912), 86.

37. A. I. Reviakin, "A. N. Ostrovskii i tsenzura," *Uchenye zapiski Moskovskogo Gorodskogo Pedagogicheskogo Instituta* 48, no. 5 (1955), 271.

38. Ibid., 274.

39. We have only Iur'ev's account of the experiment. It exerted no national "influence," remaining unpublished for a quarter of a century: S. A. Iur'ev, "Derevenskii teatr," *Artist*, no. 3 (September 1889). Perhaps Lotman's remarks on textual pragmatics of printed texts should be considered when Iur'ev's account of audience responses leaves researchers wanting confirmation. "Even when critical opinion is well documented, information on the response of readers is, as a rule, sparse and fragmentary. . . . Of course, even this meager information is valuable material for reconstructions." Iuri Lotman, "Concerning Khlestakov," 167.

40. Iur'ev, "Derevenskii teatr," 46.

41. See Gary Thurston, "Theatre and Acculturation in Russia from Peasant Emancipation to the First World War," *Journal of Popular Culture* 18, no. 2 (Fall 1984), 4–7.

42. See Marc Raeff, "Kliuchevskii—Historian of the Eighteenth Century," *Canadian-American Slavic Studies* 20, nos. 3–4 (1986), 391–92.

43. Lidiia M. Lotman, *A. N. Ostrovskii i russkaia dramaturgiia ego vremeni* (Moscow and Leningrad, 1961), 338. Quoting Ostrovsky (*Sobranie sochinenii*, 12:255), she notes that Chekhov would try to shatter the illusion of "the clarity of life."

44. See Richard Thorpe, "The Management of Culture in Revolutionary Russia: The Imperial Theaters and the State, 1897–1928" (Ph. D. diss., Princeton University, 1990), 20–23.

45. "Zapiska o polozhenii dramaticheskogo isskusstva v Rossii v nastoiashchee vremia," in A. N. Ostrovskii. *Sobranie sochinenii v desiati tomakh* (Moscow, 1960), 10:168–86.

46. Ivan Shcheglov, *Narod i teatr* (Saint Petersburg, 1911), 78.

47. See Joseph Macleod, *Actors Cross the Volga* (London, 1946), 63–66.

48. Ostrovskii, "Zapiska," 170.

49. "They neither understand plays nor their performance, and attend merely for appearances' sake. Yet they have ruined the Maly's repertoire, because playwrights have begun to write for their taste, 'plays that would have no significance for healthy people.'" Ibid., 179.

50. Ibid., 181. "Historical dramas and chronicles work even more powerfully on this virgin audience: they develop peasant self-knowledge and inculcate conscious love for the fatherland. The public is thirsty to know its history. The historian transmits *what was;* the dramatic poet shows *how it was,* making the viewer a participant in the action."

51. Diogenes Laertius, *Lives of Eminent Philosophers* (London, 1925), 2:327–29.

52. *Oxford Dictionary of English Etymology* (Oxford, 1966), 916. "Theory . . . Gr. *theoria,* contemplation, speculation, sight. . . . *theâsthai* look upon, contemplate (cf. THEATRE)."

53. A generation ago Ortega y Gasset called attention to the unique status of the text in literary theatre, which the actors cannot see but which summons the audience to contemplation. No one would today endorse his opening proposition, but he was surely correct to join great moments of achievement in theatre and surges in its public's literacy. "The book as an industrial and public entity had been invented . . . toward the middle of the fifth century . . . in order to 'publish' the most important tragedies. [Likewise] in our seventeenth century, the 'parts' of Lope de Vega were published and the collections of the 'most famous comedies.' It would seem that the dramatic work would have its maximum form of existence on the stage, and it would be less urgent than for any other production to give it another form of life in a book. In both cases, however, the contradictory happened, and this fact invites us to reflect upon the phenomenon, because it may perhaps put us on the track of what is the true (and problematical) condition of dramatic art." "The Difficulty of Reading," *Diogenes* 28 (Winter 1959), 15 n. 23.

54. Charles Segal, "Tragedy, Orality, Literacy," in *Oralità: Cultura, Literatura, Discorso: Atti del Convegno Internazionale a cura di Bruno Gentili e Giuseppe Paioni* (Rome, 1986), 205.

55. Ibid., 216–17. "The struggle between oral and literate cultures is, in one sense, the subject of tragedy."

56. Jean-Pierre Vernant, "Tensions et ambiguïtés dans la tragédie greque," in *Mythe et tragédie en Grèce ancienne* (Paris, 1981), 35–36.

57. Eugene Bristow, ed. and trans., *Five Plays of Alexander Ostrovsky* (New York, 1969), 22–23.

58. These contexts had to be rediscovered in Russia in the twentieth century. In 1910 Stanislavsky prepared himself to play the role of Krutitsky, studying the period with Nemirovich, then on his own. "How many photographs, sketches, portraits I was shown, how many did I find for myself that seemed to correspond with the external appearance of the role. We even managed to find out which general Ostrovsky had taken as a model when creating Krutitsky." Jean Benedetti quotes, in *Stanislavsky: A Biography* (London, 1988), 210. He goes on to add, "When the play opened on March 9 the role was recognized as one of his most significant achievements.

Not only had he created the individual personality of this decaying general, who had power without sense, but had symbolized a whole era and a whole section of Russian society."

59. Daniel Brower, "L'urbanisation Russe à la fin du XIXe siècle," *Annales, Economies, Sociétés, Civilisations,* no. 1 (January–February 1977), 70.

60. At the turn of the century economists and statisticians published studies demonstrating the increasing influence of urban areas upon peasants. Arcadius Kahan, "Determinants of the Incidence of Literacy in Rural Nineteenth Century Russia" in *Education and Economic Development,* ed. C. Arnold Anderson and Mary Jean Bowman (Chicago, 1965), 301.

61. Alchevskaia, *Peredumannoe,* 111.

62. See Jeffrey Brooks, *When Russia Learned to Read,* 330–51.

63. N. I. Nikolaev, "Po povodu odnoi ankety" (1904), in his *Efemeridy* (Kiev, 1912), 136.

64. A. L. Volynskii, "Staryi i novyi repertuar" (1901), in *Kniga velikago gneva* (Saint Petersburg, 1904), 225.

65. Iu. Aikhenval'd, *Siluety russkikh pisatelei* (Moscow, 1908), 2:168.

66. Bristow, *Five Plays,* 206.

67. Richard Seaford, *Reciprocity and Ritual: Homer and Tragedy in the Developing City State* (Oxford, 1994), 204–5, 216–17.

68. A. N. Ostrovsky, *Sobranie sochinenii,* (Moscow, 1959), 2:257. Boulevard seems inappropriate as a translation for *bul'var* because it connotes tree-lined. F. D. Reeve gives "avenue"; see his *Nineteenth-Century Russian Plays* (New York, 1973), 366.

69. Peter Borsay, "The Rise of the Promenade: The Social and Cultural Use of Space in the English Provincial Town c. 1660–1800," *British Journal for Eighteenth-Century Studies* 9 (1986), 125–26.

70. Ibid., 132, 126.

71. Keith Thomas, *Man and the Natural World* (London, 1983).

72. Borsay, "Rise of the Promenade," 130.

73. Ostrovsky, *Sobranie sochinenii,* 2:224, 229, 268, 260.

74. Two books with descriptive titles are Erving Goffman, *The Presentation of Self in Everyday Life* (Edinburgh, 1956) and Richard Sennett, *The Fall of Public Man* (New York, 1977).

CHAPTER THREE

1. Bunakov named his son born in 1874 Alexander, in honor of the "Tsar Liberator." Years later, when he found himself obliged to litigate in order to force a credit society to disgorge his savings, he reflected in his diary that he owed the quick and efficient recovery of his money to the reorganized court system that emerged from the 1864 judicial reform.

2. Three provincial statistical commissions elected Bunakov to membership: Vologda in 1861, Voronezh in 1866, and Kostroma in 1874. Numerical data figured prominently in his writings for educational journals.

3. In 1863 and 1864 he published two articles in the journals *Den'* (The day) and *Russkaia Stsena* (The Russian stage) whose titles indicate that his interest in the theatre and in its relevance for children actually predate his entry into the teaching profession: "Deti na stseny" (Children on stage) and "Priobreteniia nashego teatra v 1864" (Gains of our theatre in 1864).

4. V. Latyshev, "Bunakov, Nikolai Fedorovich," in *Kritiko-Biograficheskii Slovar' Russkikh Pisatelei i Uchenykh*, 5 (1889), 367. Rezener's school was soon closed by government order, along with all other tuition-free schools.

5. Bunakov's memoirs, based on diaries he kept, are a major source on culture and education for the period; *Zapiski N. F. Bunakova. Moia zhizn', v sviazi s obshche-russkoi zhizn'iu, preimushchestvenno provintsial'noi. 1837–1905* (Saint Petersburg, 1909). His second wife, née Mikhailova, wrote the introduction. Hereafter cited in chapter as Z.

6. During the Crimean War, the commander of the Second Army ordered a school established at Voronezh for the training of cadets. Opened in 1856, it devoted an unprecedented amount of time to imparting general education, including history, and nurturing moral development. An intensive program was initiated in the study of the Russian language, with emphasis on reading, writing, and grammar exercises. Courses in civil and military law figured as well. Other schools soon copied the Voronezh curriculum. When Miliutin became minister of war he separated the new programs for general education from higher courses for professional military training. The gymnasia would eliminate their military organization and replace company commanders with faculty members. See Forrest Miller, *Dmitrii Miliutin and the Reform Era in Russia* (Nashville, Tenn., 1968), 108–21.

7. One of his students, G. V. Plekhanov, attested to this. "The Father of Russian Marxism," also recalled of Bunakov that "he instilled in me a love of literature and taught me to speak and write correctly, definitely, clearly and simply." Quoted in S. H. Baron, *Plekhanov* (Stanford, Calif., 1963), 7. Bunakov, after reading one of his compositions, told Plekhanov that he had the potential to become a great writer. Baron surmises that it was Bunakov who introduced him to the writings of Belinsky, Chernyshevsky, and Dobroliubov. When V. I. Lenin began his study of the Russian peasantry in the 1890s, he took as his starting point the orthodox Russian Marxist position that Plekhanov had set down in an article written in 1887. Esther Kingston-Mann points out that Plekhanov's attitude was characterized by "disgust with peasants who rejected the enlightenment offered them by a generation of revolutionaries"; *Lenin and the Problem of Marxist Peasant Revolution* (New York, 1985), 33.

8. "As you look closely at our peasantry you think in spite of yourself, 'Lord, how this people has been turned into cattle' [because] it was easier to turn them into cattle than to humanize them"; Z 202.

9. Latyshev, "Bunakov," 366.

10. After a revision in 1899, his most popular text sold upward of eighty thousand copies annually. E. N. Medynskii, *Istoriia Russkoi pedagogiki do velikoi oktiabr'skoi sotsialisticheskoi revoliutsii* (Moscow, 1938), 281. In that year it won special recommendation as a primary school text from the Scholarship Committee of the Ministry of Education (whose members he described in his memoirs as "complete nitwits").

11. Elvira Wilbur selected Voronezh province, "in an area generally agreed to be one of the poorest and most traditional in the empire," as the basis for her inquiry into the peasantry's economic progress and prospects from the late 1880s. "The data," she found, "almost without exception, reveal austere but still viable peasant institutions." "Peasant Poverty in Theory and Practice: A View from Russia's 'Impoverished Center' at the End of the Nineteenth Century," in *Peasant Economy, Culture, and Politics of European Russia, 1800–1921,* ed. Esther Kingston-Mann and Timothy Mixter (Princeton, N.J., 1991), 105.

12. Z 173. Bunakov's desire to enhance country singing suggests an affinity to French teachers in the 1850s who worked to supplant songs in regional dialect with singing in French. Eugen Weber estimates that "French . . . songs helped the singers pick up elementary notions of the national language, perhaps encouraged them to learn more of it, but also bolstered their self-esteem." "Who Sang the Marseillaise?" in *My France* (Cambridge, Mass., 1991), 97. Of course Russian peasants spoke (and sang) Russian, but their version could never be mistaken for that of the educated. In Bunakov's view, peasants who refined their singing somehow enhanced their status and merited self-esteem.

13. M. S. Lapatukhin, "N. F. Bunakov i ego Metodicheskaia Sistema," *Russkii iazyk v shkole,* no. 6, (1974), 52.

14. N. F. Bunakov, "Nechto o krest'ianskikh vozzreniiakh na gramatnost' i shkolu," in *Izbranye pedagogicheskie sochineniia* (Moscow, 1953), 269.

15. "Sel'skaia shkola i narodnaia zhizn'," *Russkii nachal'nyi uchitel',* no. 2 (1890).

16. On the comparative severity of the famine in Voronezh Province and other central black earth provinces, see Richard Robbins, *Famine in Russia, 1891–1892* (New York, 1975), 2.

17. Z 216–17. See also "Desiatiletie sel'skoi shkoly i obiazatel'noie vseobshche obuchenoe," in *Russkii narodnyi uchitel',* nos. 6–7 (1895), 294.

18. As confidence in the peasant commune as a bulwark of stability collapsed, peasant literacy came to be seen as a panacea for curing military,

agricultural and industrial backwardness. See Ben Eklof, *Russian Peasant Schools* (Berkeley and Los Angeles, 1986), 83, 102–7.

19. N. F. Bunakov, "Sel'skaia shkola i narodnaia zhizn'. Stat'ia X. Opyt narodnago teatra." *Russkii nachal'nyi uchitel',* no. 1 (1892), 7.

20. He thought the language counterbalanced the rather pale and superficially drawn characters. "Opyt narodnago teatra," in *Izbrannye pedagogicheskie sochineniia* (Moscow, 1953), 305.

21. Bunakov and Mikhailova used the second edition, published in 1887. Quotations here are from the Saint Petersburg edition of 1897 (edited by N. P. Karbasnikov). I discuss the play in "Theatre in the Village School: The Bunakovs' Discoveries," in *School and Society in Tsarist and Soviet Russia,* ed. Ben Eklof (New York, 1993).

22. *When Russia Learned to Read: Literacy and Popular Literature, 1861–1917* (Princeton, N.J., 1985), 166.

23. "Opyt," in *Izbrannye pedagogicheskie sochineniia,* 309.

24. Ibid., 310.

25. I have used the text published in Saint Petersburg by Dobrodeks in 1895.

26. In its day the play was widely praised for the verisimilitude of its peasant speech, which was in the Kostroma dialect. It incorporated the texts of two songs and the title of a third, more familiar one. Sonia Ketchian, "The Plays of Alexsej Potexin," 385–86, 96.

27. *Chuzhoe dobro,* 97.

28. Ibid., 85.

29. V. P. Ostrogorskii, "Dobryi pochin. K voprosy o narodnom teatre," *Obrazovanie* (March 1892), 69.

30. N. F. Bunakov, "Razmyshleniia po povodu vystavki narodnago teatra ustroennoi v Moskve v 1895," in *Narodnyi teatr. Sbornik.* (Moscow, 1896), 171.

31. Bunakov, "Razmyshleniia," 171.

32. L. Bunakova, "Zametki o narodnom teatre," *Teatr i iskusstvo,* no. 36 (1910), 663.

33. Ibid., 664.

34. L. Bunakova, "Istoriia Petinskago Nar. Doma" [a report read to the All-Russian Popular Theatre Congress, 3 January 1916], in *Trudy Vserossiiskogo s"ezda deiatelei narodnogo teatra v Moskve, 27 dekabria 1915–5 ianvaria 1916* (Saint Petersburg, 1919), 157–58.

35. Bunakov, "Razmyshleniia," 172.

36. For biographical details: N. Ia. Frid'eva, *Zhizn' dlia prosveshcheniia naroda* (Moscow, 1963).

37. Ibid., 7-8.

38. Quoted in ibid., 11. It is not clear from the context whether she encouraged them to reason or to argue and debate. She already understood

that the classroom rigidities and intimidating emphasis of the typical gentry school instruction for peasants induced a pervasive laziness in people unaccustomed to any kind of intellectual constraint. See Ben Eklof, "Peasant Sloth Reconsidered: Strategies of Education and Learning in Rural Russia before the Revolution," *Journal of Social History* 14, no. 3 (Spring 1981), 360.

39. As Sidney Monas observes, Herzen had done much to establish journalistic standards of honesty in Russia before he emigrated. He can justly be called "the first really effective champion of a free public opinion in Russia." "The Twilit Middle Class of Nineteenth-Century Russia," in *Between Tsar and People: Educated Society and the Quest for Public Identity in Late Imperial Russia,* ed. Edith W. Clowes, Samuel D. Kassow, and James L. West (Princeton, N.J., 1991), 29. Alchevskaia may have directed her communication to Herzen because she shared his faith in social action. See Lydia Ginzburg: "Herzen sought his basic criteria neither in utility, nor in pleasure, nor in Feurbachian love, but in action (the demand for 'creative action' was a principal one for him in the 1840s). That action was of course not conceived as mere activity without an object, but as an act that had historical and social significance. Herzen was unable . . . to substantiate the necesssity for the humanistic goals of that action, although that necessity remained obvious to him, reflecting as it did the practical concerns of the liberation movement." *On Psychological Prose,* 327.

40. *Peredumannoe i perezhitoe* (Moscow, 1912), 89. On her contribution to the expansion of literacy in Russia, see Jeffrey Brooks, "Readers and Reading at the End of the Tsarist Era," in *Literature and Society in Imperial Russia, 1800–1914,* ed. William Mills Todd III (Stanford, Calif., 1977), 130ff. Also Martha Bohachevsky-Chomiak, *Feminists Despite Themselves: Women in Ukrainian Community Life, 1884–1939* (Edmonton, Canada, 1988).

41. Frid'eva, *Zhizn' dlia prosveshcheniia naroda,* 47.

42. See Richard Stites, *The Women's Liberation Movement in Russia* (Princeton, N.J., 1978), 89: "In the broadest sense, Chernyshevsky's novel . . . was a Bible for all advanced Russian women with aspirations toward independence."

43. See Frid'eva, *Zhizn' dlia prosveshcheniia naroda,* 19–22.

44. The censorship apparently kept her from including an account of reactions to the Ukrainian dramatist Kropovnitsky's *Pauk (Spider)* in *Chto chitat' narodu?* See 2:532. Hereafter cited in text as *Ccn?*

45. She used the phrase in a letter to Tolstoy, quoted in Frid'eva, *Zhizn' dlia prosveshcheniia naroda,* 42.

46. "Istoriia otkrytiia shkoly v derevne Alekseevke Mikhailovskoi volosti," *Iuzhnyi Krai,* nos. 53 and 54 (February 1881). Reprinted in *Peredumannoe,* 201–25. Hereafter cited in text as "Istoriia."

47. Kh. D. Alchevskaia, *Dramaticheskiia proizvedeniia: Ostrovskii v primenenii k chteniiu v narode* (Saint Petersburg, 1887). Hereafter cited in text as *Dp*.

48. Aleksandra Efimenko, "Zhenshchina v krestianskoi sem'e," in *Issledovaniia narodnoi zhizni,* vol. 1, *Obychnoe pravo* (Moscow, 1884), 92.

49. Ibid., 122. In the north the nuclear family, while supplanting the extended family, had inherited many of its conceptions and principles. Where no employment was available in industry for women, they remained in complete subjugation to their husbands. Yet where the northern countryside was penetrated by good communications, near towns and in places where post stations had long been established, men beat their wives hardly at all, and women maintained a more independent outlook (67, 87).

50. Ibid., 101–2.

51. S. A. An-skii, *Narod i kniga* (Moscow, 1913), 54.

52. Efimenko, "Zhenshchina," 99. Beatrice Farnsworth concluded after studying *volost'* court records from four provinces of European Russia that "peasant women . . . asserted and exercised rights, and instigated family and community change to a degree not hitherto recognized." "The Litigious Daughter-in-Law: Family Relations in Rural Russia in the Second Half of the Nineteenth Century," in *Russian Peasant Women,* ed. Beatrice Farnsworth and Lynne Viola (New York, 1992), 102.

53. *Ccn?* 2:529. (But Grandpa Brusko objected, "Why are they gabbing about the old days? Maybe she acted of her own accord.")

54. M. N. Saltykova, ed., *Khronika voskresnykh shkol* (Moscow, 1900), 183.

55. N. Vlasenko, "O poseshchenii moimi uchenitsami teatra," ibid., 269 (emphasis added).

56. Its population had doubled between 1850 and 1870. Evan Mawdsley, writing of its significance in the year before Alchevskaia's death, describes it as "the main political and industrial center of the eastern Ukraine and one of the most important towns in Russia." *The Russian Civil War* (London, 1987), 171.

57. V. R. Leikina-Svirskaia, *Russkaia intelligentsia v 1900–1917 godakh* (Moscow, 1981), 187.

58. Vladimir Filippov, "Ostrovskii v Teatre Statistichestie materialy," in *A. N. Ostrovskii. Dnevnik i pis'ma. Teatr Ostrovskogo* (Moscow and Leningrad, 1937), 267.

59. Ibid., 272.

60. E. P. Karpov and N. N. Okulov, *Organizatsiia narodnogo teatra i poleznykh razvlechenii dlia naroda* (Saint Petersburg, 1899), 5. Other cities with Societies included Saratov, Samara, Orel, Tambov, Novgorod, and Penza. The city's leadership in theatre continued into the war years. The All-

Russian Congress held in Moscow in 1915, which in a sense marked the culmination of the Russian popular theatre movement, was preceded by a preparatory organizational meeting in Kharkov. Vladimir Filippov, *Zadachi narodnogo teatra i ego proshloe v Rossii* (Moscow, 1918), 44.

61. M. N. Saltykova, ed., *Khronika,* 187.

62. For example, a Saint Petersburg newspaper article in 1894 alluded to Alchevskaia's discoveries in calling for public support for theatres for the people in the capital that would provide uplifting entertainment. A. N. Kremlev, "O narodnom teatre v S. -Peterburge," *Novosti,* no. 276 (1894), 1.

63. For an introduction to the range of perspectives on the folk, see Ben Eklof, "Ways of Seeing: Recent Anglo-American Studies of the Russian Peasant (1861–1914)," *Jahrbücher für Geschichte Osteuropas* 36, no. 1 (1988).

64. Cathy Frierson, "Crime and Punishment in the Russian Village: Rural Concepts of Criminality at the End of the Nineteenth Century," *Slavic Review* 46, no. 1 (Spring 1987), 58.

65. C. A. Frierson, "Rural Justice in Public Opinion: The *Volost'* Court Debate, 1861–1912," *Slavonic and East European Review* 64, no. 4 (October 1986).

66. Stephen Frank, "Popular Justice, Community and Culture Among the Russian Peasantry, 1870–1900," *Russian Review* 46, no. 3 (July 1987), 264 n. 77.

67. Ibid., 263.

68. Stephen Frank, "'Simple Folk, Savage Customs?' Youth, Sociability, and the Dynamics of Culture in Rural Russia, 1856–1914," *Journal of Social History* 25, no. 4 (1992), 712.

69. Christine Worobec, *Peasant Russia: Family and Community in the Post-Emancipation Period* (Princeton, N.J., 1991), 9.

70. Cathy Frierson, *Peasant Icons: Representations of Rural People in Late Nineteenth Century Russia* (New York, 1993), 11, 193.

71. "Confronting the Domestic Other: Rural Popular Culture and Its Enemies in Fin-de-Siècle Russia," in *Cultures in Flux: Lower-Class Values, Practices, and Resistance in Late Imperial Russia,* ed. Stephen P. Frank and Mark D. Steinberg (Princeton, N.J., 1994), 79, 93, 98, 107.

72. Cathy Frierson, "From Narod to Kulak: Peasant Images in Russia, 1870–1885" (Ph.D. diss., Harvard University, 1985), 307.

73. Cathy Frierson, "Rural Justice," 537.

74. Ibid., 529, 538–44. The *volost'* courts were restructured and their judges put under Land Captains appointed by the Ministry of Interior in 1889, when the justices of the peace were abolished.

75. She mentions the tutelary aspect of Kiselev's work in peasant justice, without explaining his point of departure. On this see Gary Thurston,

"P. D. Kiselev and the Development of a Russian Legal Consciousness," *Canadian-American Slavic Studies* 19, no. 1 (Spring 1985), esp. 3–5 and 23–24.

76. A. A. Sinitsyn, "Iz vospominanii starogo vracha," *Russkaia Starina* 155 (July 1913), 144. Unlike the *volost'* courts, which served peasants only, the justices had jurisdiction over all estates in cases involving prison sentences of less than one year and fines less than 300 rubles. On the creation of justices of the peace see Eugene Pyziur, "Michael N. Katkov: Advocate of English Liberalism in Russia, 1856–1863," *Slavonic and East European Review* 45 (July 1967).

77. Sinitsyn, "Iz vospominanii starogo vracha," 144.

78. Ibid., 146.

79. Cathy Frierson, *Peasant Icons,* 64. "What was the level of development of the peasant's legal consciousness—indeed, did he have a legal consciousness?"

80. *Democracy in America,* ed. Phillips Bradley, 2 vols. (New York, 1945), 2:118.

81. *The Ancien Régime and the French Revolution,* trans. Stuart Gilbert (Manchester, 1966), 120–21.

82. See Alexis de Tocqueville, *Selected Letters on Politics and Society,* trans. James Toupin and Roger Boesche, ed. Roger Boesche (Berkeley and Los Angeles, 1985), 358.

83. Stephen Frank, "Confronting the Domestic Other," 92.

84. See the Introduction, esp. notes 51 and 68.

85. Alain Corbin, *The Foul and the Fragrant: Odor and the French Social Imagination* (Cambridge, Mass., 1986), 229, 56–58. Two of his examples show what he means by a perceptual revolution (27, 203). "[When Rousseau first visited Paris—in 1731 or 1732—] the quays revolted the sense of smell; excrement was everywhere: in alleys, at the foot of milestones, in cabs." "A respectable old lady was disturbed to find in the Saint-Cloud of Louis XVIII the excremental odors that prevailed in the Versailles of Louis XVI. She confided to Viollet-le-Duc that this mark of aristocratic indifference to the stench of excrement awoke nostalgia for her lost youth and the vanished days of the ancien régime." By the 1840s, Corbin found, the stench from the village was a common French literary theme. "The sensory change within the elite and the flood of discourse it provoked were to bring about the revolution in public health, the road to modernity (155)."

86. Donald Nathanson, *Shame and Pride: Affect and the Birth of the Self* (New York, 1992), 319.

87. A teacher in Alchevskaia's Kharkov Sunday school characterized the level of conduct of the Old Believers she knew as "much higher, cleaner, and better than that of the Russian Orthodox she knew. "Instead of a pious attitude," she wrote, "[the Old Believers] possess definite *concepts* of how

one must live and act." I. I. S-v, in M. N. Saltykova, *Khronika voskresnykh shkol* (Moscow, 1900), 212.

88. *Narod i kniga,* 57–58.

CHAPTER FOUR

1. Catriona Kelly, *Petrushka: The Russian Carnival Puppet Theatre* (Cambridge, 1990), 55, 81.

2. Nina Froud and James Hanley, eds., *Chaliapin: An Autobiography as told to Maxim Gorky* (London, 1967), 45.

3. In a 1929 article comparing the reception and impact of written literature and folk poetry, "Die Folklore als eine besondere Form des Schaffens," Roman Jakobson and Petr Bogatyrev compared the writer's freedom to depart from the poetic canon of the day and the oral poet's need to conform and observed that "in the domain of political economy so-called production for the market provides a close parallel to the relationship of literature to the consumer," while in folklore, the relationship "is closer to production on demand" (in Peter Steiner, *Russian Formalism: A Metapoetics* [Ithaca, N.Y., 1984], 227–29).

4. Kelly, *Petrushka,* 68–69. "The characters live in the present, and their identity is limited to their function: they are there to beat or be beaten."

5. A. N. Kremlev, "O narodnom teatr v S. Peterburge," *Novosty,* no. 276 (1894), 1.

6. F. Danilov, "Iarmarochnyia narodnyia razvlecheniia," *Obrazovanie,* nos. 7–8 (1897), 238.

7. Ibid., 239.

8. V. Serova, "Vstrecha s L. N. Tolstym na muzykal'nom poprishche," *Russkaia muzykal'naia gazeta,* no. 4 (1894), 83.

9. E. Karpov, *Desiatiletie narodnykh gulianii za Nevskoi zastavoi. Ocherki deiatel'nosti Nevskago Obshchestva ustroistva narodnykh razvlechenii* (Saint Petersburg, 1895), 4.

10. "The Tsar, traumatized by his own father's libertine life and violent end, was convinced that Tolstoy was right about the link between sex and murder." Donald Rayfield, "Peasant Reforms," *Times Literary Supplement,* 25 April 1997, p. 19.

11. K. N. Lomunov, *Tvorchestvo L. N. Tolstogo* (Moscow, 1959), 523.

12. Quoted ibid., 526.

13. As late as 1903 a special request to perform it in a popular theatre was denied. Finally a frightened censorship approved a request that it be authorized for popular theatres in December 1905.

14. See E. Anthony Swift, "Fighting the Germs of Disorder: The Censorship of Russian Popular Theater, 1888–1917," *Russian History* 18, no. 1 (Spring 1991), 3–4.

15. E. Anthony Swift, "Theater for the People," 257.

16. A. Avseenko, quoted ibid., 260.

17. *Russkie narodnye gulian'ia po rasskazam A. Ia. Alekseeva-Iaskovleva v zapisi i obrabotke Evg. Kuznetsova* (Leningrad and Moscow, 1948), 99–100.

18. Swift, "Theater for the People," 259, 287, 249. But see below for the fairground survivals in Saint Petersburg Temperance Trusteeship theatres.

19. E. N. Medynskii, *Vneshkol'noe obrazovanie, ego znachenie, organizatsiia i technika* (Moscow, 1916), 288. G. A. Khaichenko, *Russkii narodnyi teatr,* 96.

20. N. Bekkerevich, "Pervaia popytka ustroistva professional'nago teatra v sele," in *Narodnyi teatr. Sbornik.* (Moscow, 1896), 133–50.

21. Ibid., 136.

22. It should be noted that many of the first *cultivated* audiences had difficulty accepting that the play was over when the final curtain fell, still expecting the romantic loose ends to be tied up. See Milton Ehre, ed., *The Theater of Nikolay Gogol* (Chicago, 1980), xxi.

23. Bekkerevich, "Pervaia popytka," 144.

24. In 1872 a wealthy landowner opened a theatre in Odessa for the common folk. It had a commercial thrust, being operated in conjunction with a circus. Police refused to allow it to be officially designated "popular." The census takers referred to its actors as "dung beetles" *(navozniki).* Khaichenko, *Russkii narodnyi teatr,* 22.

25. N. F. Bunakov, *Zapiski,* 228.

26. Quoted in L. Gorev, "Provintsial'naia pechat'," *Severnyi Vestnik,* no. 6 (1896), 300.

27. Quoted from a manuscript memoir in Khaichenko, *Russkii narodnyi teatr,* 54.

28. Ibid., 122.

29. E. V. Lavrova, "Narodnye spektakli v derevne," *Obrazovanie,* nos. 5–6 (1897), 68. She also published separate articles on *Boris Godunov* and *Poverty Is No Vice* in this journal, which were reprinted in *Narodnyi teatr. Sbornik.*

30. Emer [M. V. Rklitskii], "K voprosy ob organizatsii narodnykh trupp dlia teatral'nykh predstavlenii," *Russkoe bogatstvo,* no. 7 (June 1898), 82. The author of this account fails to identify his own social background, but apparently was a member of the nobility.

31. Ibid., 85.

32. A. Sindeev, "O narodnom spektakle," *Obrazovanie,* nos. 5–6 (1896), 110.

33. Ibid., 111.

34. L. M. Kleinbort, *Ocherki rabochei intelligentsii,* 2 vols. (Saint Petersburg, 1923), 2:11.

35. N. Tamarin, "Narodnyi teatr," *Zhizn',* no. 1 (1897), 104.

36. Ivan Shcheglov, *Narodnyi teatr v ocherkakh i kartinkakh* (Saint Petersburg, 1898), 58.

37. E. P. Karpov and N. N. Okulov, *Organizatsiia narodnago teatra i polezhnykh razvlechenii dlia naroda* (Saint Petersburg, 1899), 17.

38. Nikolai Popov, "O repertuare narodnogo teatra," in *Narodnyi teatr. Sbornik.* (Moscow, 1896), 239.

39. E. Karpov, *Desiatiletie narodnykh gulianii,* 5.

40. Ibid., 7.

41. Shcheglov, *Narodnyi teatr,* 8.

42. Tamarin, "Narodnyi teatr," 106. "You would see how a crowd of a thousand watches a play, some sitting, others standing, pressed tightly against one another. The silence is broken only at especially interesting places, when exclamations come from the audience, or general laughter, or surprise or terror."

43. N. K. Mikhailovsky, "Literatura i zhizn'," *Russkoe bogatstvo,* no. 6 (June 1896), 52.

44. Chargonin, "Neskol'ko slov o repertuare narodnago teatra," *Teatr i iskusstvo,* no. 32 (August 1905), 513.

45. Mikhailovsky, "Literatura i zhizn," 55.

46. Ibid., 58.

47. "And what a wonderful array of holidays there was, at least from the peasant point of view . . . !" remarks T. H. VonLaue, who enumerates them in his "Russian Labor between Field and Factory, 1892–1903," *California Slavic Studies* 3 (1964), 53–54.

48. *P'ianstvo, kak sotsial'nyi nedug i bor'ba protiv nego* (Saint Petersburg, n.d.), 49. See also Iu. M. Lotman, "Dekabrist v povsednevnoi zhizni," in *Literaturnoe nasledie Dekabristov,* ed. V. G. Bazarov (Leningrad, 1975), 52: "Among the merchantry, the strict propriety of everyday life was juxtaposed to the 'drinking binge' [*zagul*] that knew no limit. The requirement that social masks be exchanged meant that if in everyday life someone belonged to the humiliated and downtrodden classes, then going on a spree required him to play the role of a man for whom 'the sky's the limit'. . . ." On the social controls implemented to deal with ritual drinking in Russia in the late nineteenth century, see Patricia Herlihy, "Joy of the Rus': Rites and Rituals of Russian Drinking," *Russian Review* 50, no. 2 (April 1991).

49. Mikhailovsky, "Literatura i zhizn," 58.

50. The phrase "real person" retains a resonance in Russian that it lacks in either British or American English. Vera Dunham, writing of the 1940s, observed: "Middleclass language now began to manipulate the difference between a 'simple person' *(prostoi chelovek),* an 'average person' *(srednii chelovek),* and a 'real person' *(nastoyashchii chelovek).* These terms were not merely descriptive but became value judgments, laden with emotion. Nor have they become identical in sense throughout the social struc-

ture." *In Stalin's Time: Middleclass Values in Soviet Fiction* (Cambridge, 1976), 95.

51. In 1894 *Woe from Wit* had to be repeated three times to satisfy audience demands, and at each successive performance Chatsky's monologue received greater applause. Tamarin, "Narodnyi teatr," 116.

52. Ibid., 102.

53. A. N. Kremlev, "O narodnom teatre v S.-Peterburge," *Novosti,* no. 276 (1894), 2.

54. L. Gorev, "Provintsial'naia pechat'," *Severnyi Vestnik,* no. 6 (June 1896), 298.

55. Andrew Donskov, *Mixail Lentovskij and the Russian Theatre* (East Lansing, Mich., 1985), 3

56. Quoted ibid., 34. See the description by a journalist in the 1880s of patrons of the New Theatre and the Moscow Paradis operetta, managed by an employe of Lentovskii: "A fast living, jaded audience—old debauchees, scrutinizers of bare torsos, peering through opera glasses to see if the actresses' tights had split anywhere. An audience trained at night clubs, music halls and theatrical masquerades." Quoted in Laurence Senelick, ed., *National Theatre in Northern and Eastern Europe, 1746–1900* (New York, 1991), 404. Lentovskii persisted with the idea of perfecting a purifying space for public entertainment. In 1897 he proposed to the Moscow Duma that it lease him Samotek Boulevard—a haunt for undesirables—and part of Ekaterininskii Park so that he could develop the area and transform it with an all-purpose theatre auditorium. He pointed out that western Europeans had long appreciated the need for municipal gardens and public entertainment. (See Donskov, 56–60, on his rejected proposal.)

57. Iu. A. Dmitriev, *Mikhail Lentovskii* (Moscow, 1978), 227.

58. Ibid., 238.

59. Quoted in Donskov, *Mixail Lentovskij,* 83.

60. Reprinted in *Narodnyi teatr,* 76–77.

61. "Old Gentleman" [A. V. Amfitreatov], "Vlast' t'my pered narodom," *Novoe Vremia,* no. 7107 (10 December 1895). Maxim Gorky defended Tolstoy against charges that he had exaggerated the potential for bestiality of peasant life in the *Samara Gazette* in 1895. Citing cases of peasant brutality known to him, he concluded that the facts bore Tolstoy out: "in real life things may be even worse than they are depicted in Lev Nikolaevich's drama." By 1900 Gorky had decided that the play itself was "repulsive, grotesque" and full of crudeness. *Sobranie Sochinenii v tridtsati tomakh,* (Moscow, 1954), 28:112.

62. "Old Gentleman," "Vlast' t'my pered narodom."

63. Tsentral'nyi Gosudarstvennyi Istoricheskii Arkhiv SSSR (hereafter TsGIA) fond 575, opis 11, ed. khr. 207. The document bears no date, but appears to have been compiled in 1902 and updated in 1903.

64. The most famous name on the list of industrialists operating factory theatres is Savva Morozov. His grandfather, S. V. Morozov, had been the first merchant to import English spinning equipment, along with English technical specialists, to Russia. The family textile factories employed thirty thousand workers at the turn of the century.

65. Aleksei Iartsev, "Pervye fabrichnye teatry v Rossii," *Istoricheskii vestnik* (May 1900), 649–52.

66. Ibid., 652.

67. The catalogue, by N. Timkovskii and N. Popov, "Pervaia vystavka narodnago teatra. Obzor vystavki.," was reprinted in *Narodnyi teatr. Sbornik.*

68. "Ob organizatsii razvlechenii dlia rabochikh. Doklad, prochitannyi na vtorom s"ezd russkikh deiatelei po tekhnicheskomu i professional'nomu obrazovaniiu v Moskve, 31 dekabria 1895 g.," *Teatral,* no. 65 (1896), 52.

69. *Teatr i iskusstvo,* no. 11 (1897), 212.

70. *Protokoly Osobogo soveshchaniia, uchrezhdennogo pod predsedatel'stvom D. F. Kobeko, dlia sostavleniia novogo ustava o pechati (10 fevralia–4 dekabria 1905 g.)* (Saint Petersburg, 1913), 391. The word *pornographic* seems to have been employed not in its literal sense (of depicting harlots) but rather as an extreme synonym for lewd in *its* literal sense: common, low, vulgar.

71. Vladimir Filippov, *Zadachi narodnogo teatra i ego proshloe v Rossiii* (Moscow, 1918), 44.

72. Karpov and Okulov, *Organizatsiia,* 5.

73. See Vera Gottlieb, *Chekhov and the Vaudeville* (Cambridge, 1982).

74. Quoted in Lomunov, *Tvorchestvo L. N. Tolstogo,* 550.

75. Quoted in Khaichenko, *Russkii narodnyi teatr,* 155.

76. "Moskovskii obshchedostupnyi teatr," in V. I. Nemirovich-Danchenko, *Stati. Rechi. Besedy. Pis'ma.* (Moscow, 1952) 63–71. The Moscow Imperial Technical Society, a private group chartered by the tsar that investigated social and technical problems, published the report in 1898, along with others in support of a general access theatre for the city.

77. G. A. Khaichenko, "Narodnyi teatr," in *Russkaia khudozhestvennaia kul'tura kontsa XIX–nachala XX veka,* ed. A. D. Alekseev (Moscow, 1968), 1:223.

78. Vladimir Nemirovich-Dantchenko, *My Life in the Russian Theatre,* trans. John Cournos (New York, 1936), 181. P. M. Pchel'nikov, the censor for private theatre productions, in a report on the private theatres in Moscow in 1901–2, insisted that the Art Theatre had copied the Korsh management in distributing large numbers of low-priced or free tickets at educational institutions and declared factory workers its *second* most desirable category of viewers—after educated youths. TsGIA, fond 776, op. 25, ed. khr. 624, l. 53.

79. Robert W. Thurston, *Liberal City, Conservative State. Moscow and Russia's Urban Crisis, 1906–1914* (New York, 1987), 8.

80. See Joseph Bradley, "The Moscow Workhouse and Urban Welfare Reform in Russia," *Russian Review* 41, 4 (October 1982), 427–44.

81. [Omega], "Liubimoe detishche upravy," *Moskovskie vedomosti*, no. 264 (1902), 2.

82. "Vzgliad na ideal'nyi teatr i ego zadachi v nashe vremia," in *Narodnyi teatr. Sbornik.*, 224.

83. "Kakiia razvlecheniia blagotvorno vliiaiut na rabochikh?" in *Obrazovatel'no–vospitatel'nyia uchrezhdeniia dlia rabochikh* (Moscow: Imperatorskoe Russkoe Tekhnicheskoe Obshchestvo, 1898), 41.

84. *Rukovodiashchie ukazaniia dlia deiatel'nosti popechitel'stva o narodnoi trezvosti, odobrennye ministrom finansov 28 ianvaria 1897 goda.*

85. *Polnoe Sobranie Zakonov Rossiiskoi Imperii,* 3d collection, vol. 18, no. 13744, (1897), 64.

86. Ibid., no. 14751, 681–83.

87. TsGIA, fond 776, op. 25, ed. khr. 624. Memorandum of E. M. Pchel'nikov, 27 January 1901.

88. "Zagadki peterburgskago narodnago teatra," *Novoe Vremia,* no. 9698 (5 March 1903).

89. F. W. J. Hemmings describes the career of the French *cafés-chantants,* which first appeared in the middle of the nineteenth century: "The *café-chantant* or *café-concert*—the latter term eventually prevailed—was a peculiarly Parisian institution; attempts to popularize it in the provinces never seem to have come to anything. . . . [T]heir numbers were swelled immensely in the course of the Second Empire, thanks in part to the destruction of the little theatres on the Boulevard du Temple, whose former audiences sought their quota of amusement for preference in the cafés, but chiefly owing to the decree of 1864 which resulted in an immense expansion of the *café-concert* industry. . . . [B]y 1911 . . . the more successful of the *cafés-concerts* . . . had . . . transformed themselves into theatres." *Theatre and State in France,* 200–203.

90. TsGIA, fond 776, op. 25, ed. khr. 624, l. 21.

91. "Teatr i muzyka," *Novoe Vremia,* no. 9119, (25 July 1901).

92. "In its repertoire, interior design, and advertising style, the People's House initially had much in common with the fairground theaters. . . . Rather than raising the masses to the level of art, the [Trusteeships] desacralized art by reducing it to the status of a mere spectacle." Anthony Swift, "Theater for the People," 263, 281.

93. *Vestnik popechitel'stvo narodnoi trezvosti,* no. 1 (2 August 1903), 1.

94. "Popechitel'stva o narodnoi trezvosti," *Vserossiiskii s"ezd po bor'be s p'ianstvom,* 3 vols. (Saint Petersburg, 1909–10), 2:905.

95. "Zagadki peterburgskago narodnago teatra," *Novoe Vremia,* no. 9699, (6/19 March 1903).

96. TsGIA, fond 575, opis 3, ed. khr. 4062, l. 87.
97. Ibid., l. 64.
98. Ibid, l. 69.
99. A. S. Balitskaia, "Iz derevni," *Obrazovanie* (April 1894), 144.
100. Ianzhul, *P'ianstvo,* 44–45.

CHAPTER FIVE

1. Scott Seregny, *Russian Teachers and Peasant Revolution: The Politics of Education in 1905* (Bloomington, Ind., 1989), 66.

2. Nancy M. Frieden, *Russian Physicians in an Era of Reform and Revolution, 1856–1905* (Princeton, N.J., 1981), 231. The Ninth Pirogov Congress drew 2,136 physicians to Petersburg (242). "It opened immediately after 3000 participants of a Congress for Activists in the Field of Technological Education . . . passed a set of demands for a constituent assembly, basic freedoms of speech, press and assembly; the eight-hour day; and removal of religious and ethnic discrimination."

3. Adele Lindenmeyr, "Voluntary Associations and the Russian Autocracy." *Carl Beck Papers in Russian and East European Studies,* no. 807 (June 1990), 24. Lindenmeyr observes that the Department of Police came into conflict with bureaucrats who were seeking to *encourage* independent local initiative *(samodeiatel'nost')* (45).

4. Linda Edmondson, "Was there a Movement for Civil Rights in 1905?" in *Civil Rights in Imperial Russia,* ed. Olga Crisp and Linda Edmondson (Oxford, 1989), 263.

5. Mark G. Pomar, "Anatoly Fedorovich Koni: Liberal Jurist as Moralist," *Carl Beck Papers in Russian and East European Studies,* no. 1202 (March 1996), 34.

6. Joan Neuberger, *Hooliganism: Crime, Culture, and Power in St. Petersburg, 1900–1914* (Berkeley and Los Angeles, 1993), 46.

7. Ibid., 46. In roughly a generation Russia moved from a position of last among the major European nations to first in the world in the number of titles and total copies of books published per annum. Gregory Guroff and S. Frederick Starr, "A Note on Urban Literacy in Russia, 1890–1914," *Jahrbücher für Geschichte Osteuropas* 19 (1971), 572.

8. Habermas, *Structural Transformation,* 133.

9. Ibid., 138.

10. Robert F. Byrnes, "'Between Two Fires': Kliuchevskii on Religion and the Russian Orthodox Church," *Modern Greek Studies Yearbook* 6 (1990), 162. Boris Mironov relates the rise of a feeling of personal individualism, "which was especially apparent when peasants worked in the city and established close bonds between the city and their commune," to the grow-

ing fondness for fashionable dress after 1861." "The Peasant Commune after the Reforms of the 1860s," in *The World of the Russian Peasant*, ed. Ben Eklof and Stephen Frank (Winchester, Mass., 1990), 28.

11. Frank, "Confronting the Domestic Other," 90. On hooliganism, see also Gregory Freeze, "'Going to the Intelligentsia': The Church and its Urban Mission in Post-Reform Russia," 230–31.

12. Frank, "Confronting the Domestic Other," 103: "[I]ndividualism itself, if properly channeled, could serve as the new bulwark of the social order." Louise McReynolds suggests a reading of a post-1905 collection of essays by repentant Marxists that fits it into the Habermas scheme of a collapsed or collapsing Public Sphere. "Russia's intelligentsia struggled to come to terms with the politics of individualism that accompanied modernization. Some published their confusion in the 1909 collection of essays *Landmarks (Vekhi)*, whose tone of retreat from public life to concentration on private, personal growth upset many others." "'The Incomparable' Anastasia Vial'-tseva and the Culture of Personality," in *Russia—Women—Culture*, ed. Helena Goscilo and Beth Holmgren (Bloomington, Ind., 1996), 288.

13. Shmuel Galai, *The Liberation Movement in Russia, 1900–1905* (Cambridge, 1973), 143.

14. "The 'police state,' he said, had formerly tried to control all areas of national life. This role was now antiquated." Quoted in John R. Fisher, "The Witte Conference on the Needs of Agriculture in Russia: 1902–1905" (Ph.D. diss., University of Toronto, 1978), 57.

15. Ibid., 270, 322–23.

16. Later investigation would reveal that they most often started in communes bordering noble-owned great estates and linked to them through rental arrangements. S. S. Khrulov, "Iz istorii bor'by s agrarnym dvizheniem, 1905–1906," *Krasnyi Arkhiv* 39 (1930), 83.

17. Stephen Wheatcroft, "Crisis and the Condition of the Peasantry in Late Imperial Russia," 170. "Did the government really think that the peasantry would continue to pay the hated redemption tax, once the government had foresworn the use of violence, and group pressure, and once it had forgiven those who had earlier refused to pay?" Wheatcroft answers his own question: "This soft line contributed to the collapse of state authority in the countryside" (167).

18. Ibid., 170.

19. Randall McGowan examines the transition from gallows to prison in England. He finds that doctors and lawyers presenting themselves as spokesmen of progress and the spread of politeness and refinement in all aspects of life effectively attacked the practice of concentrating punishment on the body of the offender. With surprising rapidity, the individual body came to be identified as the locus of rights and autonomy. As public ritual lost its significance in the life of the community, reformers envisioned a new soci-

ety founded on sympathy, promoting "reciprocal integrity, benevolence, and charity between man and man" [Henry Dagge, *Considerations on Criminal Law* (Dublin, 1772)] and reducing instances of opposition and violence in human interaction. "The Body and Punishment in Eighteenth-Century England," *Journal of Modern History* 59, no. 4 (December 1987), 668, 670, 675.

20. Ben Eklof considers that the public campaign against child abuse at this time "typifies the way Russians in general . . . overstated the degree of their own 'backwardness' in educational matters." "Worlds in Conflict: Patriarchal Authority, Discipline and the Russian School, 1861–1914," in *School and Society in Tsarist and Soviet Russia*, ed. Ben Eklof (London, 1993), 107.

21. The prestigious juridical weekly *Pravo* (Right) said in April 1903 that the greatest need in the agrarian field was for the peasant "to consider himself an individual, not only provided with inalienable rights but also bearing unavoidable responsibilities" and observed in January 1904 that attention to the personality of the peasant had become a "banner of the times." Quoted in Fisher, "Witte Conference," 195.

22. Ibid., 376.

23. Bunakov, *Zapiski*, v.

24. Seregny, *Russian Teachers*, 44.

25. Fisher, "Witte Conference," 168. In assessing the Voronezh affair Fisher examined an account by a zemstvo statistician published in Stuttgart in 1903 and (from the Central State Historical Archive) Plehve's report to Nicholas II dated 24 November 1902.

26. *Osvobozhdenie*, no. 12 (2 and 15 December 1902), 186.

27. *The Times*, 28 February 1903, 8. The paper's Saint Petersburg correspondent was expelled from Russia shortly thereafter.

28. L. Bunakova, "Istoriia Petinskago Nar. Doma" [a report read to the All-Russian Popular Theatre Congress, 3 January 1916], in *Trudy Vserossiiskogo s"ezda deiatelei narodnogo teatra v Moskve, 27 dekabria 1915–5 ianvaria 1916* (Petrograd, 1919), 160. In her introduction to her husband's memoir she says cryptically, "At this time there were many masters at the people's house, but N. F. was not one of them." *Zapiski*, xi.

29. Richard Pipes called this November gathering "the equivalent in the Russian Revolution of the French National Assembly of 1789," because it furnished a majority of the country's only elected officials the opportunity to vote to demand a representative legislative body. *Struve: Liberal on the Left, 1870–1905* (Cambridge, Mass., 1970), 366.

30. *Sobranie sochinenii v tridtsati tomakh* (Moscow, 1954), 28:332. Hereafter cited in chapter as G, *Ss*.

31. See Seregny, *Russian Teachers*, 30: "The zemstvo gentry, as it turned out, was not . . . democratic. Their commitment to political opposition was provisional and their understanding of enlightenment (and the role of the teacher) rather limited."

32. Galai gives percentages of district and provincial committees proposing particular reforms. *Liberation Movement,* 153.

33. The 1865 censorship reform had removed Russian drama censorship from the jurisdiction of the police and put it under the Main Administration on Press Affairs. A "temporary regulation" in May 1888 had created the special censorship for popular theatres: those which, because of low admission prices, attracted "mainly unsophisticated people." Interested authors, translators, and directors could request approval for their plays by submitting a stamped application to the Main Administration. Not until 1897 did the Main Administration get around to issuing a list of plays approved for popular theatres. It contained eighty-one titles. The Second Complete Alphabetical List, with 570 titles (340 of which were one-acts), came out in 1903. But it did not include plays approved with cuts. A popular theatre interested in doing a work not listed would have to buy special tax stamps and apply, in order to learn whether the censors had sanitized a text they deemed flawed but retrievable. For E. Anthony Swift's reading of the censors' reports see "Fighting the Germs of Disorder: The Censorship of Russian Popular Theater, 1888–1917," *Russian History* 18, no. 1 (Spring 1991) and "Theater for the People," 83–156.

34. TsGIA, fond 776, op. 25, ed. khr. 624, l. 7.

35. "Leninskaia 'Iskra' i teatr," *Teatral'noe nasledstvo* (Moscow, 1956), 120.

36. *Protokoly . . . pechati,* 8.

37. Ibid., 376.

38. V. A. Tsinkovich, "Narodnyi teatr i dramaticheskaia tsenzura," in *Teatral'noe nasledstvo* (Moscow, 1956), 381.

39. *Protokoly . . . pechati,* 406.

40. Seven years earlier, for example, speakers at the First All-Russian Conference of Theatre Personnel had voiced baldly undemocratic claims for the advantages of expertise over the benefits of a free marketplace of ideas. One recommended that the Russian Theatrical Society petition the Main Administration to "forbid persons incompetent in questions of art" to write theatre reviews in periodical publications. Another proposed that reviewers be required to hold higher eduction degrees in history and philosophy, have worked in dramatics and possess material security and independence. *Trudy pervago vserossiiskago s"ezda stsenicheskikh deiatelei* (Moscow, 1898), 318.

41. TsGIA, fond 776, op. 25, ed. khr. 624, l. 157.

42. Martin Malia estimates that the intelligentsia numbered between 200,000 and 300,000 on the eve of the 1905 revolution. *Comprendre la révolution russe* (Paris, 1980), 57.

43. An actor who authored many vaudevilles, Lenskii followed Eugène Scribe's methods for making comedies of manners into *pièces bien faite.* His "Sinichkin" is considered "a direct precursor of Ostrovsky's plays por-

traying theatrical customs." Vera Gottlieb, *Chekov and the Vaudeville* (Cambridge, 1982), 202.

44. *Protokoly . . . pechati*, 386.

45. TsGIA, fond 776, op. 25, ed. khr. 815.

46. V. I. Charnoluskii, ed., *Sbornik zakonov i spravochnykh svedenii o pechati, sobraniiakh, s"ezdakh, lektsiiakh, narodnykh chteniiakh, kursakh dlia vzroslykh, obshchestvakh, soiuzakh, bibliotekakh, knizhnoi torgovle, teatr, uveseleniiakh, i.t.d.* (Moscow, 1907), 92; emphasis in original.

47. Khaichenko, *Russkii narodnyi teatr*, 101.

48. Chargonin, "Neskol'ko slov o repertuare narodnago teatra," *Teatr i iskusstvo*, no. 32 (7 August 1905), 513.

49. "Suvorov the Stationmaster" and "Charles XII before Poltava." TsGIA, fond 776, op. 26, ed. khr. 24; 17 March 1905.

50. Ibid., 28 August 1905.

51. Pchel'nikov stated in his 1903–4 report that the Temperance trustees had greatly increased the production of operas and that the number of dramatic productions in Moscow had declined steadily since 1901. TsGIA, fond 776, op. 25, ed. khr. 624, l. 28.

52. *Structural Transformation*, 174.

53. A. P. Chekhov, *Sobranie sochinenii* (Moscow, 1960), 9:486. Hereafter cited in chapter as C, *Ss*.

54. For the audience, no particular point of view is privileged. For the actors, the "minor" characters with few lines are often as fully realized and capable of being brought to life by nonverbal means as the characters taking sides and sides of dialogue.

55. TsGALI, Memoirs of P. P. Gaideburov. Fond 991, op. 60, ed. khr. 348, l. 12. The elder Gaideburov had as a student been expelled from Saint Petersburg University for participating in a demonstration, and as editor fought an incessant battle with the tsarist government, which closed *Nedelia* before he died in 1893. He had been a successful amateur actor in his younger years and approved of his son's theatrical interests.

56. E. P. Karpov i N. N. Okulov, *Organizatsiia*, 4.

57. A leading member of the Bolshoi company, professor at the Conservatory and reputedly the best voice teacher in Moscow, Komissarzhevskii had given the adolescent Stanislavsky (Alekseev) lessons. The young man's natural sense of phrasing greatly impressed him. For Mussorgsky's views on the relation between music and the inflections of speech, see Caryl Emerson, *Boris Godunov* (Bloomington, Ind., 1986), 157–64.

58. "Polveka s Chekhovym" (1946), in *Na stsene*, 136. His description points up Chekhov's genius for examining aspirations, or directing the viewer to do so. Perceiving discrepancies promotes practical action.

59. TsGALI, Gaideburov memoir. Fond 991, op. N 267, ed. khr. 335.

60. Ibid., 12.

61. "Polveka s Chekhovym," 141. On atmosphere in Chekhov and Levitan see Paul Debreczeny, "Chekhov's Use of Impressionism in 'The House with the Mansard,'" in *Russian Narrative and Visual Art: Varieties of Seeing*, ed. Roger Anderson and Paul Debreczeny, (Gainesville, Fla., 1994), 105–8.

62. Wolfgang Pailer, *Die frühen Dramen M. Gor'kijs in ihrem verhältnis zum dramatischen Schaffen A. P. Čechovs* (Munich, 1978), 2. Pailer compares the six plays Gorky had written by 1907, which he claims represent a unity, to the great Chekhov dramas.

63. Pailer calls it a "Romantic relic." But could the didactic speechifying have been rooted in the oral culture Gorky had from his grandmother? Pailer, *Die frühen Dramen,* 18.

64. Mary Louise Loe finds he "portrayed [them] as the strongest men in Russia because they . . . have had the courage to follow their own desires." "Gorky and Nietzsche" in *Nietzsche in Russia,* ed. Bernice Glatzer Rosenthal (Princeton, N.J., 1986), 267.

65. In a 1916 essay he wrote to try to explain why the Russian is a poor worker, for instance, he started out by saying, "the social and political systems bear some responsibility for this." M. Gorky, *Polveka dlia knigi* (Moscow, 1916), 26.

66. In the late 1880s he worked for a Populist who opened a general store in Krasnovidovo. This altruistic *intelligent* aimed not for profits but to create a place where peasants could buy goods at low prices and gather in their spare time for serious talk. Peasant suspicion of outsiders doomed the enterprise. The building in flames, young Peshkov and his employer found themselves fleeing for their lives in the darkness before a pursuing vigilante band. Bertram D. Wolfe, *The Bridge and the Abyss* (New York, 1967), 33.

67. B. Bialik, *M. Gor'kii—dramaturg* (Moscow, 1977), 37.

68. See Loe, "Gorky and Nietzsche," 270–71.

69. N. I. Gitovich, ed. *M. Gor'kii i A. Chekhov, Perepiska, stati, vyskazyvaniia* (Moscow, 1951), 71.

70. S. Balukhatyi, "Prikhod M. Gor'kogo v teatr. Rabota ego nad p'esoi 'Meshchane,'" in *"Meshchane" M. Gor'kogo* (Moscow, 1941), 70.

71. *Maksim Gor'kii . . . Perepiska,* 74. This to Chekhov, who had corresponded with Shcheglov for years and was on friendly enough terms to address him as "Dear little staff captain with mustaches."

72. Ibid., 99–100.

73. That is, lack of education, boorishness, lack of respectability; in its adjectival form, uncultivated.

74. *Ss,* 86. Note the similarity in Gorky's choice of words to Bunakov's scandalous assertion that Russia was not a well-ordered European nation. An earlier draft of Nil's speech had him say, "I know this and I don't like it. It upsets me. I do not want this order [*etogo poriadka*]!" Balukhatyi, "Prikhod M. Gor'kogo v teatr," 78.

75. M. Khorosh, "Tolstoi o Gor'kom," in *Na literaturnom postu* (Moscow, 1928), 29.

76. Maxim Gorky, *Reminiscences of Tolstoy* (New York, 1946), 50.

77. Khorosh, "Tolstoi o Gor'kom," 32.

78. V. Charskii, "Khudozhestvennyi teatr," in Iu. M. Stekiov, ed., *Krizis teatr. Sbornik statei* (Moscow, 1908), 133.

79. Gorky, *Reminiscences*, 20.

80. Khorosh, "Tolstoi o Gor'kom," 30–31.

81. Ibid., 29.

82. *Arkhiv A. M. Gor'kogo* (Moscow, 1960), 8:33. Edith Clowes kindly called this comment to my attention.

83. Thomas Mann, *Diaries, 1918–1939* (New York, 1982), 263–64 (3 December 1936).

84. On the tonal values that date Nöel Coward's immortal line, see George Steiner, *After Babel* (London, 1975), 15–17.

85. S. A. Orlov and A. V. Sigorskii, "A. M. Gor'kii i bor'ba za narodnyi teatr," in *Liudi russkogo isskustva* (Moscow, 1960), 102.

86. "Leninskaia 'Iskra' i teatr," in *Teatral'noe nasledstvo* (Moscow, 1956), 132.

87. S. Markov's recollections appeared in the 12 February issue of *Leningradnaia gazeta.* E. Gigushvili and A. Iufit, *Bol'shevistskaia pechat' i teatr* (Leningrad and Moscow, 1961), 44–45 n. 3.

88. Tat'iana Prozerova, "Teatr Gor'kogo v Nizhnem Novgorode," *Teatr*, no. 5 (1967), 92.

89. Quoted ibid., 94.

90. Quoted ibid., 100.

91. Benedetti, *Stanislavski*, 143.

92. Abraham Ascher, *The Revolution of 1905* (Stanford, Calif., 1988), 85.

93. Samuel N. Harper Collection, University of Chicago Library, Box 24, Folder 19. Harper's father, a biblical scholar, was the founder and first president of the University of Chicago. Harper first went to Russia with a Chicago industrialist. He became interested in the country, and studied Russian language and literature in Paris 1901–3. He had read *The Lower Depths* there and made extensive notes on it.

94. Quoted in L. K. Dolgopolov, "Vokrug 'Detei solntsa'," in *M. Gor'kii i ego sovremenniki*, ed. K. D. Muratova (Leningrad, 1968), 103.

95. See George L. Mosse, "Nationalism and Respectability," *Journal of Contemporary History* 17 (1982), 235. "The movement attempted to return to the so-called genuine forces of life, and to reform man and society through vegetarianism, anti-alcoholism, nature-healing, land reform." Compare Bal'mont's famous line: "I came into this world to see the sun."

96. L. K. Dolgopolov, "Vokrug 'Detei solntsa'," 81.

97. See L. K. Dolgopolov, *Na rubezhe vekov (*Leningrad, 1977), 71.

98. *Ss* 374. But Gorky reprises his old theme that the existing social structure is a gross impediment to the realization of human potential. As Dolgopolov puts it, "The *narod* are not [bright and clear], and the reason is rooted in the most basic social structure." *Na rubezhe vekov,* 88.

99. Critics chastised Gorky for introducing cholera—but peasant violence directed at physicians was only somewhat anachronistic, such occurrences being not uncommon in Russia in the early 1890s. G. M. Gigolov, *Dramaturgiia M. Gor'kogo. 1902–1906 gg. v sovremennoi ei kritike i publitsistike* (Tbilisi, 1975), 220–21.

100. Alexander Kaun, *Maxim Gorky and His Russia* (New York, 1931), 370.

101. Dolgopolov emphasizes Gorky's assault on the symbolists: "The cholera riot shattered the illusory harmony of Protasov's world. Gorky revealed the disingenuousness of the symbolists, according to whom harmony could be achieved by separating personality from the mass, isolating it from everyday life by means of promoting individual self satisfaction." *Na rubezhe vekov,* 93.

102. *Ocherki rabochei intelligentsii* (Saint Petersburg, 1923), 2:56.

103. L. N. Kleinbort, "Maksim Gor'kii i chitatel' iz nizov," *Vestnik Evropy,* no. 12 (December 1913), 171–93.

104. A report to the Seventh Congress on Alcohol Abuse in Paris in 1899 explained that Moscow's first temperance society had organized tea rooms and several plays: "It is interesting to note that the plays enjoyed colossal success only with the artisans and *meshchane.* Factory workers and the crowd (simple folk) prefer religious discussion." Alexandre Korowin, "La Tempérance en Russie," *Septième Congrès contre l'abus des boissons alcooliques* (Paris, 1899–1900), 285. I am grateful to Patricia Herlihy for bringing this report to my attention.

105. K. V. Skorobogatov, *Zhizn' i stsena* (Leningrad, 1970), 202. He achieved fame as a professional actor after the revolution.

106. Tsentral'nyi gosudarstvennyi arkhiv literatury i iskusstva SSSR (TsGALI). Data on the first decade of the Ligovsk People's House. Fond 991, op. 1, ed. khr. 1018.

107. O. V. Kaidanova, *Ocherki po istorii narodnogo obrazovaniia v Rossii i SSSR na osnove lichnogo opyta i nabliudenii,* 2 vols. (Berlin, 1938, 1939), 2:509. Their influence troubled her paternal grandmother, who petitioned the empress to have Sofia taken from her mother's custody and sent for schooling to the Saint Petersburg Institute for Young Ladies of the Nobility. The authorities acceded to the request, apparently agreeing that it might be dangerous to leave a woman of her enormous wealth under the influence of a man who had often been arrested and exiled. Petrunkevich had long campaigned for a constitution and alone among the liberals had gone so

far as to approach revolutionaries for support (though insisting that they abandon the use of terror).

108. "Istoriia Ligovskogo narodnogo doma Sofii Vladimirovny Paninoi" [n.d., 1913?] TsGALI, fond 991, op. 1, ed. khr. 1018.

109. If only all the patrons had, like Browning's nuns, left a signifying garment by the door, it might be possible to guess in what proportion skilled workers and unskilled, lower-white-collar employees, the *meshchane* owners of small properties and intelligentsia mingled and how they influenced each other. Joseph Bradley breaks out occupational listings from the 1902 and 1912 Moscow censuses and shows relative rates of increase and decline in *Muzhik and Muscovite* (Berkeley and Los Angeles, 1985), 154. Daniel Orlovsky discusses the urban lower middle classes and their "alliances with workers and peasants, as opposed to the bourgeoisie" in "The Lower Middle Strata in Revolutionary Russia," in *Between Tsar and People.*

110. Quoted in N. F. Skarskaia and P. P. Gaideburov, *Na stsene i v zhizni* (Moscow, 1959), 26.

111. S. V. Panina and P. P. Gaideburov, "Iskusstvo v narodnoi auditorii," *Russkaia shkola,* nos. 5–6 (1914), 168.

112. Ibid., 151.

113. Gaideburov and Skarskaia drew 250 rubles a month, at a time when provincial directors earned ten times as much as actors. E. D. Golovinskaia, "Peredvizhnoi teatr P. P. Gaideburova (Iz vospominanii)" in *Zapiski o teatre* (Leningrad and Moscow, 1960), 206.

114. Ibid., 206.

115. Iu. Petr, "Desiatiletie teatra Narodnogo doma gr. Paninoi," *Teatr i iskusstvo,* no. 45 (1913), 930.

116. For an account of how the censorship cut an earlier Ibsen play that became a great favorite of the General-Access Theatre, *An Enemy of the People,* see B. A. Shaikevich, *Dramaturgiia Ibsena v Rossii* (Kiev, 1968), 46. They owed some of their popularity to the novelty of *Ghosts.* The tragedian P. N. Orlenev had persuaded the censorship to lift its performance ban on the play early in 1904 and toured the provinces with it. Orlenev emphasized in his portrayal the complete breakdown of Oswald's personality under the impact of congenital syphilis. Gaideburov's Oswald, however, underscored the character's "zest for life, straining for the sun with joyful, happy expressions" (*Na stsene,* 38). He played the entire last scene with his back turned to the audience. Skarskaia emphasized the destructiveness of Mrs. Alving's compromise and her personal tragedy. Audiences flocked to the new production, keen to compare it to the Orlenev version still fresh in their memories.

117. N. N. Khodotov, *Blizkoe-dalekoe* (Moscow and Leningrad, 1962), 293 n. 211.

118. He noted that some of the most talented actors, though well disposed to the idea of popular enlightenment, declined to join companies for

popular theatre on account of its very limited repertory. "It is the greatest misfortune," he said, "that under prevailing conditions of development, the business of popular theatre is beginning to be recognized as hopeless." *Sobranie sochinenii* (1958), 5:280.

119. "Za pervyi god deiatel'nosti peredvizhnogo teatra," *Biblioteka pervago dramaticheskago peredvizhnogo teatra* Seriia 1905 goda, Vyp. 5 (Saint Petersburg, 1907), 10.

120. Gaideburov described the Itinerant Theatre in a piece he wrote for a cooperative newspaper in 1918, "Nashim budushchim zriteliam." It is reprinted in *Pavel Pavlovich Gaideburov: literaturnoe nasledie,* ed. Simon Dreiden (Moscow, 1977), 221–24.

121. A few specifics chosen more or less at random may indicate how the revolution failed to live up to his expectations. Kathleen Prevo discovered that strikes that began in Voronezh on 5 February were motivated by the success of strikes elsewhere, rather than by outrage or political frustration. Picketers there actually attacked intelligentsia speakers calling for a political stand against the government. "Worker Reaction to Bloody Sunday in Voronezh," in *1905: La première révolution russe* (Paris, 1986), 171. John Bushnell concluded that soldiers mutinied "when they believed the regime's writ had expired. . . . When they believed the regime's authority to be intact, they repressed civilians." *Mutiny Amid Repression: Russian Soldiers in the Revolution of 1905–1906* (Bloomington, Ind., 1985), 226. Maureen Perrie, reviewing hundreds of responses to the Free Economic Society's questionnaire on the revolution, found that peasants from Pskov province who worked in Saint Petersburg supported the revolutionary movement because it was the only way they could achieve equal rights with members of the other estates, but that their perception was atypical for peasants in 1905. "The Russian Peasant Movement of 1905–7: Its Social Composition and Revolutionary Significance." *Past and Present,* no. 57 (November 1972), 126.

122. Golovinskaia, "Peredvizhnoi teatr," 204.

CHAPTER SIX

1. Alexander Blok, "O teatre," in *Sobranie Sochinenii v vos'mi tomakh* (Moscow and Leningrad, 1962), 5:276. Two important books on what appeared to contemporaries to be a turning point in Russian theatre also appeared in 1908: *Teatr. Kniga o novom teatre. Sbornik statei.* (Saint Petersburg) and the Marxist-oriented *Krizis teatra* (Moscow).

2. Ibid., 276. In Ibsen's play, Solness became a master builder through willpower, forcing others to serve him by enlisting the aid of "the helpers and the servers." The aging Solness confessed his fear of youth, his premonition that youth would topple him, that youth was retribution for his defiant and single-minded achievement.

3. The tone and the contempt for privilege expressed by the Olonetsk poet are not unlike those Dostoevsky had encountered among illiterate convicts in Siberia half a century earlier: "The likes of us are not in the least shy of 'you,' but simply envy you and hate you, and if we put up with your presence amongst us it is only for so long as we see some 'profit' to be had of you. Oh, how fierce is the pain of your presence, what an infinite-accursed sorrow it is to know that there is still no doing without 'you.' This knowledge is what is at the root of the sorrow, the yearning, the angry brooding that gnaws away at us. . . . The awareness that we cannot do without 'you' is the only reason for our failure to communicate with you. . . . The awareness that 'you' are everywhere, that 'you' can whereas we 'must' . . . that is the insurmountable barrier that prevents us from entering into communication with you. But what reasons are there on your side? None—except for profound contempt and purely physical revulsion." Quoted in Avril Pyman, *The Life of Aleksandr Blok* (London, 1980), 2:21.

4. The turning point came in 1908, when they played more of the repertory that the Saint Petersburg Nardom audiences preferred and emphasized the classics. The company toured with *The Storm, Antigone, Hamlet, The Cherry Orchard,* Hauptmann's *Poor Heinrich,* and Shaw's *The Devil's Disciple.* Dreiden, *Pavel Pavlovich Gaideburov,* 43.

5. Quoted in Pyman, *Life of Aleksandr Blok,* 2:26.

6. Samuel N. Harper Collection. Box 24. Folder 13.

7. Ibid., p. 19.

8. Ibid., Box 24. Folder 33 (1906).

9. Ibid., Box 24. Folder 21.

10. Marc Szeftel, *The Russian Constitution of April 23, 1906; Political institutions of the Duma monarchy* (Brussels, 1976), 362. Deliberations in the Council of State that gave rise to this crucial reform suggest that the change in rules on voluntary associations had nothing to do with appreciation of civic initiative as an absolute value but related instead to a feeling that once unshackled, such associations would eschew extremism and give active support to the government. *Otchet po deloproizvodstvu Gosudarstvennago Soveta za sessiiu 1905–1906 gg.*, quoted in Jacob Walkin, *The Rise of Democracy in Pre-Revolutionary Russia* (New York, 1962), 140.

11. Laura Engelstein, *The Keys to Happiness: Sex and the Search for Modernity in Fin-de-Siècle Russia* (Ithaca, N.Y., 1992), 245–81.

12. Roberta Manning, *The Crisis of the Old Order in Russia* (Princeton, N.J., 1982), 304.

13. Francis W. Wcislo, "*Soslovie* or Class? Bureaucratic Reformers and Provincial Gentry in Conflict, 1906–1908," *Russian Review,* 47 (1988), 3.

14. G. Khaichenko, "Narodnyi teatr i dooktiabr'skaia 'Pravda,'" in *Voprosy teatra. Sbornik statei i materialov* (Moscow, 1970), 141.

15. D. N. Borodin, "Popechitel'stva o narodnoi trezvosti," in *Vserossiiskii s"ezd po bor'be s pianstvom,* 3 vols. (Saint Petersburg, 1909–10), 2:905.

16. TsGIA, fond 575, op. 3, ed. khr. 4111, 19 November 1909.

17. On the novel and its reception: Engelstein, *Keys to Happiness,* 383–87.

18. TsGIA, fond 575, op. 3, ed. khr. 4111, l. 2 May 1912,.

19. Khaichenko, *Narodnyi teatr,* 292. Among the unauthorized works were *The Lower Depths* and *Meshchane,* and Schiller's *The Robbers* and *Maria Stuart.*

20. The typescript survives in the manuscript collection of the Library of the All-Russian Theatrical Society in Moscow. Klepikov apparently first wrote an account of his theatrical activities with the cooperative societies and the Section to Promote Village, Factory, and School Theatre during the turbulent period from 1916 to 1920. This document of some thirty pages is entitled "From Theatrical Reminiscences." It is incorporated into his larger "At the Dawn of Independent Theatre," which begins with his first visit to a theatre at the age of seven in the mid-1870s and runs to seventy-nine pages. Tsentral'naia nauchnaia biblioteka V.T.O. Sektor redkoi knigi i rukopisei. Fond teatral'nykh memuarov. A. K. Klepikov, "Iz teatral'nykh vospominanii" VTO/584 and "Na zare samodeiatel'nogo teatra" VTO/K48.

21. A. K. Klepikov, "Na zare," 32.

22. The title of his memoir would likely be read by a Russian who saw it cited as "At the Dawn of Amateur Theatre," because in its adjectival form *samodeiatel'nyi* is used to mean *amateur* in reference to the performing arts. But the noun *samodeiatel'nost'* is translated as "independent action, spontaneous activity." (*Samodeiatel'nyi* as a category used in the census designated that part of the population not basing their livelihood on another's earnings.) The 1961 Academy of Sciences *Dictionary* gives as its first definition "manifestation of personal initiative, a creative beginning of some kind," and as its second, "artistic creativity of persons who are not professional artists" (Akademiia Nauk SSSR. *Slovar Russkogo iazyka* [Moscow, 1961], 4:21). It furnishes two (undated) historical examples of the first usage: Saltykov-Schedrin, "If society is deprived of *samodeiatel'nost',* then it becomes incapable of conducting its affairs"; and Gorky, "A will to *samodeiatel'nost',* an active life, is rising in the masses." With this in mind it is easy to see why anyone who had read Klepikov's memoir and had to render its title in English would chose something along the lines of "At the Dawn of Independent Action."

23. A. K. Klepikov, "Na zare," 22.

24. Notes were taken by Aleksei Petrovich Sergeenko, son of P. A. Sergeenko, who wrote *How Count L. N. Tolstoi Lives and Works.* The younger Sergeenko met Tolstoy in 1900, when he was fourteen. He worked for Tolstoy's secretary, V. G. Chertkov, near Iasnaia Poliana in 1907. In 1908 he worked in London on the Tolstoy archive. He was at the Optina Pustyn and Osta-

povo with Tolstoy and published his recollections. This fragment from his archive dealing with Tolstoy and the Golitsyn circle was published for the first time in 1982.

25. A. Sergeenko, "O narodnom teatre," *Oktiabr* (Moscow), no. 10 (1982), 196.

26. E. Poliakova, "Tolstoi i teatr," *Tiatr*, no. 8 (1978), 15. But in the course of a sleepless night he decided instead that he would have to write something for the cinema. This was a medium that could be understood by the broad masses, all peoples. And one could compose not four or five, but ten or fifteen "pictures."

27. This was the same Orlenev who had badgered Censor Litvinov to lift his ban on *Ghosts* in 1904 by going personally to the official, whose son had committed suicide, and threatening to shoot himself then and there if he did not grant permission to play Oswald. With the help of a doctor friend, he studied mental patients in preparation for touring in the role. Some thought his performance "more pathological than psychological." A. P. Matskin, *Orlenev* (Moscow, 1977), 217.

28. P. N. Orlenev, *Zhizn i tvorchestvo russkogo aktera* (Leningrad and Moscow, 1961), 221–22.

29. In 1913 Orlenev bought a piece of land near the Vostriakovo station of the Riazan-Ural'sk railroad and constructed an open-air theatre there. After filming *Brand* in Norway, he promised the Bakhrushin theatrical museum moving pictures of his work there. Two camera operators assembled to film his performance of *Tsar Fëder Ioannovich* on 15 August 1915, along with the audience's reactions. But stormy weather prevented filming. Bakhrushin himself came and saw the next presentation four days later. Orlenev fled to escape his creditors, and the filming was never done. Orlenev did build one more open-air theatre (in Odintsov), when he was in funds after another tour. Unfortunately, the Bakhrushin has nothing on his production of *Tsar Fëder*, nor any material on Russian popular theatre between 1905 and 1917, except for plays (personal communication from V. V. Gubin, director, 26 April 1990).

30. Sektsiia sodeistviia ustroistvu derevenskikh i fabrichnykh teatrov, *Sbornik retsenzii p'es dlia narodnago teatra* Vyp. I (Moscow, 1914) [87 plays] and Vyp. II (Moscow, 1916) [47 plays].

31. Catherine Salzman, "Consumer Societies and the Consumer Cooperative Movement in Russia, 1897–1917" (Ph.D. diss., University of Michigan, 1977), 62.

32. A. S. Irisov, *Kooperatsiia i tekushschi moment* (Moscow, 1917), 6.

33. *Trudy pervago vserossiskago s"ezda deiatelei obshchestv narodnykh universitetov i drugikh prosvetitel'nykh uchrezhdenii chastnoi initsiativy, S. Peterburg, 3–7 Ianvaria 1908* (Saint Petersburg, 1908), 25.

34. Ibid., 113. Totomiants would write to Tolstoy describing the ethical and economic bases of cooperatives in hopes of securing his endorsement.

Tolstoy replied: "I am bound to admit that cooperative activity, the founding of cooperatives and participation in them is the only social activity which a moral, self-respecting person who doesn't wish to be a party to violence can take part in our time. . . . If I were young I would take up this task, and even now I don't despair of doing what I can among the peasantry who are near and dear to me." R. F. Christian, *Tolstoy's Letters*, 2:696 (23 January 1910). Totomiants inaugurated Russia's first university courses in cooperation in 1910 and gave courses on the history and theory of cooperation. After teaching two years in higher colleges of commerce and the Polytechnic Institute in Saint Petersburg, he moved to Moscow and lectured at Moscow University and the Moscow Institute of Commerce. E. M. Kayden and A. I. Antsiferov, *The Cooperative Movement in Russia during the War* (New Haven, Conn., 1929), 163.

35. "Allocations per society and per member both more than doubled." Salzman, "Consumer Societies," 201–2.

36. Anita B. Baker, "Rural Education in Russia: *Vneshkol'noe Obrazovanie* and the Cooperatives," *Slavic and European Education Review*, no. 1 (1977), 20–21.

37. I. Zhilkin noted in mid-1914 that a number of provincial newspapers had begun devoting substantial space to the cooperative movement, and that the "living pulse of local social interaction" was shifting from the zemstvos to the pervasively growing cooperatives. "Now the cultural and educational initiative is coming from below." In his regular column for *The Messenger of Europe*, he summarized information from several newspapers on the growth of cooperation across the empire. "Provintsial'noe obozrenie," *Vestnik Evropy*, no. 5 (1913), 367–69.

38. A. K. Klepikov, *V "Nizinakh." Stseny iz derevenskoi zhizni.* (Moscow, 1912), 6.

39. Ibid., 13.

40. See Seregny: "Teachers' lack of rights *(bespravie)* was most evident in . . . matters of transfers and dismissals, where teachers lacked the right of self-defense before local school boards and even of being informed of the motives behind disciplinary action." *Russian Teachers*, 16.

41. *V "Nizinakh,"* 33.

42. "Tiatr i potrebitel'nyia o-va," ibid., 58.

43. A. Tikhii, "Derevenskii teatr pod Moskvoiu," *Shkola i zhizn'*, no. 24 (16 June 1914), 661.

44. Ibid., 662.

45. *Vtoroi Vserossiiskii S"ezd po kooperatsii v g. Kieve 1–7 avgusta 1913 g. Trudy*, Vyp. I (Kiev, 1915), 28.

46. This sort of People's House can be seen as the ultimate response to the anomaly on which Gogol constructed *Revizor:* the provincial town provided by the center with an array of services the locals neither want nor understand very clearly.

47. *Vtoroi Vserossiiskii S"ezd,* 29.

48. E. V. Sakharova, ed., *Vasilii Dmitrievich Polenov Pisma, dnevnik, vospominaniia* (Moscow, 1950), 411.

49. A. K. Klepikov, "Na zare," 35.

50. The booklet he published on simple stage production circulated widely. N. V. Skorodumov, *Novyi metod uproshchennykh postanovok: ustroistvo stseny i dekoratsii* (Moscow, 1913).

51. O. A. Laskovskaia, *V. D. Polenov 1842–1927* (Moscow, 1946), 45.

52. E. Tikhii, "Derevenskii teatr," 662.

53. A. K. Klepikov, "Na zare," 38.

54. *Trudy pervago vserossiiskago s"ezda deiatelei obshchestv narodnykh universitetov i drugikh prosvetitel'nykh uchrezhdenii chastnoi initsiativy S.-Peterburg 3–7 ianvaria 1908 g.* (Saint Petersburg, 1908), 117, 26, 140.

55. *Vserossiiskii s"ezd po bor'be s pianstvom,* 3 vols. (Saint Petersburg, 1909–10), 2:517.

56. Sakharova, *Vasilii Dmitrievich Polenov,* 414. He had given some cause for imperial displeasure when the Academy of Arts was reorganized in the early 1890s. Alexander III had ordered the Wanderers brought in, and Polenov was one of the five, along with Repin, who sat on the commission that drafted the new statute. Polenov fought hard to remove all the Academy positions from imperial patronage and make them elective. He failed, and was himself excluded from the teaching staff. Elizabeth Kridl Valkenier, *Russian Realist Art* (New York, 1989), 134. Valkenier calls Polenov "culturally . . . the most sophisticated Peredvizhnik."

57. V. V. Tikhonovich, "Narodnyi teatr po soobshcheniiam s mest," *Uchitel' i shkola,* nos. 17–18 (September 1914).

58. Ibid., 19.

59. TsGALI, fond 991, op. 1, ed. khr. 843.

60. "S.-V.," in *Ekho otvetnoe* (Saint Petersburg, 1913), 23.

61. TsGALI, file on the 1913 jubilee. Fond 991, op. 1, ed. khr. 978.

62. Leningradskii Gosudarstvennyi Institut teatra, musiki i kinematografii. Kabinet rukopisnykh i ikonograficheskikh materialov. Fond 32, op. 1, ed. khr. 119.

63. Petr, "Desiatiletie teatra," 930.

64. Ibid., 931.

65. TsGALI, fond 2413, op. 1, ed. khr., 1059.

66. A. Mashirov-Samobytnik, "Istoriia proletkul'ta (1905–1917)," *Voprosy literatury,* no. 1 (1958), 174. A. S. Popov published the notes, based on recollections written down in 1933.

67. Quoted in N. F. Skarskaia and P. P. Gaideburov, *Na stsene i v zhizni* (Moscow, 1959), 24.

68. Quoted ibid., 27.

69. Quoted ibid., 19, from "Terek," no. 4309 (8 May 1912).

70. I. V. Shuvalov mentioned this in his 1958 recollections.

71. Quoted in Dreiden, ed., *Pavel Pavlovich Gaideburov,* 31.

72. Golovinskaia, "Peredvizhnoi teatr," 204.

73. Petr, "Desiatiletie teatra," 930.

74. S. V. Panina, *Narodnyi Dom* (Saint Petersburg, 1918), iii.

75. "Organizatsiia narodnykh teatrov," ibid., 187–211, 191.

76. Iurii Il'ich Kir'ianov, *Zhiznennii uroven' rabochikh Rossii (konets xix–nachalo xx vv.)* (Moscow, 1979), 55, 80. "In Moscow province the proportion of workers on the job more than eleven hours a day decreased from 80 percent in 1895 to only 6 percent in 1908" (63).

77. L. N. Kleinbort, *Ocherkii rabochei intelligentsii,* 2 vols. (Saint Petersburg, 1923), 2:12.

78. Joseph Macleod, *Actors Cross the Volga* (London, 1946), 37.

79. N. I. Nikolaev, "Po povodu odnoi 'ankety,'" in his *Efemeridy* (Kiev, 1912), 134.

80. L. N. Kleinbort, "Rabochaia intelligentsiia i iskusstvo," *Vestnik Evropy,* no. 8 (1913), 228.

81. Ibid., 221–22.

82. Kleinbort, *Ocherkii rabochei intelligentsii,* 43.

83. A. K. Klepikov, "Na zare," 46.

84. Kleinbort, "Maksim Gor'kii i chitatel iz nizov," 172. Gorky took part in organizing instruction for workers at the Kornilov Sunday school and in the workers club "Znanie i svet," which was "a refuge for revolutionaries on the eve of the 1905 events." Skorobogatov, *Zhizn' i stsena,* 201.

85. Tikhonovich, "Narodnyi teatr," 6.

86. Kleinbort, "Rabochaia intelligentsia," 218.

87. "O raskole v rabochem teatre," *Put' pravdy,* 27 April 1914.

88. D. Lentsov [D. Odintsov], "Rabochii teatr," *Put' pravdy,* 20 April 1914, p. 4.

89. A. Mashirov-Samobytnik, "Istoriia proletkul'ta (1905–1917)," 174.

90. "Gor'kaia sud'bina Pisemskago v 'Rabochem teatre,'" *Rabochii* (25 May 1914).

91. Tikhii, "Derevenskii teatr," 664.

92. A. A. Cherepnin, "Gde-zhe obshchedostupnye teatry?" *Kopeika-Moskva,* no. 98 (13 August 1909).

CHAPTER SEVEN

1. V. Kh. Davatts, *K voprosu o postroike narodnago doma v g. Vol'ske* (Vol'sk, 1915), 1–3. He pointed out that the need for education and "free cultural unification" had special priority, and that People's Houses with theatres responded directly to the need.

2. Khar'kovskoe Obshchestvo Gramotnosti, *Narodnyi Dom, ego zadachi i obshchestvennoe znachenie. Doklad . . . V. Ia. Danilevskago* (Kharkov, 1915), 33.

3. E. Zviagintsev, *Komu i zachem nuzhny narodnye doma?* 2d ed. (Moscow, 1918), 14–15.

4. P. P. Gaideburov, "Predislovie," *Zapiski Peredvizhnogo Obshchedostupnago Teatra,* no. 1 (March 1914), 1.

5. V. R. Leikina-Svirskaia, *Russkaia intelligentsiia,* 183–84. She quotes V. A. Teliakov to the effect that although noble homes remained closed to them, "artists, painters and musicians began to be regarded in the same way as doctors, priests, engineers, [and] superintendents of power stations."

6. V. V. Tikhonovich, *Samodeiatel'nyi teatr* (Vologda, 1922), 27–28.

7. Zviagintsev, *Komu i zachem,* 36.

8. V. V. Tikhonovich, "Vopros narodnago teatra," *Uchitel' i shkola,* nos. 15–16 (1915), 17, 19.

9. Walkin, *The Rise of Democracy,* 139–40. "The first congress of cooperative societies in 1908 was greeted with great enthusiasm, so much so that the government closed it before it had completed its work. The second congress, held in 1912, was likewise very active. Although the leaders of the consumers' cooperatives could not participate, unofficially they took part in the work of the congress. The third congress, in 1913, which again included all cooperative societies, was greeted with even more enthusiasm than the first, although its chairman was a government appointee."

10. *Trudy sozvannogo Khar'kovskim obshchestvom gramotnosti 7–12 iiunia 1915 g. v g. Khar'kove s"ezda po voprosam organizatsii razumnykh razvlechenia dlia naseleniia Khar'kovskoy gubernii* (Kharkov, 1915). Hereafter cited in chapter as *TsK.*

11. Zemstvo budgets had risen an average 14 percent per year from 1903 to 1913. Zemstvo interest in People's Houses represented a recent development.

12. Tikhonovich, *Samodeiatel'nyi teatr,* 28. The proceedings of the Iaroslavl conference were not published.

13. TsGIA, fond 1284, opis 188, ed. khr. 53; 10 June 1915.

14. Klepikov, *Na zare,* 55.

15. *Trudy Vserossiiskogo s"ezda deiatelei narodnogo teatra v Moskve, 27 dekabria 1915–5 ianvaria 1916* (Petrograd, 1919). Hereafter cited in chapter as *TV.*

16. *TV,* 220. (The report of the theatre of the Rublevsk Pumping Station, which consisted mainly of employees and their families, stated that they performed mainly Ostrovsky plays and Chekhov vaudevilles.[29])

17. Salzman, "Consumer Societies," 4.

18. Lydia Armand, "Narodnyi teatr i kooperatsiia," *TV,* 73–81.

19. Salzman, "Consumer Societies," 194. "In the fall, the union was told privately that the police were planning to arrest several of its leaders and was considering banning all cultural activity."

20. "Organizatsiia derevenskogo teatra kruzhka i ego truppy," Otdel Rukopisei, Gos. Biblioteka Im. Lenina (Moscow) Fond 300, 17172-1/AC, Papka No. IVb, 5, l. 16.

21. Ligovsk Narodnyi Dom Panina, *Narodnyi Dom* (Petrograd, 1918), 403.

22. Zviagintsev, *Komu i zachem nuzhnye narodnye doma?* 7.

23. Ibid., 36–37. Besides youths, this drama group attracted older peasants in their thirties and even a man age seventy.

24. Panina, *Narodnyi Dom,* 379. In the Baltic provinces, where agricultural societies, temperance societies, and cultural circles played a role comparable to that of the cooperatives in the central provinces, the "people's house" designation was not used. Hereafter cited in chapter as *ND.*

25. Davatts, *K voprosom o postroike narodnago doma,* 4.

26. L. Armand and A. Nikitin, *Narodnye Doma* (Moscow, 1918), 13.

27. Zviagintsev, *Komu i zachem,* 14.

28. Otdel Rukopisei, Gos. Biblioteka Im. Lenina. Fond 300, 17172-1/AC, Papka No. VII, 58.

29. Zviagintsev, *Komu i zachem,* 41.

30. Ernest Poole, *The Village* (New York, 1918). Although Poole published a book-length profile of the village, he failed to name it. To get there took five hours by eastbound train, then a few hours more by steamer up an unnamed river. It may reasonably be assumed that Tarasov's village lay in Iaroslavl province. Hereafter cited in chapter as *V.*

31. Samuel N. Harper Collection. Box 61, File 10. Typescript: "A Week with the Russian Army," 7.

32. Ibid., Box 27, File 22, 122. He summarized remarks on the food question by economist S. N. Prokopovich.

33. E. V. Sakharova, *V. D. Polenov,* 413–14.

34. See J. L. H. Keep, *The Russian Revolution: A Study in Mass Mobilization* (New York, 1976), 167, 169.

35. The condition of the army and the cumulative effect of political propaganda within its ranks must remain a question for specialists. But the private impression of a Moscow professor who began to keep a diary in 1917 is worth noting. "The destruction of the army, undertaken in the name of underground slogans that were designed for the struggle against tsarism, has of course brought forth the fruit it was meant to yield: transformation of an army that had fought for two and a half years into a crowd of propagandized bandits." Terence Emmons, ed. and trans., *The Time of Troubles: The Diary of Iurii Vladimirovich Got'e* (Princeton, N.J., 1988), 27. (From Got'e's entry dated 8/16 July 1917.)

36. A. A. Bardovskii studied the surviving *ankety* and wrote a book about the tour based on memoirs, articles, extracts, letters, and a collective diary: *Teatral'nyi zritel' na fronte v kanun oktiabria* (Leningrad, 1928). Hereafter cited in chapter as *Tz*.

37. P. P. Gaideburov and N. F. Skarskaia, "Na frontovykh spektakliakh v predoktiabr'skie dni," *Neva*, no. 11 (1967), 210–11.

38. *Tz*, 74. The success of Bolshevik propaganda among the soldiers emerges clearly in the responses to the Wanderers. Richard Pipes speaks to the magnitude of their print campaign: "In early July [1917], the combined printing of the Bolshevik press was 320,000 copies. In addition, *Soldatskaia Pravda* [their soldiers' newspaper initiated 15 April 1917] printed 350,000 pamphlets and broadsheets. This was a most remarkable achievement, considering that in February 1917 the Bolsheviks had had no press." *The Russian Revolution* (New York, 1990), 410.

39. René Morax, *Tell* (Lausanne, 1914). The Russian translation was published in Petrograd in 1920.

40. Keep, *The Russian Revolution*, 456.

41. Ernest Poole, *The Dark People* (New York, 1918), 107–8.

42. Lars Kleberg, "'People's Theatre' and the Revolution: On the History of a Concept before and after 1917," in *Art, Society, Revolution: Russia 1917–1921*, ed. N. A. Nilsson (Stockholm, 1979), 193. Speaking of the subordination of popular theatre and festivals to bureaucratic control in 1919, James von Geldern remarks: "The people's culture could not be trusted to the people." *Bolshevik Festivals, 1917–1920* (Berkeley and Los Angeles, 1993), 136.

43. Kleberg, "People's Theatre," 194.

44. N. B. Volkova, "Teatral'naia deiatel'nost' Proletkul'ta," in *Russkii sovetskii teatr* (Leningrad, 1968), 329.

45. Lynn Mally, *Culture of the Future: The Proletkult Movement in Revolutionary Russia* (Berkeley and Los Angeles, 1990), 50–51. "The popularity of this cultural movement astounded even its most optimistic supporters. New organizations sprang up 'like mushrooms after a spring rain.'"

46. Ibid., 67.

47. Kleberg, 191.

48. Ibid., 195. The congress meeting had to be postponed until November.

49. *Izvestiia*, no. 199 (751), 9 September 1919. A new central theatrical organ, Tsentroteatr, had been formed 26 August to provide repertorial direction. Richard Thorpe, *The Management of Culture*, 164.

50. Otdel Rukopisei, Gos. Biblioteka Im. Lenina. Fond 300, 17172-1/AC, Papka No. 1, 50.

51. Ibid.

52. M. D. Shishkin, *Iz vospominanii kooperativnykh i politicheskikh* (New York, 1960), 38. Besides his seminal contribution to the Golitsyn circle, Shishkin had worked for Tsentrosoiuz helping to organize independent peasant theatre circles. He pointed out that in Lenin's mind, "cooperation was a laboratory for Menshevism" (30).

53. Writing of the administration of theatre policy in 1920, Katerina Clark notes: "The theatre under War Communism was artificially maintained at the very time it might otherwise have collapsed under dire conditions, for it was subsidized by some government agency. . . . There was an official policy that ultimately all the seats should be free, and this policy was achieved to a greater extent in Petrograd than anywhere else. The aim was to squeeze out private theatres by unfair competition." *Petersburg, Crucible of Cultural Revolution* (Cambridge, Mass., 1995), 107.

54. "Narodnye doma," *Moskva Entsiklopediia* (Moscow, 1980), 450.

55. Mally, *Culture of the Future,* 195.

56. Thomas Remington, *Building Socialism in Bolshevik Russia* (Pittsburgh, 1984), 133.

57. Michael Heller, "The First Warning," *Survey* 24 (Summer 1979), 179.

58. Dmitri Volkogonov, *Lenin: A New Biography* (New York, 1994), 367 (quoted from the Archives of the President of the Russian Federation).

59. Heller, "First Warning," 182. The Decree on Administrative Exile was not promulgated until 10 August 1922. The number of those exiled remains uncertain, but Heller notes (186) that "Agricultural studies . . . suffered severe losses . . . and the leaders of the cooperative movement."

60. Volkogonov, *Lenin,* 136 (quoted from Party Central Committee Archives).

61. V. V. Tikhonovich, *Samodeiatel'nyi teatr. Posobie dlia samodeiatel'nomu teatr i teatral'nomu prosveshcheniiu* (Vologda, 1922), 8.

62. Lidiia Spiridonova, "Gorky and Stalin (According to New Materials from A. M. Gorky's Archive) (trans.)," *Russian Review* 54, no. 3 (July 1995), 412–13.

63. Norman Stone, *The Eastern Front, 1914–1917* (New York, 1975), 285. See also Norman Stone, *Europe Transformed, 1878–1914* (Cambridge, Mass, 1984), 334–39.

64. Stone, *Eastern Front,* 284–85. "Even the building industry, normally one to be hit in wartime, employed 1,500,000 people in 1917, a rise of one third."

65. Ibid., 204.

66. On the muting of patriotism after 1914 and the increasing reliance of patriotic culture on folklore and nostalgia: Hubertus Jahn, *Patriotic Culture in Russia during World War I* (Ithaca, N.Y., 1995), 171.

67. Stone, *Eastern Front,* 283.

68. Thomas Porter and William Gleason, "The *Zemstvo* and Public Initiative in Late Imperial Russia," *Russian History* 21, no. 4 (Winter 1994), 435.

CONCLUSION

1. Norbert Elias, *The Civilizing Process,* 2 vols., trans. Edmund Jephcott (New York, 1978, 1982), 2:316–19. Hereafter cited in chapter as *CP.*

2. Norbert Elias, *The Court Society,* trans. Edmund Jephcott (New York, 1983), 242–43. Hereafter cited in chapter as *CS.*

3. Ibid., 252.

4. Edward Gibbon, *Memoirs of My Life* (Harmondsworth, Middlesex, Eng., 1984), 136.

5. Lawrence Stone called attention to the similarity in literacy rates—between one-third and two-thirds—in France before 1789 and England before its seventeenth-century revolution. Literacy was in the same range in Russia in 1917. Lawrence Stone, "Literacy and Education in England 1640–1900," *Past and Present,* no. 42 (February 1969), 138.

6. Jack Goody and Ian Watt, "The Consequences of Literacy," in *Literacy in Traditional Societies,* ed. Jack Goody (Cambridge, 1968), 62–63.

7. Jesper Svenbro, *"Phrasikleia": Anthropologie de la lecture en Grèce ancienne* (Paris, 1988), 187–88.

8. Vladimir Fillipov, *Zadachi narodnogo teatra i ego proshloe v Rossii* (Moscow, 1918), 5.

9. *Protokoly . . . pechati,* 383.

10. Konstantin Paustovsky, *The Story of a Life* (New York, 1964), 55.

11. Poole, *The Dark People,* 224.

12. Reginald Zelnik, ed. and trans., *A Radical Worker in Tsarist Russia: The Autobiography of Semën Ivanovich Kanatchikov* (Stanford, Calif., 1986), 48.

13. But also see G. Freeze: "The acute concern for 'social origin' in the early Soviet state, especially the disfranchisement of entire categories on the grounds of their legal origin (the *lishentsy*), represented a kind of inverted *soslovie* policy until formal abandonment of the exclusion in 1936. As has indeed been noted before, in this and other respects Soviet social policy evinced some significant continuities . . . with the *ançien regime.*" "The *Soslovie* (Estate) Paradigm and Russian Social History," *American Historical Review* 91, no.1 (1986), 35 n. 88.

14. Quoted in Bernard Williams, *Shame and Necessity* (Berkeley and Los Angeles, 1993), 163. Hereafter cited in chapter as *SN.*

15. See above, Introduction, note 61.

16. Richard Seaford, *Reciprocity and Ritual* (Oxford, 1994), 360. Hereafter cited in chapter as *RR.*

17. The plays themselves addressed the disparity between cultivated and natural or unconsidered behavior. As an Italian scholar put it, "The world of Russian literature is . . . comprehended between two universally opposing forces: the world of European culture and the world of ideal (or idealized) 'primitive' life." Vittorio Strada, "K teorii Russkogo romana," *Rossiia/Russia* (Turin), no. 4 (1980), 166. This is as true of Russian plays as it is of the Russian novel.

18. James Riordan supplies the scenario for "Indians, British, and Reds," acted out south of Moscow in 1924 in *Sport in Soviet Society* (Cambridge, 1977). For the scenario for "The Mystery of the Emancipation of Labor" (1920), see *Russkii sovetskii teatr,* 263–64.

19. See Katerina Clark: "The first revolutionary mass spectacles were meant to function as crucibles for transforming consciousness among the illiterate masses, to break down the gulf between actors and audience, between cultural professionals and the masses. It was believed that if the masses participated in a ritual reenactment of revolution, they might experience a revolution of their very psyches." *Petersburg, Crucible of Cultural Revolution,* 243.

20. Ken Jowitt, *The New World Disorder: The Leninist Extinction* (Berkeley and Los Angeles, 1992), 249.

21. Calhoun, *Habermas and the Public Sphere,* 471.

22. "Solving problems by dialogue, process, law, and debate requires certain shared beliefs that did not flourish in an atmosphere of suspicion and mistrust. Yet there can be no doubt that a public sphere was developing. It was neither rooted enough nor powerful enough to overcome the crises that called forth the ultimate resort to repression and violence." Samuel D. Kassow, "Russia's Unrealized Civil Society," in *Between Tsar and People,* 370.

23. A. K. Klepikov, *"Na zare,"* 25.

24. See T. Shanin's foreword to Tatyana Zaslavskaya, *The Second Socialist Revolution* (Bloomington, Ind., 1990), xi–xiv.

25. Basile Kerblay, *Modern Soviet Society* (New York, 1983), 278–79.

26. Havelock, *The Muse Learns to Write,* 120.

Works Cited

ARCHIVES

Tsentral'nyi Gosudarstvennyi Istoricheskii Arkhiv (Leningrad)

TsGIA	Fond 575	Glavnoe upravlenie neokladnykh sborov i kazennoi prodazhi pitei
	Fond 770	Karpov
	Fond 776	Glavnoe upravlenie po delam pechati
	Fond 1284	Kantseliariia Ministra Vnutrennykh Del Glavnoe upravlenie po delam mestnago khoziastva

Tsentral'nyi Gosudarstvennyi Arkhiv Literatury i Iskusstva (Moscow)

TsGALI	Fond 991	Bibliotek. Peredvizhnogo Teatra

Tsentral'naia Nauchnaia Biblioteka Vserossiiskoe Teatral'noe Obshchestvo. Sektor redkoi knigi i rukopisei. (Moscow)

TsNB Fond teatral'nykh memuarov (Klepikov)

Leningradskii Gosudarstvennyi Institut Teatra, Muzyki i Kinematografii.

LGITMik	Fond 32	Kabinet rukopisnykh i ikonograficheskikh materialov

Gosudarstvennaia Biblioteka im. Lenina. Otdel rukopisei. (Moscow)

GBL	Fond 300	Tolbuzin

University of Chicago Library. Department of Special Collections
Samuel Harper Collection

UNPUBLISHED MEMOIRS AND DISSERTATIONS

Fisher, John R. "The Witte Conference on the Needs of Agriculture in Russia: 1902–1905." Ph.D. diss., University of Toronto, 1978.

Frierson, Cathy. "From Narod to Kulak: Peasant Images in Russia, 1870–1885." Ph.D. diss., Harvard University, 1985.

Gaideburov Memoirs. TsGALI Fond 991. Op. 60, ed. khr. 348.

Gasparov, Irina Paperno. "The Individual in Culture: N. G. Chernyshevsky. A Study in the Semiotics of Behavior." Ph.D. diss., Stanford University, 1984.

Guffee, Ruth Meyer. "The Yasnaya Polyana School, 1859–1862: Its Place in Leo Tolstoy's Development as a Thinker." Ph.D. diss., Yale University, 1982.

Harper Collection (S. N.). University of Chicago. Typescript: "A Week with the Russian Army." Box 61, File 10.

Ketchian, Sonia. "The Plays of Alexsej Potexin." Ph.D. diss., Harvard University, 1974.

Klepikov, A. K. "Iz teatral'nykh vospominanii." "Na zare samodeiatel'nogo teatra." Tsentral'naia nauchnaia biblioteka V.T.O. Sektor redkoi knigi i rukopisei. Fond teatral'nykh memuarov. VTO/584 and VTO/K48.

Machan, Helen W. "The Popular-Theatre Movement in France." Ph.D. diss., University of Illinois, 1950.

Salzman, Catherine. "Consumer Societies and the Consumer Cooperative Movement in Russia, 1897–1917." Ph.D. diss., University of Michigan, 1977.

Shakanov, A. Ia. "Vospominaniia ob Obshchedostupnom teatre." TsGALI. Fond 2413. Op. 1, ed. khr. 1059.

Swift, Anthony. "Theater for the People: The Politics of Popular Culture in Urban Russia, 1861–1917." Ph.D. diss., University of California, Berkeley, 1992.

Thorpe, Richard. "The Management of Culture in Revolutionary Russia: The Imperial Theaters and the State, 1897–1928." Ph.D. diss., Princeton University, 1990.

PUBLISHED ESSAYS

Aikhenval'd, Iu. "Otritsanie teatra." In *Sporakh o teatre. Sbornik,* 11–38. Moscow, 1914.

Akimova, T. M. "Russkii narodnyi teatr v issledovaniiakh poslevoennykh let." *Sovetskaia etnografiia* 5 (1976): 100–106.

Alchevskaia, Kh. D. "Istoriia otkrytiia shkoly v derevne Alekseevke Mikhailovskoi volosti." *Iuzhnyi Krai,* nos. 53–54 (February 1881). Reprinted in her *Peredumannie i perezhitoe,* 201–25. Moscow, 1912.

Armand, Lydia. "Narodnyi teatr i kooperatsiia." In *Trudy Vserossiiskogo s"ezda deiatelei narodnogo teatra v Moskve, 27 dekabria 1915–5 ianvaria 1916,* 73–80. Petrograd, 1919.

Baker, Anita B. "Rural Education in Russia: *Vneshkol'noe Obrazovanie* and the Cooperatives." *Slavic and European Education Review,* no. 1 (1977): 10–22.

Balitskaia, A. S. "Iz derevni." *Obrazovanie* (April 1894): 139–45.

Balukhatyi, S. "Prikhod M. Gor'kogo v teatr. Rabota ego nad p'esoi 'Meshchane.'" In *"Meshchane" M. Gor'kogo*, 68–90. Moscow, 1941.

Bekkerevich, N. "Pervaia popytka ustroistva professional'nago teatra v sele." In *Narodnyi teatr. Sbornik*, 133–50. Moscow, 1896.

Blok, Aleksandr. "O teatre." In *Sobranie Sochinenii v vos'mi tomakh*, 5:241–76. Moscow and Leningrad, 1962.

Borodin, D. N. "Popechitel'stva o narodnoi trezvosti." In *Vserossiiskii s"ezd po bor'be s p'ianstvom*. 3 vols., 2:905. Saint Petersburg, 1909–10.

Borsay, Peter. "The Rise of the Promenade: The Social and Cultural Use of Space in the English Provincial Town c. 1660–1800." *British Journal for Eighteenth-Century Studies* 9 (1986): 125–39.

Bradley, Joseph. "The Moscow Workhouse and Urban Welfare Reform in Russia." *Russian Review* 41, no. 4 (October 1982): 427–44.

Brooks, Jeffrey. "Readers and Reading at the End of the Tsarist Era." In *Literature and Society in Imperial Russia, 1800–1914*, edited by William Mills Todd III, 97–150. Stanford, Calif., 1977.

Brooks, E. Willis. "The Improbable Connection: D. A. Miljutin and N. G. Ĉernyŝevskij, 1848–1862." *Jahrbücher für Geschichte Osteuropas* 37, no. 1 (1989): 21–44.

Brower, Daniel. "L'urbanisation Russe à la fin du XIXe siècle." *Annales, Economies, Sociétés, Civilisations*, no. 1 (January–February 1977): 70–86.

Bunakov, N. F. "Desiatiletie sel'skoi shkoly i obiazatel'noie vseobshche obuchenoe." *Russkii narodnyi uchitel'*, nos. 6–7 (1895): 275–96.

———. "Nechto o krest'ianskikh vozzreniiakh na gramatnost' i shkolu." In his *Izbranye pedagogicheskie sochineniia*, 194–210. Moscow, 1953.

———. "Opyt narodnago teatra." In his *Izbrannye pedagogicheskie sochineniia*, 298–318. Moscow, 1953.

———. "Razmyshleniia po povodu vystavki narodnago teatra ustroennoi v Moskve v 1895." In *Narodnyi teatr. Sbornik*, 168–75. Moscow, 1896.

———. "Sel'skaia shkola i narodnaia zhizn'. Stat'ia X. Opyt narodnago teatra." *Russkii nachal'nyi uchitel'*, no. 1 (1892): 7–27.

Bunakova, L. "Istoriia Petinskago Nar. Doma." In *Trudy Vserossiiskogo s"ezda deiatelei narodnogo teatra v Moskve, 27 dekabria 1915–5 ianvaria 1916*, 156–62. Petrograd, 1919.

———. "Zametki o narodnom teatre." *Teatr i iskusstvo*, no. 36 (1910): 663–66.

Burns, Alfred. "Athenian Literacy in the Fifth Century B.C." *Journal of the History of Ideas* 42, no. 3 (1981): 371–87.

Bushnell, John. "Peasants in Uniform." *Journal of Social History* 13, no. 4 (Summer 1980): 565–76.

Byrnes, Robert F. "'Between Two Fires': Kliuchevskii on Religion and the Russian Orthodox Church." *Modern Greek Studies Yearbook* 6 (1990): 157–85.

Chargonin, A. "Neskol'ko slov o repertuare narodnago teatra." *Teatr i iskusstvo*, no. 32 (7 August 1905): 513–15.
Charskii, V. "Khudozhestvennyi teatr." In *Krizis teatr. Sbornik statei*, 126–56. Moscow, 1908.
Cherepnin, A. A. "Gde-zhe obshchedostupnye teatry?" *Kopeika-Moskva* (13 August 1909): 8.
Cohen, Adir. "The Educational Philosophy of Tolstoy." *Oxford Review of Education* 7, no. 3 (1981): 241–51.
Danilov, F. "Iarmarochnyia narodnyia razvlecheniia." *Obrazovanie*, nos. 7–8 (1897): 231–39.
Danilov, S. S. "Materialy po istorii russkogo zakonodatel'stva o teatre." In *O teatre. Sbornik statei*, 177–203. Moscow and Leningrad, 1940.
Debreczeny, Paul. "Chekhov's Use of Impressionism in the 'House with the Mansard.'" In *Russian Narrative and Visual Art: Varieties of Seeing*, edited by Roger Anderson and Paul Debreczeny, 101–23. Gainesville, Fla., 1994.
Derzhavin, G. R. "Zapiski." In *Russkie memuary: izbrannye strannitsy XVIII vek*, edited by I. I. Podol'skaia, 117–67. Moscow, 1988.
Dmitrievskii, V. N. "Nekotorye voprosy metodiki izucheniia interesov i redaktsii teatral'nogo zritelia." In *Khudozhestvennoe vospriiateie. Sborniky*, edited by B. S. Meilakh, 366–85. Leningrad, 1971.
Dolgopolov, L. K. "Vokrug 'Detei solntsa'." In *M. Gor'kii i ego sovremenniki*, edited by K. D. Muratova, 79–109. Leningrad, 1968.
Donskov, Andrew. "L. N. Tolstoy as an Editor of Literature by Peasant Writers." In *Crisis and Commitment: Studies in German and Russian Literature in Honour of J. W. Dyck*, edited by John Whiton, 41–47. Waterloo, 1983.
———. "The Peasant in Tolstoi's Thought and Writings." *Canadian Slavonic Papers* 21, no. 2 (1979): 183–96.
Drizen, N. V. [Osten-] "Vliianie teatra na detei i iunoshei shkol'nogo vozrasta." *Russkaia shkola*, no. 1 (1911): 38–52.
Edmondson, Linda. "Was there a Movement for Civil Rights in 1905?" In *Civil Rights in Imperial Russia*, edited by Olga Crisp and Linda Edmondson, 263–85. Oxford, 1989.
Efimenko, Aleksandra. "Zhenshchina v krestianskoi sem'e." In her *Obychnoe pravo*. Vol. 1 of *Issledovaniia narodnoi zhizni*, 49–123. Moscow, 1884.
Eklof, Ben. "Peasant Sloth Reconsidered: Strategies of Education and Learning in Rural Russia before the Revolution." *Journal of Social History* 14, no. 3 (Spring 1981): 355–85.
———. "Ways of Seeing: Recent Anglo-American Studies of the Russian Peasant (1861–1914)." *Jahrbücher für Geschichte Osteuropas* 36, no. 1 (1988): 57–79.
———. "Worlds in Conflict: Patriarchal Authority, Discipline and the Russian School, 1861–1914." In *School and Society in Tsarist and Soviet Russia*, edited by Ben Eklof, 95–120. London, 1993.

Ely, Geoff. "Nations, Publics, and Political Cultures: Placing Habermas in the Nineteenth Century." In *Habermas and the Public Sphere,* edited by Craig Calhoun, 289–339. Cambridge, Mass., 1992.

Emer [M. V. Rklitskii]. "K voprosy ob organizatsii narodnykh trupp dlia teatral'nykh predstavlenii." *Russkoe bogatstvo,* no. 7 (June 1898): 80–88.

Emmons, Terence. "The Tsar's Reforms." Review of *The Great Reforms,* by W. Bruce Lincoln. *Times Literary Supplement,* 27 December 1991, p. 19.

Farnsworth, Beatrice. "The Litigious Daughter-in-Law: Family Relations in Rural Russia in the Second Half of the Nineteenth Century." In *Russian Peasant Women,* edited by Beatrice Farnsworth and Lynne Viola, 89–106. New York, 1992.

Filippov, Vladimir. "Ostrovskii v teatre. Statisticheskie materialy." In *A. N. Ostrovskii. Dnevnik i pis'ma. Teatr Ostrovskogo,* 263–84. Moscow and Leningrad, 1937.

Fisher, David J. "The Origins of the French Popular Theatre." *Journal of Contemporary History* 12 (1977): 461–97.

Florovsky, Georges. "The Problem of Old Russian Culture." *Slavic Review* 21, no. 1 (March 1962): 1–15.

Frank, Stephen. "Confronting the Domestic Other: Rural Popular Culture and Its Enemies in Fin-de-Siècle Russia." In *Cultures in Flux: Lower-Class Values, Practices, and Resistance in Late Imperial Russia,* edited by Stephen P. Frank and Mark D. Steinberg, 74–107. Princeton, N.J., 1994.

———. "Popular Justice, Community and Culture Among the Russian Peasantry, 1870–1900." *Russian Review* 46, no. 3 (July 1987): 239–65.

———. "'Simple Folk, Savage Customs?' Youth, Sociability, and the Dynamics of Culture in Rural Russia, 1856–1914." *Journal of Social History* 25, no. 4 (1992): 711–36.

Freeze, Gregory. "'Going to the Intelligentsia': The Church and its Urban Mission in Post-Reform Russia." In *Between Tsar and People: Educated Society and the Quest for Public Identity in Late Imperial Russia,* edited by Edith Clowes, Samuel Kassow, and James West, 215–32. Princeton, N.J., 1991.

———. "The *Soslovie* (Estate) Paradigm and Russian Social History." *American Historical Review* 91, no. 1 (1986): 11–36.

Frierson, C. A. "Rural Justice in Public Opinion: The *Volost'* Court Debate, 1861–1912." *Slavonic and East European Review* 64, no. 4 (October 1986): 526–45.

Frierson, Cathy. "Crime and Punishment in the Russian Village: Rural Concepts of Criminality at the End of the Nineteenth Century." *Slavic Review* 46, no. 1 (Spring 1987): 55–69.

Gaideburov, P. P. "Nashim budushchim zriteliam." In *Pavel Pavlovich Gaideburov: Literaturnoe nasledie,* edited by Simon Dreiden. 221–24. Moscow, 1977.

———. "Organizatsiia narodnykh teatrov." In *Narodnyi Dom. Sbornik,* 187–211. Petrograd, 1918.

———. "Polveka s Chekhovym." In *Pavel Pavlovich Gaideburov: Literaturnoe nasledie,* edited by Simon Dreiden, 134–59. Moscow, 1977. Reprint, *Teatral'nyi al'manakh* 7 (1946): 302–27.

———. "Predislovie." *Zapiski Peredvizhnogo Obshchedostupnago Teatra,* no. 1 (March 1914): 1.

———. "Za pervyi god deiatel'nosti peredvizhnogo teatra." *Biblioteka pervago dramaticheskago peredvizhnogo teatra,* seriia 1905 goda, 5 (Saint Petersburg, 1907): 3–34.

Gaideburov, P. P., and N. F. Skarskaia. "Na frontovykh spektakliakh v predoktiabr'skie dni." *Neva,* no. 11 (1967): 209–15.

Gogol', N. V. "Peterburgskaia stsena v 1835–36 g." In *Sobranie sochinenii v semi tomakh,* 6:455–65. Moscow, 1978.

Golovinskaia, E. D. "Peredvizhnoi teatr P. P. Gaideburova (Iz vospominanii)." In *Zapiski o teatre,* 199–216. Leningrad and Moscow, 1960.

Goody, Jack, and Ian Watt. "The Consequences of Literacy." In *Literacy in Traditional Societies,* edited by Jack Goody, 27–84. Cambridge, 1968.

Gorev, L. "Provintsial'naia pechat'." *Severnyi Vestnik,* no. 6 (1896): 298–306.

"Gor'kaia sud'bina Pisemskago v 'Rabochem teatre.'" *Rabochii,* 25 May 1914, p. 2.

Gorky, M. "*." In *Polveka dlia knigi. Literaturno-khudozhestvennyi sbornik,* 29–32. Moscow, 1916.

Grigorev, A. "O natsional'nom znachenii tvorchestve A. N. Ostrovskago." In *Sobranie Sochinenii,* 11:iii–61. Moscow, 1915.

Guroff, Gregory, and S. Frederick Starr. "A Note on Urban Literacy in Russia, 1890–1914." *Jahrbücher für Geschichte Osteuropas* 19 (1971): 520–31.

Heller, Michael. "The First Warning." *Survey* 24 (Summer 1979): 159–89.

Henis, Wilhelm. "Goethe, Goya and the Threat of Modernity." *Times Literary Supplement,* 11 November 1994, pp. 15–16.

Herlihy, Patricia. "'Joy of the Rus'': Rites and Rituals of Russian Drinking." *Russian Review* 50, no. 2 (April 1991): 131–47.

Holquist, James M. "The Metaphor of Literacy in Late Tolstoi." *Canadian-American Slavic Studies* 12, no. 4 (Winter 1978): 549–70.

Hutchinson, J. F. "Science, Politics and the Alcohol Problem in post-1905 Russia." *Slavonic and East European Review* 58, no. 2 (April 1980): 232–54.

Iartsev, Aleksei. "Pervyi fabrichnye teatry v Rossii." *Istoricheskii vestnik* (May 1900): 645–53.

Iur'ev, S. A. "Derevenskii teatr." *Artist,* no. 3 (September 1889): 46–50.

Kahan, Arcadius. "Determinants of the Incidence of Literacy in Rural Nineteenth Century Russia." In *Education and Economic Development,* edited by C. Arnold Anderson and Mary Jean Bowman, 298–302. Chicago, 1965.

Kaiser, Friedhelm. "Der europäische Anteil an der russischen Rechtsterminologie der petrinischen Zeit." *Forschungen zur osteuropäischen Geschichte* 10 (1965): 75–333.

Kassow, Samuel D. "Russia's Unrealized Civil Society." In *Between Tsar and People: Educated Society and the Quest for Public Identity in Late Imperial Russia,* edited by Edith Clowes, Samuel Kassow, and James West, 367–71. Princeton, N.J., 1991.

Kastorskii, S. V. "Pisatel'-dramaturg A. A. Potekhin." In *Iz istorii russkikh literaturnykh otnoshenii xviii–xx vekov,* edited by S. V. Kastorskii, 177–98. Moscow, 1959.

Khaichenko, G. A. "Narodnyi teatr." In *Russkaia khudozhestvennaia kul'tura kontsa XIX–nachala XX veka,* edited by A. D. Alekseev, 1:218–37. Moscow, 1968.

———. "Narodnyi teatr i dooktiabr'skaia 'Pravda.'" In *Voprosy teatra. Sbornik statei i materialov,* 138–53. Moscow, 1970.

Khorosh, M. "Tolstoi o Gor'kom." In *Na literaturnom postu,* 26–32. Moscow, 1928.

Khrulov, S. S. "Iz istorii bor'by s agrarnym dvizheniem 1905–1906." *Krasnyi Arkhiv* 39 (1930): 76–107; 40 (September 1930): 41–48.

Kleberg, Lars. "'People's Theatre' and the Revolution: On the History of a Concept before and after 1917." In *Art, Society, Revolution: Russia 1917–1921,* edited by N. A. Nilsson, 179–97. Stockholm, 1979.

Kleinbort, L. N. "Maksim Gor'kii i chitatel' iz nizov." *Vestnik Evropy,* no. 12 (December 1913): 171–93.

———. "O raskole v rabochem teatre." *Put' pravdy,* 27 April 1914, p. 6.

———. "Rabochaia intelligentsiia i iskusstvo." *Vestnik Evropy,* no. 8 (1913): 215–28.

Klinchin, A. P. "Narodnyi teatr na politekhnicheskoi vystavke v Moskve." In *Teatral'noe nasledstvo. Soobshcheniia. Publikatsii,* 447–74. Moscow, 1956.

Konechnyi, A. M. "Peterburgskie narodnye gulian'ia na maslenoi i paskhal'noi nedeliakh." In *Peterburg i guberniia: Istoriko-etnograficheskie issledovaniia,* 21–52. Leningrad, 1988.

Korowin, Alexandre. "La Tempérance en Russie." In *Septième Congrès contre l'abus des boissons alcooliques,* 276–99. Paris, 1899–1900.

Kremlev, A. N. "O narodnom teatre v S.-Peterburge," *Novosti,* no. 276 (1894): 1–2.

Kuleshov, V. I., and A. A. Gozenpud. "Provintsial'nye gastroli M. S. Shchepkina." In *Teatral'noe nasledstvo,* 266–80. Moscow, 1956.

Lapatukhin, M. S. "N. F. Bunakov i ego Metodicheskaia Sistema." *Russkii iazyk v shkole,* no. 6 (1974): 51–56.

Latyshev, V. "Bunakov, Nikolai Fedorovich." *Kritiko-Biograficheskii Slovar' Russkikh Pisatelei i Uchenykh* 5 (1889): 363–75.

Lavrova, E. V. "Narodnye spektakli v derevne." *Obrazovanie,* nos. 5–6 (1897): 62–76.

Leifert, A. V. *Balaganyy.* Petrograd, 1922.

"Leninskaia 'Iskra' i teatr." In *Teatral'noe nasledstvo,* 115–35. Moscow, 1956.

Lentsov, D. [D. Odintsov]. "Rabochii teatr." *Put' pravdy,* 20 April 1914, p. 4.

Leskov, N. S. "Tupeinyi khudozhnik." In *Sobranie sochinenii,* 7:220–42. Moscow, 1958.

Lidtke, Vernon. "Nationalism and Socialism in Germany." *American Historical Review* 79, no. 1 (1974): 14–37.

Lindenmeyr, Adele. "Voluntary Associations and the Russian Autocracy." In *Carl Beck Papers in Russian and East European Studies,* no. 807 (June 1990): 23–45.

Loe, Mary Louise. "Gorky and Nietzsche: The Quest for a Russian Superman." In *Nietzsche in Russia,* edited by Bernice Glatzer Rosenthal, 251–74. Princeton, N.J., 1986.

Lomunov, K. N. "L. N. Tolstoi i narodnyi teatr." In *Tvorchestvo L. N. Tolstogo,* 502–58. Moscow, 1959.

Longo, Oddone. "The Theater of the *Polis.*" In *Nothing to Do with Dionysos?* edited by John J. Winkler and Froma Zeitlin, 13–19. Princeton, N.J., 1989.

Lotman, Iu. M. "Bytovoe povedenie i tipologiia kul'tury v Rossii xviii v." In *Kul'turnoe nasledie drevnei rusi,* 292–97. Moscow, 1976.

———. "Concerning Khlestakov." In *The Semiotics of Russian Cultural History,* edited by A. D. Nakhimovsky and A. S. Nakhimovsky, 150–87. Ithaca, N.Y., 1985.

———. "Dekabrist v povsednevnoi zhizni (Bytovoe povedenie kak istoriko-psikhologicheskaia kategoriia)." In *Literaturnoe nasledie Dekabristov* edited by V. G. Bazarov, 25–74. Leningrad, 1975.

———. "Teatr i teatral'nost v stroe kultury nachala xix veka." In *Stat'i po tipologii kul'tury,* 2:42–73. Tartu, 1973.

Lounela, Pekka. "Theatre by the People for the People: Amateur Theatre in Finland." *Cultures* 2, no. 3 (1976): 81–95.

McGowan, Randall. "The Body and Punishment in Eighteenth-Century England." *Journal of Modern History* 59, no. 4 (December 1987): 651–79.

Malnick, Bertha. "Russian Serf Theatres." *Slavonic and East European Review* 30, no. 75 (June 1952): 393–411.

Mashirov-Samobytnik, A. "Istoriia proletkul'ta (1905–1917)." *Voprosy literatury,* no. 1 (1958): 172–76.

———. "Peredvizhnoi teatr (k 20-letiiu khudozhestvennoi deiatel'nosti)." *Rabochii i teatry,* no. 13 (1925): 11.

McReynolds, Louise. "'The Incomparable' Anastasiia Vial'tseva and the Culture of Personality." In *Russia—Women—Culture,* edited by Helen Goscilo and Beth Holmgren, 273–94. Bloomington, Ind., 1996.

Mikhailovsky, N. K. "Literatura i zhizn'." *Russkoe bogatstvo,* no. 6 (June 1896): 42–61.

Mironov, Boris. "The Peasant Commune after the Reforms of the 1860s." In *The World of the Russian Peasant,* edited by Ben Eklof and Stephen Frank, 7–43. Winchester, Mass., 1990.

Monas, Sidney. "The Twilit Middle Class of Nineteenth-Century Russia." In *Between Tsar and People: Educated Society and the Quest for Public Identity in Late Imperial Russia,* edited by Edith W. Clowes, Samuel D. Kassow, and James L. West, 28–37. Princeton, N.J., 1991.

Mosse, George L. "Nationalism and Respectability." *Journal of Contemporary History* 17 (1982): 221–46.

"Narodnye doma." *Moskva Entsiklopediia.* 1980 ed.

Nemirovich-Danchenko, Vladimir. "Moskovskii obshchedostupnyi teatr." In his *Stati. Rechi. Besedy. Pis'ma,* 63–71. Moscow, 1952.

Nikolaev, N. I. "Po povodu odnoi 'ankety.'" In his *Efemeridy,* 132–37. Kiev, 1912.

Nikulina-Kositskaia, L. P. "Zapiski L. P. Nikulinoi-Kositskoi, artistki Imperatorskikh Moskovskikh Teatrov." *Russkaia starina* 21 (1878): 65–80, 281–304.

Novikov, Nikolai. "O vospitanii i nastavlenii detei." Translated by V. Snow. In *Russian Intellectual History,* edited by Marc Raeff, 61–86. New York, 1966.

Obodriaiushchii. "'Gor'kaia sud'bina' Pisemskago v 'Rabochem teatr.'" *Rabochii,* 25 May 1914, p. 2.

"Old Gentleman" [A. V. Amfitreatov]. "Vlast' t'my pered narodom." *Novoe Vremia,* no. 7107 (10 December 1895): 4.

Orlov, S. A., and A. V. Sigorskii. "A. M. Gor'kii i bor'ba za narodnyi teatr." In *Liudi russkogo isskustva,* 91–112. Moscow, 1960.

Orlovsky, Daniel. "The Lower Middle Strata in Revolutionary Russia." In *Between Tsar and People: Educated Society and the Quest for Public Identity in Late Imperial Russia,* edited by Edith Clowes, Samuel Kassow, and James West, 248–68. Princeton, N.J., 1991.

Ortega y Gasset, José. "The Difficulty of Reading." *Diogenes* 28 (Winter 1959): 1–17.

Ostrogorskii, V. P. "Dobryi pochin. K voprosy o narodnom teatre." *Obrazovanie,* no. 3 (March 1892): sec. 2, pp. 69–74.

Ostrovskii, A. N. "Zapiska o polozhenii dramaticheskogo isskusstva v Rossii v nastoiashchee vremia." In *Sobranie sochinenii v desiati tomakh,* 10:168–86. Moscow, 1960.

Panina, S. V., and P. P. Gaideburov. "Iskusstvo v narodnoi auditorii." *Russkaia shkola,* nos. 5–6 (1914): 150–73.

Perrie, Maureen. "The Russian Peasant Movement of 1905–7: Its Social Composition and Revolutionary Significance." *Past and Present,* no. 57 (November 1972): 123–55.

Petr, Iu. "Desiatiletie teatra Narodnogo doma gr. Paninoi." *Teatr i iskusstvo,* no. 46 (1913): 930–31.

Poliakova, E. "Tolstoi i teatr." *Tiatr,* no. 8 (1978): 15–26.

Polner, T. "Kakiia razvlecheniia blagotvorno vliiaiut na rabochikh?" In *Obrazovatel'no- vospitatel'nyia uchrezhdeniia dlia rabochikh,* 38–49. Moscow, 1898.

Pomar, Mark G. "Anatoly Fedorovich Koni: Liberal Jurist as Moralist." In *Carl Beck Papers in Russian and East European Studies,* no. 1202 (March 1996): 1–34.

Popov, N. A. "Ob organizatsii razvlechenii dlia rabochikh. Doklad, prochitannyi na vtorom s"ezd russkikh deiatelei po tekhnicheskomu i professional'nomu obrazovaniiu v Moskve, 31 dekabria 1895 g." *Teatral,* no. 65 (1896): 23–37.

Popov, Nikolai. "O repertuare narodnogo teatra." In *Narodnyi teatr. Sbornik,* 237–56. Saint Petersburg, 1896.

Porter, Thomas, and William Gleason. "The *Zemstvo* and Public Initiative in Late Imperial Russia." *Russian History* 21, no. 4 (Winter 1994): 419–37.

Prevo, Kathleen. "Worker Reaction to Bloody Sunday in Voronezh." In *1905: La première révolution russe,* edited by F.-X Coquin and C. Gervais-Francelle, 165–78. Paris, 1986.

Prozerova, Tat'iana. "Teatr Gor'kogo v Nizhnem Novgorode." *Teatr,* no. 5 (1967): 91–100.

Pyziur, Eugene. "Michael N. Katkov: Advocate of English Liberalism in Russia, 1856–1863." *Slavonic and East European Review* 45 (July 1967): 439–56.

Raeff, Marc. "Kliuchevskii—Historian of the Eighteenth Century." *Canadian-American Slavic Studies,* 20, nos. 3–4 (1986): 383–98.

Rayfield, Donald. "Peasant Reforms." *Times Literary Supplement* 25 April 1997, p. 19.

Reid, Douglas A. "Popular Theatre in Victorian Birmingham." In *Performance and Politics in Popular Drama,* edited by David Bradby, Louis James, and Bernard Sharratt, 65–89. Cambridge, 1980.

Revel, Jacques. "The Uses of Civility." In *A History of Private Life,* edited by Roger Chartier, 3:167–205. Cambridge, Mass., 1989.

Reviakin, A. I. "A. N. Ostrovskii i tsenzura." *Uchenye zapiski Moskovskogo Gorodskogo Pedagogicheskogo Instituta* 48, no. 5 (1955): 267–98.

Roosevelt, Priscilla. "Emerald Thrones and Living Statues." *Russian Review* 50, no. 1 (January 1991): 1–23.

Rousseau, J. J. "J. J. Rousseau à M. d'Alembert sur son article GENEVE, dans le VIIe volume de *l'Encyclopédie* sur le projet d'établir un théâtre de comédie en cette ville." In *Oeuvres complètes,* 16:5–283. Paris, 1791.

"Samodeiatel'nost'." *Slovar Russkogo iazyka.* Vol. 4. Moscow, 1961.

Segal, Charles. "Tragedy, Orality, Literacy." In *Oralità: Cultura, Literatura, Discorso: Atti del Convegno Internazionale a cura di Bruno Gentili e Giuseppe Paioni,* 199–226. Rome, 1986.

Senelick, Laurence. "The Erotic Bondage of Serf Theatre." *Russian Review* 50 (January 1991): 124–34.

———. "Russian Serf Theatres and the Early Years of Mikhail Shchepkin." *Theatre Quarterly,* no. 38 (Summer 1980): 8–16.

Sergeenko, A. "O narodnom teatre." *Oktiabr* [Moscow], no. 10 (1982): 195–99.

Serova, V. "Vstrecha s L. N. Tolstym na muzykal'nom poprishche." *Russkaia muzykal'naia gazeta,* no. 4 (1894): 477–83.

Shatz, Marshall. "The Noble Landowner in Russian Comic Operas of the Time of Catherine the Great: The Patriarchal Image." *Canadian Slavic Studies* 3, no. 1 (Spring 1969): 22–38.

Shcheglov, Ivan. "Zagadki peterburgskago narodnago teatra." *Novoe Vremia,* no. 9698, (5 March 1903): 3.

Shchepkin, M. O. "Nashy Manilovy i narodnyi teatr." *Russkaia letopis,* no. 9 (2 March 1870): 327–32.

Sindeev, A. "O narodnom spektakle." *Obrazovanie,* nos. 5–6 (1896): 109–11.

Sinitsyn, A. A. "Iz vospominanii starogo vracha." *Russkaia Starina* 155 (July 1913): 140–46.

Sleptsov, Vasilii. "Neizvestnyi stranitsy." *Literaturnoe nasledstvo* 71 (March 1963).

Spiridonova, Lidiia. "Gorky and Stalin (According to New Materials from A. M. Gorky's Archive) (trans.)." *Russian Review* 54, no. 3 (July 1995): 413–23.

Stanislavskii, K. S. "O tsenzure." *Sobranie sochinenii v vos'mi tomakh,* 5:274–84. Moscow, 1958.

Stepanov, D. "Vzgliad na ideal'nyi teatr i ego zadachi v nashe vremia." In *Narodnyi teatr. Sbornik,* 224–28. Saint Petersburg, 1896.

Stone, Lawrence. "Literacy and Education in England, 1640–1900." *Past and Present,* no. 42 (February 1969): 76–139.

Strada, Vittorio. "K teorii Russkogo romana." *Rossiia/Russia* [Turin], no. 4 (1980): 159–71.

Struve, Peter. *Osvobozhdenie,* 2 December/15 December 1902, p. 186.

Swift, E. Anthony. "Fighting the Germs of Disorder: The Censorship of Russian Popular Theater, 1888–1917." *Russian History* 18, no. 1 (Spring 1991): 1–49.

Tamarin, N. "Narodnyi teatr." *Zhizn',* no. 1, (1897): 97–117.

"Theory." *Oxford Dictionary of English Etymology.* 1966 ed.

Thomas, Keith. "The Meaning of Literacy in Early Modern England." In *The Written Word: Literacy in Transition,* edited by G. Baumann, 97–131. Oxford, 1986.

Thurston, Gary. "Alexis de Tocqueville in Russia." *Journal of the History of Ideas* 37, no. 2 (April–June 1976): 289–306.

———. "The Impact of Russian Popular Theatre, 1886–1915." *Journal of Modern History* 55 (June 1983): 237–67.

———. "P. D. Kiselev and the Development of a Russian Legal Consciousness." *Canadian-American Slavic Studies* 19, no. 1 (Spring 1985): 1–27.

———. "Theatre and Acculturation in Russia from Peasant Emancipation to the First World War." *Journal of Popular Culture* 18, no. 2 (Fall 1984): 3–16.

———. "Theatre in the Village School: The Bunakovs' Discoveries." In *School and Society in Tsarist and Soviet Russia,* edited by Ben Eklof, 70–94. New York, 1993.

Tikhii, A. "Derevenskii teatr pod Moskvoiu." *Shkola i zhizn',* no. 24 (16 June 1914): 659–64.

Tikhonovich, V. V. "Narodnyi teatr po soobshcheniiam s mest." *Uchitel' i shkola,* nos. 17–18 (September 1914): 1–20.

———. "Samodeiatel'nost' naseleniia v oblasti vneshkol'nogo obrazovaniia." *Uchitel' i shkola,* nos. 9–10 (1915): 33–44.

———. "Voprosy narodnago teatra." *Uchitel' i shkola,* nos. 15–16 (1915): 16–32.

Tsinkovich, V. A. "Narodnyi teatr i dramaticheskaia tsenzura." In *Teatral'noe nasledstvo,* 375–401. Moscow, 1956.

Tynianov, Iurii. "O literaturnoi evoliutsii." In his *Arkhaisty i novatory,* 1:30–47. Leningrad, 1929.

Vernant, Jean-Pierre. "Tensions et ambiguïtés dans la tragédie greque." In his *Mythe et tragédie en Grèce ancienne,* edited by J.-P Vernant and P. Vidal-Naquet, 21–40. Paris, 1981.

Vestnik popechitel'stvo narodnoi trezvosti, 1, no. 1 (2 August 1903): 1.

Vlasenko, N. "O poseshchenii moimi uchenitsami teatra." In *Khronika voskresnykh shkol,* edited by E. V. Saltykova, 268–70. Moscow, 1900.

Volkova, N. B. "Teatral'naia deiatel'nost' Proletkul'ta." In *Russkii sovetskii teatr,* 328–69. Leningrad, 1968.

Volynskii, A. L. [A. L. Flekser]. "Staryi i novyi repertuar." In *Kniga velikogo gneva,* 219–25. Saint Petersburg, 1904.

VonLaue, T. H. "Russian Labor between Field and Factory, 1892–1903." *California Slavic Studies* 3 (1964): 33–65.

Wcislo, Francis W. "*Soslovie* or Class? Bureaucratic Reformers and Provincial Gentry in Conflict, 1906–1908." *Russian Review* 47 (1988), 1–24.

Weber, Eugen. "Who Sang the Marseillaise?" In his *My France,* 92–102. Cambridge, Mass., 1991.

Wettlin, Margaret. "Alexander Ostrovsky and the Russian Theatre before Stanislavsky." In *Alexander Ostrovsky. Plays,* 7–79. Moscow, 1974.

Wheatcroft, Stephen. "Crisis and the Condition of the Peasantry in Late Imperial Russia." In *Peasant Economy, Culture, and Politics of European*

Russia, 1800–1921, edited by Esther Kingston-Mann and Timothy Mixter, 128–72. Princeton, N.J., 1991.
Wilbur, Elvira. "Peasant Poverty in Theory and Practice: A View from Russia's 'Impoverished Center' at the End of the Nineteenth Century." In *Peasant Economy, Culture, and Politics of European Russia, 1800–1921,* edited by Esther Kingston-Mann and Timothy Mixter, 101–127. Princeton, N.J., 1991.
Wortman, Richard. "Theatricality, Myth, and Authority." *Russian Review* 50, no. 1 (January 1991): 48–52.
Zelnik, Reginald. "The Sunday School Movement in Russia, 1859–1862." *Journal of Modern History* 27 (June 1965): 151–70.
Zhilkin, I. "Provintsial'noe obozrenie." *Vestnik Evropy*, no. 5 (May 1914): 367–79.
Zhirkevich, I. S. "Zapiski." *Russkaia starina* 13 (1875): 567–70.
Omega. "Liubimoe detishche upravy." *Moskovskie vedomosti,* no. 264 (1902): 2.

BOOKS AND PAMPHLETS

Adrados, Francisco. *Festival, Comedy and Tragedy.* Leiden, 1975.
Aikhenval'd, Iu. *Siluety russkikh pisatelei.* Vol. 2. Moscow, 1908.
Alchevskaia, Kh. D. *Dramaticheskiia proizvedeniia: Ostrovskii v primemenii k chteniiu v narode.* Saint Petersburg, 1887.
———. *Peredumannoe i perezhitoe.* Moscow, 1912.
Anisimov, Evgenii. *The Reforms of Peter the Great.* Armonk, N.Y., 1993.
Anskii, S. A. *Narod i kniga.* Moscow, 1913.
Argutinskii-Dolgorukii, N. E. *K istorii Gorodskogo Narodnago Doma imeni K. Ia. Zubalova.* Tiflis, 1909.
Arkhiv A. M. Gor'kogo. Vol. 8. Moscow, 1960.
Armand, L., and A. Nikitin. *Narodnye Doma.* Moscow, 1918.
Ascher, Abraham. *The Revolution of 1905.* Stanford, Calif., 1988.
Auerback, Berthold. *Schwarzwälder Dorfgeschichten.* Stuttgart, 1843–53.
Bailey, Peter. *Leisure and Class in Victorian England: Rational Recreation and the Contest for Control, 1830–1885.* London, 1978.
Bardovskii, A. A. *Teatral'nyi zritel' na fronte v kanun oktiabria.* Leningrad, 1928.
Baron, S. H. *Plekhanov.* Stanford, Calif., 1963.
Barsukov, N. P. *Zhizn' i trudy M. P. Pogodina.* Vol. 12. Saint Petersburg, 1891.
Beck, Henning. *When Men Meet.* Chicago, 1997.
Belinskii, Vissarion. *Polnoe sobranie sochinenii.* Vol. 12. Moscow, 1956.
Benedetti, Jean. *Stanislavsky: A Biography.* London, 1988.
Bialik, B. *M. Gor'kii—dramaturg.* Moscow, 1977.

Bohachevsky-Chomiak, Martha. *Feminists Despite Themselves: Women in Ukrainian Community Life, 1884–1939*. Edmonton, Canada, 1988.

Boyle, Nicholas. *Goethe: The Poet and the Age*. Oxford, 1991.

Bradby, David, and John McCormick. *People's Theatre*. London, 1978.

Bradley, Joseph. *Muzhik and Muscovite*. Berkeley and Los Angeles, 1985.

Bristow, Eugene, ed. and trans. *Five Plays of Alexander Ostrovsky*. New York, 1969.

Brooks, Jeffrey. *When Russia Learned to Read: Literacy and Popular Literature, 1861–1917*. Princeton, N.J., 1985.

Brower, Daniel. *The Russian City between Tradition and Modernity, 1850–1900*. Berkeley and Los Angeles, 1990.

Brown, Frederick. *Theater and Revolution*. New York, 1980.

Bunakov, N. F. *Zapiski N. F. Bunakova. Moia zhizn', v sviazi s obshcherusskoi zhizn'iu, preimushchestvenno provintsial'noi. 1837–1905*. Saint Petersburg, 1909.

———. *Izbrannye pedagogicheskie sochinenii*. Moscow, 1953.

Bushnell, John. *Mutiny Amid Repression: Russian Soldiers in the Revolution of 1905–1906*. Bloomington, Ind., 1985.

Calhoun, Craig, ed. *Habermas and the Public Sphere*. Cambridge, Mass., 1992.

Charnoluskii, V. I., ed. *Sbornik zakonov i spravochnykh svedenii o pechati, sobraniiakh, bibliotekakh, knizhnoi torgovle, teatr, uveseleniiakh, i.t.d.* Moscow, 1907.

Chartier, Roger. *The Cultural Origins of the French Revolution*. Translated by Lydia G. Cochrane. Durham, N.C., 1991.

Christian, R. F. *Tolstoy's Letters*. Vol. 2. New York, 1978.

Clark, Katerina. *Petersburg, Crucible of Cultural Revolution*. Cambridge, Mass., 1995.

Corbin, Alain. *The Foul and the Fragrant: Odor and the French Social Imagination*. Cambridge, Mass., 1986.

Davatts, V. Kh. *K voprosu o postroike narodnago doma v g. Vol'ske*. Vol'sk, 1915.

Davies, Cecil W. *Theatre for the People*. Austin, Tex., 1977.

Delany, Paul. *British Autobiography in the Seventeenth Century*. New York, 1969.

Dmitriev, Iu. A. *Mikhail Lentovskii*. Moscow, 1978.

Dolgopolov, L. K. *Na rubezhe vekov*. Leningrad, 1977.

Dolgorukov, P. V. *Des réformes en Russie*. Paris, 1862.

Donskov, Andrew. *Mixail Lentovskij and the Russian Theatre*. East Lansing, Mich., 1985.

Dostoevskii, F. M. *Zapiski iz mertvogo doma*. In *Polnoe sobranie sochinenii v tridsati tomakh*, Vol. 4. Leningrad, 1972.

———. *Moia tetradka katorzhnaia: 'Sibirskaia tetrad.'* Krasnoiarsk, 1985.

Dowler, Wayne. *An Unnecessary Man: The Life of Apollon Grigor'ev.* Toronto, 1995.
Dreiden, Simon. *Pavel Pavlovich Gaideburov: Literaturnoe nasledie.* Moscow, 1977.
Dunham, Vera. *In Stalin's Time: Middleclass Values in Soviet Fiction.* Cambridge, 1976.
Dynnik, Tat'iana. *Krepostnoi teatr.* Moscow, 1933. Reprint, Leipzig, 1977.
The Earlier Life and Chief Earlier Works of Daniel Defoe. Ed. Henry Morley. London, 1889.
Efros, Nikolai. *M. S. Shchepkin.* Saint Petersburg, 1920.
Ehre, Milton, ed. *The Theater of Nikolay Gogol.* Chicago, 1980.
Eikhenbaum, Boris. *Lev Tolstoi.* 3 vols. Leningrad, 1928, 1931, 1960.
Eklof, Ben. *Russian Peasant Schools.* Berkeley and Los Angeles, 1986.
Elias, Norbert. *The Civilizing Process.* Translated by Edmund Jephcott. 2 vols. New York, 1978, 1982.
———. *The Court Society.* Translated by Edmund Jephcott. New York, 1983.
Emerson, Caryl. *Boris Godunov.* Bloomington, Ind., 1986.
Emmons, Terence, ed. and trans., *The Time of Troubles: The Diary of Iurii Vladimirovich Got'e.* Princeton, N.J., 1988.
Engelstein, Laura. *The Keys to Happiness: Sex and the Search for Modernity in Fin-de-Siècle Russia.* Ithaca, N.Y., 1992.
Fanger, Donald. *The Creation of Nikolai Gogol.* Cambridge, Mass., 1979.
Farber, Leonid M. *A. M. Gorkii v Nizhnem Novgorode. 1889–1904.* Volgo-Viat., 1968.
Fergusson, Francis. *The Idea of a Theatre.* Princeton, N.J., 1949.
Fedotov, A. F. *Predislovie k knige: D. I. Fonvizin. Nedorosl'.* Moscow, 1886.
Filippov, Vladimir. *M. S. Shchepkin i ego rol' v istorii russkogo teatra.* Moscow and Leningrad, 1938.
———. *Zadachi narodnogo teatra i ego proshloe v Rossii.* Moscow, 1918.
Fisher, David. *Romain Rolland and the Politics of Engagement.* Berkeley and Los Angeles, 1988.
Frank, Joseph. *Dostoevsky: The Stir of Liberation, 1860–1865.* Princeton, N.J., 1986.
Frid'eva, N. Ia. *Zhizn' dlia prosveshcheniia naroda.* Moscow, 1963.
Frieden, Nancy M. *Russian Physicians in an Era of Reform and Revolution, 1856–1905.* Princeton, N.J., 1981.
Frierson, Cathy. *Peasant Icons: Representations of Rural People in Late Nineteenth Century Russia.* New York, 1993.
Froud, Nina, and James Hanley, eds. *Chaliapin: An Autobiography as Told to Maxim Gorky.* London, 1967.
Fussell, Paul. *The Great War and Modern Memory.* New York, 1975.
Gaideburov, P. P. *Narodnyi teatr (Pervye itogi).* Saint Petersburg, 1918.

Galai, Shmuel. *The Liberation Movement in Russia, 1900–1905.* Cambridge, 1973.
Gibbon, Edward. *Memoirs of My Life.* Harmondsworth, Middlesex, Eng., 1984.
Gigolov, M. *Dramaturgiia M. Gor'kogo. 1902–1906 gg. v sovremennoi ei kritike i publitsistike.* Tbilisi, 1975.
Gigushvili. E., and A. Iufit. *Bol'shevistskaia pechat' i teatr.* Leningrad and Moscow, 1961.
Ginzburg, Lydia. *On Psychological Prose.* Translated by Judson Rosengrant. Princeton, N.J., 1991.
Gitovich, N. I., ed. *M. Gor'kii i A. Chekhov. Perepiska, stati, vyskazyvaniia.* Moscow, 1951.
Gleason, Abbott. *Young Russia: The Genesis of Russian Radicalism in the 1860s.* New York, 1980.
Goffman, Erving. *The Presentation of Self in Everyday Life.* Edinburgh, 1956.
Gorky, Maxim. *Polveka dlia knigi. Literaturno-khudozhestvennyi sbornik.* Moscow, 1916.
———. *Reminiscences of Tolstoy.* New York, 1946.
Gottlieb, Vera. *Chekhov and the Vaudeville.* Cambridge, 1982.
Griboedov, A. S. *Gore ot uma.* Moscow, 1984.
Gusev, V. E., ed. *Narodnyi teatr: sbornik statei.* Leningrad, 1974.
Habermas, Jürgen. *The Structural Transformation of the Public Sphere: An Inquiry into a Category of Bourgeois Society.* Translated by Thomas Burger. Cambridge, Mass., 1991.
Hacking, Ian. *The Taming of Chance.* Cambridge, 1990.
Havelock, Eric. *The Muse Learns to Write.* New Haven, Conn., 1986.
———. *The Literate Revolution in Greece and its Cultural Consequences.* Princeton, N.J., 1982.
Hemmings, F. W. J. *Theatre and State in France: 1760–1905.* Cambridge, 1994.
———. *The Theatre Industry in Nineteenth-Century France.* Cambridge, 1993.
Hubner, Zygmunt. *Theater and Politics.* Evanston, Ill., 1992.
Ianzhul, I. I. *P'ianstvo, kak sotsial'nyi nedug i bor'ba protiv nego.* Saint Petersburg, n.d.
Ingram, David. *Habermas and the Dialectic of Reason.* New Haven, Conn., 1987.
Irisov, A. S. *Kooperatsiia i tekushschi moment.* Moscow, 1917.
Ivanov, I. *A. N. Ostrovskii.* Saint Petersburg, 1900.
Jackson, Robert Louis. *The Art of Dostoevsky.* Princeton, N.J., 1981.
Jahn, Hubertus. *Patriotic Culture in Russia during World War I.* Ithaca, N.Y., 1995.

Jowitt, Ken. *The New World Disorder: The Leninist Extinction.* Berkeley and Los Angeles, 1992.

Kaidanova, O. V. *Ocherki po istorii narodnogo obrazovaniia v Rossii i SSSR na osnove lichnogo opyta i nabliudenii.* 2 vols. Berlin, 1938, 1939.

Kallash, V. V. *Stranichka iz istorii russago narodnago teatra.* Moscow, 1903.

Karlinsky, Simon. *Russian Drama from Its Beginnings to the Age of Pushkin.* Berkeley and Los Angeles, 1985.

Karpov, E. *Desiatiletie narodnykh gulianii za Nevskoi zastavoi. Ocherki deiatel'nosti Nevskago Obshchestva ustroistva narodnykh razvlechenii.* Saint Petersburg, 1895.

Karpov, E. P., and N. N. Okulov. *Organizatsiia narodnogo teatra i poleznykh razvlechenii dlia naroda.* Saint Petersburg, 1899.

Kaun, Alexander. *Maxim Gorky and His Russia.* New York, 1931.

Kayden, E. M., and A. I. Antsiferov. *The Cooperative Movement in Russia during the War.* New Haven, Conn., 1929.

Keep, J. L. H. *The Russian Revolution: A Study in Mass Mobilization.* New York, 1976.

Kelly, Catriona. *Petrushka: The Russian Carnival Puppet Theatre.* Cambridge, 1990.

Kennedy, Emmet. *A Cultural History of the French Revolution.* New Haven, Conn., 1989.

Kerblay, Basile. *Modern Soviet Society.* New York, 1983.

Khaichenko, G. A. *Russkii narodnyi teatr kontsa xix—nachala xx veka.* Moscow, 1975.

Khar'kovskoe Obshchestvo Gramotnosti. *Narodnyi Dom, ego zadachi i obshchestvennoe znachenie. Doklad . . . V. Ia. Danilevskago.* Kharkov, 1915.

Khodotov, N. N. *Blizkoe-dalekoe.* Moscow and Leningrad, 1962.

Kingston-Mann, Esther. *Lenin and the Problem of Marxist Peasant Revolution.* New York, 1985.

Kir'ianov, Iurii Il'ich. *Zhiznennii uroven' rabochikh Rossii (konets xix–nachalo xx vv.).* Moscow, 1979.

Kizevetter, A. A. *M. S. Shchepkin.* Moscow, 1917.

———. *Pervyi obshchedostupnyi teatr v rossii.* Moscow, 1904.

———. *Teatr i Ocherki. Razmyshleniia. Zametki.* Moscow, 1922

Kleinbort, L. M. *Ocherki rabochei intelligentsii.* 2 vols. Saint Petersburg, 1923.

Klepikov, A. K. *V "Nizinakh." Stseny iz derevenskoi zhizni.* Moscow, 1912.

Kliuchevskii, Vasili. *Kurs russkoi istorii.* Vol. 4. Moscow, 1958.

Kruger, Loren. *The National Stage.* Chicago, 1992.

Laertius, Diogenes. *Lives of Eminent Philosophers.* London, 1925.

Laskovskaia, O. A. *V. D. Polenov, 1842–1927.* Moscow, 1946.

Leikina-Svirskaia, V. R. *Russkaia intelligentsia v 1900–1917 godakh.* Moscow, 1981.

Lemke, M. K. *Ocherki osvoboditel'nogo dvizheniia 'shestidesiatykh godov.'* Saint Petersburg, 1908.
Lerner, Daniel. *The Passing of Traditional Society*. Glencoe, Ill., 1964.
Ligovsk Narodnyi Dom. *Narodnyi Dom.* Petrograd, 1918.
Lincoln, W. Bruce. *The Great Reforms.* DeKalb, Ill., 1990.
———. *In the Vanguard of Reform.* DeKalb, Ill., 1982.
Lloyd, G. E. R. *Demystifying Mentalities.* Cambridge, 1990.
Lomunov, K. N. *Tvorchestvo L. N. Tolstogo.* Moscow, 1959.
Lotman, Lidiia M. *A. N. Ostrovskii i russkaia dramaturgiia ego vremeni.* Moscow and Leningrad, 1961.
Lucas, Victor. *Tolstoy in London.* London, 1979.
Macleod, Joseph. *Actors Cross the Volga.* London, 1946.
Madariaga, Isabel de. *Russia in the Age of Catherine the Great.* New Haven, Conn., 1981.
Malia, Martin. *Comprendre la révolution russe.* Paris, 1980.
Mally, Lynn. *Culture of the Future: The Proletkult Movement in Revolutionary Russia.* Berkeley and Los Angeles, 1990.
Mann, Thomas. *Diaries, 1918–1939.* New York, 1982.
Manning, Roberta. *The Crisis of the Old Order in Russia.* Princeton, N.J., 1982.
Marchioness of Londonderry and H. Montgomery Hyde, eds. and introd. *The Russian Journals of Martha and Catherine Wilmot.* New York, 1971.
Marker, Gary. *Publishing, Printing and the Origins of Intellectual Life in Russia, 1700–1800.* Princeton, N.J., 1985.
Maroger, Dominique. *Les idées pédagogiques de Tolstoi.* Lausanne, 1974.
Matskin, A. P. *Orlenev.* Moscow, 1977.
Mawdsley, Evan. *The Russian Civil War.* London, 1987.
Mazade, Charles de. *La Russie sous l'Empereur Alexandre II: La crise d l'autocratie et la société Russe.* Paris, 1862.
Mazaev, A. I. *Prazdnik kak sotsial'no-khudozhestvennoe iavlenie.* Moscow, 1978.
McCormick, John. *Popular Theatres of Nineteenth-Century France.* London, 1993.
McReynolds, Louise. *The News Under Russia's Old Regime.* Princeton, N.J., 1991.
Medynskii, E. N. *Istoriia Russkoi pedagogiki do velikoi oktiabr'skoi sotsialisticheskoi revoliutsii.* Moscow, 1938.
———. *Vneshkol'noe obrazovanie, ego znachenie, organizatsiia i technika.* Moscow, 1916.
Miller, Forrest. *Dmitrii Miliutin and the Reform Era in Russia.* Nashville, Tenn., 1968.
Miller, O. F. *Materialy dlia zhizneopisaniia F. M. Dostoevskago.* Saint Petersburg, 1883.

Minihan, Janet. *The Nationalization of Culture.* New York, 1977.
Morax, René. *Tell.* Lausanne, 1914.
Morley, Henry, ed. *The Earlier Life and the Chief Earlier Works of Daniel Defoe.* London, 1968.
Nathanson, Donald. *Shame and Pride: Affect and the Birth of the Self.* New York, 1992.
Nekrylova, A. F. *Russkie narodnye gorodskie prazdniki, uveseleniia i zvelishcha: konets xviii nachalo xx veka.* Leningrad, 1984.
Nemirovich-Danchenko, Vladimir. *My Life in the Russian Theatre.* Translated by John Cournos. New York, 1936.
Neuberger, Joan. *Hooliganism: Crime, Culture, and Power in St. Petersburg, 1900–1914.* Berkeley and Los Angeles, 1993.
O repertuare narodnago teatra, razrabotannom komissiei Komiteta gramotnosti. Moscow, 1870.
Okenfuss, Max. *The Discovery of Childhood in Russia.* Newtonville, Mass., 1980.
Orlenev, P. N. *Zhizn' i tvorchestvo russkogo aktera.* Leningrad and Moscow, 1961.
Pailer, Wolfgang. *Die frühen Dramen M. Gor'kijs in ihrem verhältnis zum dramatischen Schaffen A. P. Čechovs.* Munich, 1978.
Panina, S. V. *Narodnyi Dom.* 3d ed. Saint Petersburg, 1918.
Paperno, Irina. *Chernyshevsky and the Age of Realism.* Stanford, Calif., 1988.
Pasternak, Boris. "Okhrannaia gramota," 203–63. In *Proza 1915–1958, Povesti rasskazy, autobiograficheskie proizvedeniia.* Ann Arbor, Mich., 1961.
Patouillet, J. *Ostrovsky et son théâtre de moeurs russes.* Paris, 1912.
Paustovsky, Konstantin. *The Story of a Life.* New York, 1964.
Pinch, Alan, and Michael Armstrong, eds. *Tolstoy on Education: Tolstoy's Educational Writings, 1861–62.* Rutherford, N.J., 1982.
Pipes, Richard. *The Russian Revolution.* New York, 1990.
———. *Struve: Liberal on the Left, 1870–1905.* Cambridge, Mass., 1970.
Polignac, François de. *Cults, Territory, and the Origins of the Greek City-State.* Chicago, 1995.
Polnoe Sobranie Zakonov Rossiiskoi Imperii. 3d collection. Vol. 18. Saint Petersburg, 1897.
Poole, Ernest. *The Dark People.* New York, 1918.
———. *The Village.* New York, 1918.
Pottécher, Maurice. *Théâtre du peuple à Bussang.* Paris, 1913.
Protokoly Osobogo soveshchaniia, uchrezhdennogo pod predsedatel'stvom D. F. Kobeko, dlia sostavleniia novogo ustava o pechati (10 fevralia–4 dekabria 1905 g.). Saint Petersburg, 1913.
Pyman, Avril. *The Life of Aleksandr Blok.* Vol. 2. London, 1980.

Raeff, Marc. *Understanding Imperial Russia.* New York, 1984.
Reeve, F. D. *Nineteenth-Century Russian Plays.* New York, 1973.
Remington, Thomas. *Building Socialism in Bolshevik Russia.* Pittsburgh, Pa., 1984.
Riordan, James. *Sport in Soviet Society.* Cambridge, 1977.
Robbins, Richard. *Famine in Russia, 1891–1892.* New York, 1975.
———. *The Tsar's Viceroys.* Ithaca, N.Y., 1987.
Robson, Roy. *Old Believers in Modern Russia.* DeKalb, Ill., 1995.
Rolland, Romain. *Le Théâtre du peuple.* Paris, 1926. (Originally published 1903.)
Roosevelt, Priscilla. *Life on the Russian Country Estate.* New Haven, Conn., 1995.
Rowell, George. *The Old Vic Theatre.* Cambridge, 1993.
Russkie narodnye gulian'ia po rasskazam A. Ia. Alekseeva-Iakovleva v zapisi i obrabotke Evg. Kuznetsova. Leningrad and Moscow, 1948.
Russkii sovetskii teatr. Leningrad, 1968.
S.-V. *Ekho otvetnoe.* Saint Petersburg, 1913.
Sackett, Robert Eben. *Popular Entertainment, Class, and Politics in Munich, 1900–1923.* Cambridge, Mass., 1982.
Sakharova, E. V., ed. *Vasilii Dmitrievich Polenov Pisma, dnevnik, vospominaniia.* Moscow, 1950.
Sakhnovskii, V. G. *Teatr A. N. Ostrovskogo.* Moscow, 1919.
Saltykova, M. N., ed. *Khronika voskresnykh shkol.* Moscow, 1900.
Savushkina, I. I. *Russkii narodnyi teatr.* Moscow, 1976.
Seaford, Richard. *Reciprocity and Ritual: Homer and Tragedy in the Developing City State.* Oxford, 1994.
Sektsiia sodeistviia ustroistvu derevenskikh i fabrichnykh teatrov. *Sbornik retsenzii p'es dlia narodnago teatra.* Vol. 1, Moscow, 1914; Vol. 2, Moscow, 1916.
Senelick, Laurence, ed. *National Theatre in Northern and Eastern Europe, 1746–1900.* New York, 1991.
———. *Serf Actor: The Life and Art of Mikhail Shchepkin.* Westport, Conn., 1984.
Sennett, Richard. *The Fall of Public Man.* New York, 1977.
Seregny, Scott. *Russian Teachers and Peasant Revolution: The Politics of Education in 1905.* Bloomington, Ind., 1989.
Shaikevich, B. A. *Dramaturgiia Ibsena v Rossii.* Kiev, 1968.
Shcheglov, Ivan. *Narod i teatr.* Saint Petersburg, 1911.
———. *Narodnyi teatr v ocherkakh i kartinkakh.* Saint Petersburg, 1898.
Shchepkin, M. S. *Zapiski, pis'ma. Sovremenniki o M. S. Shchepkine.* Edited by A. P. Klinchin and S. N. Durylin. Moscow, 1952.
Shishkin, M. D. *Iz vospominanii kooperativnykh i politicheskikh.* New York, 1960.

———. *Teatr i potrebitel'nyia obshchestva.* [Moscow, 1912].
Skarskaia, N. F., and P. P. Gaideburov. *Na stsene i v zhizni.* Moscow, 1959.
Skorobogatov, V. *Zhizn' i stsena.* Leningrad, 1970.
Skorodumov, N. V. *Novyi metod uproshchennykh postanovok: ustroistvo stseny i dekoratsii.* Moscow, 1913.
Sleptsov, Vasilii. *Neizvestnyi stranitsy.* "O teatre," "K teatru mozhno otnosit'sia razlichnym obrazom," and "Trudy i razvlecheniia v obshchestvennoi zhizni." *Literaturnoe nasledstvo* 71 (March 1963): 124–32, 147–52, 359–67.
Snell, Bruno. *The Discovery of Mind: The Greek Origins of European Thought.* Cambridge, Mass., 1953.
Solov'ev, S. M. *Istoriia Rossii s drevneishikh vremen.* Moscow, 1961.
Steiner, George. *After Babel.* London, 1975.
Steiner, Peter. *Russian Formalism: A Metapoetics.* Ithaca, N.Y., 1984.
Steklov, Iu. M., ed. *Krizis teatra.* Moscow, 1908.
Stites, Richard. *The Women's Liberation Movement in Russia.* Princeton, N.J., 1978.
Stone, Norman. *The Eastern Front, 1914–1917.* New York, 1975.
———. *Europe Transformed, 1878–1914.* Cambridge, Mass, 1984.
Svenbro, Jesper. *"Phrasikleia": Anthropologie de la lecture en Grèce ancienne.* Paris, 1988.
Szeftel, Marc. *The Russian Constitution of April 23, 1906; Political Institutions of the Duma Monarchy.* Brussels, 1976.
Thomas, Keith. *Man and the Natural World.* London, 1983.
Thomas, Rosalind. *Literacy and Orality in Ancient Greece.* Cambridge, 1992.
Thurston, Robert W. *Liberal City, Conservative State. Moscow and Russia's Urban Crisis, 1906–1914.* New York, 1987.
Tikhonovich, V. V. *Narodnyi teatr. Demokratizatsiia teatra.* Moscow, 1918.
———. *Samodeiatel'nyi teatr. Posobie dlia samodeiatel'nomu teatr i teatral'nomu prosveshcheniiu.* Vologda, 1922.
Tocqueville, Alexis de. *The Ancien Régime and the French Revolution.* Translated by Stuart Gilbert. Manchester, 1966.
———. *Democracy in America.* Edited by Phillips Bradley. 2 vols. New York, 1945.
———. *Selected Letters on Politics and Society.* Translated by James Toupin and Roger Boesche. Edited by Roger Boesche. Berkeley and Los Angeles, 1985.
Tolstoi, Peter A. *The Travel Diary of Peter Tolstoi: A Muscovite in Early Modern Europe.* Translated by Max Okenfuss. DeKalb, Ill., 1987.
Tolstoy, Nikolai. *The Tolstoys.* New York, 1983.
Tomalin, Nichols, and John Elsom. *History of the National Theatre.* London, 1978.
Trudy pervago vserossiiskago s"ezda stsenicheskikh deiatelei. Moscow, 1898.

Trudy sozvannogo Khar'kovskim obshchestvom gramotnosti 7–12 iiunia 1915 g. v g. Khar'kove s"ezda po voprosam organizatsii razumnykh razvlechenia dlia naseleniia Khar'kovskoy gubernii. Kharkov, 1915.
Trudy pervago vserossiskago s"ezda deiatelei obshchestv narodnykh universitetov i drugikh prosvetitel'nykh uchrezhdenii chastnoi initsiativy S.-Peterburg 3–7 ianvaria 1908 g. Saint Petersburg, 1908.
Trudy Vserossiiskogo s"ezda deiatelei narodnogo teatra v Moskve, 27 dekabria 1915–5 ianvaria 1916. Saint Petersburg, 1919.
Valkenier, Elizabeth Kridl. *Russian Realist Art, the State and Society.* New York, 1989.
Varnike, B. V. *Zametki ob Ostrovskom.* Odessa, 1912.
Veyne, Paul. *Did the Greeks Believe in Their Myths?* Chicago, 1988.
Volkogonov, Dmitri. *Lenin: A New Biography.* New York, 1994.
Vserossiiskii s"ezd po bor'be s pianstvom. 3 vols. Saint Petersburg, 1909–10.
Vsevolodskii-Gerngross, Vsevolod. *Istoriia russkogo teatra.* Leningrad and Moscow, 1929.
Vtoroi Vserossiiskii S"ezd po kooperatsii v g. Kieve 1–7 avgusta 1913 g. Trudy. Vol. 1. Kiev, 1915.
Walkin, Jacob. *The Rise of Democracy in Pre-Revolutionary Russia.* New York, 1962.
Warner, Elizabeth A. *The Russian Folk Theatre.* The Hague, 1977.
Watt, Ian. *The Rise of the Novel.* London, 1957.
Weber, Eugen. *Peasants into Frenchmen.* Stanford, Calif., 1967.
Wettlin, Margaret, introd. *Alexander Ostrovsky. Plays.* Moscow, 1974.
Wiener, Leo. *The Contemporary Drama of Russia.* Boston, 1924.
Williams, Bernard. *Shame and Necessity.* Berkeley and Los Angeles, 1993.
Winkler, John J., and Froma Zeitlin, eds. *Nothing to Do with Dionysos? Athenian Drama in its Social Context.* Princeton, N.J., 1989.
Woehrlin, William. *Chernyshevsky, The Man and the Journalist.* Cambridge, Mass., 1971.
Wolfe, Bertram D. *The Bridge and the Abyss.* New York, 1967.
Woodfield, James. *English Theatre in Transition, 1886–1914.* Beckenham, Kent, 1984.
Worobec, Christine. *Peasant Russia: Family and Community in the Post-Emancipation Period.* Princeton, N.J., 1991.
Zaslavskaya, Tatyana. *The Second Socialist Revolution.* Bloomington, Ind., 1990.
Zelnik, Reginald, ed. and trans. *A Radical Worker in Tsarist Russia: The Autobiography of Semën Ivanovich Kanatchikov.* Stanford, Calif., 1986.
Zguta, Russel. *Russian Minstrels: A History of the Skomorokhi.* Philadelphia, 1978.
Zviagintsev, E. *Komu i zachem nuzhny narodnye doma?* 2d ed. Moscow, 1918.

Index